WILLIAM PITT BALLINGER

WILLIAM PITT BALLINGER

Texas Lawyer, Southern Statesman

1825–1888

BY JOHN ANTHONY MORETTA

Foreword by Don E. Carleton

Texas State Historical Association

Austin

For Chris

Copyright © 2000 by the Texas State Historical Association, Austin, Texas. All rights reserved. Printed in the United States of America.

Library of Congress Cataloging-in-Publication Data
Moretta, John Anthony
    William Pitt Ballinger: Texas lawyer, southern statesman 1825–1888/ by John Anthony Moretta.
    p. cm.
    Includes bibliographical references and index.
    ISBN 978-0-87611-199-4
    1. Ballinger, William Pitt, 1825–1888. 2. Lawyers--Texas--Galveston--Biography. 3. Texas--History--1846–1950. I. Title. II. Series.
    KF368.B3135 M67 2000
    340'.092--dc21
    [B]   00-026845

10 9 8 7 6 5 4 3 2

Published for the Center for American History by the Texas State Historical Association in Cooperation with the Center for Studies in Texas History at the University of Texas at Austin.

Number seven in the Barker Texas History Center Series
Senior editor, Don E. Carleton

Book design by Janice Pinney. Dustjacket design by David Timmons.

The paper used in this book meets the minimum requirements of the American National Standard for Permanence of Paper for Printed Library Materials, Z39.48-1984.

This book was made possible in part by grants from the Center for American History at the University of Texas at Austin, and the Galveston, Texas, law firm of Mills, Shirley, Eckel & Bassett, L.L.P.

Contents

	Acknowledgments	vii
	Foreword *by Don E. Carleton*	xi
	Introduction	1
1.	"He was my lungs"	11
2.	"To bestow honour and dignity upon the family"	25
3.	"Allow me to become an ordinary citizen again"	49
4.	"As if I was caught up in a maelstrom"	63
5.	"My life is now fulfilled"	89
6.	"Secession is Revolution"	111
7.	"With every energy of the body consecrated"	133
8.	"The spirit of the people are ready for submission"	169
9.	"To fill the full measure of my ambitions"	191
10.	"The Lawyer of Texas"	223
11.	"As a Gentleman, Citizen, and Lawyer"	255
	Selected Bibliography	263
	Notes	285
	Index	321

ACKNOWLEDGMENTS

Rarely does one earn the distinction of having written a book without the invaluable support of friends, relatives, colleagues, and mentors. Thus, it is a pleasure to thank the many people who helped me with this biography. My first, most sincere thank you goes to the late S. W. Higginbotham of Rice University, who first introduced me to the idea of specializing in Texas and Southern history. He not only guided me down this different path, but then suggested that biographical history is always an interesting and sound dissertation topic, if done well. After convincing me to change fields and then recommending that I do a biography, he next found Ballinger for me. One of his former students, Louis Marchiafava, who is presently the director of the Houston Metropolitan Research Center, called "Higgs" one day and informed him that he had struck an historical gold mine: the center had just acquired the complete legal and various personal papers of Ballinger and Jack. Professor Higginbotham was overjoyed at the news and told Louis that one of his graduate students was on his way downtown to visit him. Thus, the Ballinger story began.

I took my first note card on Ballinger in the spring of 1982, and after research at the Rosenberg Library in Galveston, Texas, and at the Barker Texas History Center (now the Center for American History) on the campus of the University of Texas at Austin, I completed my dissertation three years later. It was at this juncture that another crucial individual in the Ballinger saga stepped forward: Professor John B. Boles, also of Rice University, who became my second mentor. From the moment he read Ballinger in dissertation form, he encouraged me to take it to the next level—a book on the life and times of one of Texas's relatively unknown but key historical figures. With such support, I began to dig as deep as I could into every facet of Ballinger's life and times, and after close to a decade of writing and research, the complete William Pitt Ballinger has finally emerged. In the process, both John and Higgs took time out from their busy lives to read every page of the early manuscript. Their comments, criticisms, and exhortations were invaluable in helping me to continue with this project.

I also had the good fortune while a graduate student at Rice Univeristy to have had the tutelage of Professors Ira Gruber, Tom Haskell, and Marty Wiener. From all three I not only learned a great deal of history, ranging from English history to American colonial to social and intellectual theory, but perhaps more important, each, in his own special, unique way, served as a great model for what it means to be totally dedicated to the life of the mind.

I would not have been able to complete this book without the trust and beneficence of the late Ballinger Mills Jr., William Pitt's great-grandson. For several weeks, usually over lunch at Clary's, his favorite Galveston restuarant, he shared with me, and eventually allowed me complete access to, numerous letters and other Ballinger family documents never released to the public. In those boxes and files were some of the most revealing and personal thoughts and feelings of William Pitt on a variety of issues ranging from his relationships with his wife and children and slaves, to the secession crisis and civil war. Ballinger's thoughts on a variety of other issues affecting his life were also found in those papers, and in the end, I was able to flesh out so much more of a complete human being, thanks to his great-grandson's generosity and confidence in my abilities as an historian.

I would also like to thank William Pitt Ballinger's law firm, the present-day partnership of Mills, Shirley, Eckel, and Bassett, who still practice in the same building that once housed Ballinger and Jack. The firm has the distinction of being the oldest continuous legal establishment in Texas. I am especially grateful to senior partner John Eckel, who not only met with me and discussed the book, but who, together with the other partners, was responsible for helping in the funding of its publication. I must also thank Beverley Vidrine, also of Mills, Shirley, Eckel, and Bassett, who was responsible for procuring some of the most important photographs of William Pitt Ballinger and his partners. Beverley also helped me sort through a hundred other details that seemed at times to be more confounding than the actual writing of the book.

A number of friends and colleagues were always there for me, never wavering in their support and confidence in my abilities as a scholar. In this most crucial area, I am especially indebted to Joe Glatthaar and Jim

Acknowledgments

Jones of the University of Houston, two of the most disciplined, prolific, and wonderfully gifted scholars in the profession. We have been close friends, associates, and fellow baseball and sports enthusiasts for several years. Their friendship and support knew no boundaries, as they encouraged me at some of my lowest ebbs to keep going. They took the time from their own scholarship to read, discuss, and criticize the manuscript. Jim exhorted me to write a bold biography by putting Ballinger on the couch and exploring what animated him from childhood to adolescence to adulthood. Over literally hundreds of miles of daily running, Joe and I discussed this biography. Through those miles he never tired of me bouncing ideas off him, nor did he hesitate to offer insights and criticisms that forced me to go beyond where I was in my own thinking about Ballinger's time and place in history. I thank them both profusely for believing in me as an historian and for forcing me to raise my intellectual sights several notches. Also of great help was another University of Houston associate, Eric Walther. Eric, like Jim and Joe, took time out of his schedule and away from his scholarship to read the manuscript and offer invaluable advice in a variety of different areas, most of which were taken to heart and made part of the final manuscript.

Within my home department at Central College of the Houston Community College System, I received the kind of support that represents the college at its best. David Wilcox and Susan Hult who served as department chairs during the years I worked on this book supported the project in every way possible. I thank them for teaching schedules and committee and other duty assignments that allowed me to pursue my scholarship. For being interested colleagues and good listeners, I want to thank Steven Walmsley, Mike McCormick, Cheryl Peters, Pat Johnson, and Brenda Jones. I am also grateful to Steven Pitts and Richard Goselin of Central College's Economics Department for their computations of nineteenth-century incomes and prices, as well as for the financial data that was incorporated into the book. For helping me to better understand Ballinger's personality and behavior, I would like to thank Denise Boyd of Central College's Psychology Department. Denise not only offered her own thoughts on Ballinger's personality traits, but suggested as well an invaluable array of sources which were consulted and incorporated into the Ballinger story. My thanks, too, to Julann Sam for a thousand kindnesses.

George Ward, my editor at the Texas State Historical Association, has been a pleasure to work with. From the start, he recognized Ballinger's importance to Texas and Southern history. He encouraged me to write a book that would bring Ballinger's importance out as one of the most compleat men of his time. Over countless phone conversations George contributed insights and criticisms that sharpened my focus and analysis and saved me from endless rewrites. I also wish to thank Janice Pinney, my amazingly thorough and gifted copy editor. A special thank you must be extended to Anna Peebler and Shelly Henley-Kelly of the Rosenberg Library, who helped procure the wonderful photographs of Ballinger, his wife, and other important Galvestonians, as well as views of the city. Their assistance helped make this biography more real and personal.

Family members provided unfailing support. I am especially indebted to my mother-in-law, Ms. Gail Tycer, whose seminars on effective written communication proved indispensable to the actual writing of this book. A marvelous editor as well, Mom always took the time on her business trips to Houston, and even on her vacations, to inquire about Ballinger, and after reading a chapter or two, offered invaluable insights into his personality. I also owe a great deal of who I have become as an adult to my deceased maternal grandmother, an Italian immigrant, Aurelia "Rosie" Rosotti. From childhood she taught me the importance of hard work and perseverance, and instilled in me the confidence that I could accomplish almost anything if I maintained "forza e animo"—strength and spirit.

Our four children—Christina, Michelle, Rachel, and Lisabeth Rose—have filled my life with much happiness. Over the years I have worked on this book, I watched Christina and Michelle mature into delightful adults, and I have watched Rachel and Lizzy develop into wonderful teenagers. I love them all for being themselves and for reminding me what matters most in life.

Of all the encouragement I received to complete this undertaking, no one was more reassuring and confident in my ability to do so than my wife Chris, to whom I dedicate this book. To her patience with my frustrating starts and stops, to her understanding of weekends away from home for research, to her reading of every paragraph—she was always there, never hesitating to help in whatever way she could. She was my sharpest critic, most determined advocate, best editor, and closest friend and confidante. No written tribute could ever express my deep appreciation for the faith, patience, and love she has demonstrated throughout twenty-four years of marriage.

FOREWORD

John Anthony Moretta's *William Pitt Ballinger: Texas Lawyer, Southern Statesman, 1825-1888* is the seventh volume in the Barker Texas History Center Series, a cooperative publication program of the University of Texas at Austin Center for American History (CAH) and the Texas State Historical Association. CAH is a special collections library, archive, and museum that facilitates research and sponsors programs on the historical development of the United States. The Center has four units: the Research and Collections Division, located on the campus of UT-Austin; the Sam Rayburn Library and Museum in Bonham, Texas; Winedale Historical Center near Round Top, Texas; and the John Nance Garner Museum in Uvalde, Texas. Among the components of CAH's Research and Collections Division are the Littlefield Southern History Collections, the Congressional History Collections, and the Barker Texas History Collections. CAH supports research and education by acquiring, preserving, and making accessible research collections and by sponsoring exhibitions, conferences, symposia, oral history projects, publications, fellowships, and grant-funded initiatives. As a research collection, its areas of strength include the histories of Texas, the lower South, the Southwest, and the Rocky Mountain West.

The Barker Series was established to encourage and support the publication of historical studies based largely on CAH's Barker Texas History Collections, which includes the nation's largest Texana library as well as extensive holdings of archival, cartographic, newspaper, sound, and photographic material. We selected William Pitt Ballinger for the series because Dr. Moretta based a significant portion of his book on research conducted in the Barker Collections' Willam Pitt Ballinger Papers, an extensive manuscript collection measuring more than thirty-one linear feet of shelf space. The collection, which was donated by William Pitt Ballinger's grandson, Ballinger Mills, in 1935, is among the Center's most outstanding sources for primary research in nineteenth-century Texas and Southern history. In addition to CAH's holdings, the Houston Metropolitan Research Center and Galveston's Rosenberg Library have substantive collections of Ballinger papers that have enriched this work.

Dr. Moretta has also made excellent use of CAH's valuable collection of Guy Morrison Bryan Papers (1821–1901). A cousin of Stephen F. Austin, Bryan served in a number of public offices during his distinguished career. Dr. Moretta mined as well several other important CAH resources, including the papers of Moses Austin Bryan (1817–1895), Oran Roberts (1815–1898), and Ashbel Smith (1805–1886).

William Pitt Ballinger was a key player in the legal, political, and economic affairs of Texas and the South for more than four decades of the nineteenth century, yet his historical role has not been widely recognized. John Moretta has made a significant contribution to our knowledge of Texas history by bringing much needed attention to this important Galveston attorney. As director of the Center for American History, I am pleased that CAH resources helped to make this work a reality and that it now becomes available to the public through our Barker Texas History Center Series. Texas State Historical Association director Ron Tyler and assistant director George Ward have been supportive of this project from its earliest stages. I thank them and the Association's Executive Council for making possible the publication of *William Pitt Ballinger: Texas Lawyer, Southern Statesman, 1825–1888*.

Don E. Carleton, Director
The Center for American History

INTRODUCTION

In only a few instances in a long and illustrious career did William Pitt Ballinger have difficulty remaining calm. Ballinger prided himself on his reserve and equanimity, but on the morning of March 7, 1881, the fifty-six-year-old attorney found himself unable to maintain his composure. Arriving at his office at 7:00 A.M. (he usually did not arrive until after nine), Ballinger was a bundle of nervous energy. He could not sit still for five minutes, let alone concentrate on his work. He spent most of the morning pacing back and forth in his office, typically muttering to himself and when not pacing, he arranged and rearranged his books, an activity he habitually engaged in when trying to relax.[1]

Causing Ballinger's anxiety was his impending conference with Jay Gould, the most legendary "robber baron" of the Gilded Age, who had written Ballinger just six days earlier, telling the attorney he was coming to Galveston "to obtain the best legal advice I can. I have been told by my lawyers [the New York firm of Shearman and Sterling] that you are the best trial lawyer in the South & that your knowledge of the laws of your State relative to railroads is unsurpassed. I hope this to be true."[2]

At 12:10 P.M. Jay Gould arrived at the Galveston train station. Waiting to greet him was Ballinger and his wife and children, all dressed, according to Ballinger's daughter Betty, "in our best Sunday attire." Much to Ballinger's surprise Gould left his car and met the attorney as he approached the train. Betty remembered "standing like a statue as Papa introduced us one by one, oldest to youngest. We [Ballinger's three daughters] all bowed like good Southern ladies, while my brother shook Mr. Gould's hand. Mr. Gould commented that Papa must be very proud of us, for we all appeared to be such healthy, happy young people, which Mr. Gould believed testified to my father's success & devotion to his family."[3] Galvestonians had heard that Gould was coming, and by the time of his arrival, a sizeable crowd had gathered at the station to witness the salutations between one of their state's most respected citizens and the richest, most powerful man in the country. As Ballinger's son later recalled, "for a moment it seemed to me that all the eyes of Texas were upon my father. The group of people that had gathered stared with complete awe but silence as my father and Mr. Gould shook hands & did not leave until we all went into the car." There was an attempt at a "photo session" by local newspapermen, but according to Ballinger's son, Gould "politely but firmly told the men that he did not have time to indulge them for he was here only for business, not pleasure & that he rarely, if ever allowed himself to be photographed."[4]

As Ballinger entered Gould's car, he remembered personally "gawking most embarrassingly" and his children's "eyes popping out of their heads" (only his wife Hally maintained "her usual decorum & dignity"), at "this most magnificent display of American railroad genius." Ballinger mentally photographed every detail of Gould's car, later recalling for posterity "the oiled walnut walls, carved and gilded, etched and stained plate glass, metal trappings heavily silver-plated, seats cushioned with thick plushes, washstands of marble and walnut, damask curtains, and massive mirrors of gilded walnut. The floors were carpeted with the most costly Brussels, and the roof beautifully frescoed in mosaics of gold, emerald green, crimson, skyblue, violet, drab, and black." Gould told Ballinger that George Pullman personally designed and outfitted the car and that "he considered it a bargain at $50,000." After about "a half an hour of exchanging pleasantries and polite conversation," the Ballingers and Gould sat down to lunch. Again Ballinger recalled being "mesmerized" by the display of food before him. Ballinger and his family feasted on a twelve-course supper that included "blue-winged teal, antelope steaks, roast beef, boiled ham and tongue, broiled chicken, corn on the cob, fresh fruit, hot rolls, and corn bread."[5] After lunch the two men retired to Ballinger's downtown office to discuss Gould's acquisition of the Galveston, Houston and Henderson Railroad.

Ballinger was aware of Gould's reputation as a cold, sinister, unscrupulous "Corsair" who crushed rivals ruthlessly, betrayed close friends, and defrauded his own corporations with unmatched precision. This perception was fastened on Gould early in his career and never left him. Undoubtedly there was much truth to this image. Yet, it was also misleading and greatly exaggerated. Ballinger believed Gould's business practices were "little different from those of his associates, which seem to me to have become the standard of the day." Moreover, Ballinger liked Gould as a person, finding him "a most charming & pleasant man." He was surprised by Gould's physical appearance, believing the New Yorker to be one of "the frailest men I have ever met—he could not be more than 120 lbs." Gould confessed to Ballinger that his slight build was a result of a "total disinterest toward food," and a "very sickly childhood." Gould also had "very black, deep [set] eyes," which made it difficult for the Texan "to tell what he was thinking when I was speaking—most unnerving at times." Gould's voice in conversation was "always the same—very soft, low, yet deliberate & to the point." Ballinger also found Gould's attire to be "very modest for someone of his stature." Much to Ballinger's surprise, Gould told the jurist of his passion for gardening and flowers, which Ballinger also had, and after discovering this mutual interest, Ballinger believed their conversation "flowed more easily and productively." Like Ballinger, Gould was "devoted to his family—rarely goes out, in fact very much detests the N.Y. social scene, & does not appear to be a man of any vice or extravagance whatsoever. I think much of what has been said about him is exaggerated."[6]

After about four hours Gould left Ballinger's office with the opinion he had traveled thousands of miles to get: it would be legal for Gould to acquire the GH&H. Thirty days later Gould received Ballinger's bill for twenty-five hundred dollars. Gould replied, thanking Ballinger for his "well-conceived opinion," adding that he hoped he could continue to rely on the Galvestonian's legal services, for he needed "a lawyer with great ability and nerve." Gould then told his Texas counselor that Ballinger's rendering of the GH&H acquisition convinced him of Ballinger's ability and that the size of the attorney's bill convinced him that Ballinger had the nerve.[7]

Jay Gould was just one of the many prominent and powerful individuals Ballinger knew during his lifetime. The attorney's associations and friendships ranged literally across the nation. Over the course of his life he had befriended, corresponded with, or become personally acquainted with Secretaries of State Daniel Webster, John J. Crittenden, and William H. Seward; Mexican War generals William Worth and Zachary Taylor; Confederate generals Albert Sidney Johnston, John Bankhead Magruder, and Edmund Kirby Smith; Confederate president Jefferson Davis and Confederate officials Josiah Gorgas, Stephen Mallory, and Judah P. Benjmain; Union generals William Tecumseh Sherman, Philip Sheridan, Edward S. Canby, Gordon Granger, and Winfield S. Hancock; President

Andrew Johnson; and business magnates Samuel Colgate, Alexander T. Stewart, Bowen McNamee, and a host of other Northeastern financiers, lawyers, and politicians. Also on the national level, Ballinger's brother-in-law was Supreme Court justice Samuel Miller, whom he frequently turned to for support and counsel on a variety of issues. Within Texas, Ballinger's list of friends and relatives read like a "Who's Who" of the mid-nineteenth century: Michel Menard, Samuel May Williams, Robert and David Mills, Hamilton Stuart, Willard Richardson, William Marsh Rice, James Bell, James Throckmorton, Andrew Jackson Hamilton, Morgan Hamilton, Ferdinand Flake, James Love, Sam Houston, Elisha Pease, Francis Lubbock, Pendleton Murrah, George Paschal, Richard Coke, Fletcher Stockdale, Charles Syndor, Ashbel Smith, Oscar Farish, Edmund Davis, and Guy Bryan.

As Gould's visit confirmed, by the 1880s Ballinger had national acclaim for his expertise in tort and railroad law. His counsel on such matters was sought regularly by some of the largest, most prestigious legal establishments in the country. But Ballinger's life was not just about the law, it was about living life to its fullest, regardless of physical limitations, and in the process of doing that, William Pitt Ballinger became one of the most compleat men of his time—lawyer, soldier, public servant, and civic leader; author, editorialist, philosopher, botanist, naturalist, education reformer, and bibliophile. Ballinger was impassioned by all these interests and many more. Though accomplished in many diverse areas, the law was, without question, what energized Ballinger and made him who he was.

It is no easy task for the historian, over a century removed from Ballinger's prime at the Texas bar, to capture and assess his professional standing. The cold, mute trial records of courtroom victories and defeats, his personal notes, diary, correspondence, briefs, his entry books of earnings and fees, all give a most inadequate picture of Ballinger's ability and genius as an advocate. To reanimate the power, persuasiveness, and personality that distinguished Ballinger, and to discover why he was proclaimed by many of his peers to have been "the best all-around lawyer of his day,"[8] it is best to summon as witnesses friends and colleagues who saw him in action. Through these individuals' testimonies we are able to see that rare combination of qualities, moral and intellectual, essential to the making of a great lawyer. They will also attest to Ballinger's deep reverence for the law as well as his high professional standards.

Therewith, history's first witness will be Chief Justice Oran Roberts of the Texas State Supreme Court. Roberts presided over many of Ballinger's cases, some of them pivotal in the Galvestonian's career. Roberts declared that "In all the elements that constituted a lawyer William Pitt Ballinger had few if any equals." Roberts was certain that no Texas attorney who appeared before him "posessed Ballinger's knowledge of the law. He seized the strong points of a cause and presented them with clearness and great compactness." Roberts was impressed not only by Ballinger's cogency of argument, but by the attorney's conviction "to the right and justice of the matter which he advocated. When so convinced, whether the cause was great or small he was unusually successful. He had in the highest possible degree the art of persuasion and power of conviction."[9]

One of Ballinger's closest associates was one of his law partners, Marcus Mott, who practiced law with Ballinger for twenty years. In that time Mott became convinced that "Will Ballinger was the finest lawyer I ever knew and of a professional bearing so honorable that he was the model worthy of the closest imitation."[10]

Another of Ballinger's peers and close friends, Walter Botts of the Houston firm Baker & Botts, stated that when he first became acquainted with Ballinger in the late 1850s, the Galvestonian already "had a very strong hold upon popular affection, and stood high in the confidence of the people of the State. He was the leader of the bar—he was the star; he stood above and beyond them all."[11]

Defeats and victories in legal contests too often depend on other antecedent facts and circumstances, and thus reveal little about the respective abilities of the lawyer combatants. Neither unusual success in winning cases nor profound knowledge of the law alone suffice to make a great lawyer. Each is an element but there are other equally important factors. The famous English jurist Lord Coke opined that true legal sages were men who not only possessed a superior knowledge of the law but had also "sucked from the breasts of that divine knowledge, honesty, gravity, and integrity."[12]

This essential quality of the great lawyer, Ballinger unquestionably possessed. Indeed, his sense of truth and justice prevented even greater fame, for Ballinger was unwilling to sacrifice his principles in order to win a case. Ballinger simply lacked that mercenary or "killer" instinct that enables a lawyer to fight on the one side of a cause as well as on the other, and on a bad as well as a good one. As Marcus Mott revealed, "If to Ballinger a thing seemed untrue he could not in his nature simulate truth. This extreme conscientiousness robbed him of much so-called success at the bar."[13]

Ballinger possessed a keen, unique intellect that hated quibbles and evasions. He would no more tolerate dishonest reasoning than unscrupulous dealing. The same conscience that drove his own life can be seen in the advice he gave to clients and friends. Ballinger was honest with them, with the court and jury, and most important, with himself. A faithful adviser, a fearless defender ready to use his skill and every opportunity for his clients' protection, Ballinger never forgot his duty as a citizen and remained always honest with the public.

Ballinger possessed something greater than the mere abstract knowledge of the law. He sought to win his cases on prosaic ground of hard practical sense and logical demonstration through clearness of exposition, and a style of expression distinguished by its rare simplicity. Ballinger could brush aside all the nonessentials of a case and instinctively determine the vital and controlling principles. All his colleagues agreed that for lucidity of statement, clear reasoning power, and analogy Ballinger had no superior at the Texas bar.

What perhaps made Ballinger one of the most effective trial lawyers of his day was his possession of the essential and indispensable qualities of a great jury pleader—a strong personality, a readiness of wit and invention, and a flair for the dramatic. He repressed his identity as the paid advocate and assumed instead the role of juror, counseling and pleading with his fellows in the jury box. He made the jury feel that they, not he, were trying the case. He learned early in his career that if he appeared to be trying too hard to protect his client's interests, it usually resulted in defeat. He avoided anything that might give the impression he was employing his every wile to prevent his client's guilt from becoming known. From the very outset of his cases, he created an atmosphere of honesty, candor, and fair dealing. In his summations he seemed to be speaking personally to each juror, taking them individually into his confidence. They were invariably convinced that this rather homely barrister, speaking their own language, was really one of their own kind, rather than a member of a professional aristocracy. Ballinger appeared to them as a fair-minded, noble man in pursuit of truth and justice, and whom they could trust implicitly.

Ballinger was a lawyer by his own choice. This decision took courage, as he was criticized by family who hoped he would choose a different occupation. Ballinger was called to the law by a craving for power—power in order to create a stable, ordered, and prosperous life not only for himself but for his world as well. Ballinger needed both courage and stamina to discipline that craving, to manage himself so he could earn the chance to manage others. This demanded what he called character, a splendid word which he never fully defined but never hesitated to use. Ballinger selected a profession that satisfied his temperament and brought to it a perceptive practicability about the ways of utilizing the law for the purpose of justice. From the start of his first partnership, Ballinger's legal career was a testament to the law's obligation to balance public and private interests. To do so justly the law must secure individual rights against public intrusion and vest society with the institutions and authority to protect those rights. In an 1874 speech before a gathering of Texas attorneys, Ballinger proclaimed that "liberty" was "meaningless" unless "the weak are protected against the strong, and justice is armed with the power of defending the innocent and punishing the guilty." Law was "the very bond of society" originating in the "moral relations of man, and its spirit and essence consist of the principles of natural equity and justice."[14] By practicing what he called "positive law," Ballinger sought to promote national strength and stability while assuring to each individual unfettered opportunity to attain the dignity and satisfactions of honest work.

Throughout his long career Ballinger found that sometimes his just causes were not so just. Frequently he found himself enmeshed in legal matters that violated his personal code of ethics. In some instances, when confronted with such a dilemma, he looked the other way, rationalizing that he was doing what was in his client's best interest, which was a lawyer's first and foremost responsibility. In his heart Ballinger felt he was wrong, but like any complex human being, he allowed personal ambition and aggrandizement to overcome his principles. More often than not, however, Ballinger took the moral high ground, whether it was in law or politics, and in almost heroic fashion, sacrificed his own well-being for the sake of others or for a cause he believed in.

Ballinger witnessed in his lifetime the bankruptcy of public policy produced by a callous disregard of morality. Honesty, he knew, was always an issue. Corrupt public servants, whether they were lawyers or politicians, he found intolerable. When aroused by such breeches of the public trust, Ballinger's actions were forceful, for they were animated by his high personal and professional standards. In that combination, Ballinger had faith he could set things right. Nowhere, perhaps, was this more evident than in Ballinger's struggle against secession. Ballinger was devoted to the Union, yet, during the crises of the 1850s, he was steadfast in his commitment to remain apolitical. Nothing was as guaranteed to arouse Ballinger's ire as lawyers turned ambitious politicians. When he finally realized that his apoliticism had allowed the secessionists to gain momentum, Ballinger typically threw off his restraint and plunged heart and soul into trying to prevent Texas from leaving the Union. In speeches and broadsides, Ballinger argued against secession, warning Texans and Southerners, that it would only lead to a horrible conflict of arms and the end of the Southern way of life. Even though public opinion was against him, and he risked censorship and ostracism for his unionism, Ballinger nonetheless committed himself to the Unionist cause. Texas's withdrawal from the Union caused Ballinger great personal grief. However, he concluded that the will of the people had spoken, and thus it was his civic duty to now devote himself with equal energy and passion to the cause of Southern independence. Few Texans or Southerners were as passionate a Rebel as Ballinger. To the jurist, the Confederate cause became a revolutionary struggle to preserve a way of life and a culture from which he could not separate himself.

The Confederacy's defeat saddened Ballinger, yet he knew from the beginning of the war that the likelihood of a Southern victory was remote. He thus urged fellow Texans to put the past behind them, accept defeat, rejoin the Union, and get on with their lives. During the upheaval of Reconstruction, Ballinger personally adjusted to the significant social changes brought about by the war, not only accepting the end of slavery, but championing as well civil rights for black folk. Though such a position seemed disingenuous for a former slaveowner, Ballinger, ever the pragmatist, realized such an accommodation was essential not only for his own peace of mind, but for the well-being of all Southerners, white and black.

The end of Reconstruction brought interesting professional possibilities into Ballinger's life. No sooner was the new regime in power, than Gov. Richard Coke appointed Ballinger to the Texas Supreme Court. For a moment Ballinger considered the position, but after consulting with his beloved Hally, he turned it down. Three years later, an even grander opportunity for national acclaim was before him when his name came up for possible nomination to the bench of the Supreme Court of the United States. Yet, again, after conferring with his wife, Ballinger decided to remain "a simple lawyer."

William Pitt Ballinger's life not only provides us with a look into the rise of a great lawyer, but, perhaps more important, it gives us a window through which we can examine many other historical issues and events that were part and parcel of Ballinger's time. For example, through Ballinger we can watch the evolution of Texas from a rural and agrarian slave society into one of the fastest growing commercial states in postwar America.

Introduction

Though Texas's postwar economic development accelerated significantly, we can see through Ballinger's experiences, that politically the Lone Star state remained tied to its antebellum past. Through Ballinger we can travel North during the prewar and postwar periods and witness firsthand the impact Northern life had on Southerners. Ballinger's life and career in Galveston give us a wonderfully rich portrait of Texas's premier antebellum city. Through Ballinger's professional activities, especially during the Gilded Age, we observe the rise of the corporation via the railroad industry, and the effect industrialization had on American political, economic, and social life. In short, Ballinger's full and varied life is a story that encompassed some of the most crucial, formative decades in the Republic's history.

Whatever his shortcomings, Ballinger's actions had enduring value. Durable and sinewy were thus the roots of his career. They had to be, for the roots of his convictions were tough. From his rustic youth, from his Quaker-Victorian God, from the Jesuits at St. Mary's College, from nature, from romantic and realist novels, and from the history he read and helped shape, he abstracted in life the principles of behavior which he honored to his death. He did not always abide by them; no individual could. Yet, he attempted to uphold his ethos, refusing either to abandon what he considered right or to let that consideration immobilize him. To his generation, as he would himself have said, he proved his truth by his endeavor.

William Pitt Ballinger. *Photograph by Rose and Zahn of Galveston, ca. 1870s. Courtesy Rosenberg Library, Galveston, Texas.*

Chapter One

"HE WAS MY LUNGS"

In the summer of 1843, a wheezing, gaunt youth of eighteen stepped off the latest packet from New Orleans to behold the bustling port city of Galveston, Texas. It had taken nearly four weeks for the young Kentuckian to reach the Texas Gulf Coast from his hometown of Barbourville, nestled in the southeastern highlands. Along his overland journey Will Ballinger suffered three asthma attacks, the last forcing him "to take to bed" for several days in Madisonville while cousins nursed him back to health with various home remedies. Finally, after a week's postponement, Ballinger was well enough to continue his journey. At Paducah he caught the "paddle-wheel" that took him down the Mississippi to New Orleans. From the Crescent City he picked up one of the steamers travelling weekly to Galveston.[1]

As young Will Ballinger jostled his way through the busy throng of the wharf area anxiously searching for his uncle, James Love, he little realized that fifteen years later he would be defending the owners of the Port of Galveston before the Texas Supreme Court. No one knew, least of all Ballinger, that he was entering the "promised land" of the Southwestern frontier to begin a great career in American law. By the eve of the Civil War Ballinger had emerged as one of Texas's premier trial lawyers as well as a leading specialist in Texas realty law. By the 1880s he had become one of the nation's most respected railroad attorneys. That the son of a minor Kentucky civil servant could rise so quickly to such prominence makes Ballinger's life a fascinating reflection of the time and place in which he lived. He not only succeeded professionally in antebellum Galveston, an intensely competitive commercial city within an agricultural slave state, but attained even greater success and notoriety in the postwar decades when the country underwent its most profound economic changes. In many ways, Ballinger's professional and personal accomplishments were testimony to the American creed that believed hard work was in itself a virtue, and whatever this hard work did was right. Ballinger also believed that humanity had continuously progressed so that his generation lived in the best of all possible times. The external forces of time, place, and people interacted with his own aspirations, talents, and emotional needs to create a life of continuing change and development.

Upon his arrival in Galveston, Ballinger's meager appearance and homespun suit gave little indication of his remarkable qualities. Even in later years when he could easily afford more expensive, fashionable attire, Ballinger chose to keep his modest appearance. Indeed, for several years he had only a few suits, wearing them constantly until they became so threadbare that his wife would not let him leave the house unless he changed clothes. Even when dressed in new attire, Ballinger still somehow appeared disheveled and "country," prompting his wife and others to remark that he "looked more the itinerant preacher than a distinguished member of the Bar."[2]

Ballinger was rather tall for the time, over six feet. Severe asthma, however, caused him to become stooped-shouldered, so he appeared shorter than he really was. His affliction was also responsible for his angular figure: Ballinger never weighed more than 150 pounds, and even then he looked emaciated. He had a peculiar gait, "stately but swinging," as his son later described it.[3] His eyes were a piercing blue-gray but were surrounded by such deep, dark black circles from asthmatic sleeplessness that they lost much of their lustre and warmth. More often than not, Ballinger appeared haggard, drawn, and ready to collapse from exhaustion. His complexion was fair, but it too was affected by his asthma, causing it to take on a yellow-gray patina. In later life, an appropriately stylish beard concealed much of the sallowness caused by years of physical affliction. He had thick, wavy, black hair which was kept fairly short and parted on the left side. Ballinger's nose was undoubtedly his "most remarkable" feature, as he himself confessed. It was rather large, crooked, and swollen much of the time because of his illness. All in all, Will Ballinger was not the most handsome and dashing of men.

Little about Ballinger's early life seemed extraordinary, much less heroic. The greatest influences of his early years were not wars or politics but the more mundane affairs of daily existence—physical affliction, the loss of a parent, going off to college, filial reconciliation, and deciding upon a career. Such early experiences are hardly epic, nor do they seem to represent a life worthy of a biography. But taken together they reflect the dauntlessness of an individual determined to accomplish more than the ordinary. Perhaps it was the imprint left by his Quaker heritage that provided Ballinger with the inner strength to persevere and ultimately triumph over personal adversity.

Of all the European settlers who migrated across the Atlantic and settled in English North America in the seventeenth century, the Quakers best personified the image of the continent as a land of simple, innocent, independent, and virtuous folk. Among the thousands of Quaker emigres who resettled in North America was Henry Ballinger, the patriarch of the Ballinger clan, and William Pitt Ballinger's great-great-grandfather. Henry joined the first wave of Quaker settlers who relocated in North America in 1678 in the recently acquired Quaker proprietary colony of West Jersey. Four years earlier, George Fox and William Penn, the two Englishmen most responsible for transplanting thousands of English Quakers in North America, purchased West Jersey from its original owners Lord John Berkeley and Sir George Carteret. Henry Ballinger and his family finally settled in Burlington County, West Jersey. Here, despite several more years of bewildering exchanges of proprietary shares, divisions and subdivisions of land, changing governments, and the influx of non-Quaker and non-English Europeans and Africans, Henry not only prospered as a merchant, but dabbled in local politics as well. Elected a member of the assembly beginning in 1697, Henry continued to serve as his county's representative until his death in 1733. He was also appointed special tax collector for Burlington County in 1701, holding that position as well for the remainder of his life.[4]

Upon his death, Henry left a tidy sum to his four sons. Joseph, the youngest, took his meager share of the inheritance, forty pounds sterling, and moved to Amherst County in central Virginia in 1760. By the 1770s Joseph had parlayed his endowment into a burgeoning tobacco plantation maintained by a retinue of twenty slaves. By the time of his death in 1802 at the age of seventy-two, Joseph's estate, including slave property, approached several thousand dollars. It was Joseph, Ballinger's great-grandfather, who first violated one of his faith's most fundamental tenets: opposition to human slavery. According to family history, Joseph's "betrayal" caused "great despair & upheaval. From what has been said, his brothers were most disturbed by his leaving of the family—moving to Va. &c—and his taking up of slaves was the greatest blow to them because of the Quaker opposition to the inst."[5] Despite his brothers' protest, the lure of the West and the profitability of plantation slavery were too tempting for Joseph to resist. Breaches of faith were common, especially among those Europeans born in the New World. The vast opportunities for individual accrual presented first-generation Americans with a dilemma. Continued adherence to their parents' Old World creeds would gain only a modest existence in a land of plenty, while the development of their own more profane standards was better suited for conquering the wilderness. As Joseph Ballinger's transformation from humble Quaker to Virginia squire exemplified, once the choice was made, first generation Anglo-Americans quickly dispensed with those ideals restricting their material aggrandizement.

In his will, Joseph somewhat atoned for his faithlessness by manumitting fifteen of his twenty slaves. The remaining five were bequeathed to his only daughter, Elizabeth, who was to take possession of them upon "her marriage to a Gentleman of Proper standing." Until that time the five slaves were entrusted to the care of a Samuel Groff. Groff was found to be mistreating the slaves, and thanks to the intercession of Richard Ballinger, the eldest of Joseph's four children and Ballinger's paternal grandfather, the slaves were not only saved from Groff's cruelty, but were also freed by young Ballinger. Apparently, when it came to bondage, Richard, unlike his father or his brothers or even his great-grandson, remained true to his Quaker heritage and its long-standing opposition to human slavery.[6]

During the Revolutionary War, Richard served briefly in the Continental Army, seeing action in the war's final battle at Yorktown. Upon the war's conclusion, Richard returned to the security of the Virginia gentry, married, and had three children—before deciding he had had enough of planter gentility. In 1786 Richard sold his plantation (and most of his other possessions) and moved his family across the Blue Ridge Mountains, through the Cumberland Gap, to the "blue grass" of Kentucky.[7]

Although thousands of pioneers regarded the Kentucky wilderness with its fertile soil, virgin forests, and plentiful game as the promised land, Richard Ballinger found his new life in Kentucky unfulfilling. He soon discovered that he disliked being a yeoman farmer as intensely as he had disliked the propriety of the Virginia gentry. Soon after settling in Kentucky, Richard struck off again, indulging in what was to become a family fondness for military adventure. During the Indian wars of the early 1790s, "Colonel Dick" served as aide-de-camp to Arthur St. Clair, governor of the Northwest Territory. The Washington admininstration dispatched St. Clair to put down a British-incited uprising of the northern Indians.

"He was my lungs"

General St. Clair Marched against the tribes in the autumn of 1791, and on March 4, 1791, the Indians surprised St. Clair's camp and quickly turned the battle into a melee in which over nine hundred men were killed or wounded. "Colonel Dick" was one of the few officers who survived one of the costliest defeats of the campaign.[8]

After the war, Richard returned to Kentucky and became the first clerk of the courts of Knox County, which was created in 1799. His fellow Kentuckians elected him to the state senate, and by the time of his death at seventy-five, Colonel Ballinger had become one of the most respected and influential citizens of the county.[9]

His son James Franklin Ballinger, Will's father, carried on the family tradition of public service. James also displayed the Ballinger taste for military adventure, enlisting in the War of 1812 at the age of seventeen. Unfortunately, James did not escape a disastrous American defeat by the Indians as easily as his father. James was one of 866 Kentuckians under Col. William Dudley, whom William Henry Harrison ordered to break the British siege at Fort Meigs on the Maumee River near Lake Erie in northern Ohio. On their way to the fort, Dudley's Kentuckians were ambushed by Tecumseh's Indians, and 630 of the relievers were killed, wounded, or captured. James was taken prisoner and kept his scalp by successfully "running the gauntlet."[10]

After the war James returned to Barbourville, the Knox County seat, and assumed his father's position as clerk of the courts. He won the confidence of his compatriots as much by his physical prowess at county games as by his professional talents. Blessed with many friends but few profitable enterprises, James earned his living from the fees of his official duties as clerk of the courts. Like his father, James served in state politics. In 1837 he was elected to the Kentucky legislature; in 1840 he became an elector on the national Whig ticket. James remained in Barbourville until 1867. There, as a young widower, he raised two daughters and two sons, the eldest of whom was born on September 25, 1825, and was named after the famous English statesman, William Pitt.[11]

Unfortunately, very little information has survived concerning Ballinger's mother, Olivia Adams, and her family. First Ballinger, in his "Family Notes" (which are personal compilations taken from various sources over a period of years as Ballinger attempted to reconstruct his family heritage while he lived), and then later his daughter Betty, who did the most extensive research on her lineage, had difficulty authenticating Olivia's family history. Ballinger had to rely almost exclusively on his grandmother, Sarah Herndon, for his information. Betty fared better fifty years later with the help of a professional genealogist, but she too had to depend on the oral tradition for much of her account. Due to the dubious nature of his source, Ballinger accepted only information that could be confirmed by other relatives. Still, he was able to establish that John Adams, the clan's elder, migrated from England sometime in the 1730s, settling first in Maryland and then moving to Virginia in the 1740s. By the 1760s John Adams had become a fairly wealthy tobacco planter. His son, Thomas Randolph, migrated to Kentucky sometime after the Revolution. Ballinger's mother's father was Randolph Adams, Thomas's firstborn. Sometime in the 1790s Randolph went back to Henry County, Virginia, working as a clerk of the courts. There in 1805 he met and married Sarah Herndon. Two years later the couple moved to Knox County, Kentucky, where Ballinger's mother, Olivia was born in 1807. Randolph Adams eventually became a lay judge of the circuit court of Kentucky and died in 1865.[12]

Olivia Adams married James Ballinger in 1824. At the age of twenty-eight, Olivia died giving birth to her fourth child, Ballinger's youngest sister, America.[13] Young Will Ballinger was only nine years old when his mother died, remaining more a vision than flesh and bones in his memory. His mother's death at Ballinger's vulnerable age undoubtedly affected his early years. Like most antebellum youths, Ballinger had already witnessed the deaths of several of his relatives, and was aware that death was an omnipresent feature of frontier existence. However, his mother had been there to calm the fears. Now suddenly she too was gone, leaving him no aegis against the awful finality of death. Although Ballinger had the comfort of ceremonial mourning provided by his mother's public funeral, he nevertheless spent the rest of his life trying to reconcile the awful anxieties of this trauma.

Ballinger sanctified his mother. "She was as gentle as a dove, & as true, kind & brave as any individual I have known. When the news of her death reached me, I at first did not believe it. When I finally accepted that she had died, I felt utterly alone—helpless, & abandoned by someone who loved me deeply but could not be with me all the time because of her illnesses & genl. frail constitution."[14] For Ballinger, the fact that his mother was bedridden most of her adult life as a wife and mother only added to the trauma of her departure. Her prolonged convalescence and the births of his brother and sister deprived Ballinger of the bonding between a mother and child that is so crucial to a child's development. When not with their father the Ballinger children were placed in the home of a local uncle and an aunt who assumed the role of surrogate mother until the children were returned to their mother's care. Will's younger siblings accepted "Aunt Nancy's" role as mother but Ballinger did not. Since Ballinger had no way of getting closer to his mother he naturally turned to his father for love and attention. Although Ballinger's asthma probably had a physical base, the difficulty in breathing was a cry for closeness and care, and he found that his father's solicitude intensified during his attacks. Years later Ballinger recalled that "My affliction was so bad that I remember I could not go to school very much, nor was I allowed to run & play &c. with the other children for fear that such activity would bring on another attack. When the attacks came, I would sit up in bed gasping with Mother & Father trying to help. I remember Father carrying me in my distress, in my battle to just breathe—pacing the floor all night until I was able to finally breathe or passed out from the fatigue of it all. Father was a pillar of strength, of life, he was my lungs."[15]

Closeness through physical infirmity unfortunately had limited benefits for Ballinger. By his early teens, his father expected him to have "grown out" of his malady, and convalescence now was regarded to be within his own power. James Franklin Ballinger was the epitome of the rugged, virile, frontier male, whose physical strength and athletic ability were legendary in the Kentucky highlands. As Will recalled, his father "was the fastest runner in all the surrounding area as a young man, & some say in the entire State. He was a magnificent woodsman & hunter, and at local fairs, he always won the various games that tested one's strength. He was truly a physically remarkable fellow."[16]

Even though Ballinger's asthma abated as he grew older, it remained a lurking specter easily unleashed by overexertion or a stressful situation. By the time Will entered his teens, James Franklin was convinced that robust physical activity would eventually cure his son's affliction. Ballinger did not possess the strength or stamina to endure his father's exercises, and the constant pressure upon him to rise to those expectations usually precipitated an attack. Will tried manfully to keep up with his father and the other male members of his family on rigorous outdoor excursions and activities. Unfortunately, his father rarely noticed his efforts. Ballinger recollected a "ten mile hike in which I stayed with everyone the entire time. That night however I collapsed from asthma & Father refused to help relieve my distress. He said I could do it myself that I was a man now [Will was fifteen at the time]. The next day, tho I felt better, I had to remain behind with some of the younger boys & girls & help prepare the supper."[17] Will's father, apparently, had punished him for his recent display of weakness. Unable to ventilate his anxieties externally through athletics, Ballinger's frustration turned inward. It was during his adolescence that Ballinger began focusing his energies on gaining recognition for his intellectual prowess and scholarly accomplishments, which he hoped his father would accept as compensation for his lack of physical attributes. Ballinger's asthma reinforced his solitary tendencies because he could rarely, if ever, maintain the rigorous physical life his father seemed to believe was an essential component of masculine maturation. As a result, physical tests of manhood usually ended up with Ballinger feeling isolated from the other male members of his family, and that isolation, abetted by his father's often emasculating chastisements, probably helped push him further toward being a loner. Throughout his adult life Ballinger resolved anxieties and feelings of isolation through boundless activity, incredible self-discipline, and an inordinate control over passions unbefitting his stature.

Ballinger was fortunate to spend his early years in Barbourville rather than in one of Kentucky's more remote areas. The town rests on the east bank of Richland Creek, above the creek's mouth at the Cumberland River in southeast Kentucky—the perfect location to receive settlers moving west from Virginia and the Carolinas via the Cumberland Gap turnpike. The scenery about the town was not breathtaking but pleasant and reposeful, with rolling green hills and a large park built by city fathers during the 1820s to show off the natural beauty of the area's flora and fauna. Barbourville's economy was sustained by livestock production, sugar, grain, some cotton and tobacco, and of course, sourmash whiskey, which became one of the town's most profitable enterprises by the time of the Civil War.[18]

The grandiloquence of Ballinger's name was in keeping with the town's cultural pretensions. Although it numbered fewer than two hundred inhabitants in the 1830s and 1840s, Barbourville boasted a vigorous intellectual atmosphere. For example, in 1837, the town's intelligentsia organized a debating society which met every Saturday evening at the courthouse to discuss some question of current interest. Though the society's format was rather formal, members wasted little time at their weekly meetings bantering mundane or esoteric topics. Instead, they addressed current political issues such as "Is it constitutional and expedient for the United States in their federative capacity to make internal improvements?" Or, "Would it be politick to admit Texas as a member of this confederacy, provided she establishes her independence?" On October 28, 1837, a Dr. U. S. Williams read "an instructive essay on the Science of Phrenology," which was followed by debate on the question: "Have the acts of Andrew Jackson been of more benefit than injury to the United States?"[19]

The final answers were never in doubt, for Knox County was a Whig stronghold. Few important public issues went unexplored by the debaters, and for the society's more avid and impressionable spectators like Will Ballinger, the evening courthouse speeches were not only exciting but also provided the foundation upon which Ballinger subsequently constructed his own political philosophy.

Due to his severe asthma, Ballinger's formal childhood education was rudimentary at best. Most of his early learning took place either at home under his father's tutelage or as Ballinger later recalled "down at the Court House where I would go every Sat. evening & memorize the lectures, debates, &c. without missing a word."[20] Ballinger also made the most of Barbourville's and his father's well-chosen library. James Franklin directed his son's reading toward the classics, most especially Plutarch's *Lives*. Here young Ballinger encountered the men of ancient Greece and Rome, complex and sophisticated individuals whom the historian portrayed as neither complete heroes nor total villains.[21] That balanced presentation provided Will Ballinger with insights into himself and his kinsmen. His reading also gave him a way to grapple with the reality of his life in Barbourville. It was a far better preparation for life than his occasional attendance at nearby country schools.

In 1840, at the age of fifteen, Ballinger was invited by the Jesuit fathers to attend St. Mary's Catholic College in Bardstown, Kentucky. This was a rare privilege indeed for a young lad from a small, rural community. American colleges and universities were still a long way from realizing the democratic ideal of higher education. During Ballinger's youth only one man in a thousand (no women at all) had access to any college education. Those few who did attend colleges or universities were almost exclusively members of prosperous, propertied families.

St. Mary's had been established in 1837 by French Jesuit emigrés under the auspices of Benedict Flaget, the first bishop of the Kentucky diocese. Early Catholic colleges like St. Mary's engaged in an array of educational activities that today would be the responsibility of several different types of schools. The fact that these institutions served both as secular education centers and seminaries for prospective clergy was the main reason for the lack of differentiation and specialization. Even more revealing was the makeup of the student population: exclusively young males ranging in age from eight to twenty-two years old. Such a combination of young and old students required the college to offer instruction in a curriculum ranging from elementary courses in spelling, penmanship, and basic English grammar to higher level work for the older students in Latin, Greek, philosophy, history, mathematics, and geography.[22]

Because frontier America was overwhelmingly Protestant, colleges like St. Mary's, if they wished to survive, had little choice but to admit Protestant students. These institutions routinely solicited young Protestant males of "quality rearing." Ballinger was not the only non-Catholic in his class. In fact, one-third of his classmates were Protestants, whose affiliations ranged from Ballinger's Quaker background to Baptists, Methodists, Presbyterians, and as Will noted, "a lad from Pleasant Hill reputed to be a practicing Shaker."[23]

No sooner did Ballinger arrive at St. Mary's than he found himself immersed in his studies. "I took courses in European history, geography, mathematics and Latin my first year," he recalled years later in a series of letters to his son Thomas Jack Ballinger. "I liked them all but mathematics which I find to this day still confounding. It seemed at the time that I read from the moment I awoke until I went to sleep at night & even then I would often awake with the day's subjects racing thro my mind. I would light the candle by my bedside & read until I fell asleep again."[24]

Despite the rigors required of his studies, Ballinger stood second and then first in his class. He also found time to join a debating society which he found "most illuminating & enjoyable. It provided a wonderful tho only temporary escape from our real purpose which was our books."[25] As a debater Ballinger learned to think on his feet, to develop his own ideas in rational discourse, and to respond to challenges from his peers. The debate topics, though often trivial, provided Ballinger with opportunities to apply insights and concepts learned in the classroom to contemporary issues. Ballinger thus sharpened his understanding of the world in which he would live his adult life. Here, too, in debates over capital punishment for debtors and the nonremoval of manumitted slaves, his later preoccupation with law and justice took shape.

Unfortunately Ballinger's severe asthma forced him to leave St. Mary's and return to Barbourville in the winter of 1843. Although his exposure to higher education was brief, it left him with a passion for learning that remained with him for life. At times, especially with his favorite subjects—law, history, and philosophy—Ballinger became obsessed with absorbing all he could. Even after exhausting all available sources on a particular topic, he wanted to learn more. As a result, Ballinger became a voracious, extensive reader, who developed a fierce concentration and a photographic memory. Throughout his adult life relatives and friends were overwhelmed by his breadth of knowledge on a variety of topics, ranging from history and philosophy to botany and zoology. More impressive was his remarkable recall, often verbatim, of virtually everything he had read on a particular subject. As his son remembered, "Papa could recite perfectly, not a sentence or word missing, entire pages from books he had read. It did not matter what the topic was—if he believed it was important or of great interest, he committed as much of the text as was possible to memory & could recall whatever information he needed, word for word at an instant's notice even tho [sic] he had read the book years ago. He possessed this remarkable ability down to the end of his life."[26]

Perhaps more important than inculcating Ballinger with a yearning for knowledge and reflection was the Jesuits' expostulation for religious tolerance. Much to the chagrin of many rabid Kentucky fundamentalists, the Jesuits, whose own missionary zeal was legendary, wisely restrained their passion for conversion. The Catholic Church was acutely aware of its precariousness in revivalist Kentucky, and thus to avoid even the slightest accusation of a "Roman conspiracy," the clergy assiduously reassured their Protestant hosts that their communities were safe from their proselytizing.[27] As Ballinger later recalled, "the Jesuit Bros. were always very careful about preaching the Catholic faith & instead encouraged us to keep our hearts & minds open—to keep ourselves free of religious bigotry & embrace all in the brotherhood of man. I have endeavored & believe I have been true to those teachings throughout my life."[28]

Throughout his adult life Ballinger believed education was an essential bulwark of civilization. It was especially imperative in a republic. Its widespread accessibility determined not only individual fate but society's survival as well. Ballinger was particularly keen on a classical curriculum which, he believed, stimulated "the investigation of truth, the observation & the study of the causes of things, and most important, the stretching to the limit, the powers of rational & creative thought." As he further told his son, any young man who has pursued a liberal education will "know himself & will know the principles governing the moral & physical world. It is the key to unlocking the mysteries of Nature." Such individuals become the intellectual leaders "upon whose shoulders will come to rest civilization." That was why in a republic, which "depends on the voices of the many rather than the few," education is "the most important subject for society—not to the individual only, but to the community."[29]

Once the decision was made to leave St. Mary's, Ballinger remembered "being as despondent & remorseful as the day Mother died. I could not bear the thought of having to leave the place & return to Barbourville. I believed Father would be disappointed & look upon me as someone who could not rise above his affliction & be something."[30] Despite feelings of trepidation about his return home, Ballinger was proud of his accomplishments at St. Mary's, not all of which were academic. Most important to Ballinger was his ability to deal with his asthma alone, and in the process, bring it under better control. During his first two years at college, he suffered only three asthma attacks, only one of which forced him to miss several days of class while recuperating in bed. According to Ballinger, the other two were "of the mildest nature that I had little difficulty attending lecture & pursuing my studies as usual. Indeed, I was fully recovered in both instances in less than a day & found myself even more intensely engaged in my life at the college." While at St. Mary's Ballinger led the most physically active life he could remember during his adolescence. "Running constantly everywhere with all the other lads. Long hikes as well—fishing, hunting in the wilderness—things I never enjoyed before for fear they would bring on the asthma."[31] It seems that being away from his father and in the nurturing and accepting arms of the Jesuits helped Ballinger to build his self-confidence. Gaining better control over his asthma taught Ballinger unforgettable lessons in relying on his own powers and believing in his abilities. Altogether, Ballinger's childhood could have served as another exemplary tale of surmounting odds and rewarding compensations.

Much to Ballinger's surprise, James Franklin had changed considerably, largely as a result of his marriage to Elizabeth Jenkins in 1840. Apparently, five years a widower with four children to raise was too much even for the most hearty of frontiersmen. James Franklin remarried during Ballinger's first year at St. Mary's. When Ballinger received the news of his father's wedding, he recalled being "very disturbed. I asked how could he do that to my mother. How could he disgrace himself in such a fashion, & defile her honor & memory. But I later realized how foolish & juvenile such thoughts were—I was jealous & angry. I never realized how lonely he was & the help he needed with all of us."[32]

In Ballinger's mind, his father's new wife could never take the place of his idealized real mother. Yet, as he later admitted, Elizabeth's "strength &

relentless patience & gentleness," caused James Franklin to change his conception of Ballinger. When Will arrived home his father greeted him with such affection that he was "awe struck." His stepmother was equally warm in her reception. As Ballinger later recalled, "from the moment we first met, she treated me as if I was her son & always came to my defence if she believed Father was being unkind or unreasonable. I grew to greatly admire & respect her." More important to Ballinger was Elizabeth's affect on his father. He believed that "She was the person most responsible for Father having changed his feelings toward me." Thanks to Elizabeth, Ballinger and his father "became closer—companions in a strange sort of way, & I believe he truly respected me & was proud of what I had accomplished. For the first time since a small child I felt close to him."[33]

Will and his father indeed became close. After a few months of convalescense, Ballinger went to work for James Franklin as deputy clerk. As such, Ballinger had the opportunity to study law, and he daily immersed himself in the works of the great jurists like Blackstone. The struggle against his asthma played an important part in directing Ballinger's interests and ambitions. From adolescence on, the law absorbed Ballinger. Except for an earlier fascination with ships and the sea,[34] he had no other interests until adulthood. The timing of his attraction to the law was also a reflection of his newly gained confidence in his own powers. While at home under his father's tutelage, Ballinger began envisioning a legal career for himself. Above his desk in his room he put up a portrait of Daniel Webster, considered one of the nation's greatest antebellum advocates as well as the stalwart of the Whig Party. Ballinger joked with friends and relatives that one day aspiring young attorneys would have his portrait above their desks.[35]

Since James Franklin's legal training was rudimentary at best, and his legal skill equally modest, Ballinger's education under his father's direction was severely limited. It must be remembered that during the antebellum period the legal profession was one of the easiest to enter, particularly if one lived in a rural settlement. The vast majority of antebellum advocates, whether they lived in a rural or urban environment, received their training, as Ballinger did, under the auspices of an established attorney. For a fee, they read Blackstone and Coke, and they copied legal documents. If lucky, the apprentices benefited, as Ballinger did, from watching the lawyer do his work and hopefully do it well. Some lawyers were conscientious about their clerks, anxious like James Franklin to give them proper training. However, a good number of established lawyers who accepted clerks had only marginal training themselves and were thus ill-qualified to properly prepare future advocates. Regardless of their mentor's qualifications, young aspirants simply "read the law" until they were ready to take the bar exam. The exam was usually orally administered by a local judge and two other established lawyers. After satisfactorily answering questions of the most common jurisprudence, the inquisitors pronounced the individual qualified to become a member of the bar; he could now "hang out his shingle" anywhere in the state and receive clients. Although Ballinger's training might have been a little more formal because his father was associated with the local court system, it nevertheless was fundamentally the same.[36]

Ballinger did not want to follow family precedent, spending most of his life dealing in writs and warrants. He was grateful to his father for giving him the opportunity to learn law and court procedure, but he wanted more than just a peripheral knowledge of the nation's legal system. He wanted to become a "legitimate" jurist. Moreover, Will Ballinger, like so many young Americans in the 1840s, was restless and wanted adventure. Thanks to his years at St. Mary's, Ballinger was confident that he could make it on his own anywhere. He had outgrown Barbourville and the Kentucky highlands and now was ready to move on to a larger world of opportunity and challenge. Chance, in the form of an uncle, opened that door for him.

In the summer of 1843 Ballinger was contacted by his uncle, James Love, inviting him to come to Galveston, Texas, and finish his legal training under Love's auspices. "Uncle Jimmy" had moved to Texas in 1837 and soon emerged as a man of many talents, not all of which were related to his legal practice. By the time Will Ballinger arrived in Texas, Love had become a cotton planter and slaveowner, whose plantation on Oyster Creek in Brazoria County added a tidy sum to his legal fees. He was also an intensely partisan politician, whose home served as a base of operations for the opponents of Sam Houston.[37] There he welcomed his eighteen-year-old nephew, and for more than two years Will Ballinger learned many things not found in his law books.

Chapter Two

"TO BESTOW HONOUR AND DIGNITY UPON THE FAMILY"

No sooner did Ballinger arrive in Galveston than his uncle had him reading every standard legal text of the era. James Love was a small, thin man, with a wrinkled, wizened face. He was always meticulously and fashionably attired and coifed. As Ballinger further recalled, "his voice was shrill, sharp & unpleasant, and he had not a single grace of oratory. But when he spoke, he always had interested & attentive listeners. Underneath this curious exterior was a gigantic intellect." Methodical, industrious, particular, painstaking, and precise, Love imposed on his nephew a regimen of study that made even "the most stern of the Jesuit fathers easier task-masters."[1] At times, Ballinger found his reading to be "distressfully boring," but he labored through it because "Uncle Jimmy watched over me constantly & when I started to fall asleep, I would hear a thunderous boom from the corner of his office—'William stand tall on those books or you'll not succeed at this profession."[2] Apparently his uncle's admonishments were effective, for even when Ballinger walked about the town or the beach, he carried a book with him, and though he "pleasantly responded to interruptions," he promptly went back to his reading. "He read so much—was so studious—& took so little physical exercise—was so laborious in his studies," James Love remembered," that he became emaciated & even I was afraid that he would craze himself."[3]

In his studying, Ballinger soon realized that his most difficult task was reducing the enormous amount of diffuse material to some kind of system that he could memorize. The idea he hit upon was to compose a practice manual summarizing procedures and the essential points of laws under major headings, such as Damages, Process, Judgment and Execution, Pleas, Venue, and so on. After writing the manual, Ballinger then memorized it in his usual manner, pacing to and fro and reciting aloud to himself. Ballinger found the beach rather than his uncle's law office to be the best place to concentrate in such a fashion. Daily for several hours Ballinger would stroll on the beach talking to himself. Suffice it to say, many Galvestonians found Ballinger's study habits a bit peculiar, but as he later recalled, he rarely noticed their stares, and if he did, he would "stop, smile at them cordially, respond to their query, if they had one, and then continue along my course. I believe I became a familiar site after awhile, and soon everyone stopped thinking I was crazed & understood what I was attempting to do."[4] In addition to his reading, his uncle insisted that he attend local court proceedings. Observing the highly informal procedures and learning that most of the leading lawyers were self-educated doubtless led Ballinger to believe that this was a forum in which he could successfully compete.

Ballinger had almost completed his legal apprenticeship when the United States declared war on Mexico in the spring of 1846. Like so many Texans, Will Ballinger was eager to participate in the conflict. At his uncle's home he restlessly listened to reports of military activities along the Rio Grande and watched the departure of volunteers responding to Gen. Zachary Taylor's April 26th call for the creation of three Texas regiments to be mustered into regular service for a three-month period.[5] The outbreak of the Mexican War stirred Ballinger's romantic spirit. In a letter to his father, Ballinger not only displayed his own enthusiasm for the war and the opportunity he would have to gloriously uphold the family's martial tradition, but at the same time reassured his father that he would "return from the field, safe & sound and resume my legal studies. I know Uncle Jimmy wrote to you strongly protesting my desire to enlist in one of the companies already being formed here [Galveston]. This is the moment every young man waits for in his life—the opportunity to bravely serve his country & by his deeds performed in battle bestow honour and dignity upon the family name. Please do not deny me this glorious moment to do that for our family. I could not bear to live with myself if I could not join in & prove myself worthy of true manhood."[6]

Ballinger had been waiting since childhood to prove his masculinity to his father, and the Mexican War gave him the opportunity to erase any lingering doubts his father still harbored about his manliness. Will believed if he could endure the physical, moral, and psychological challenges of warfare, James Franklin would have no choice but to accept his son as an equal, for Will would have proved himself in that one arena of universal acceptance: valor on the battlefield. Thus for reasons more personal than patriotic, twenty-one-year-old Will Ballinger set out to prove his mettle. Despite his uncle's continued solicitations, on Saturday, May 16, 1846, Ballinger, along with seventy-two other Galvestonians, enlisted as a private in a volunteer unit, Company D, under the command of Capt. Ephraim W. McLean.[7]

Unable to get passage by sea, Ballinger and his compatriots set forth by horse on a three-hundred-mile journey to Fort Polk, the name given to the installation at Point Isabel, which served as the rendezvous point for all the Texas volunteer companies. Joining Ballinger's Galvestonians en route were other Texas contingents, as well as individual Texans whom, as Ballinger remarked, "had joined up just for the chance to fight Mexicans who they appear to have a very deep hatred for. These men come from all over the State & are a very rough bunch in their behaviour. They should do well when the fighting actually begins. Right now they are an unpleasant lot to be around."[8] After thirty-eight days of travel, Ballinger's outfit arrived at Point Isabel.

At Point Isabel on the Gulf of Mexico, Ballinger found an abundance of sand, heat, and confusion. The center of activities was Fort Polk, a hastily erected earthwork located on a thirty-foot bluff overlooking the sea. Encamped in the open around the fort were the volunteers, including throngs of Texans who were arriving daily in parties similar to the one that Ballinger joined. Gov. J. Pinckney Henderson, commander of all the Texas forces, had not arrived, so the Texans were still on their own. Much to the governor's chagrin, the legislature required that officers be elected by the troops, not appointed by him.[9]

Not until June 18th did Henderson arrive and the regimental organization occur. At that time, Ballinger's company was combined with seven other smaller companies and mustered into the regular army for three-month's service as Company D of the First Regiment of Texas Foot Rifles. Albert Sidney Johnston, an intimate of James Love whom Ballinger had also befriended, was unanimously elected colonel of the regiment, and Ballinger and Oliver C. Hartley were elected first and second lieutenants respectively. Ballinger remained a field officer for only a few weeks. On July 1 Johnston appointed him to his regimental headquarters staff as adjutant, and together they prepared for the Battle of Monterrey.[10]

Though honored by his appointment as adjutant, Ballinger was initially reluctant to accept it as it would limit his opportunity to see combat and win glory—something he believed essential at this juncture in his life. As adjutant he managed both Johnston's and volunteer commander Brig. Gen. William O. Butler's administrative affairs, wrote much of their official correspondence, and carried out a variety of special assignments, including reconnaissance and raiding forays. He also ensured that both his fellow officers' and regular soldiers' achievements were recognized and rewarded. At the same time, he helped discipline troops and, through assiduous administrative labors, saw to their being as appropriately uniformed, provisioned, and regularly paid as was possible during a war that saw more American soldiers die from disease, malnutrition, and general carelessness than from combat. Ballinger's experience as adjutant taught him something about himself, which rankled even as it contributed to his maturity. Much as he yearned to prove his worth on the battlefield, he was forced to recognize that he could contribute far more as an administrator. He was a man who could run things, and that talent was in great demand and short supply. Although he had no field command, Ballinger repeatedly knew the thrill and danger of combat and thus had opportunites to distinguish himself in the heat of battle.[11]

Ballinger and his compatriots remained at Point Isabel for more than a month. The battles of Palo Alto and Resaca de la Palma occurred before his arrival, and the defeated Mexican army had already retreated deeper into Mexico. Occupying Matamoros, Taylor prepared to strike into the interior of Mexico as soon as he collected troops, equipment, and transportation for such a campaign. In late July, Taylor pressed up the Rio Grande for an assault on the Mexican army concentrating at Monterrey. Taylor's army of over six thousand troops comprised two divisions of regulars and one of volunteers. Ballinger and a portion of his regiment embarked on August 5th on a steamboat up the Rio Grande for Camargo, the site of Taylor's advance base.[12]

For more than three hundred miles the transport wound its way up the river, allowing Ballinger time to observe and reflect upon the country and people he saw. It was the first time Ballinger had traveled beyond the civilized confines of semitropical southeast Texas. He now found himself in a completely opposite environment, where his appreciation for the rugged beauty of the Mexican soil contrasted sharply with his disregard for the people who worked it. "As a race the inhabitants are inferior," he wrote, "resembling in color and general make up the indians of the United States & not much superior to some of them in civilization. Such exposures to other peoples makes one appreciate our Anglo-Saxon heritage which has elevated us far above many other people."[13]

The nativism if not outright racism revealed in Ballinger's observations of Mexican culture was not atypical. His perceptions were similar to those held by numerous Anglo-Americans caught up in the fervor of national expansionism and the turgid rhetoric of "manifest destiny," which has since become a label for the whole complex of attitudes, concepts, and actions that swept American dominion to the shores of the Pacific Ocean. At the heart of this impulse was an exuberant faith in the democratic creed: Anglo-Americans were a chosen race, and their appointed mission was to extend the area of freedom.[14] Thus young Will Ballinger, animated by his own feelings of Anglo-Saxon superiority, was prepared to help relieve Mexico of a large measure of her national domain.

Disappointment awaited Ballinger in Camargo. Arriving in mid-August, he found a scene of sickness, death, and demoralization. The town lay on the San Juan River a few miles above the point where this stream flows into the Rio Grande. Sweltering in unbearable heat, plagued with myriad insects, and supplied with impure water, the raw recruits died daily from exhaustion and disease. Years later, in a letter to his brother-in-law, Guy Bryan, who was serving in the Confederate army, Ballinger recalled the conditions at Camargo, which he believed were similar to those afflicting Confederate forces by 1864. "Few understand the ravages & perils of war. They are not found in the reports of the battle field; these account for but a small portion of the tragic waste of life. Privations without number, hard marches under a burning sun or in the chilly hours of the night, or the dead of winter, make up a bill of mortality treble that of the fiercest combat."[15]

At this moment of misery, Ballinger's regiment was reduced further by the end of the enlistment period for most of the Texas volunteers. Out of a regiment of over five hundred men, 318 volunteers, including an entire company of German-Americans who had suffered much sickness, left for home. Though having suffered through two asthma attacks and enduring a serious bout of diarrhea, Ballinger was determined to persevere, at least until the army reached Monterrey, where he hoped he would see some fighting. From the moment he enlisted his purpose was to prove his masculinity in combat. To give up now—even though his enlistment was up—and return home, would result only in his feeling "ashamed & unworthy of the respect & dignity offered to those who actually fight for their country." As he further told his uncle, "no matter what other maladies or hardships I must endure, I will not quit this army until I have earned that right by facing the enemy in battle." With such resolve Ballinger prepared to leave Camargo and, in late August, began the march toward Monterrey.[16]

On the morning of September 21, 1846, the Battle of Monterrey commenced. Gen. William J. Worth with a division of regulars, advanced on El Soldado. Taylor ordered the remainder of the army to attack from the east. Another division of regulars under Col. David Twiggs moved first, engaging the Tenería redoubt and Fort Diablo before being stopped by heavy enemy fire. Seeing this assault momentarily halted, Taylor committed Butler's division of volunteers to the attack.[17]

The volunteers advanced under severe bombardment from the Citadel. Ballinger, accompanying Johnston and Butler, joined forces (mostly Texans) with those of Brig. Gen. Thomas L. Hamer, commanding another volunteer unit, the First Ohio Volunteers. Their object was to take Fort Diablo. Resistance everywhere was fierce. Every street was barricaded and reinforced by artillery and musketry; concealed on the flat roofs of the stone houses were enemy troops firing point-blank into the Americans. Butler tried breaking through the walls from house to house in order to escape the Mexicans' fire, but the attempt failed, and the volunteers endured intense enemy fire. The heaviest American losses of the Battle of Monterrey occurred here. In two hours of fighting, the combined division of Ohio and Texas volunteers lost one-fourth—125—of its soldiers killed or wounded.[18]

According to Ephraim McLean, who was a member of Ballinger's regiment, despite the "noise, smoke, and confusion," young Will Ballinger "remained in his saddle and was a perfect target for the enemie [sic]. Altho his horse was struck in several places he was unharmed and continued on foot until another horse was brought, to encourage the men to hold on. He moved from position to position, always in the line of fire, shouting orders amid the uproar in an effort to keep the assault moving."[19] Despite the gallant performances of young officers like Ballinger, all was in vain. Taylor, seeing the futility of further advances, reluctantly ordered the entire army, except those forces occupying the Tenería, to withdraw.[20]

As the Americans retreated from the edge of the city, a column of Mexican mounted lancers counterattacked what was left of the Ohio-Texas regiment. The lancers were reputed to be the most formidable of Mexican soldiers. Sweeping across the plain and killing stragglers with their javelins or sabres as they came, the Mexican hussars spread panic among the retreating volunteers. Many of the Americans threw aside their arms and fled pell-mell through the nearby cornfield.[21]

Watching this rather ignoble retreat from the battlefield was young Ballinger. Aware that this was no way for a respectable soldier to withdraw, he took the initiative to try to save his men from not only disgrace but certain death. He was separated from his commander during the confusion, and instead of waiting for his superior to reappear with orders, which might not be for some time, Ballinger rode among the frightened troops, urging them to turn and form a line against their pursuers. Once again his courage and air of command provided his comrades with the inspiration they needed. They took positions behind a fence and opened fire on the lancers, killing a good number of them and sending the remainder volte-face.[22]

In a letter to James Love, Albert Sidney Johnston, Ballinger's commanding officer, wrote of his lieutenant's dauntlessness during the skirmish. "It was through your nephew's presence & personal valor, mainly, that our men ceased their hasty & ignominious retreat. Young Ballinger exhorted them to take up positions & fire at the Mexican charges instead of running from the field of battle. His coolness and courageous performance saved our men from a cruel slaughter & left an impression on the minds of many that will not be forgotten. Upon return to camp, 'three cheers' went up for Lt. Ballinger from those men whose lives he undoubtedly helped to save & restore dignity to. You should be proud of his bravery & the honour he has bestowed upon your Family."[23]

Though failing to take Monterrey in one decisive battle and losing 394 men in the assault, Taylor inflicted more damage upon his adversary than he knew. The Mexican commander, Gen. Pedro Ampudia, retreated deeper into the city with his forces and the Americans controlled the Saltillo road, completely cutting him off from supplies and reinforcements. This was apparent by the second day of battle. After a relentless artillery barrage, the Americans penetrated the city with ease, meeting only token Mexican resistance as they moved toward the Central Plaza. Realizing that further attempts to hold the city would be futile, General Ampudia surrendered his army on the morning of September 24, 1846. According to the terms finally agreed upon, Monterrey was to be surrendered to the Americans and all Mexican troops had to fall beyond Rinconada Pass. An armistice of eight weeks was to be observed by both sides. Considering the weakened and exhausted condition of the American army and the near depletion of its materiel, Taylor wisely accepted the conditions.[24] Victory at Monterrey made heroes of Worth and Taylor. Worth was the "highcombed cock" of the army; Taylor was on his way to the White House; and William Pitt Ballinger had proved his valor on the battlefield.

After the storming of Monterrey, Ballinger's term of enlistment expired and he returned to Galveston to continue his legal studies. After a few more months of intense preparation, he was finally ready to take his bar examination. On November 12, 1846, after an examination in open court by a committee of three established attorneys (Joseph A. Lovett, Henry Potter, and Jonas Butler), William Pitt Ballinger, age twenty-two, was pronounced "possessed of sufficient skill and learning in the science of law to entitle him to admission as an attorney & counselor at law," which was issued the following day by his uncle, Judge James Love, of the First Judicial District.[25] Two months after Ballinger passed his bar Uncle Jimmy secured a partnership for him with Jones and Butler (John B. Jones and Jonas Butler), a well-established firm, reputed to have one of the most extensive practices in the Galveston area. This was a rare opportunity for a young lawyer with little experience. Unlike most beginning lawyers who had to hunt around for business or accept cases that no one else would want, Ballinger began with a very full practice.

Ballinger quickly impressed Jones and Butler with his abilities. He had no difficulty performing routine office work, like drafting wills or writing deeds; as he had done a certain amount of this for his uncle even before he was admitted to the bar. Moreover, comprehensive knowledge of the law was not required of Ballinger. Litigation was then very simple; the state's judicial system was still in its infancy, with no voluminous collection of precedents to master and no array of authorities to cite. Most lawsuits were extremely simple and involved small sums of money. Technical training was not yet essential for a lawyer. Railroads, corporations, trusts, big business did not trouble the profession as they would in Ballinger's later years with their countless abstruse and subtle legal problems. The fundamental principles of Blackstone and Chitty, together with a fine intellect, ability to marshal facts, power of reasoning, common sense, and tenacity of purpose, were more than sufficient to make Ballinger a worthy assistant to Jones and Butler. Thus, within months of his joining the practice, Jones and Butler entrusted to Ballinger's care the account of Samuel May Williams. Williams was one of the wealthiest and most influential members of Galveston's ruling elites who had kept Jones and Butler on retainer for several years. Ballinger's services for Williams ranged from note payments and land sales, to the paying of personal debts and judgments, and even the discretionary apportioning of a monthly stipend to Williams's son

"To bestow honour and dignity upon the family"

Jonas Butler, Ballinger's law partner, 1846–1854. Though at times Ballinger was disturbed by his partners' sleight-of-hand activities, he nonetheless learned much about the law from them. *Photograph courtesy Mills, Shirley, Eckel & Bassett, L.L.P., of Galveston, Texas.*

"Beaver" (William Henry Williams), who was attending Harvard.[26]

Of more legal substance than managing the familial affairs of prominent Galvestonians, was Ballinger's involvement in the vexing issues of land titles. Perhaps no other question was as confounding yet potentially lucrative for Texas attorneys than determining the legitimacy of the various land grants issued throughout Texas's history. What made this such a contentious area of jurisprudence was that, since the days of Mexican rule, land was literally given away in order to attract settlers. First Mexico, then the Republic, and finally the state of Texas all gave generous portions of the public domain away at no cost. Depending on the time a settler came to Texas, he received land ranging anywhere from 640 to four thousand acres. The problem was, however, which of the grants—Mexican, Rebublican, or those awarded by the state of Texas—took precedence when they conflicted. Adding to the confusion was the dubious legitimacy of many of these grants. Speculation and fraud had resulted in the issuance of patents, especially by the Republic and state, granting land far in excess of what was legally sanctioned. Thus millions of acres of Texas public domain had disputed or "unquiet" titles, requiring protracted litigation to determine the proper owner.[27]

It was in this area of Texas law that the tutelage of Jones and Butler proved most beneficial to Ballinger. The research he was required to do proved to be an invaluable introduction to the intricacies of emerging Texas realty law. Thanks to his exposure at Jones and Butler, once on his own Ballinger rapidly transformed his practice into one that was noted for its expertise in Texas land law.

As Ballinger soon discovered, lawyers were integral members of the capital-based Anglo elite that dominated the post–Mexican War Texas economy. It was Anglo lawyers who organized the land market in the new territories, and in the process, became the critical intermediaries between the land-based Mexican elite and capital-based Anglo merchants. Firms such as Jones and Butler, who were well-versed in Spanish and Mexican land law, were especially effective in winning suits for their Anglo-American clients against Mexican Nationals and Tejanos who claimed title to land granted by the state of Coahuila-Texas in the last years of Mexican rule. These grants totaled about five million acres along the lower Texas Gulf Coast and the United States-Mexican border. Because of their location, they were referred to as the "littoral and border leagues." In a display of antipathy for Mexican authority, the convention declaring Texas independence simultaneously nullified all littoral and border grants. The convention argued that most of these grants were spuriously acquired since they violated the Mexican national law of 1824 forbidding the granting of land to any settler if it was within "twenty border leagues" of the Texas Gulf Coast or the United States-Mexican border. Many current claim holders believed their conveyance was official because it had been issued by the governor of Coahuila-Texas, an authorized representative of the Mexican government. To compound an already messy situation, much of the land, because of "double-dealing," had been acquired by Anglo-American speculators, some of whom did not even reside in Texas.[28]

In 1841 the Texas Congress decreed that all persons claiming Mexican land grants had one year to bring suit against the Republic to determine their claim's legitimacy. If they failed to bring suit in the allotted time, all further claims under Mexican grants would be abjured. In 1842 the government declared all unclaimed land as public domain and began disbursing it to Anglo settlers claiming certificates from the Republic. It must be remembered that the Republic was money poor but land rich. In order to attract homesteaders to develop Texas's vast acreage, it was crucial that much of the public domain be free so it could be dispersed to as many individuals as possible. Of course, Anglo-Americans were given priority as preferred settlers. They were already credited with transforming Mexican Texas from a forgotten, unproductive wasteland into one of the most promising sources of agricultural wealth in the Southwest. The Texas state legislature and local courts made sure that any disputed land, particularly if it was held by a Mexican or Tejano, became part of the public domain and was quickly sold or given to Anglo-Americans.[29]

It made no difference to Jones and Butler, or to the majority of Anglo firms, whether Tejano claimants had substantial documentation legitimizing their claim. Some Tejanos even tried negotiating "compromises" with Anglo practitioners (offering them, directly, sizeable portions of their land) in hopes of at least keeping some of their original grant. All was in vain. Anglo-Texans were determined to strip all Mexicans of their land and wealth, reducing them to economic vassals.[30]

Such were the conditions of two cases in which Ballinger was directly involved. The claimants, Leonardo Manso and Joaquin Arguelles, tried for months to convince Ballinger of the legitimacy of their respective claims. Writing their entreaties mostly in Spanish (which Ballinger mastered by the end of his tenure with Jones and Butler), both men inundated the firm with what they believed was more than adequate proof of their right to their land. Their efforts were in vain. After nine months of litigation, the state Supreme Court nullified both the Manso and Arguelles grants. Each man lost a league and labor of land, or roughly five thousand acres. According to Jones, Butler and Ballinger, Manso and Arguelles had no right to the land because their grant violated the Mexican law of 1824 by being less than twenty leagues from the United States-Mexican border: the Sabine River in east Texas where the disputed property was located. After the court ruled against Manso and Arguelles, their land then became part of the public domain.[31]

Once the property became public domain, Jones and Butler instructed Ballinger to contact prospective Anglo buyers, who supposedly held certificates from the Republic. Those contacted about the land's availability were the speculator friends of Jones and Butler to whom the firm wanted to sell the land before homesteaders had access to it. Within a matter of weeks, both the Manso and Arguelles grants were purchased (for two dollars an acre), not by any hardy Anglo yeomen, which was the decree's original intent, but by an East Texas cotton and timber baron, Peter Powell of

Tyler. Suffice it to say Powell was elated by his acquisition. He was so delighted that he displayed his gratitude by not only giving Jones and Butler "all my future business &c," but also assuring the two attorneys that he would "refer your names as reliable & effective land agents to other individuals who wish to purchase good land at such bargain prices. You have proven yourselves worthy of your reputation as men interested in promoting the development of our State."[32]

The law nullifying Mexican grants was not only prejudiced but spurious as well. Ballinger's complicity in these shady dealings was thus inexcusable. Even if his involvement was a result of his naivete, his actions were nonetheless disreputable, and Ballinger knew it. He was also disheartened by his partners' conspiracy with speculators to ensure their acquisition of the forfeited land. Uncle Jimmy wanted him to "learn first hand" the profession's many facets; Ballinger was now getting more experience than he cared for. Before joining Jones and Butler, Ballinger's only exposure to the law was as a clerk in rarefied Kentucky courtrooms. Antebellum Texas was a wide-open frontier environment where the rule of law was still with a Colt revolver, and where professional niceties were rarely observed. It is no wonder Ballinger became despondent soon after the close of the Manso and Arguelles cases. Though knowing his uncle was not a very sympathetic man, Ballinger nonetheless was so distraught that he wrote to him anyway, hoping for solace. "Tho I fully understand that my principal responsibility at all times is to serve the law, & to display loyalty to Messrs. Jones & Butler, I regret my latest endeavor. I believe both men [Manso and Arguelles] were treated unfairly. I wish there was something that could be done. An injustice has been done to these men & to others as well. Is this what the practice of law is all about?"[33]

As predicted, Love was wholly unsympathetic to his nephew's situation, and in fact, reprimanded him for his "juvenile notions about the Law. The law is not your's to ponder its meaning or purpose, but to uphold & enforce at all times. We [lawyers] do not make the laws, the People do, & if they wanted them changed then it is their responsibility to do so. Your job as a lawyer is to ensure the People's wishes—nothing else. If you hope to succeed in this profession, I urge you to remember what I have said & pursue your career accordingly."[34]

After his uncle's scolding, Ballinger quickly absolved himself of his sentimentality and reassured James Love that he understood and appreciated "the advice of your last letter. I will endeavor henceforth to keep my patron's interest first & foremost, regardless of personal sentiments or dis-

"To bestow honour and dignity upon the family"

agreement with its [the law's] intention."³⁵ This was not the last time in his career that Ballinger would have to wrestle with the morality of his professional conduct. Time and again Ballinger would have to make difficult choices whether to uphold a questionable law or to defend a client clearly in the wrong. Even though he remained true to his uncle's conception of a lawyer's fundamental responsibility, Ballinger's decision often caused him anguish. Perhaps his uneasiness was the result of the popular image of lawyers in the antebellum period.

Throughout most of the nation's history, including the present, the lawyer has been many creatures. He has been called a Tory, parasite, usurer, land speculator, corrupter of the legislature, note shaver, panderer to corporations, tool of the trusts, ambulance chaser, and loan shark. Some of his negative image is a result of his role as hired hand. Individuals of wealth and property need lawyers to protect their interests, as well as to help insulate them from the masses. And since the upper classes have the money to retain them, lawyers are thus popularly regarded as the lackeys of the rich. Lawyers were also perceived as aggressive, upwardly mobile opportunists, using the law to line their own pockets at the people's expense. The American lawyer never has been known for his scholarliness. Only a handful during the antebellum period attended college and graduated. Even fewer attended legitimate law schools upon receiving their undergraduate degrees. The antebellum practitioner was a man of action and cunning, not a learned doctor of laws. In short, the American jurist has played a useful role, sometimes admired, but rarely loved.

In only a few instances throughout his long career did Ballinger resemble any of the above characters in his professional conduct. Nonetheless he was stigmatized by the very nature of his occupation. Perhaps this was why he was so distraught by his partners' perfidy in the Manso and Arguelles cases and his tacit complicity in their guile. After his uncle's chastisement for his naivete, Ballinger accepted that he had idealized his profession's purpose. Like most young professionals of his time, he was sensitive to public opinion, wanting to be held in the highest esteem. Ballinger hoped to help change the popular image of lawyers as shysters and land speculators who cared not for the sanctity of the law but only how they might benefit from its perversion. Combining a scholarly ethicality with a devotion to justice, Ballinger strove to keep his reputation for personal integrity unblemished throughout his career. However, his conscientiousness and veneration of the truth did not mean that he always listened to his heart at the expense of his head. He was no heavenly agent of justice and knight-errant of law and equity, scorning the proffered fees of the rich and powerful in order to help the weak and distressed. Ballinger was a realist—shrewd, practical, and matter of fact. Although he was eager to right a wrong whenever it was in his power to do so, he did not go out of his way in search of cases of injustice to combat. He did not withdraw from cases in which he doubted success, nor did he look with suspicious scrutiny on all cases that came into his office. Inherently honest himself, he suspected no guile in others, and like any other lawyer, welcomed the general run of business. In short, Ballinger was ambitious for himself, his country, and his state, and thus knew well the complexity of sustaining convictions in action.

Although much of Ballinger's time was devoted to assisting Jones and Butler in land claim disputes, he was involved in a variety of other legal matters as well. For example, in the summer of 1848 he defended the right of the Galveston German Association to build a church and school on land to which the city claimed title. Apparently city fathers were alarmed by the increasing number of German Catholics in Galveston, and in a move reflecting their nativism, they attempted, on the most specious charges, to nullify the association's original grant. In their petitions, city aldermen accused the association of falsifying their "pretended documents" by which they claimed title to the land. Some letters even intimated that Galveston Germans were a fifth column of "conspirators," who came to the Island City "not to become American citizens & obey our laws," but to help prepare the way for a massive Catholic invasion of the United States through Texas, "the perfect, unsuspecting place for a popish plot to be hatched." One councilman even accused Ballinger of "base fraud & forgery," maintaining that the attorney knew the papers were falsified and that he was going to profit from the deal because the association was supposedly planning to give the firm some of the land in lieu of payment. Jones, Butler and Ballinger, after "raising the price to an exorbitant rate," were then going "to offer it to the City, or to anyone who will buy it at a significant profit to them."[36]

Ballinger knew the city's accusations were rubbish. If there was one thing guaranteed to rouse Ballinger to a cause, it was religious bigotry. Despite the city's harsh charges to the contrary, this time the firm of Jones, Butler and Ballinger was not involved in any clandestine wheeling and dealing. Indeed, much to Ballinger's relief, Jones and Butler turned down an offer from the German Association to give them a portion of the land in question in lieu of money for their services. Inspired by a renewed faith in his partners, as well as by the city's anti-Catholicism, Ballinger was determined to uphold the association's right to its property. Despite Ballinger's commitment, many association members were ready to give in, fearing nativist-inspired reprisals if they did not. In the minds of the Germans a few city blocks was not worth incurring the wrath of their Anglo-Protestant neighbors. Ballinger convinced the German Association that it had nothing to fear, "that the law is on your side & you have all the documents &c. essential to establish your right to the property. Once this overwhelming evidence is presented to the City, they will have no choice but to allow you the land. You must for now dismiss all other accusations against you—they are the designs of evil men." After inundating city officials with letters and documents, substantiating the German Association's right to the land, the city finally relinquished its claim, allowing the association to construct their church and school.[37]

Ballinger was not successful in every case he handled. One case in particular proved embarassing for his firm, for it involved the violation of federal customs and slave laws by a local merchant who was a close friend and business associate of Jones and Butler. Ballinger was assigned to defend a James Merrill of Galveston against the charges of the deputy collector of customs at Galveston—that Merrill was involved in smuggling slaves from Cuba, and importing other merchandise without paying the appropriate duties. The collector confiscated all the contraband, including the ten Africans, and was then ordered by Secretary of the Treasury Robert Walker, "to sell at public auction all the illegal merchandise, except the negroes, who are to be returned to Cuba on the next available vessel leaving for that place." Merrill pleaded innocent of all charges, accusing the customs collector of "vindictiveness for my refusal to pay his usual bribe that others of this place are willing to do in order to have their merchandise free of charge. He has turned on me."[38]

Initially, Ballinger believed Merrill's story that the customs official was on the take, not an uncommon practice in major port cities. However, Ballinger's investigation revealed that the collector, James Cocke, was "clean." Merrill still insisted that he knew nothing of the Africans on the ship captained by a man named White, and that as far as the other goods were concerned, "rum, cigars, silk, Spanish port, French linens, & other finery," he was assured by White that all duties had been paid.[39] The types of goods Merrill attempted to smuggle into Galveston reflect the relative affluence of many of the islanders during the antebellum period. Galveston was a lucrative market for the retailers of fine goods, and boasted as well a thriving black market for contraband. The more involved Ballinger became with the Merrill case, the more suspicious he grew of his client's trustworthiness. Merrill finally confessed that he lied about the slaves "because there was good money to be made on the island selling negroes—I could easily get $1,000 to $2,000 a piece for them."[40]

"Good money" indeed. By the 1850s Galveston was regarded as one of the most profitable markets for the illegal African slave trade. The trade's revival resulted from the incessant demand of Texas planters to cultivate the rich bottom lands of the Gulf Coast. To these potential cotton barons, federal and state laws forbidding the importation of African slave labor appeared as obstacles to progress. Those individuals actually involved in the slave trade were in it for immediate profit. The fact that by the 1850s (and even earlier, as Merrill declared) a prime field hand could be sold in Texas for as much as fifteen hundred dollars made the trade especially attractive. The importers based their "merchandising" on interesting market principles. Because the demand for slave labor was so great in Texas, even under the most brutal conditions of the Middle Passage, it was possible to bring African labor directly to the Texas coast for about a dollar a pound, even after absorbing "shrinkage" costs. Thus, the profit on an African male weighing 150 pounds might be as much as $1,350.[41]

Though betrayed by Merrill, Ballinger accepted his responsibility, as Merrill's attorney, of at least mitigating his client's punishment. Merrill had been caught red-handed violating several federal laws, including bribery of a United States official. Ballinger was rapidly learning the difficulty of defending a client who was guilty—yet that was a lawyer's duty, like it or not.

More disconcerting to Ballinger than Merrill's chicanery was the revelation several months later that Jones, Butler, Merrill, and several other prominent Galvestonians were part of a smuggling operation bringing Africans into Galveston to be sold as slaves to mainland planters. Ballinger found this out from his Uncle James Love after plea bargaining with Secretary Walker not to hold his client accountable for all the infractions. Walker was apparently in a conciliatory mood, for he discounted any charges of bribery and Merrill's failure to pay the duties on the imported luxuries. Walker, however, would not overlook Merrill's involvement in the smuggling of Africans. On this infraction he flatly rebuffed Ballinger's overture to negotiate. Walker told the attorney that "both men [Merrill and White] must be punished for their violation of the Government's laws on the importation of Africans into this country to be sold as slave labor.

This office finds such an attempt to be the greatest offence in this case. I am determined to discourage with the severest penalties the illegal entry of Africans into this country." Merrill was fined two hundred dollars for his complicity in the affair, while White had his ship confiscated and sold at auction for being "the original procuror & carrier of the Africans."[42]

Both White and Merrill were fortunate to have received such light sentences. Their punishment would have been much harsher had they committed their crimes in an earlier period. Had Walker been willing to use the full force of the original 1807 statute, both men faced imprisonment as well as the paying of fines. In fact, White could have been executed for piracy under the revised statute of 1820. Yet, as Ballinger and most Southern attorneys were aware, the federal government made only perfunctory efforts at enforcing the statutes. Only sporadically did federal agencies come down hard on violators. Moreover, in most instances, such action was merely a display of empty executive bravado designed to muzzle the abolitionists. By the time of Merrill's and White's escapades, the illicit traffic reached such proportions that it virtually constituted the trade's reopening. Many slavers were outfitted openly in northern ports such as New York, and their cargoes often unloaded without any attempt at secrecy. Even if White and Merrill were indicted and hauled before a judge and jury, the likelihood of their conviction in a Texas court was remote. Indeed, the first conviction and execution for piracy under the 1820 law occurred after the outbreak of the Civil War.[43]

Even though successful in negotiating a slap on the hand for Merrill, Ballinger was distraught by his partners' clandestine involvement in the slave trade. He was not disturbed by their activity because he opposed slavery. Quite the contrary; what distressed him was the mockery of their oath to uphold the law. Yet Ballinger never took his partners to task for their transgressions. Perhaps he felt that to do so would only call attention to his association with such rogues and possibly ruin his career. The accounts of Jones's and Butler's illegal gambits were buried deep in Ballinger's papers as if he wanted us to know of his experiences and discomfort but was ashamed to admit he had worked with such men. Perhaps in retrospect Ballinger recognized that, despite their unethical conduct, Jones and Butler unquestionably were shrewd, knowledgeable attorneys from whom he had learned valuable lessons, not all of which were bad.

By 1850 Ballinger had grown weary of his partnership with Jones and Butler. In fact, he was so disillusioned that he briefly considered returning to Kentucky to practice law. James Love, however, quickly drove that notion from his mind, telling his bewildered nephew that returning home "would not be a very wise or profitable decision. Galveston is rapidly developing & the opportunities here are boundless for someone in your position."[44] Love believed the best way to relieve a bemused Ballinger of his anxiety (and keep him in Texas), was to provide him with another professional outlet. With that in mind, in the spring of 1850, the wily Love, with a little help from his friends, secured Ballinger a federal appointment. Upon the recommendation of the Texas Supreme Court, the state legislature, and prominent Texans, Ballinger was appointed by Secretary of the Interior Thomas Ewing to be the new United States district attorney for Eastern Texas. Unquestionably Ballinger's appointment was political, the successful result of personal lobbying by James Love to secure the vacated position for his nephew. Love's prestige among leading Texas Whigs was especially helpful. In their letters, prominent party members presented Ballinger as "a warm and zealous friend of the Administration," and as a "young man of uniform devotion to Whig principles." In his prefaces, J. L. Bates, the assistant to Secretary Ewing, described the Texans sanctioning Ballinger as "devout Whigs," "gentlemen of high standing in Texas," and as "warm and decided supporters of the Administration." Ballinger's referees also reserved ample space to comment on his personal attributes as well. He was described as having a "steady and diligent devotion to his business, a thorough knowledge of his profession, and exceptional character as a gentleman eminently suited for this station."[45]

That Ballinger's appointment was political is not to suggest that he was undeserving of the position. The wide range of recommendations attested to Ballinger's competence and knowledge of the law, as well as his respect among clients and peers. Nonetheless, Ballinger received the position as a result of direct party affiliation. Throughout most of the antebellum period the majority of federal appointments—such as United States district attorney—were the result of the "spoils system." Both Democrats and Whigs rewarded loyal party supporters with political office, ranging from secretary of state to assistant clerk in the Patent Office.

Rotation of office was just one of the ways by which continued party allegiance was maintained. If Ballinger had any remaining tendencies toward wanderlust and adventure, these were soon eclipsed by his romance with the "belle of the Brazos," Harriet Patrick Jack. In a society in which personal contacts were invaluable, Ballinger was fortunate in his family connections. Uncle Jimmy helped him secure his position in the firm of Jones and Butler as well as his appointment as United States attorney, and with his uncle's assistance, Ballinger's future in Texas grew even more promising with his engagement to "Hally" Jack in the summer of 1849.

Harriet Patrick Jack, daughter of Col. William Jack and Laura Harrison, was born in 1829 in Jefferson County, Alabama. The Jacks came to Texas in 1830, settling for a number of years at San Felipe where William Jack practiced law. Jack fought in the rebellion against Mexico, earning distinction for valor at the Battle of San Jacinto. After Texas won its independence, Jack purchased a plantation near Velasco where he prospered as a cotton planter and entrepreneur, speculating in land and a variety of other ventures. By the 1840s, the Jacks had emerged as one of the most influential families in the state.[46]

Although barely five feet tall and weighing less than ninety pounds, Hally's slender figure was no reflection of her feisty, robust personality. The red-haired, blue-eyed beauty was hardly the demure Southern belle. She was athletic, spirited, and incredibly self-possessed and, in many ways, the very antithesis of her more reserved and introspective fiancé. Hally was also every bit her future husband's intellectual equal. William Jack had not slighted his eldest daughter's education because of her gender. For five years "at the North," in an exclusive Boston school "for young ladies," Hally Jack learned more than ninety percent of her American female counterparts ever imagined possible. When she returned to Texas only a year before meeting Ballinger, she had become quite the renaissance woman. She was fluent in French, was well versed in rhetoric and the European classics, and, according to Ballinger, could play the piano "as well as most concert performers." Though enlightened beyond the norm, Hally nevertheless was also instructed in the more "acceptable" pursuits of watercolor, sewing, needlepoint, flower arrangement, and a variety of other traditional female activities. Thus, Hally not only returned academically enriched but more genteel and "lady-like" as well. It was no wonder that upon their first meeting at his uncle's house young Will Ballinger recollected being "completely enchanted & a bit intimidated. All through the day & into supper she captivated me with her charm, grace, & wit. By the end of the evening I knew I wanted to marry her."[47]

Ballinger's deep attraction to Hally sprang from her high-spiritedness, inner calm, and sensitivity, an unusual combination that inspired Ballinger to keep moving forward. Hally was remarkably nurturing and solicitous of Ballinger, not because she believed him weaker, but rather out of a sincere desire to help him overcome the emotional pain and self-doubt stemming from his traumatic childhood. Ballinger unquestionably loved

Harriet "Hally" Ballinger, Ballinger's beloved wife for thirty-four years. *Photograph by Rose and Zahn of Galveston, ca. 1880s. Courtesy Rosenberg Library, Galveston, Texas.*

and respected Hally as an individual and remained in love with her the rest of his life. To Ballinger, Hally was the perfect mate because she so cleverly offset his intense, methodical, and reflective temperament. She was gregarious, unflappable, and energetic. Refusing to let Ballinger retreat into himself, as he frequently did when feeling anxious, she drew him out of his brooding by making fun of him for taking himself too seriously. Although never coddling Ballinger or catering to his moodiness, Hally was always there for him—exhorting him when he was down, supporting him in whatever project he undertook, and caring for him when he was stricken with asthma. She was never condescending or patronizing, and when arguing, freely expressed herself without fear that Ballinger would think less of her for displaying her temper. Hally and Ballinger were close friends, enjoying each other's company, and longing for that companionship when separated. Hally was Ballinger's confidante in whom he had complete trust and faith.[48] Their deep, abiding love for each other gave them the strength to endure the loss of several children, indefinite separations, the trauma of war, prolonged financial crisis, epidemics, natural disasters, and myriad other problems part and parcel of nineteenth-century American life.

From the evidence found in Ballinger's papers, it appears that he and Hally enjoyed a fairly unsupervised courtship and were never pushed into matrimony. They grew to feel genuine romantic love for each other and entered into their marriage emotionally bonded by mutual love, respect, and compatibility. However, in the minds of both James Love and Laura Jack, Hally's mother (William Jack died in 1844), there lingered a more pragmatic attitude toward marriage among the upper classes. Laura Jack expected her only daughter to marry "well"—that is, to a male who was eligible by reason of family background and earning potential. Love assured Laura Jack that his nephew's new job as United States district attorney would provide Ballinger with enough income to support a wife and family.[49] Despite their parents' economic concerns, neither Hally nor Ballinger any longer viewed parental consent as a prerequisite for a happy relationship. Like most young couples of the mid-nineteenth century, Hally and Ballinger chose each other as spouses on the more secure basis of emotional commitment than for economic reasons.

On April 30, 1850, at the Jacks' Brazoria County plantation, Oak Grove, Ballinger and Hally were married by the Reverend J. H. Young of the Episcopal Church of Velasco. Later that day, over two hundred friends and relatives gathered to celebrate their union. One of Ballinger's new Harrison kin, "Uncle Tommy," described the reception as "one of the most splendid and joyous events given in this local [*sic*] for several years. I think it will be some time before we will see again such a fine display of grace & elegance, of fine food and beverage, and of gaity—all in celebration of the start to what everyone toasted would be the long & prosperous life for Mr. and Mrs. William Pitt Ballinger."[50]

After only seven years in Texas, Will Ballinger had achieved much. He had studied law, fought in a national war, returned with honor, become a respected lawyer, and married into one of the state's leading families. Before migrating to Texas, Ballinger acquired from his father, and the Jesuits at St. Mary's, the belief that honest labor was a virtue in any social class. As a result, he disdained the dilettantism he too often saw displayed by many of his professional peers. Although spending the last several years living in the affluence and security of his uncle's home, Ballinger nonetheless had little reverence for the wealth and power surrounding him. While working with Jones and Butler, Ballinger was exposed daily to a variety of individuals, many of whom earned their riches illegally or by brazenly exploiting others. For such individuals Ballinger had only contempt. From the moment he entered the legal profession until his death, Ballinger was determined to make it on his own. He pursued his career and conducted his personal life by principle and relentless application of effort rather than expedience.

Despite his resolve to be self-reliant, Ballinger's marriage stirred a latent fear of succumbing to the corruptibility of easy money. The Jacks' wealth could have easily secured Ballinger's financial future. As it was, they beseeched the newlyweds constantly, wanting to help "the children get started." Ballinger graciously refused their overtures, determined to make it on his own both professionally and personally. In only one recorded instance did Ballinger accept his in-laws' largesse. After much cajoling by the Jacks, he finally accepted his mother-in-law's offer to build Hally and him a home on the island. Ballinger's new residence was a "modest" six-room, two-storied abode on Avenue H, complete with servants' quarters, gardens, and a new carriage and team of four horses to go with it. Apparently, the Jacks feared their poor Hally would have to rough it while her husband established himself![51]

By 1850 Ballinger was a thorough urbanite and, like many other Galvestonians, was detached from the problems of the rest of the state. Indian depredations and lawlessness on the western pale were of little concern to Galvestonians unless they were forced to personally confront its reality. Thus, during the decade of the 1850s, Ballinger devoted himself to his family, to his profession, and to making his city "the Queen of the Gulf coast." However, before he could focus his energies on those activities, he had to endure three years of service on his government's behalf, chasing revolutionaries and filibusterers across South Texas and northern Mexico. It was while serving as United States attorney that Ballinger experienced the real Texas frontier of violence and lawlessness that forever chastened his urban smugness.

Chapter Three

"ALLOW ME TO BECOME AN ORDINARY CITIZEN AGAIN"

L awyers and politicians. The two were synonymous in the minds of most nineteenth-century Americans. The nation's antebellum political leadership was overwhelmingly drawn from the rank of its jurists. Perhaps because of their connections with the courts and as the interpreters and guardians of the nation's laws, lawyers were traditionally believed to be the best-qualified men for public office. Thus a political career, not the practice of law, became an obsession for many antebellum practitioners.

What attracted so many lawyers to office-holding? Perhaps it was the glamor of public life that captivated them. Or ambition—ambition fueled by the lust for power, authority, and patronage; the coveting an office for prestige and honor. For some it was an innate altruism: a desire to serve the people, to carry out their wishes, and to protect them from unscrupulous forces. Any one of these reasons, or a combination of them, could have lured the practitioner into public office. However, not all lawyers found politics or political jobbing to their liking; they eagerly awaited the opportunity to return to private practice and remain out of politics in any capacity forever. Contrary to the contemporary stereotype of lawyers being ambitious office-seekers, Will Ballinger's short career as a public servant proved the opposite could also be true.

Remarkably soon after his appointment, Ballinger had second thoughts about his role and responsibilities as a public servant. In fact, he had reservations the moment James Love and his friends began lobbying on his behalf. Once confirmed, however, Ballinger felt trapped. He had to accept the position, or his uncle and "all those who supported my candidacy would feel affronted by my lack of desire. This is a rare opportunity for a young lawyer, and to shun such a position because of fear of failure or disinterest" would be incomprehensible to a political animal like James Love. The majority of Ballinger's peers coveted such opportunities, believing anyone who eschewed them, for whatever reason, to be supremely foolish. Moreover, as Ballinger further revealed to his wife, his income would "go very far in my ability to provide adequately for you and baby."[1] Ballinger's first child, Laura Jack was born in January 1851. With such pressures upon him, Ballinger accepted the office, placating his politically ambitious uncle, but forcing him to postpone what he wanted to do most—practice law.

In retrospect, Ballinger appreciated his uncle's solicitude and the exposure this job gave him to another facet of the nation's legal system. However, at the time the experience only seemed lonesome, tedious, and grueling. In San Augustine the hotel was a "vile, ill-smelling place, with the dirtiest dining room." In Clarksville the proprietor so "liked his liquor" that guests had "to make do themselves—prepare their own meals &c." Everywhere the cooking was "villainous" and the bedbugs abundant.[2] In letters to Hally, Ballinger expressed his anxiety and the physical and mental fatigue that were part and parcel of his job. "It has been a cold bad day—a severe norther is now blowing. I feel fatigued and weary—chilled to the bone. Bowels are troubling me again. Have not eaten properly the last few days. . . . I find myself thoroughly sick and disgusted with the case [*Jackson v. Lamphire*]. Last night I slept poorly—have never felt so oppressed by a case. I have spent weeks preparing & now find myself so tired, anxious I only wish a decision to be made."[3]

Despite the hardships from the moment he took office in 1850 until resigning three years later, Ballinger faithfully dispatched his every assignment, committed to upholding federal laws as they pertained to conditions in Texas. Unfortunately, only a handful of Ballinger's letters have been preserved by the Attorney General's Office and the State Department, revealing Ballinger as the government's principal attorney and emissary in a potentially explosive international controversy. Ballinger's determined efforts to prosecute the Mexican revolutionist, José María Jesús Carvajal, and his Anglo-American accomplices earned him lasting recognition in the annals of the federal government.

Largely as a result of Mexico's centralist-versus-federalist conflict, by the early 1850s the lower Rio Grande Valley had become an especially troublesome area. The allure of lucrative smuggling operations and Indian raids against the settlers of both countries added to the general disorder.

Compounding the region's chaos was the chronic instability of the Mexican political scene, which, since 1822, witnessed one tottering regime after another fall to revolution or coup d'etat. Mexico never had effectively governed the vast Borderlands (Alta California, New Mexico, Arizona, and Texas prior to 1835), and after the war she found herself unable to maintain order in her provinces immediately south of the Rio Grande—the states of Coahuila, Tamaulipas, and Nuevo León. Even before the war, Mexican separatists from the region had conspired with Anglo-Texans from across the river to establish an independent northern republic forged out of these states.[4] One of the most legendary and genuine of these insurgents was José María Jesús Carvajal, who, together with his Anglo-Texans allies, kept the lower Rio Grande in a constant state of insurrection between 1851 and 1853.

No sooner did Ballinger assume his position than the "trivial border broils" (the assessment of Robert Hughes, Ballinger's predecessor) escalated into a potentially explosive international crisis with the emergence of Carvajal. For five years beginning in 1848, Carvajal and his followers tried to separate the northern states of Tamaulipas and Nuevo León and form a new state called the Republic of the Sierra Madre. Carvajal was able to rally many Anglo border dwellers to his cause by promising land and loot. Of great concern for the United States was the ability of revolutionaries like Carvajal to raise recruits from ex-officers and ex-soldiers of the United States Army. For a variety of reasons, Anglo-Texans, especially ex–Texas Rangers, found filibustering a particularly appealing new career. In September 1851, in his *plan de la Loba*, Carvajal formally "pronounced" against the Mexican government. Soon after announcing his plan, Carvajal fled to Brownsville, where he immediately negotiated with local Anglo merchants to supply him with the guns and other goods he needed to separate the northern states.[5]

At this juncture the new secretary of state, Daniel Webster (Webster, replacing John Clayton, was serving for his third and final time as the nation's chief foreign-policy maker), asked Ballinger to conduct a series of investigations of the state of affairs along the Rio Grande. Webster instructed Ballinger to keep the State Department informed "of all those who may be found within your district engaged in expeditions against the possessions of a friendly power, as well as any other unlawful acts committed by U.S. citizens in the area."[6] Webster's directive took Ballinger by surprise, for he too was under the impression, based on Hughes's reports, that all was relatively calm along the Rio Grande. Ballinger had just taken over from Hughes when he received Webster's letter, and consequently confessed to the secretary that his inquiry had been "carried on in a very hasty & cursory manner." Ballinger nevertheless reassured Webster that both he and other federal officers "may be relied on as ready and determined to do everything in our power to prevent any such movement from this state against Mexico."[7]

While Ballinger was busy with his fact-finding, Carvajal began his revolution. In late September 1851, Carvajal with an army of one hundred Mexicans and seventy Anglo-Americans, easily captured the village of Camargo, remaining there until early October. The surrounding towns of Mier and Guerrero also fell to the insurgents. Ballinger did not hear of Carvajal's taking of Camargo and the participation of the seventy Americans until three weeks after the town was occupied. He quickly sent a message to Webster, but it was too late for the Fillmore administration to take "preventive action."[8] Realizing Camargo was of little strategic or even symbolic value to his cause, Carvajal evacuated the town on October 9, proceeding with his reinforced army of four hundred men to Matamoros. Carvajal's original 170-man contingent was augmented by the arrival of about fifty ex-Rangers, as well as other Anglo-Texan adventurers lured by Carvajal's promise of land and loot.[9]

As Carvajal's uprising continued, Ballinger curiously became more sympathetic toward the rebel leader and his cause. Perhaps it was his desire to see justice prevail for an oppressed people, or a manifestation of his belief in the American democratic creed that accounted for his approbation of Carvajal's movement. As he related to Webster, Carvajal's claim of being a liberator was proving "to be of greater truth than was first assumed." Ballinger believed that *norteños* had "real grievances" against the centralist regime in Mexico City. "Corruption and treachery among Mexican officials, both civilian & military, is well known & all are equally despised by the people. There are conditions here which would cause the greatest outcry in our country. Perhaps even a rising of the citizenry against such abuses & tyranny." Though inclined to accept Carvajal as a legitimate revolutionary, Ballinger questioned "the true motives & desires" of *el jefe's* Anglo-American accomplices. To the attorney, most of these men were "brigands out for plunder."[10]

After failing to take Matamoros in the fall of 1851, and then Camargo in February 1852, Carvajal was back in Texas and supposedly safe. However, on March 1, a detachment of United States dragoons surprised the rebel leader at his camp, arresting Carvajal and eleven of his followers for their repeated violations of United States neutrality laws.[11] When Ballinger heard the news of Carvajal's capture he hurried to Brownsville. He wanted to quickly bring the rebel leader and his Anglo cohorts before a grand jury, which he was confident would indict the filibusterers for their violation of the neutrality laws. After presenting all the evidence he had gathered on Carvajal's activities, Ballinger was elated when the grand jury indicted *el jefe* and his Anglo officers. In a letter to Hally, Ballinger discussed his momentary victory. "After only one day of deliberation, and after I had presented the court with the most thorough account on their [Carvajal's band] looting & plundering, the grand jury ruled in our favor. I am very pleased & hope to see the whole thing finished before long."[12]

Unfortunately Ballinger's initial excitement over the indictment soon turned to disappointment. As he prepared his case he realized he lacked sufficient evidence to bring Carvajal and his followers to trial. As he confessed to Webster, "such evidence that is necessary is insurmountable to obtain because we will have to largely rely on Mexicans who do not understand our language, as well as many who are sympathisers with Carvajal." Evidently Carvajal still had significant Anglo support on the border—more than most United States officials were willing to concede. Perhaps Ballinger sensed this and therefore tried to convince his government that, since the bulk of his witnesses supported Carvajal, it would be impossible to get an indictment. Ballinger also could not charge Carvajal's Anglo conspirators for their violations of United States laws. According to the attorney, these individuals had "evaded but not violated the neutrality laws of the U.S." because they had not "organized into companies, electing officers &c. until they had crossed into Mexico." Had Carvajal organized his Anglo forces on the Texas side of the river with the purpose of invading Mexico, then Ballinger could have charged them with violating the 1818 Neutrality Acts. Since that was not the case, Ballinger regrettably informed Webster that he could not "pursue them legally any further than what I have already accomplished." On March 8, 1852, Carvajal and all eleven of his Anglo associates were released on bail of five thousand and three thousand dollars each, respectively.[13]

Carvajal's release infuriated the Mexican government. Most disturbing to Mexican officials was "the demonstration of public sympathy" displayed by Anglo-Texans for Carvajal and his men after they were released. According to the Mexican minister to the United States, Manuel Larrainzar, such popular approval only emboldened the filibusterers "to show themselves everywhere and boast of their actions, and the evils they have occasioned." After reproaching both the Fillmore and present Franklin Pierce administrations for their failure to "condign punishment" to Carvajal and his accomplices, Larrainzar heaped praise on Ballinger's efforts "of organizing a jury at Brownsville which proceeded to make proper investigations," which resulted in Carvajal's and his followers' arrests. "This was put into effect by the efforts of the United States Attorney, Mr. Ballinger, whose devotion to principle and duty we congratulate."[14]

In March 1853, Carvajal sent another force across the Rio Grande to the already beleaguered town of Reynosa, in an insignificant raid led by the Anglo, A. Howell Norton. After sacking Reynosa, Norton's band retreated to the town of Rio Grande City on the Texas side of the border. Five days later a United States infantry company arrested Carvajal in a surprise raid on his headquarters at Roma, Texas. The real culprit, Norton, managed to escape. However, over the next three days, all of Carvajal's Anglo followers, including Norton, were apprehended and sent to Fort Brown to await arraignment before the United States commissioner at Brownsville, Frederick Cummings.[15]

The filibusterers were held in custody for six weeks at Fort Brown before appearing in court. Once again they were released on bail (ten thousand dollars for Carvajal and five thousand dollars each for his Anglo co-conspirators) because of a "legal technicality": Ballinger, in his excitement about their capture, did not file the affidavits against them properly; consequently Commissioner Cummings had no choice but to free them immediately. Ballinger was so upset at his lapse that even his wife could not console him. In a response to a letter she had written him after the news of Carvajal's latest release in which Ballinger blamed himself "for this most dreadful debacle," he now told Hally that the filibusterers' discharge represented "the most humiliating experience I have had as a lawyer & servant of the U.S. government. I cannot think of when I have felt so aggrieved by my own inadequacies. If more trouble occurs it will be as a result of my failing to do what every lawyer knows is fundamental. There is nothing I can do to amend this calamity & personal disgrace."[16]

Nothing caused Ballinger greater despondency than believing he had faltered. Driven by an obsession with achievement and dominated by a passion for order and stability, Ballinger's every decision was carefully weighed and each detail scrutinized in his determination to escape the disquieting feeling of having fallen below his own expectations. Believing himself deficient in character plunged Ballinger into self-reproach and depression. Unable to bear the thought that he had fallen short in the eyes

"Allow me to become an ordinary citizen again"

of those who loved him and depended on him, his diary entries were filled with his fear of not "living up to my potential. I do not force myself to exertion—this I must conquer. My success of character requires the faculty of hard work—not only constant application but hard work. I must apply myself faithfully to whatever I undertake—to do anything less would lead to disappointment & failure."[17] With such self-imposed pressure it is no wonder Ballinger was distressed by his inattention in the Carvajal affair. To Ballinger, any omission was an irrevocable setback since he might not have the opportunity to ever correct it.

Although Ballinger believed he had failed, local newspapers praised his numerous efforts over the past year to bring Carvajal and his band to justice. The Brownsville *American Flag* especially lauded his work. "Every praise is due to the always prompt, energetic and strictly impartial manner in which the United States District Attorney, W. Pitt Ballinger, has discharged the many and arduous duties incumbent upon his office. Mr. Ballinger is an eminent and loyal Texan, a brave and gallant officer of the Government, in whose worthy hands have been placed the responsibility of justice meted out."[18]

Despite public accolades, the filibusterers were free, and as long as they were, "the distrust and bitter feeling with which the Mexican people indiscriminately regard the American population of this side of the river will continue." In his review of events to Attorney General Caleb Cushing of the Pierce administration, Ballinger expressed his "deep" belief that the United States government must "put forth a rigid and prompt execution of the law against those who so repeatedly trampled under foot the laws of their country and the dearest rights of humanity. I impress upon your Honor the urgency of this whole affair, which I regret to have helped perpetuate by my own omissions."[19]

The above communiqué was one of Ballinger's last official reports as United States district attorney. Three days after his letter to Cushing, dated April 6, 1853, he drafted his formal letter of resignation and sent it to "Washington City." In his note Ballinger requested "to be relieved" of his duties "effective the 1st of July 1853, or upon the appointment of an individual to assume my position, whichever may come first."[20]

Undoubtedly Ballinger's sense of personal inefficacy at having failed to bring Carvajal to justice was the principal reason for his resignation. Although only briefly mentioning his "omissions of duty" in his resignation letter to Cushing, Ballinger revealed to Hally how disturbed he was by "the whole Carvajal business. I cannot express to you the deep feelings of disgrace, nor how oppressed I feel by the weight of my present position. I think it is time that I leave this position. I am no longer capable of continuing—I can no longer perform the duties incumbent upon me to the best of my abilities. My despair has become too great. Allow me to become an ordinary citizen again."[21]

Ballinger remained in his position ex officio for another two months, helping his successor, Samuel Hay, "to become acquainted with the rigors of this postion which I believe no one truly is capable of understanding until it is too late to change one's mind."[22] According to Hay, Ballinger's assistance was "invaluable," for without it, Hay was certain he would not have been able to keep the Pierce administration "as well informed, especially on the movements of the 'Filibusters' on the Rio Grande. Mr. Ballinger's suggestions were most helpful in determining what line of action should now be taken."[23]

In 1854 Hay finally had enough evidence to bring Carvajal to trial after the Mexican consul at Brownsville again reported to American officials that *el jefe* was organizing men and supplies for a new invasion. This time Hay made sure everything was filed properly. Hay had waited too long for this moment to let any oversights prevent what he and Ballinger had worked hard toward for the past three years. Wanting Ballinger to share in his joy at Carvajal's apprehension, Hay immediately contacted the Galveston attorney, asking Ballinger for his assistance at the forthcoming trial. In his letter to Caleb Cushing, requesting Ballinger's services, Hay told the attorney general that "it would be useless to say that there are not many other persons in Texas of equal ability with Messr. Ballinger, but I do say that in my opinion, there is no other whom, under the circumstances it would be proper to retain." Cushing approved Hay's retaining of Ballinger, and the payment of two thousand dollars for his services.[24] Ballinger, however, declined the offer. Apparently he had had enough of Carvajal's separatist movement. In a brief note to Hay, Ballinger first thanked the attorney for his "kindness & sincere esteem for my qualifications," but "regretted" having to tell his colleague that, since he was "presently engaged in private practice, time and pecuniary matters prevent me from coming to your assistance. I have the fullest confidence in your ability & congratulate you and wish you all the success that you deserve."[25]

More than likely Ballinger declined Hay's offer because he knew that, after two years of chasing Carvajal all around South Texas, there was not enough evidence to convict the rebel leader or any of his Anglo accomplices for their violations of United States neutrality laws. There was always some act of omission or a legal technicality overlooked that allowed Carvajal and his band to slip through the law's grasp. Moreover, as Ballinger realized, from the beginning of his exploits Carvajal was a popular leader on both sides of the Rio Grande, and thus, regardless of having all legal loose ends secured, a South Texas jury, regardless of its ethnic composition, would be unlikely to convict an individual (or his accomplices) whose cause they still supported. Knowing this, Hay requested and received a change of venue to Galveston for Carvajal's trial. In January 1854, Carvajal and all eleven of his Anglo co-conspirators were brought to trial for their violations of United States neutrality laws. Even though the trial was held in Galveston, and despite Hay's repeated entreaties to have Ballinger "sit by my side—this [Carvajal's trial] is something we had both labored for & now the moment has finally arrived, and our vindication is near," Ballinger refused to even attend the proceedings.[26] As he confided to his diary, he believed his presence at the trial would only remind him of his own "failure to have ended this business. My sincerest wish is to see them found guilty but I believe that will not be the outcome. Jury here is too unfamiliar with their past acts—Hay hasn't enough evidence to put before them to win conviction."[27]

Ballinger's prediction was correct. Despite the overwhelming evidence against Carvajal and his band, corroborated by both Anglo-American and Mexican witnesses, the jury nevertheless found the filibusterers innocent of the charges of violating United States neutrality laws.[28] Carvajal was once again free to pursue his revolution.

After resigning his position as United States attorney, Ballinger decided he needed a brief hiatus from the law. Three years of public service on the Texas frontier had exhausted Ballinger both mentally and physically. As a result, the thought of immediately returning to private practice was the furthest thing from his mind. He was so drained of energy that soon after arriving home from Brownsville he suffered a severe asthma attack, forcing him to bed for several weeks. This was the first serious attack Hally had witnessed in two years, causing her great alarm. She had seen her husband afflicted before, wheezing for several hours before regaining his ability to breathe normally. She was there for him, comforting him and helping him to relax in order to ease the lung spasms. She was calm and strong, assured her husband would rebound and pursue life with his usual intensity. This time, however, it was different. The wheezing and difficulty in breathing lasted for several days instead of going away in a few hours. No matter what Hally did, she could not relieve Ballinger's suffering. Each day saw her husband growing weaker. Hally was afraid Ballinger was dying. Several local doctors were called in, but they could do little more than Hally. There were no miracle drugs for asthma—no inhalers or pills to open the constricting bronchial passages. Watching her husband in such pain caused the unflappable Hally to break down. According to Ballinger's recollection, Hally "could no longer bear to see me in such a condition. She cried for days & had to be cared for by her mother. For the first time she was not at my side, day & night until I recovered. I was alone & remembered that when I was younger I had to get better on my own strength. I could hear Hally crying in the other room, and knew I had to get well for her & the sake of our family."[29] As in the past, and as he would countless times in the future, Ballinger pulled himself through this latest ordeal.

To help Ballinger recover, Hally sent "for the finest physician that could be found—a specialist in afflictions of the lungs. A Dr. Mirabeau came, reputed to have been one of Andrew Jackson's physicians." After spending over a week treating the lawyer with various medicines, including "a liquid concoction of brandy, honey, citrus fruits, & an assortment of ground herbs, given to me liberally every few hours—the taste was unmentionably horrible!," the good doctor told Hally that "complete rest was absolutely essential—several weeks of confinement before I should be allowed to return to my work."[30]

Hally knew that if her husband remained in Galveston while recuperating, he would not get the rest he needed. Friends, relatives, and those eagerly awaiting his return to private practice, hopefully as their partner, would be at the house constantly. Moreover, because of his "constant sense & pressure of duty" and the fear of not having his "independence pecuniarily established," Ballinger would return to work prematurely, believing he could pursue his practice with the same intensity as before. Within a few days of his return to work, Ballinger would suffer a relapse, causing him to prolong his convalescence. This became a familiar pattern for Hally in dealing with her husband's recovery, and she was greatly frustrated by his refusal to heed her ministrations. Consequently, beginning in 1853 and continuing for the next several decades, Hally insisted that Ballinger's rehabilitation take place away from Galveston, on family vacations. Hally knew that if she could get him away from the island his chances of complete recovery would increase dramatically, for he would be removed from all the distractions and temptations preventing his total recuperation.[31]

Hally played on Ballinger's strong sense of familial obligation.

"Allow me to become an ordinary citizen again"

Knowing how much he always wanted to please her, Hally never hesitated to use any such wiles when Ballinger was being especially obstinate about leaving the island for an extended holiday. More than likely Ballinger's stubbornness was a display of obligatory masculine bravado, for he knew the only reason Hally insisted on getting away from Galveston was to improve his health. Moreover, Ballinger loved to travel and sightsee, and was an especially avid tourist when accompanied by his family. He liked nothing better than showing off to his children how much he knew about the nation's history, and when journeying to such illustrious cities as Boston or Philadelphia, he was in his glory. Once away from the island and his work, Ballinger quickly absolved himself of all misgiving, pleased at spending the time with his family. With recuperation and relaxation foremost on her mind, as soon as Ballinger could travel, Hally whisked her husband and daughter aboard a steamer bound for New Orleans. From there they took a "paddle wheel" up the Mississippi to Kentucky, where Hally met the legendary James Franklin and the rest of the Ballinger clan.[32]

Ballinger was returning to his native state for the first time since leaving ten years earlier. James Franklin and Elizabeth Jenkins had had three sons and a daughter over the course of their thirteen years together. A decade was a long time to be absent from home, and in the course of that time, people usually change dramatically. Though Ballinger and his father had reconciled before he left for Texas, the attorney still wondered if his father had reverted to the brusque, unapproachable autocrat of his youth.[33] For the moment, Ballinger submerged his trepidation about the impending family visit, escaping into the natural beauty of the Mississippi Valley as the riverboat wound its way upstream toward Kentucky.

In a special diary, later incorporated into his "Sketchbook," he meticulously recorded all he saw. From the decks of the paddle wheel Ballinger observed the majesty of the Mississippi and the serenity and unaffected charm of the surrounding countryside and its people. And having to travel the entire length of the state of Kentucky until reaching his home gave Ballinger ample time to reflect upon the things he had missed about the Blue Grass State over the past ten years. Not a single person, tree, flower, animal, bird, or rock formation escaped his keen, descriptive eye. Ballinger's "Sketchbook" is filled with beautifully crafted prose, describing the flora and fauna of the Mississippi Valley and his beloved Kentucky. He would spend paragraphs, sometimes even pages, describing in most vivid detail a rock formation, an expanse of wildflowers, or a small rural hamlet and its people. To Ballinger the Romantic, few things in nature or life were as simple or unadorned as they appeared. An ancient rock formation reminded him of "a Gothic cathedral, standing the test of time immemorial—through the ages past, it remains, there for all to pay homage to its simple, majestic splendor, to awe us, to give us a sense of permanence and belonging with nature." Ballinger found even the simplest of country folk enchanting: "Tho' they may be of the humblest origins, they possess a strength of character, an inner peace, a passion for life, that few of us who are more fortunate can say we have as well. Behind their weather-beaten faces, flushed with the day's toil, lies the true essence of humanity—a being who despite his meager existence, has found within himself dignity and pride."[34]

Back in Galveston, Ballinger was an avid butterfly collector, loved wild animals (yet was not a hunter), and was an amateur botanist whose knowledge of Gulf Coast plant life was well known. In fact, Ballinger reputedly assembled at his Galveston home one of the finest displays of exotic plants, trees, and flowers to be found anywhere in the antebellum South. While in Kentucky, he gathered a variety of native wildflowers and seeds, hoping to see them flourish even more splendidly in Galveston's balmy, moist climate.[35]

For all his passionate love of nature and life's simplicity, Ballinger's infatuation with the Romantic impulse ended there. He was not as enveloped by the Romantic spirit as his musings and literary meanderings may indicate. More than likely his veneration of nature and the simple life was a means to escape the tediousness and uncertainty of his own existence. Critical of most Romantic literature, Ballinger was not inclined to embrace the notion of man's inherent goodness and perfectibility; most of the time he believed the opposite about his fellow man. By education and temperament Ballinger was too logical and scholastic to reconcile the more transcendant dimensions of the Romantic creed.

Ballinger could escape the purpose of his trip to Kentucky for only a few weeks. The time was fast approaching after landing at Louisville when he would have to come to grips with the reality of seeing his family after a ten-year absence. All of his earlier anxieties consumed him once again as he and Hally made their way across Kentucky. Ballinger travelled from Louisville by rail to Lexington then by stagecoach to Barbourville, arriving there on August 24, 1853.[36] When Ballinger finally reached his childhood home, several townspeople, led by James Franklin greeted him and Hally, treating them with such fanfare that Ballinger later recalled feeling like "visiting foreign potentates!" Within a matter of hours all of Ballinger's anxieties dissipated regarding his father. James Franklin was elated by his son's return home, bursting with pride at Ballinger's accomplishments. As Ballinger remembered years later, James Franklin "told everyone, perfect strangers from around the area, that 'this is my son from Texas, a United States Attorney & hero of the late war with Mexico.'"[37]

It seemed to Ballinger that all over Barbourville, "Everyone was so pleased to see me & roundly congratulated me on my professional success at every occasion we attended." He was so pleased by his visit that he momentarily contemplated staying in Barbourville, close to his family, and practicing law. Much to his surprise, James Franklin told him that "this was no place for me. You have done well in Texas—remain there, for Barbourville did not offer the opportunities for professional success that he believed were manifold in Texas." Ballinger knew his father was correct, that Texas was a land of opportunity. He promised his father he would return to Texas after his visit. For the moment, however, the practice of law was the last thing on Ballinger's mind; he was too busy enjoying his vacation.[38]

After spending two months in Kentucky, Ballinger was "ready to return to Galveston—feel fully rested & invigorated—never realized how exhausted I had become & how much I missed all my family here. Hally was right—this was what I needed most. Confident that our trip has helped me to regain the devotion to my career essential for success."[39]

Chapter Four

"AS IF I WAS CAUGHT UP IN A MAELSTROM"

Upon returning to Galveston in the fall of 1853, Ballinger resumed his association with Jones and Butler rather than joining a new firm. News of his return to Jones and Butler disappointed many local advocates who had hoped to garner his talents. Especially solicitous of Ballinger was the firm of Thompson and Goldthwaite, reputed to have one of the most extensive practices in the area. At least twice a week for several weeks, Ballinger received notes and letters from the firm, offering him not only an immediate full partnership, but also "a 1/3 split of all business profits," including any land that might come into the firm as a result of acquisition in lieu of payment. Ballinger was momentarily enticed by Thompson and Goldthwaite's offer, but after conferring with his uncle, decided to rejoin Jones and Butler.[1] Jones and Butler was still the island's most respected establishment, whose volume of business, especially in realty law, was unmatched. By the time of Ballinger's return, the firm's reputation extended beyond the Gulf Coast and even the state of Texas.[2]

Ballinger returned from Kentucky with a dramatically changed outlook toward his fellow practitioners and the legal profession in general. Perhaps the long conversations with his father, combined with three years of public service on the Texas frontier, sobered Ballinger to the realities of his occupation. Ballinger now realized that a successful practice took patience, luck, and skill, and that along the way few attorneys questioned what was appropriate for their pride or for maintaining their personal decency—whatever was lucrative to these attorneys was fair game. To men like his father and uncle, and to Jones and Butler, all trained in the rough and tumble world of a developing legal system, where animal cunning and larceny often took precedence over professional probity, the underhanded activities of many of his colleagues were hardly surprising and certainly were not worth outbursts of righteous indignation. Since he hoped to have his own practice someday, perhaps he should take his uncle's advice and for now "look the other way at those things not pertinent to your legal education." As James Love further reminded Ballinger upon his rejoining Jones and Butler, his partners' "connexions within the legal fraternity here & around the State are more numerous than one can imagine. They can be helpful to you in this area—do not jeopardize their friendship & trust—do not be distracted by any other thoughts. The strictest devotion to the practice of law should be foremost on your mind."[3]

Ballinger's return to his former partners was a decision of momentary convenience, made at a pivotal, transitional period in his life. He knew when he rejoined Jones and Butler that it was only temporary, until he felt more assured of his own abilities and financially more stable. His family's welfare took precedence over his own ambitions. Moreover, he had been away from the private sector for three years, and was thus unfamiliar with many of the changes that had occurred in Texas law. It would be foolish to strike out on his own without acquiring a greater understanding of this re-ordering. Until the time was right to establish his own practice, why not continue to benefit from the experience of two veteran attorneys whose knowledge of emerging Texas law was superior to that of anyone in the area.

There was another reason for Ballinger to delay starting his own practice. His brother-in-law, Thomas Jack, a recent Yale University graduate, had been reading law under Ballinger's supervision but would not be ready for his bar exam until the spring of 1854. Until Jack was ready and Ballinger agreed that he was, Ballinger would remain with Jones and Butler.[4]

Tom Jack, Hally's only brother, was a short, stout, blond-haired, blue-eyed, freckled-faced lad of eighteen when he first met Ballinger during the jurist's courtship of his sister. He was every bit as athletic, energetic, and fun-loving as his adored sister. Indeed, he and Ballinger were almost in every way exact opposites. Ballinger was taller, slower-moving and woefully careless in dress. Jack was almost frenetic in his actions and a dandy when it came to his attire. Daily he sported the latest in men's fashions. Whether it was patent-leather shoes or a silk shirt imported from Europe, Jack was legendary around town for his haute couture. Ballinger disliked generalities, and his mind cautiously moved in logical progression from one fact to the next, while Jack leapt ahead, using intuition to arrive at his conclusions. Tom was the family practical joker who found Ballinger's serious temperament to be an especially appealing target for his pranks. Tom's antics frequently annoyed the more austere Ballinger, but he usually took it all in good humor, thoroughly enjoying Tom's companionship. Like Hally, Tom helped Ballinger not to take life so seriously, drawing him out of his penchant for brooding by his quick wit and jocularity. Despite the dissimilarities in thought, habits, and temperament, Ballinger and Jack possessed much in common. They respected each other as comrades and helped each other by their fellowship and contact. Ballinger, by nature secretive and reticent, often poured out his soul to Jack.[5] In short, Ballinger and Jack formed a well-nigh perfect combination from both a professional and personal standpoint. In the fall of 1854 after Jack passed his bar, Ballinger severed his connection with Jones and Butler, forming a new partnership with his brother-in-law.

Jones and Butler unquestionably missed Ballinger's talents, finding no one qualified to replace him for five years. Finally, in 1859, John Jones's son, Gustavus (George) Armstrong Jones, joined the firm as the third partner. However, one of Galveston's oldest and most respected practices was in decline. The health of both of its senior partners was failing and the work load was simply too much for young Jones and a few clerks to keep up with. In 1863, after the death of his father (Jonas Butler had died in 1858), George Armstrong Jones decided to dissolve the firm. Instead of allowing Jones to terminate one of Texas's oldest legal establishments, Ballinger offered to buy Jones's practice, which would allow him to absorb into his own practice his former partners' clients and business. Since the firm owed Ballinger over fifteen thousand dollars in past fees, Ballinger used that money along with a small loan from his uncle to purchase Jones and Butler. Ballinger's acquisition of Jones and Butler was a shrewd financial move, for it allowed him to begin Ballinger & Jack with a ready-made clientele.[6]

From the beginning of his partnership with Jack, until his brother-in-law's death in 1880, Ballinger was the recognized senior partner. This was especially true in the early years. Ballinger interviewed most of the clients, wrote the important legal papers, and pleaded the suits in court. Jack, still the student, performed routine jobs; he answered inquiries, managed the office, preserved the records, and kept the files straight. As Ballinger told James Love, Jack had "system and keeps our things in order. This is an invaluable contribution for our success."[7] Over time, Jack became an effective lawyer in his own right and Ballinger came to consider his brother-in-law an equal. But Jack's esteem for Ballinger was so great that their working relationship remained more filial than professional. Tom Jack worshipped Ballinger, believing him to be "the most honorable & courageous man I have known. He is compassionate, sincere & devoted to his family & profession. I can think of no one else that I presently know, or have known, that I have been willing to devote my fullest energies in order to have their approbation. Will is truly my ideal."[8] Although awed by Ballinger, Jack was never jealous of his brother-in-law's renown, for he did not possess the same obsession to prove himself. Unlike the compulsive Ballinger, Tom Jack was too much the free spirit to allow his career to consume him. Yet, Jack knew that next to his family, nothing else was as important to Ballinger as the law. Consequently, out of a sincere concern for Ballinger's welfare, Jack willingly deferred to his brother-in-law's more controlling personality and Ballinger's quest for validation through his work.

In the formative antebellum years of his practice, Ballinger handled everything from assault cases to divorce suits. Legal specialization was then unknown, and a lawyer's ability to adapt himself to all types of litigation, problems, and courts measured his success. Ballinger's early cases were of a class common in a new and sparsely settled country—litigation arising from disputed land titles, neighborhood quarrels, probate, and the like. Knowledge of the fundamental elements of common law and principles of natural justice were mainly relied on to dispose of the simple litigation that arose. Ballinger understood that such cases were the "bread-and-butter" of his practice and that it would be foolish to ignore such matters while waiting to prove to more worthy patrons that his legal talents were superior to most of his colleagues'. Most of Ballinger's days were routine, and many were sheer drudgery. At times the work load was almost unbearable. Would it not be better, he often mused, to be doing something else than "to be fighting for existence without a moment's respite?" Always the answer was no: "I wouldn't give one day of this work, no matter how miserable it may be for a dozen droned away in some other occupation." Sometimes he was on his feet three or four days in a row searching titles. He spent three nights supervising the auction of a bankrupt merchant's stock for a fifty-dollar commission. And several times he would cross to the mainland through driving rain or piercing wind to see a client. No less frustrating was the tendency of judges to hold cases over until the next term without giving prior notice.[9] As Ballinger later told his son, his first years of private practice felt as if he was "caught up in a maelstrom of petitons, probate, & suits from which I w.d never emerge."[10]

"As if I was caught up in a maelstrom"

By the time Ballinger began his practice, the Galveston bar was "crowded to overflowing" as Royall T. Wheeler, an associate justice of the Texas Supreme Court stated in the spring of 1855. Despite the presence of much "mediocrity,"[11] in time an adaptive, vigorous bar emerged in the West, a bar made up of shrewd, adventuruous young operators. Most of Ballinger's peers established a general practice, doing whatever their noses sniffed out as promising and lucrative. Although Ballinger handled a variety of cases and represented a wide range of clients, he was not the typical frontier practitioner, scrounging around for any niche that required his skill. Since competition for clients would be keen, Ballinger realized that the best way of ensuring success was to specialize in matters other Galveston attorneys shied away from or lacked the expertise to oversee. With this objective in mind, Ballinger and Jack set about establishing themselves as specialists in Texas realty law, making their firm's priority the execution of land claims and related transactions.

Like many Texas lawyers, Ballinger realized that land was his state's economic base, whether it was town land or country land. Who else if not a lawyer, could decipher titles? Who else could master the maze of rules on grants, on the sale and transfer of tracts, especially in Texas where the continuing validity of Spanish and Mexican grants, compounded by the intricacies of Anglo-Saxon jurisprudence, created myriad legal problems for businessmen, legatees, and the general public? By combining the best from these two realms of law, Texas devised a system of jurisprudence that was both original and tractable, particularly in the area of realty law. Liberal Spanish and Mexican policies granted a league and labor of land (over forty-six hundred acres) to hundreds of early settlers. After the Texas rebellion, the original Spanish and Mexican titles remained far away in Mexico City. The result was a rash of speculation and conflicting private claims threatening to destroy the public domain.[12] The enterprising lawyer who could unravel this ambiguity would have mastered the emerging Texas law.

Soon after establishing himself as a specialist in realty law, Ballinger became involved in one of the more protracted land claim disputes in Texas legal history—the Peter W. Grayson suit. Ballinger was first introduced to the Grayson dispute while still a member of Jones and Butler. At that time, Frederick William Grayson, nephew and heir to Peter Grayson's estate, approached Jones and Butler for counsel. They declined to represent him, and thus he had to await counsel until Ballinger established his own firm.[13] Perhaps Jones and Butler were right in refusing Fred

View of Port of Galveston and Harbor. *Photograph by Shche and Potter, 1860–1861. Courtesy Rosenberg Library, Galveston, Texas.*

Grayson as a client. It was doubtful that Ballinger grasped the magnitude of the dispute when agreeing to represent him. It was only after spending several months of preparatory and investigative work, unraveling all the arrangements and machinations that had already occurred, that Ballinger realized how entangled and churlish the whole affair had become.

Peter Grayson, the Texas Republic's first attorney general, acquired the disputed property in 1835 when he purchased eleven leagues of land (48,708 acres) from the original grantee, an Irish priest named Miguel Muldoon. At the time of purchase Peter Grayson made only a partial payment on the total purchase price of fifty thousand dollars. After receiving his down payment Muldoon empowered an M. Zachary of New Orleans to collect Grayson's final note through the agency of the United States consul in Mexico, a Mr. Parrott. Grayson was to pay Zachary, who was then to forward the final payment to Muldoon via Parrott. Grayson, after paying Zachary the balance owed on the property, went home to Tennessee, where he committed suicide in 1839. Parrott used the Grayson note to pay a personal debt to Zachary, causing Muldoon, who never received

"As if I was caught up in a maelstrom"

his final payment, to nullify his contract with Grayson. Grayson, however, had already willed his estate to his only heir, his nephew Frederick William Grayson.[14]

Unfortunately for Fred Grayson, his uncle was heavily in debt, and when Peter Grayson's creditors heard of his death, they inundated poor Fred Grayson with demands for payment. Fred had little choice but to sell off his inheritance to pay his uncle's debts, which totaled ten thousand dollars.[15] Until those obligations were met, Grayson knew he would never have clear title to his property.

At this juncture in 1854, Fred Grayson sought Ballinger's counsel, for no sooner did he begin selling land than hordes of claimants appeared contesting his title to the property. After several months of research, Ballinger concluded that Fred Grayson indeed did have proper title to his uncle's estate: Peter Grayson had fulfilled his contract with Muldoon when he made his final installment to Zachary, whom Muldoon had authorized to accept Grayson's payment. Ballinger proved that Grayson had paid Zachary according to Muldoon's instructions, producing as proof a copy of the final note paid and a receipt acknowledging Grayson's payment with Zachary's signature on it! Accordingly, Peter Grayson could rightfully pass it to whomever he wished. Ballinger further established that it was not Peter Grayson's fault that Father Muldoon never received final payment, for that "was an arrangement made between Muldoon and his agents. It was not the fault of Peter Grayson that Zachary & Parrott engaged in their own nefarious scheme to deprive Muldoon of his money."[16]

As the controversy evolved, Ballinger realized there was little he could do to protect Fred Grayson's inheritance from his uncle's debts. Those obligations had to be paid, and most of those creditors and their respective attorneys were willing to compromise on the amount owed if Ballinger could guarantee them a specific figure by securing it to the value of the land sold by Fred Grayson. Ballinger wanted to minimize the potential for suit by any of Peter Grayson's claimants, hoping to avoid expensive proceedings that could create doubt in the court's mind concerning the legality of the conveyance. However, there were pretenders demanding full title to the land, filing suits in the local courts in order to obtain it. When that occurred Ballinger had little choice but to negotiate a settlement or to accept a court challenge. In every suit heard before a district magistrate, Ballinger successfully defended his client's title.

Soon after upholding Grayson's title against a claim by the Catholic Church in 1859, Ballinger confessed to his client that "defending your inheritance has often caused me to do little else in my practice. I think it better, in order to relieve ourselves of further litigation which has cost us all in time and money, to sell the land."[17] Fred Grayson heeded his counselor's advice, selling hundreds of acres to Texas settlers for two dollars an acre. In 1859 Grayson moved to Philadelphia, entrusting to Ballinger's care what was left of his Texas estate.

Ballinger believed he had seen the end of what was an interminable list of claimants when much to his dismay, in 1860, the Catholic Church renewed its efforts to claim what was left of the property. The Church instructed its lawyers to "impress" upon Ballinger that "if Father Muldoon took the land at all, it was in trust for the Church. This has always been the policy of the Catholic Church here and elsewhere regarding the bequeathment of gifts, land &c. to a member of the clergy." Ballinger rejected the Church's argument, declaring Muldoon's supposed ignorance of Church policy regarding gifts was no excuse for "disposing of the property for money." Ballinger asserted that Muldoon, in order "to secure the land for the Church," needed to make "immediate arrangements for that purpose." Instead, Muldoon sold the property to Peter Grayson, "who, as it already has been established in the courts of this State," legally purchased the land. Ballinger, then, in a rare display of anger and sarcasm, born of his frustration with the case, retorted that "Muldoon, though a member of the Catholic clergy, by selling the land to Peter Grayson, displayed a cupidity far above us of less loftier stations."[18] A month after receipt of Ballinger's letter, the Church quietly dropped the whole matter, reassuring Ballinger that "No subsequent attempts will be made again by any persons affiliated with the Catholic Church of this place [Galveston] to infringe upon the rights of your client."[19]

After this latest round with the Church, Ballinger reflected in his diary that "the same matter breaks out in a fresh place every year or two—I doubt I will ever see the end of this business."[20] Ballinger never did see the end of the controversy—not until 1897, nine years after his death, was the Grayson legacy finally resolved. In that year, the Texas Supreme Court, in *League v. Nichols*, affirmed for the last time what Ballinger maintained for over thirty years: the right of Fred Grayson and his family to Peter Grayson's estate. After Ballinger died, his son, Thomas Jack Ballinger, continued to serve the Grayson family, and he too successfully defended the Grayson's right to their property. Unfortunately, by 1897 all that was left of the original eleven leagues was roughly two thousand acres, which the Graysons finally sold to the Santa Fe railroad for fifteen dollars an acre.[21]

"As if I was caught up in a maelstrom"

The Grayson controversy was undoubtedly one of Ballinger's more wearisome cases. He charged Fred Grayson a monthly retainer fee of only forty-five dollars, beginning in 1858 and continuing for the next thirty years. Ballinger never believed in exacting exorbitant fees for his services, especially when their cases were so intricate. Ballinger established a fee schedule for his services which was similar to that of other Galveston and Houston jurists during the 1850s: arguing a case in the Texas Supreme Court, $25 to $30; circuit court trials, $15; local or "police court" for felonies and misdemeanor charges, $7; written contract or deed, $5; printed contract, $2.50; preparing a will, $12 to $15; examination of title abstract, $12.50; and, collection on the average 3 to 5 percent up to $5,000, more than $5,000, 5 to 7 percent, and 3 percent on the excess.[22]

Although usually adhering to this agenda, Ballinger found that since many of his clients were chronically short of cash, he regularly negotiated his fees on an individual basis, sometimes cutting by one-third his normal rate. He never set his fees so high that only a few wealthy clients could afford his advocacy. Ballinger undoubtedly was out to earn as much money by his profession as he possibly could. Yet he rarely denied anyone his services. Although his charges differed little from the general run of fees received by his fellow practitioners, he frequently underrated his services and surprised his client by the smallness of his bill. This was especially true when Ballinger's sympathies were aroused by his client's poverty. For example, in the winter of 1855, he crossed over to the mainland and then rode several miles to draw up a will for a sick widow, for which he refused compensation other than the hot meal she provided him before he returned to the island. On another occasion, a Galveston school teacher, William Morris, asked Ballinger to handle a legal matter for him, and was amazed when Ballinger charged him only two dollars for his services. As Morris told his attorney, "I had no idea of paying less than ten dollars."[23]

Ballinger almost never demanded immediate payment or even full payment, routinely giving clients up to sixty days to either pay in full or pay an installment on their account. In only a few instances did he charge a patron interest, and when he did, it was a nominal 2 to 3 percent on the balance. By the time of his death in 1888, the firm's books revealed a substantial number of clients with balances of several thousand dollars. Many of these individuals had outstanding debts with Ballinger and Jack for over ten years and some as long as twenty.[24]

In an 1878 lecture to a gathering of law students, Ballinger expressed his attitude on compensation frankly and unblushingly. "The matter of

Michel Menard (left), and Samuel May Williams (right), co-owners of the Galveston Wharf Company. Menard was the founder of Galveston, and he and Williams, one of Galveston's most powerful city fathers, were business partners. Menard, Williams, and the Wharf Company were some of Ballinger's most important antebellum clients. *Photographs ca. 1850s. Courtesy Rosenberg Library, Galveston, Texas.*

fees in important, far beyond the mere question of necessity. Fairly and properly attended to, fuller justice is done to both lawyer and client. An exorbitant fee should never be charged. As a general rule, rarely take your entire fee in advance, nor more than a small retainer. Settle on the amount & take a note in advance—then you will feel that you are working for something and you will be <u>sure</u> to do your work faithfully & well, for that should be at all times foremost in your mind."[25]

Like most young and ambitious attorneys, Ballinger awaited that golden moment when that one client would enter his office, presenting him with the chance to become one of the most sought-after lawyers of his day. That occurred one winter afternoon in 1854 when Michel Menard, the founder of Galveston, and Samuel May Williams, Menard's business associate, walked through Ballinger's doors seeking his counsel. Within six months of going into practice, Galveston's newest and youngest partnership (Ballinger was twenty-nine and Tom Jack was twenty-four) was asked to represent the Galveston Wharf Company, This case concerned the city's most powerful private merchants and businessmen and became one of the longest civil litigation cases in nineteenth-century Texas history: *The Mayor Aldermen and Inhabitants of Galveston v. Michel B. Menard*. At the time, Ballinger little knew that it would be his adroit execution of the "Wharf Case" that would earn him a place within Galveston's ruling elite as the company's counselor. The case was also one of Ballinger's most outstanding early legal triumphs, propelling him overnight into the limelight of the Texas bar.

Why the Wharf Company chose Ballinger rather than a more experienced attorney is unknown. Although aware of the city's dispute with the Wharf Company, he did not aggressively seek to represent the company. Since Ballinger and Jack had yet to establish their credibility, solicitation of the patronage of the island's most powerful private corporation would be foolish and pretentious. Perhaps Ballinger's advantage over his more seasoned peers was that Samuel May Williams was already familiar with his abilities, having been impressed earlier by Ballinger's managing of his personal accounts while an associate with Jones and Butler. Williams's associate, Michel Menard, was initially skeptical of Ballinger's level of experience, although he believed Ballinger to be "a sincere & honest young fellow, who with a few more years of practice behind him, will I am sure be a first-rate lawyer." Menard had wanted one of Galveston's older legal establishments, Thompson and Goldthwaite, to defend the Wharf Company's property rights. He quickly changed his mind, however, after his first meeting with Ballinger. As he later told James Love, "I think we have made the right choice in young Ballinger. I believe he will prove to be a most trusted & faithful attorney who will commit to us all his energy. I am confident he will be able to relieve us of our present problems with the City."[26]

After several days of intense deliberation, in which Ballinger and Tom Jack did "little else but discuss the matter before us—last night we stayed at the office until dawn the next day," they decided that "come what may," this was an opportunity "that every young lawyer hopes will come his way. We must take it & to the devil with what everyone else may think."[27]

Ballinger's task was to defend the property and warehouse interests of the Galveston Wharf and Cotton Press Company, whose principal stockholders were Menard and Williams, against an attempt by the city of Galveston to break the company's monopoly on Galveston's waterfront area known as the "flats." Prior to 1854, the waterfront properties were in the hands of several warehouse owners and shippers. However, in February 1854, a group of Galveston entrepreneurs, led by Menard, joined to acquire control over the wharf area of the port. By various transactions, the new consortium united all the several wharf companies of Galveston into one corporation.[28]

The city of Galveston challenged the right of the Wharf Company to dominate the flats. Public officials decried the corporation as an illegal entity despoiling the city of valuable public property. The city sought the Wharf Company's dissolution, thus ending its port monopoly. The city also hoped to acquire complete control over the entire waterfront area. Ballinger's job was to prevent the municipal acquisition of his client's property. The question of hegemony over the flats was not resolved until 1859. In that year the issue finally reached the Texas Supreme Court. It was before the state's highest tribunal that the futures of both Galveston and William Pitt Ballinger were determined.

The city's attorneys hoped to secure the flats by proving that the Wharf Company usurped public property, divesting the city of land needed for its future growth and welfare. The prosecution focused its efforts on invalidating a large portion of the original land grant given to Michel B. Menard by the Republic of Texas in 1838 for the purpose of establishing the city of Galveston. The city contended that the flats or "the shore of the island" was not part of Menard's grant. The Wharf Company, by taking control of the flats, had encroached upon public property and thus must relinquish title to the city.[29]

Galveston's attorneys further argued that, when Menard incorporated the city of Galveston in 1841, he transferred to the city all personal property within what was to become Galveston's city limits. The city insisted that implicit in the charter of incorporation was the cession of the flats. The flats, thus, had always been public domain. To further substantiate their claim that the Wharf Company had expropriated public land, Galveston's attorneys resurrected the city's original plan, arguing that the layout clearly considered the flats municipal property and that Menard renounced all rights to the waterfront property when he incorporated Galveston.[30]

Ballinger focused his defense on proving that the flats were private property, not public as the city maintained. The best way to accomplish that was through an examination of the transaction granting Menard the property. Ballinger maintained that the flats were included in the "league and labor of land" given to Menard by the Republic in 1838 for the purpose establishing the city of Galveston. According to Ballinger, the Republican government was "in the extremest need of funds," that it willingly authorized the sale of its "resources, islands, etc," which included the flats.

The government agreed to sell the land to Menard for fifty thousand dollars, and for that price the government *"relinquished all the right, title and interest of the state of Texas in the premises."*[31]

Ballinger then asserted that the flats and the east end of the island where Menard established the city were "one and the same. No one, when describing the city of Galveston, has said other than it was on the east end of the Galveston island. No one has ever separated in his mind between the island and the flats." Ballinger considered it ludicrous for any Galvestonian "when describing the location of his city to a stranger, to make an independent mention of the flats." Since there was no distinction between the flats and the east end of the island, "all such averments should be considered arrant misinterpretations of Menard's original grant."[32]

Ballinger strengthened his argument by emphasizing that, at the time Menard received his charter, the Republic was following the Spanish civil codes, particularly those decrees pertaining to the issuance of land grants. Ballinger had little difficulty persuading the court to accept the legitimacy of the Spanish codes. The emerging Texas legal system, especially in the area of realty law, was an essentially hybridized arrangement of the Spanish civil codes and English common law. Ballinger maintained that since Menard's grant was issued when Spanish law prevailed, Menard not only received title to "one league and labor of land, but "the legal appurtenances, adjuncts and servitudes of the land," as well, which included the flats.[33]

Ballinger was perspicacious enough to realize that, regardless of the strength of his arguments based on the Spanish civil codes, he was involved in an area of Texas jurisprudence that was still too imprecise to be interpreted solely on the use of the Spanish corpus juris. He knew that Texas courts were increasingly uncomfortable with the Spanish system and were leaning more toward adopting the English common law procedure for the state's emerging legal disposition. Ballinger greatly strengthened his argument by expanding his definition of the shore to include an English common law interpretation, all the while aware that English common law vastly differed from Spanish civil law. Drawing from a variety of cases tried before both English and United States courts, as well as from other sources of Anglo-Saxon jurisprudence, Ballinger established that, under English common law "the shore belongs prima facie and of common right to the public; in England to the king; and in this country to the state; unless it has by grant become the property of individuals."[34] Thus, even under English common law, Menard had complete right of ownership of the shore and the flats as stipulated by his original patent.

Once Ballinger confirmed that the shore was included in Menard's grant, he then challenged the city's claim that Menard conveyed title to the flats when he incorporated Galveston. Ballinger contended that the original map outlining the City of Galveston clearly showed "a reservation to the proprietors [Menard and the Wharf Company] of the flats." He then addressed the December 1851 legislative act which the city claimed gave it title to the property. In challenging the 1851 ordinance Ballinger established the tenor of his argument: the sanctity of contracts and protection of private property rights. He argued that the 1851 legislative act violated the Constitution of the United States by allowing the state "the power of passing a law impairing the obligation of contracts." The legislature's action not only contravened Menard's grant made by the Republic of Texas, but also allowed the city "to take private property without the consent of the owner and without adequate compensation being made therefor."[35] Ballinger contended that any attempt by the city or the state to deprive Menard or the Wharf Company of legally acquired property was an encroachment upon an individual's right to dispose of his personal property as he desired. The only way the Wharf Company could be divested of its property was if the city proved that Menard's grant was "the result of fraud in obtaining it, or want of authority in the officer issuing it." As Ballinger wrote in his diary, the city's attorneys would have to declare "all legislation passed by the gov't of the Republic null & void—they would have to establish that that Republic was an illegitimate creation—that it never existed. That is a completely absurd notion & will never be accepted."[36]

From the moment litigation began, Ballinger typically questioned his ability to present an effective defense. The case consumed his every waking hour, and even at night he slept "fitfully," for he could not "get this case out of my head. I am full of despair & will be until it is over." When not in court, Ballinger spent his time preparing the next day's arguments. This also caused him anxiety because he had "great difficulty getting all the particulars together—there are so many important notes, documents &c. I must have & study. Time is running out. There is so much I still need to know." Ballinger knew his professional future would be largely determined by his performance in the "Flats Case." If he failed he was convinced he would be "doomed to a most meager & distressful existence for the rest of my life. I will be a disgrace to all those around me who have such confidence in my abilities. I cannot bear the thought of failing them & shaming my family. I must triumph. The future of Ballinger & Jack is now before me."[37]

"As if I was caught up in a maelstrom"

All Ballinger's forebodings were swept away when the Texas Supreme Court reversed the lower court's judgment, against Menard and the company, and ruled in his client's favor. According to Associate Justice Oran M. Roberts, the company's title to the flats was valid because the Republic of Texas had the legislative power "to grant that part of Galveston bay, which lies south of the channel, usually covered with salt water, which constitute what is called 'the flats' and thereby vest an exclusive right in Menard to the soil thereof, and to the full ownership of the same"[38]

Ballinger's victory in the Flats Case was one of his greatest legal triumphs. The case was pivotal in his professional career, launching him almost overnight into the limelight of the Texas bar. Being called upon to defend the interests of Galveston's ruling mercantile elite augured well for his own security and prestige. Prior to this case, Ballinger's legal reputation was confined largely to the Galveston area, where he was considered by many to be "up and coming." However, with the Flats Case and the opportunity to appear before the state's highest court, Ballinger displayed the confidence and efficacy of a veteran trial lawyer, worthy of the respect of his more seasoned peers. The exposure and notoriety enabled Ballinger to significantly expand his practice beyond the Gulf Coast. By 1860 the firm of Ballinger and Jack was known statewide for its expertise in realty law and was reputed to have as its clients some of the most prominent men in Texas. Most important, Ballinger's triumph earned him the distinction of being one of Texas's premier trial lawyers. Perhaps an excerpt from a letter written by L. A. Thompson, one of Ballinger's opponents in the Flats Case, congratulating him on his recent success, best captures the sense of respect Ballinger earned among the bar's more experienced practitioners. In that letter, Thompson not only praised Ballinger's "most extraordinary performance of legal acuity before the Court," but also informed him that "henceforth there will be very few members of the Bar who would for a moment hesitate to proclaim you to be their equal in every sense, and many, if they were honest, to have surpassed them in knowledge of the law."[39]

Ballinger's growing mastery of law became evident in his increasing appearances before the Texas Supreme Court. In his earliest cases before the court he tended to base his arguments on technicalities. In subsequent years, however, he depended less on such literalness in order to win his case. He came to feel very much at home in this court, where, as he told Tom Jack, an attorney had "ample time to read the record and gather up the facts—the issues and the law arising thereon."[40] In the antebellum period, the court required attorneys to prepare case abstracts in condensed form, thus limiting oral arguments. The court based its decisions largely on these written briefs, which were usually elaborate and extensive citations of precedents. In preparing his presentations, Ballinger took nothing for granted and frequently cited precedents that stretched back to the beginnings of both Spanish law and English common law. When years later his son asked him why he went to so much trouble, he responded: "I never trusted that the Court knew all things. I argued the case on the presumption that the Court knew nothing at all." Ballinger's thoroughness made him one of the most successful practitioners before the court, and by the time of his death in 1888, he had appeared before the Texas Supreme Court in at least 350 cases.[41]

Ballinger's compulsion for thorough preparation made him intolerant of sloppiness. "For ignorance one is allowed to forgive himself," he said on entering a case that his partner had botched, "but for carlessness never." The handful of cases he himself lost on procedural errors plunged him into depression. "I am in despair," he wrote in the summer of 1858. "I have been forced to the conclusion that the other fellow is right & again I must go out of court on a question other than the merits." Crestfallen, Ballinger told his client that he would not bill him, for "my conscience cannot allow me to charge you for services so poorly & ineffectually rendered."[42]

Ballinger's idealism went beyond his compulsion for technical perfection. Once he left court enraged but had to return in contrition. In a libel case, in which the judge found for the plaintiff, Ballinger became so infuriated by the judge's ruling that he went back to his office to look up cases to prove that the judge was "completely deficient in his knowledge of the law on such matters." However, after several hours of scouring his legal texts, he found, much to his chagrin, the judge's decision "to be sound in principle & equity." He returned to court the next day and apologized for his "most unbecoming display of temper & arrogance."[43]

As Ballinger's performance in the Flats Case confirmed, eloquence in court gained rapid attention, and attention gained new clients. Antebellum courtrooms were also places of entertainment, providing jurists with a ready audience. Depending upon the type of case and the notoriety of the advocates involved, courtrooms were often filled to capacity as inhabitants from the surrounding areas flocked to the local courthouse to hear the oratory of a famous barrister. In the days before radio and television, the public appreciated a good trial and a good courtroom speech. A potentially heated or exciting trial was an appealing diversion for many locals, for they could momentarily escape the monotony of life by attending court. Even though the session of the Texas Supreme Court hearing the Flats Case was held in Galveston, which was hardly a provincial settlement, Ballinger was surprised at "the number of people from out of the area that have attended Court. Lawyers & spectators have reportedly come from as far away as Austin to hear this session. Tom tells me that those in attendance, even those not of the profession, have been very impressed by my speeches."[44]

Though winning renown for his erudition, Ballinger also learned that the best trial lawyers utilized and enjoyed tricks, jokes, a neat technicality or two, or whatever personal wile it might take to sway the court. In the courtroom, Ballinger maintained a personal connection, seeming to speak to each juror individually and in a conversational tone. He avoided oratorical flourishes and rarely used technical language. He knew the importance of an effective closing statement. As he told a group of young lawyers, "Extemporaneous speaking should be mastered, for it is every lawyer's path to public recognition and professional acclaim." But he also warned that lawyers could not make "a more fatal error than relying solely on oratory or any other such showmanship."[45] It was the drudge work of endless research of precedents and the logical examination of the evidence that carried the day. In his concluding remarks to a jury Ballinger usually spoke from a short, carefully prepared outline. As he once warned Tom Jack in rather pedestrian terms, "Don't talk above the people—speak so the common people will understand you. They are the ones you want to reach."[46] Ballinger also gained a reputation as a superb performer. His sudden changes of mood and outbursts of humor brought witnesses up short and carried juries before him. He understood that flamboyance, ruses, and the other courtroom antics of his colleagues were more than a matter of personality. Such behavior created popularity, and any courtroom lawyer failing to impress the public and gain a reputation would be hard-pressed to survive.

Though often employing humor and other "down-home" strategies, Ballinger's rapid ascendancy to the top rank among Galveston's lawyers was based on his profound concentration, power of analysis, and comprehensive grasp of the law and all of its possible interpretations. Examination of Ballinger's arguments, briefs, and notes reveal that he did not like arguing the facts or merits of a cause nearly so much as he enjoyed doing battle on grounds of the law. His finished products—his arguments, interrogations, and final briefs—often appeared to be merely the result of native brilliance and intensive reflection. However, they were not, as Ballinger put endless hours of "hard, grinding work" into his preparation of a case.

This was especially true when he prepared for a courtroom duel on points of law.[47]

Ballinger had a natural gift (which he carefully cultivated) for making things look easier than they were; indeed he had a compulsion for doing so, even among his intimate friends. Another of his characteristics as a lawyer was that he rarely engaged in rebuttal but instead preferred to build a progression of positive propositions which came together in an unassailable structure of argument. By "carrying the war to the enemy," together with "an intuitive sense of where lay the vitals of a cause," Ballinger forced his opponents to argue on his terms—and usually lose.[48]

As a result of the Flats Case Ballinger realized that he could not afford to stray too far from litigation. Regardless of where one practiced law during the antebellum period, courtroom advocacy was the main road to prestige, to acclaim within the profession, and to becoming a leader of the local bar. It simply was the only way for a lawyer, as a lawyer, to become famous.

Besides deciphering titles and mastering the maze of rules on land grants, Ballinger also acted as an agent for numerous out-of-state and even foreign land speculators. For such clients, Ballinger bought and sold land, searched titles, and executed deeds. Although not as glamorous or challenging as the courtroom, Ballinger found that he was rewarded handsomely for his services. Indeed, his side activity as a land agent added a tidy sum to his yearly income. From 1855 when he arranged his first sale of several hundred acres near Houston to a group of Northern investors, to his final negotiation before the outbreak of civil war, Ballinger earned over seven thousand dollars in additional income, as well as receiving as payment for his services three thousand acres of land scattered on the mainland between Houston, Columbus, and Waco. Ballinger's most lucrative sale was one he prepared in the summer of 1860 for a wealthy Frenchman named Victor Girandeau, friend of the powerful Galveston financier, Robert Mills, who also purchased land through Ballinger and Jack. Ballinger transacted a sale of thirty-seven hundred acres for Girandeau in Fort Bend County. The Frenchman had been looking "for good grazing land" and was "quite pleased with the land you had selected for him." Mills further told Ballinger that Girandeau "would like to have you arrange other purchases for him in the future as he will be in need of more land for the raising of stock &c. He has great trust in your judgment & told me to give you carte blanche to make the necessary purchase, selection of the land, etc." For his efforts Ballinger received two thousand dollars. Several years later when Girandeau sold his land to the Galveston, Houston &

"*As if I was caught up in a maelstrom*"

Henderson Railroad Company, he called upon Ballinger to arrange the sale. This time Girandeau paid Ballinger with land, 370 acres valued at ten dollars an acre.[49]

Like most of his peers, Ballinger constantly sought new clients and thus believed it essential to advertise his services. Since there was no prohibition against advertising at that time, countless numbers of lawyers solicited the public for their business through notices in newspapers and other publications. The firm of Ballinger and Jack was no exception. Beginning in 1855 and for the remainder of his professional life, Ballinger annually took out several ads in both local and Northern newspapers and in professional journals or circulars, announcing his "proficiency in several areas of the law." The cost of such solicitation usually ran Ballinger one hundred dollars a year, with the average price for an ad about ten dollars. After a few years of advertising in several Texas and out-of-state newspapers (for four years Ballinger ran ads almost exclusively in major Southern publications), Ballinger found very few warranted "further subscription." Of the numerous Southern newspapers in which he advertised, only two proved worthwhile: the New Orleans *Picayune* and the Mobile *Register and Advertiser*. Ballinger continued runnning his ads in both papers until the early 1880s. As far as Northern publications were concerned, Ballinger found the New York papers, most notably the *Herald* and *Tribune*, yielded the greatest volume of new business. His greatest return for his advertising money came not from newspapers but from professional circulars such as his favorite, *The Monthly Catalogue of Reliable and Efficient Practising Lawyers*, published by the New York law firm of John Livingston. The circular was published in all major Northern and Southern cities and over the years brought Ballinger a susbstantial amount of lucrative new business. Ballinger paid only ten dollars a year to keep his firm listed in the publication.[50]

Another staple of Ballinger's practice was collection work. Like the majority of his Western colleagues, he dunned and sued, both for local people and for easterners holding debts in the form of promissory notes. Collection work was more tedious and frustrating than the arranging of land sales but was potentially more lucrative because lawyers usually paid themselves from the proceeds if they collected. Depending upon the number of clients and the amount of their claims, an effective collection attorney could earn several thousand dollars in additional income.

Ballinger faced keen competition in this field from both local commission merchants and other attorneys who processed a good number of routine claims, particularly for Northern creditors. He also concluded that advertising alone in Northern newspapers would not bring him the desired volume of collection work. Thus, in the summer of 1854, Ballinger made the first of his many subsequent sojourns to the North in hopes of obtaining a larger share of this interstate business. Over a two-and-one-half-month period he visited numerous businessmen in Boston, New York, and Philadelphia, offering to handle all their Texas accounts for a small commission. In some instances he even supplied his potential clients with lists of other possible Texas customers. Ballinger called upon a variety of Northern firms whose activities ranged from shipbuilding and shoemaking to bookselling and the dispensing of pharmaceuticals.

Ballinger's interviews with Northern businesses were not always encouraging. Some firms did little or no business in Texas, while others "preferred to retain their existing Galveston [collection] agents." A few were even openly hostile toward the Texas attorney, such as S. Cochran of S. Cochran & Company, who told Ballinger that "Texas lawyers charge too much—don't like lawyers—rather keep out of their hands." On the whole, however, Ballinger concluded that his venture had been successful. In a special diary he recorded the name and address of every prospect he called upon along with comments for future reference. Endorsements from prominent Texas politicians and businessmen paved the way for meetings with such notable Northern capitalists as Alexander T. Stewart of New York, who employed "257 persons in a dry goods business with assets over $200,000."[51] Stewart escorted Ballinger on a personal tour of his establishment before giving the Galvestonian several claims for collection. Equally responsive was the "great abolition house" Bowen McNamee & Company of Boston, which gave Ballinger all their Texas accounts. The Texan was overjoyed at receiving such a lucrative account, but he was surprised at McNamee's munificence, for his financial support of abolitionism, was "much acclaimed throughout the North." As Ballinger further told Tom Jack, McNamee had contributed "vast sums of money to that cause over the years & has made it known to many a Southern gentleman who has preceded me on business, that he detests slaveowners & and all they stand for. I did not tell the old fellow that I too owned slaves—I saw no percentage to be gained by such a declaration."[52]

Elderly soap magnate Samuel Colgate provided Ballinger not only with accounts and other contacts but with several bars of soap as well. For Colgate's business Ballinger had to endure a lengthy lecture on the more esoteric passages of scripture. He undoubtedly was bored to tears by Colgate's rambling. Yet, he graciously "thanked the old man for his business and the perfumed soaps which Hally will enjoy. He is a very kind old fellow but I think a bit senile."[53]

Ballinger's contracts varied from client to client, but a representative offer was that made to Woolf & Gillespie, a New York hardware firm. "I told Mr. Wolf I wd. collect at maturity for 1% and do his genl. collections by suit for 5." Whether or not he was able to negotiate an arrangement, Ballinger made sure he left one of his business cards on the premises as a reminder of his availability. Within a month of his return to Galveston, he began receiving collection notices from his new out-of-state clients. One of his first charges was from Binford Tate Plow Company of Philadelphia, asking Ballinger to collect over five hundred dollars owed by Texas farmers "Wood and Powers of your city [Galveston], and Messrs. Hart and Golden of Richmond, Tx. Please expedite this matter as rapidly as possible. This is money owed to us for over one year. We are anxious for collection." Within six months Ballinger collected all four notes, and for services rendered, received fifty dollars.[54]

One of Ballinger's more lucrative antebellum clients was the banking house of Johnston Brothers of Baltimore. By 1860 debts owed to them by Texans exceeded twenty thousand dollars. However, by the fall of 1861, with secession and war imminent, Ballinger had trouble collecting the debts which ranged from twenty dollars to over five hundred dollars. Johnston Brothers was desperate to collect, fearing it would never see its money if it was not collected soon. Ballinger was instructed to "lower the amount presently owed 25– 30%, or 70 cents on the dollar." Even at the reduced rate, by the outbreak of war in April 1861, Ballinger had collected only about one-third of the total owed.[55]

Not until 1862 could the full extent of Ballinger's "Northern connections" be seen. In July of that year, in compliance with the Confederate Sequestration Law, Ballinger disclosed all debts owed by Texans to "alien enemies." He reported that his firm handled the debt collection for seventy-nine business concerns in New York, thirty-eight in Philadelphia, and fifteen in Boston, with total claims against Texans in excess of two hundred thousand dollars.[56]

Ballinger's ambitious trip to the Northeast in 1854 revealed an interesting facet of Southern antebellum lifestyles and attitudes. In the four decades before the Civil War, large numbers of well-to-do and influential Southerners trekked northward for a variety of both personal and professional reasons. Many Southerners went to escape the oppressive heat and the fever-bearing mosquitoes for which Southern summers were notorious.

Others, like Ballinger, travelled north to improve their professional and financial status by extending their enterprises beyond the limited resources of their own region. Southern entrepreneurs realized that a trip "at the North" was necessary if they were to become successful businessmen. Regardless of the reasons for their sojourn, once in the North, Southerners found that they could not resist indulging in every amenity offered by the region's major cities.[57]

Although nothing in the South compared with New York, Ballinger was not as captivated by the metropolis as were most of his southern compatriots who found it to be the most dazzling and enchanting of places. Less rhapsodic in his appraisal, Ballinger, in fact, found New York to be "a very noisy & dirty city. So far I have been rather disappointed in the places & people who aren't very friendly." Yet, New Yorkers were a "very business-minded professional people whom I have found to be most taken with success & all the finery money can buy." The Texan also found New York to be a city of "such squalor—the general wretchedness of the city's poor exceeds anything I have ever imagined. No one seems to care about their condition—they say it is the way of things. They are particularly disdainful of the Irish who apparently make up most of the city's poor."[58]

Ballinger overcame his aversion to the seamier side of New York life, enjoying the city's sights and pleasantries. He stayed at the Astor House, "the most elegant of New York establishements—not even New Orleans has a finer place;" dined at "Sherry's where an order of soup costs 30 cents & oysters prepared in forty styles cost the same as the soup for a half dozen & entrees, fish and meats &c. at prices which would house one overnight in the finest hotel in Galveston;" visited Broadway, city hall, and the Stock Exchange, "where members paid $400 per year for the privilege of buying & selling stocks."[59]

Among the many pleasures Northern cities offered their Southern visitors were the opera and other professional musical performances. When in the North, Southerners rarely passed up the opportunity to attend an opera or a concert to satisfy their euphonic tastes. Ballinger too enjoyed this particularly delightful Northern amenity, the quality of which he remarked to his wife, "surpasses anything we have had for quite some time in Galveston. What has passed for opera in our city would be roundly considered a farce here. After this evening it will be very difficult to accept anything less." The opera Ballinger attended was *Don Giovanni*, performed at Jullien's, reputed to be one of the finest opera houses in all of New York, whose owner personally greeted his patrons in the most flamboyant

"As if I was caught up in a maelstrom"

attire as they poured through his doors. Ballinger enjoyed a classic production and delighted in watching one of the decade's most celebrated sopranos, Henriette Sontag, in one of the leading roles. Ballinger told his wife that the diva's performance "was truly one of the most memorable displays of the power & emotion of the human voice. I wish dearest that you had been with me to enjoy this most memorable treat."[60]

New York's numerous retail shops and ladies' boutiques also impressed Ballinger: "The extraordinarily fine quality & variety of products and prices charged exceeds anything we have in Galveston. The clothing is of exceptional quality & fashion—I shall buy Hally a dress—she will be the envy of all the City."[61]

After experiencing New York, Ballinger traveled to Boston. Boston proved less professionally promising than New York, but of the three major Northern cities Ballinger visited, he found Boston to be the most enchanting and memorable. He was especially impressed by the way Bostonians so fastidiously preserved their city's rich history while simultaneously transforming Boston into the nation's leading industrial area. Although commenting that he sometimes felt uncomfortable around "these shrewd Yankee businessmen" and was irritated by "the open acceptance of abolitionism & denigration of Southern principles," Ballinger nonetheless found Bostonians to be "a charming & gracious people who take great pride in their City's traditions & heritage, and are always willing to tell strangers about their glorious past."[62]

If there was a moment on his trip when Ballinger lost his sense of purpose, it was while in Boston. There his sojourn momentarily took on some of the characteristics of a "Grand Tour," as he visited every known landmark and historical sight: the Commons, the Navy Yard, the State House, Bunker Hill, Harvard College, and, of course, Faneuil Hall where he had "the misfortune to have heard a most vile & false speech on the horrible conditions of our negroes, given by fanatic [William Lloyd] Garrison." Despite his brief reminder at Faneuil Hall that Boston was the center of American abolitionism, Ballinger quickly forgot Garrison's tirade and proceeded to partake of the city's sense of history symbolized in its patriotic monuments and institutions. The Texan spent more time sightseeing and relishing the historic grandeur of Boston than he did soliciting new clients. As he visited the venerated sights around Boston, he reconstructed in his own mind the scene of the "massacre" of 1770 and the "tea party" three years later. He was so moved by all the history surrounding him that he wrote, "No sight was more inspiring than that which I enjoyed standing near the State House as I looked down from Beacon Street over Boston Common. It was a magnificent view of the water & beautiful city in the distance. There was not a place I visited that did not arouse in me a deep feeling of patriotism & pride in our nation's glorious past."[63]

The last city on Ballinger's agenda was Philadelphia, and there too he took time out from his work to appreciate the history and charm of the "City of Brotherly Love." He found Philadelphians to be "as intelligent & accomplished as the inhabitants of Boston, whom I believe to be the most informed in this country." He was also momentarily captivated by Philadelphia's Quaker past, for it reminded him of his own interesting connection with this part of the country where his great-great grandfather, Henry Ballinger, had first settled. Ballinger tried finding out if there were any distant relatives in the area, but as he told his wife, "They apparently had all migrated elsewhere—scattered throughout the country. I made several inquiries at different places, even found a Ballinger here & there, but alas they were of no relation to me, or so distant to me that it wd be very difficult to establish any sort of connexion. Many remarked however that they were disappointed—would like to have been associated with such a fine young gentleman."[64]

Like Boston, Philadelphia had a rich and inspiring past and like so many of his fellow Southerners, Ballinger made the pilgrimage to see the sights associated with the nation's early history. The Mint, the Old State House [Independence Hall], the Liberty Bell, the historical paintings—all claimed his attention. Being in the presence of some of the nation's most revered relics overwhelmed the Galvestonian. When he "touched the old cracked bell that brought our ancestors to arms in defence of our liberties," and when he went to Independence Hall and "thought about the great men who were there & the document they composed to liberate us from tyranny, I felt a sensation of devotion to this country that made my heart beat faster."[65]

Although Ballinger lived in a fairly cultivated and progressive urban environment, Galveston's amenities were few and meager compared to those of New York, Philadelphia, and Boston. Returning from his trip invigorated and optimistic, Ballinger found Northern cities novel and even educational. It was not long before the purpose of his trip came to fruition, substantially augmenting his professional and financial status. More important to Ballinger than the tangible rewards was the opportunity to experience a way of life and mentality very different from his own familiar Southern background. Ballinger's three-month trek to the North marked the first time he had traveled out of the South. Although Texas was on the periphery of Southern culture and displayed its own unique spirit, it was nevertheless overwhelmingly Southern in attitude and tradition. Texans shared with their Southern brethren common creeds and habits and were thus similarly affected by experiences outside of their parochial existence. Regardless of their background or the occasion for their excursion, a trip to the North, that strange and distant land, provided Southerners with opportunities to experience a way of life that was in most respects totally antithetical to their own reality. Once in the North, Southerners quickly realized the tediousness and isolation of their own lives. They wanted excitement and diversions and went north avidly seeking it.

Ballinger was so rejuvenated by his trip north that upon his return to Galveston he was confident he had "made the connexions necessary to greatly expand our practice." His junket had also allowed him time "to take stock of my career & renew in me a devotion to my practice. Now that I have seen greater possibilites for our success, I believe there will be little to prevent us from attaining all we desire. But we must be more diligent in our pursuits & not allow any distractions to take us from what is most important."[66] Although Ballinger repeatedly made such pledges, when it came to the enrichment and aggrandizement of his beloved Galveston, all such pretense rapidly dissipated. Rare was the moment when he was not vigorously involved in some "distracting" enterprise or scheme to further promote Galveston's ascendancy. By the end of the decade, Ballinger's individual and legal acclaim had won him a permanent place within Galveston's ruling oligarchy. From that position, Ballinger, along with other civic leaders, succeeded in making Galveston one of the most cosmopolitan and preeminent ports in the antebellum South.

Chapter Five

"MY LIFE IS NOW FULFILLED"

The 1850s were auspicious and lucrative years for Ballinger, both professionally and personally. Thanks largely to his legal acumen and effort, his law practice burgeoned into one of the most successful and respected in Texas. Through family connections and encouragement, Ballinger substantially augmented his professional income, investing in property and in the various mercantile and commercial enterprises sustaining Galveston's economic vitality during the decade.

From roughly 1845 to 1860 Galveston reigned as the "Queen City"—the commercial, financial, and cultural center of antebellum Texas. The combination of business and professional interests administering Galveston during the 1850s was one of the most powerful elites in Texas history. Galveston's aristocracy consisted of a small number of native Anglo-American families drawing their incomes from various commercial and professional enterprises, as well as from extensive mainland cotton plantations. Regardless of occupation, these individuals were by far the wealthiest and most ambitious members of Galveston society. These men and their families led a cosmopolitan, sophisticated life, rarely associating with others outside their small circle. They were bound together not only by an intricate network of personal ties, but by a shared sense of noblesse oblige as well. Through a variety of interesting policies the elite cultivated the allegiance of the lower classes, which consisted of small traders, clerks, mechanics, laborers, and seamen who provided the elite with essential services. These individuals displayed an unwitting confidence in the oligarchy's ability to govern the island in the best interests of all its inhabitants. This unique accord developed as a result of the island's unprecedented affluence as the state's principal entrepot. Galveston's commercial primacy allowed the privileged classes to create a fiscal structure that generally exempted both them and the lower classes from taxation. Thus, all Galvestonians had a vested interest in sustaining their city's commercial preeminence.[1]

Ballinger's acceptance within Galveston's elite was largely the result of his professional achievements. The owners of the Wharf Company as well as other city fathers were so impressed by his triumph in the Flats Case that he rapidly became their principal attorney, handling the majority of both their personal and commercial concerns, many of which extended beyond Texas and the Gulf Coast into a national network. Ballinger immersed himself in the professional and individual issues affecting the oligarchy and their administering of Galveston. He never ceased cultivating and extending relationships with his compatriots, doing all possible to augment the position of the elite which he believed essential for his city's security.[2]

An elitist by temperament and occupation, Ballinger believed in a meritocratic society in which power was wielded by the well-bred and educated. Yet, his sense of privilege was tempered by an equally strong sentiment of communal responsibility. Rarely did he display the penchant for self-indulgence and flattery so pervasive at times among the Galveston gentility. Ballinger believed individuals, especially those of "quality" and "sound character," had an obligation to subordinate individual gratification for society's welfare. He refused to accept the contention that the interests of the group and the individual were antagonistic, for men had reached the stage of "social evolution" where they felt "more shame and misery from neglect of duty" than could be offset by personal aggrandizement. To Ballinger, the development of character was the "prime factor" in social evolution, for it gave individuals the "power to attain a high degree of social efficiency." Collective effectiveness derived from a "love of order & capacity to subordinate the interests of the individual to the interests of the community." Progress, Ballinger maintained, might be assured "if we but live wise, brave, and upright lives."[3] That Ballinger was more willing than most to sacrifice personal desires for the benefit of the commonweal, is not to suggest he lived an austere, spartan existence. Nor was he naive when it came to understanding and maneuvering within the inner circles of Galveston's power elite. Once accepted, Ballinger quickly emerged as one of the oligarchy's most adept and pragmatic power brokers.

Possessed of an energetic, versatile intelligence, Ballinger turned his mind, even during his busiest times, to the broad complex of his world. He was maturing in an exciting time—an age of increasing industrialization, the beginnings of scientific scholarship, moral reform, romanticism, and unfortunately, escalating sectional tension over slavery. Omniverously curious, Ballinger studied these separate but often related phenomena. Gradually, he formed conclusions about nature, society, literature, politics, and the law. By the eve of the Civil War, these conclusions had become the controlling principles of his life and career.

Ballinger first publicly revealed his thoughts on the issues of his time in a lecture before Galveston's Young Men's Lyceum. In an 1856 address entitled "On the Necessity of Safeguarding Our Political Institutions & Laws From Those Corrupted by Power and Fame," Ballinger attacked public hyperemotionalism, which he believed, was endangering "our proud fabric of freedom." The cause was "the jealousy, envy, and avarice incident to our nature." Ballinger's thesis was the threat of social disorder—a common theme for many lyceum meetings during the late antebellum period, especially as sectional tensions mounted. These monthly convocations were important forums in which aspiring young men tested their rhetorical skill and improved their elocution before their peers.[4]

For several months Ballinger had been disturbed by the increasing outbursts of mob violence, which appeared endemic from New England to Texas. Whether such "disregard for person and property" was nativist inspired toward Irish and German immigrants or prompted by racism toward black folk and white abolitionists, Ballinger believed that "if the laws be continually despised" then "citizens' affection for their government must inevitably be alienated."[5]

Despite conveying a sense of despair, Ballinger believed there was a solution: "Let every American, every lover of liberty, every well wisher to his posterity, swear never to violate the laws of the country & never tolerate their violation by others." Respect for the laws "must be taught in every school & proclaimed from every pulpit throughout this great country," and most important to Ballinger it "must be enforced in the courts of justice." In short, he urged that respect for law and order become "the most passionate, single-minded devotion of every citizen."[6]

At this point in his lecture, when most listeners thought he had finished, Ballinger began again, asking why such violence and disrespect for the laws was greater now than it had been in the past. In the first half of his speech he offered a sociological interpretation; now he offered his audience a psychological interpretation. To Ballinger it was relatively simple and clear: the scarcity of individual character and public virtue amongst too many of his generation; in previous generations, most notably that of the founding fathers, the nation's leaders were "animated by a desire to see the great experiment in self-government succeed. Nothing else mattered to them—not fame, or fortune, or power. For they possessed great character & devotion to principle & duty." Ballinger reassured his audience that all was not hopeless, for there were still "many good & wise men who possess these qualities [like himself] & who aspire to the simplest of office so they can serve the people, whose welfare is their only concern." But, he lamented, there were still too many "among us who have been afflicted by a power-madness so great that they find simple honors only small stepping-stones toward their grand purpose of complete power." Ballinger's fear was that such men usually possessed "a towering genius" which "disdains a beaten path." Such intellect "thirsts & burns for distinction and will have it, whatever the costs to others might be." In concluding, Ballinger maintained that the only way to safeguard the nation's "security from the excesses of ambitious men" was to "arouse in every citizen the need to keep a vigilant eye" on such individuals, and when they appeared, the people must be "ready to disavow them completely." Naturally, this was to be accomplished at all times "with respect for the laws of this great Nation."[7]

Over time Ballinger became an adept public speaker, despite the onset of "quaking in his shoes" and "feeling queezy" in his stomach before delivering every address. Beginning in 1856 and ending in 1861, Ballinger gave at least a dozen lyceum and other public speeches each year on a variety of topics ranging from railroad construction and port expansion to opposition to temperance. As his oratorical skills and confidence grew, he often volunteered to give a lecture, for as he admitted years later, he was reluctant "to lose any opportunity" to advance himself. Although complaining after his every delivery that his speech was unsatisfactory, Ballinger's dignity, clarity, and straightforwardness engendered respect and conveyed conviction; by the eve of the Civil War Ballinger was one of the most sought-after public speakers in Texas.[8]

Ballinger's realization that recognition was the fastest way to new business created consternation during his early professional years. He found it "distressfully agonizing" to "cavort around with a lot of people whom you would not walk across the street to speak to."[9] Yet Ballinger put himself forward discreetly. He helped organize a variety of fund-raising activities to improve his city's "social & educational well-being," and threw himself into the Masons "on account of the opportunity it gives a man—especially a young man—to extend his acquaintances & standing."[10] Ballinger did many other things that often conflicted with his aspirations "to get on" as a lawyer and his desire to serve the community. For example, in 1858 he was asked to serve as a special judge in a disputed local election but decided not to accept the position, pleading a lack of time. However, as he confessed to his uncle, he would be labeled "a traitor if I decide one way & a coward if I decide the other."[11] The 1858 election was not the only time Ballinger refused to participate in controversy for fear of jeopardizing his professional standing and success. However, if "the chance of gaining prestige" was before him, then, as he told his son years later, he would "run those risks and do any amount of work necessary." But he also told his son "a man should never intentionally create enemies unless he is paid—& well for it."[12]

Ballinger's desire to impose rationality on public life reflected his inner struggle to bring coherence to his own, still unsettled personality. He was insecure about who he was and how he wanted to be perceived. He liked associating with Galveston's elite who gathered around the wealthy and snobbish Robert Mills and John Sydnor, but he also wanted to be "one of the boys," the young and active workingmen, shopkeepers, and other members of the middle class. For example, one of Ballinger's closest friends during the 1850s was a lay school teacher from New York, William Morris, who came to the island in 1855 to teach at St. Joseph's Catholic school. Morris and Ballinger became fast friends, for Ballinger "greatly admired his way with students" and his "keen mind." The two men spent much leisure time together, "discussing the affairs of the world," as well as playing cards and dominoes at Ballinger's home. Unfortunately, Morris had to leave the island in 1859 because of his "abolitionist dispostion." Morris's departure saddened Ballinger, and despite their differences over slavery, the two men remained in contact, even during the war years. When Ballinger visited New York on business in 1867, he stayed with Morris and his family and the two men remained close friends until Ballinger's death in 1888.[13]

Ballinger's reputation rested first and foremost on the universal belief in his absolute honesty. Throughout his career he held himself to the highest standards of truthfulness. In notes for a lecture on his procession, written in 1880, Ballinger observed with resentment, "the distorted view that all lawyers are necessarily dishonest." He then warned "let no young man who desires a career in the law submit to this notion. If he does, then he cannot become a lawyer, for a lawyer, above all people, must resolve to be honest; if he cannot then he should choose another occupation."[14]

Clients and other attorneys also respected Ballinger's incredible capacity for hard work. He drafted nearly all his own legal papers, from the purely formal praecipes to the most complex pleadings. Until the invention of the typewriter, Ballinger wrote in his own hand all necessary documents, which often involved enormous labor. In the Flats Case Ballinger drafted a forty-page response to the city's charges; a task requiring immense concentration, and his handwriting suggested that he wrote the entire answer at one sitting. Few cases warranted such intensity of labor, but Ballinger's clients rarely lost a suit because of their attorney's carelessness or inattention to detail.

Ballinger wanted to be regarded as a generous opponent, unwilling to hurt the feelings of a colleague; yet with his temper still not under complete control, when agitated he was capable of lashing out at his opponents with a lacerating barage of demeaning remarks. Like any other lawyer, he resorted to technicalities in order to save his clients. He preferred, however, to base his arguments on justice rather than on legal precedents. In court he rarely objected when opposing counsel introduced evidence. According to Tom Jack, Ballinger "would say he 'acknowledged' this or that to be admissible. Sometimes when his opponent could not quite prove what Ballinger knew to be the truth, he 'acknowledged' the truth to be so and so." Ballinger's apparent gentility did not mean he yielded essentials. As Jack noted, "What he appeared to be so blithely giving away was simply what he knew he couldn't get and keep." Many a rival lawyer was lulled into complacency by Ballinger's casual style as he would concede, say, six of seven points in argument, only to discover that the whole case turned on the seventh point. "Any lawyer who did not quickly see this as part of his [Ballinger's] strategy would realize too late he had been outwitted and was going to lose."[15]

Ballinger had the assurance that comes with great intellect and moral courage, but he needed clear and continued evidence of approval. In countless cases he expected defeat; after each victory he was almost pathologically exuberant. His constant motion both released and revealed his constant tension. The acerbity of his attacks on his critics attested to his doubts. Yet he was sure enough to respond, when challenged, with argument as well as condemnation, and sure enough to act with purpose.

As a member of Galveston's elite, it was "socially" incumbent on Ballinger to attend the several theatrical productions presented on the island throughout the 1850s. It was during the "fifty-seven-fifty-eight season" that Hamilton Stuart of the Galveston *Civilian* asked Ballinger to review the various attractions appearing at the Galveston Theatre. Beginning in December 1857 and running through March 1858, Ballinger saw every form of divertisement that came to town and "passed itself off as legitimate entertainment." Ballinger witnessed "exhibitions" ranging from "a most 'captivating' performance of Shakespeare's *Hamlet* that was applauded to the very echo," to all manner of minstrel troups, a piano concert, and finally a series of plays and comic acts "supposedly performed by some of the finest actors and comedians from New York and Boston." Writing a brief review for the *Civilian* after each engagement, Ballinger then, at the close of the season, submitted a general assessment of the plays and other attractions Galvestonians "had been subjected to the past several months." Ballinger prefaced his critique by telling his readers he "gratuitously and with pleasure" wrote his commentary for "We should be thankful that the year's productions are at last through. We have had our sensibilities affronted enough by all manner of individuals claiming to be 'artists.' During the last three months the performances at this resort have been a libel on the town and an insult to intelligent people. . . . The only legitimate drama we have had was Donetti's Acting Monkeys, and God knows they were bad enough." It was time for Galvestonians to stop applauding "these clap-trap clowns," and to cease patronizing "every humbug announced in flaming handbills." Ballinger then chastised fellow Galvestonians, asserting that their affluence had made many an "emphatically show-ridden people, and the dimes flow alike into the coffers of those who exhibit a monstrosity in the shape of a bearded woman or an equally unnatural burlesque of the histrionic art."[16] Apparently Ballinger's frequent treks to the North and his exposure there to "real theater," had greatly exalted his dramatic awareness. He no longer tolerated even the slightest abuse of those valuations, and wanted his compatriots to feel the same toward anything that was not unadulterated thespianism or a presentation of genuine bravura.

Ballinger's deep appreciation for the arts, especially literature, can be traced to his years at St. Mary's where the Jesuit fathers first inculcated him with a yearning for knowledge and reflection. His love of learning resulted in an insatiable desire for books that became an incurable bibliomania. Ballinger was very aware of his obsession with books, admitting that he too frequently "commonplaced" from his "old books," devoting many "spare moments to that occupation" rather than to his practice which "does not interest me nearly as greatly. If I devoted equal attention and pleasure to the law, how my acquirements would be increased." Even when pressed with other, more urgent responsibilities, Ballinger had difficulty resisting his books. The temptation to retreat to them became so

The Library of the W. P. Ballinger home, THE OAKS, in Galveston, where in 1891, was born the thought of the Daughters of the Republic of Texas.

Ballinger's "most favorite place" within his home, his library and study, his retreat and sanctuary from his busy professional life. By the time of his death, his library was reputed to have the most complete collection of law books, as well as general works, in the South. *Photograph courtesy Prints and Photographs Collection, CN10514, Center for American History, University of Texas at Austin.*

great during the Civil War that he finally had to "box them up & put them out of my sight—so as to think of nothing but official duties, and the events of the war." Throughout his diary Ballinger repeatedly chastised himself for not having read more professional publications and for buying more books than he could afford. He spent entire days "arranging books—putting them up—haven't arranged them properly yet." Even on the Sabbath, much to his wife's chagrin, Ballinger would skip church for the purpose of "rearranging the books at the office."[17]

As a book collector, Ballinger had two goals: to build the best law library in the state and to assemble an equally outstanding personal and miscellaneous collection at both his home and office. Beginning in 1859 and for the next two years—until the Civil War cut him off from his Northern booksellers—Ballinger devoted considerable money and time to developing his legal reviews. He ordered "115 volumes of States' reports from Armstrong's," and wrote "Little, Brown, Banks and Bros. to enclose list of law books which will give us a pretty good library—the most of the English reports and several of the states—I feel that a good library is indispensable to me."[18]

"My life is now fulfilled"

In the summer of 1860 Ballinger completed what he called "a capital bargain," for some law books. He purchased at a discount of 30 percent, from Little, Brown 265 volumes of assorted legal editions. Despite the discount, his bill ran $760. That amount was the most Ballinger paid for professional books in the prewar period. His usual purchases were considerably less, averaging between $250 to $300 every four to six months for both professional and miscellaneous volumes. In the prewar period Ballinger spent about sixteen hundred dollars annually on book purchases, representing about 26 percent of his yearly income between 1859 and 1861. Fortunately he had worked out various payment plans with his booksellers and thus rarely had to produce the full amount up front. Ballinger cared little what he paid for books, for he was determined "to make our library the best in the State. I believe my private library is now better than any I know."[19]

Despite a constant resolve not to spend any more money on books, nor to read when he should be doing something else, Ballinger's bibliomania was incurable. Even on important business trips Ballinger could not curb his passion for books. During one of his many professional sojourns "at the North," he literally ran amok visiting every book store he possibly could in Philadelphia and New York. He was so ecstatic after finding a rare volume of Samuel Taylor Coleridge's works, that instead of continuing to call on prospective clients, he cancelled the rest of his appointments, returned to his hotel room, and "read & wrote all day—so delighted to have found volume of Coleridge—intend to stay in tomorrow as well in order to finish reading."[20] Perhaps this excerpt best sums up the view of one of Texas's leading bibliophiles: "Thought I would make an end of buying books & examd at the difft book stores for such as I wished to get. I have almost a bibliomania which I must get rid of, or at least not to interfere with my duties." However, not until a week later, after spending another $182.75 for books, did Ballinger carry out his above-mentioned promise: "I shall now stop—no more good books here [Galveston] to be gotten."[21]

By the Civil War Ballinger had momentarily completed his goal of having a first-rate law library, but fell far short of what he envisioned. During the 1870s, when his practice finally recovered from the effects of war and reconstruction, Ballinger's bibliomania once again consumed him. No sooner was he financially solvent than he engaged in book-buying sprees running into the thousands of dollars for his purchases. The costs were of minimal concern to Ballinger, for by the end of the decade he accomplished what he had set out to do twenty years earlier: he had built the most thorough law library in the state, if not the Southwest.

Ballinger's bibliomania represented more than a simple passion for books and knowledge. His library was his sanctuary, a place he could easily retreat to from the daily stress of his profession. Even when at home, his study was a haven from the tumult and demands of family life. So comforting did Ballinger find his den, that he avoided "going out—I have too much a disposition to seclude myself in my office & home & among my books." Ballinger was conscious of "this great & growing fault" in his character, yet he found such great solace in isolating himself in his study, surrounded by his books, that he doubted he would "find greater comfort & reassurance in any other place."[22]

Because of his asthma Ballinger shied away from rigorous physical activity, thus channeling all his energies into his work, and gaining recognition for his intellectual rather than his physical prowess. His library became an all-important source from which, and upon which, he established his identity and self-worth. Since his asthma limited his ability to resolve aggressive drives physically, he found first the courtroom, then book collecting, the perfect catharses for such intense energy. In Ballinger's mind, his library and performance in the courtroom were symbiotic: without his legal texts he could not become the respected lawyer he so fervently desired. Professional acclaim would not only win his father's approbation but that of other, more illustrious individuals as well. Ballinger built an eclectic intellectual home, its parts connected but the whole more comfortable than integrated. It was designed to provide security for a man whose personality compelled him to act, whose profession required him to compromise, and whose moral beliefs forced him to justify everything he did.

Despite his many civic and professional activities, Ballinger managed to devote both time and attention to his home, family, and friends. In late 1858 he moved into a new home he had built a year earlier. His new residence was called "The Oaks," and here Ballinger was to live the remainder of his life. With an ever-increasing family (by 1860 Ballinger had four children—three girls—Lucy, Betty, and Harriet, ranging in age from seven years to two years, and a son, one-year-old William Pitt Jr.), and with the constant stream of guests and relatives often visiting the Ballingers for weeks at a time, a large, spacious home was essential. Although Ballinger's home was set in an urban context, its design and ambiance reflected that of a traditional Southern plantation. Indeed, the majority of Galveston's aristocracy constructed and fashioned their homes in this style. The Oaks was

"My life is now fulfilled"

W. P. Ballinger home, "The Oaks," built by Ballinger in 1858, at the corner of Avenue O at 29th Street, about a 15 to 20 minute walk from the offices of Ballinger and Jack. *Photograph taken from* Art Work of Galveston *(1894). Courtesy Rosenberg Library, Galveston, Texas.*

a white, pillared, two-story, high-ceilinged structure with wide opening doors, high windows, broad veranda doors opening from upstairs rooms and wide stairways, all designed for the greatest possible ventilation. Ballinger's home sat far back from the street—Avenue O at Twenty-Ninth Street—completely surrounded by large shade trees. At the rear of the house was a walled garden with luxurious hedges of oleander shrubs, poinsettias, bougainvillea, palm trees and other tropical trees, bushes, and plants. The Ballinger "park," was reputed to have been "one of the most exotic and lush displays of botanical beauty in all of Texas, if not the entire South. Even the foreign dignitaries frequenting our City have made it a point on their sojourns to visit regularly the Ballinger house and marvel at their gardens."[23]

Ballinger's estate was impressive, particularly when considering he enjoyed such affluence at the age of thirty-two. The Oaks not only reflected Ballinger's professional success but also his other ventures which were frequently more lucrative than his law practice. Ballinger increasingly augmented his professional income by dabbling in land speculation. "Uncle Tommy [Harrison] has made a sale of all our land below Waco—at a profit of a little over $7,000 on the purchase—to be divided between the three of us [Tom Jack, Ballinger, and Guy Bryan]," he recorded in March 1854. "The news made me feel almost rich, as it will be the first money I have ever made outside my profession. I trust, though, when I get a little more to operate with, as our town is improving rapidly, that it will not be the last." By 1860 Ballinger owned several thousand acres of land all around southeast and central Texas with an estimated value of twenty-five thousand dollars.[24]

Like the posh homes, entertainment in Galveston tended to be lavish. At times the Ballinger residence was a scene of continuous pleasantry. Almost every day Ballinger and Hally hosted afternoon tea, de rigeur among Galveston's gentility. One of Ballinger's favorite tea-time companions was the powerful merchant/financier, Robert Mills, whom Ballinger enjoyed because of the "fine talk of homes, books, and trade," as well as the playing of dominoes until dinner and sometimes until the early hours of the morning. According to Ballinger, Mills was "obsessed with the game & is most irritated when I beat him. I indulge him & continue to play until he has had enough or has sufficiently beaten me." Though many Galvestonians considered Mills to be one of the most insufferable members of the city's elite, Ballinger found him "to be a fine gentleman whose companionship I thoroughly enjoy."[25]

When the cotton crop flowed into the city each November, ships from New York and Boston, Le Havre and Liverpool crowded the harbor, their captains and supercargoes eagerly waiting to load the bales piled high on the wharves. After Christmas, mainland planters and their families arrived for the Galveston social season, which peaked in March with balls, horse races, nightly plays and concerts, and a constant round of private parties, dinners, and visits. The Ballingers hosted large, formal parties in their home, occasions reputed to be among Galveston's more notable social events. When entertaining at home, Ballinger was by no means a perfunctory host, casually assuming his wife would make all the arrangements, as well as making sure the evening ran smoothly. Ballinger was an equally attentive host, making every effort to assist his wife to ensure their party's success. Although formal entertaining was regarded as one of the most important functions of the antebellum Southern belle, Hally Ballinger did not fit that stereotype. She relied very heavily on her husband's help, particularly when it came to the guest list and the "managing of the servants." On the day of the party the Ballinger household was a whirlwind of activity. All family members, including the children, had a specific task to perform in preparation for the evening's event. Ballinger's willingness to help his wife prepare for their festivities resulted in his declaring, "Our party

"My life is now fulfilled"

went off well last night as handsomely as we could have desired. Just enough people—music good—supper superb. Our servants performed very well—with complete grace & charm. We are all delighted."[26]

Both the Galveston *News* and *Civilian* often covered the Ballinger parties, commenting that "there is little doubt that Messr. and Madame Ballinger have once again graced our City with one of the year's most memorable affairs. A sumptuous supper was served upon many tables so perfectly arranged and beautified with exotic flowers straight from the Ballinger gardens. The fare included all variety of fish and fowl, fruits and cakes and other delights—a general profusion of viands and wines which exceeded anything we have seen in Galveston for quite some time. The extent and style of the preparations was entirely due to the gracious liberality of our noted jurist and his wife."[27]

In many instances Ballinger's domestic activities and attitudes reflected the dramatic changes the American nuclear family experienced during the late antebellum period. By the mid-nineteenth century, the family had been redefined in radically new terms. No longer was it merely part of the larger network of public institutions comprising the commonweal. Instead, the family became a separate entity, a "private" retreat from the vagaries of the outside world. It was regarded as a sanctuary where virtues and emotions were rejuvenated and safeguarded against an increasingly aggressive and obtrusive outer world. It was a place where women and children were secure and where men could find relief and comfort from external stresses and recover their humanity. Although the values of independence, self-reliance, and ambition remained the essence of the American creed and appropriate for the external world of the market place, within the home, a new set of values prevailed: love, mutuality, companionship, and selflessness. By mid-century the family was no longer a microcosm of the larger society. Rather, it was a counterbalance and refuge against the acquisitiveness and corruption of the external environment.[28]

As Ballinger's developing legal career attested, the American economy was undergoing rapid material and geographic expansion during the late antebellum period. Families were being "pushed" closer together as all members searched for stability and security amidst extensive socioeconomic change. As the nation's economy became more commercial and market-oriented, the work place became less emotional and more impersonal. The home thus became a haven for the rekindling of affection and belonging.[29]

Ballinger's relationship with Hally is testimony that the older ideals of patriarchal authority and strict wifely obedience were giving way to the new standards of shared esteem, friendship, and confidence. Ballinger unquestionably regarded Hally as his most intimate friend to whom he confided his innermost thoughts and feelings. Hally was his companion for life, and as such, Ballinger treated her with the respect and dignity befitting her new status as a companionate equal. After all, it was Hally who knew Ballinger better than anyone else, and on whom he could count to be there as a devoted wife and confidant.

In his relationship with his children, Ballinger was anything but the stereotypical bewhiskered Victorian father presiding over obeisant children. In fact, Ballinger was so "permissive" that he worried he was spoiling his children "beyond tolerance." He was often away from his Galveston home for weeks and sometimes months at a time and felt compelled when finally with his children to make up for lost time by overwhelming them with attention. He rarely returned from a trip without several presents for everyone, including Hally, and when at home, Ballinger spent practically every available moment interacting with his children. Whether playing games, toys, or reading to them by the hour, Ballinger doted on his children, negating the image of the domineering patriarch. Ballinger rarely, and not without feeling horribly distressed, verbally reprimanded his children. Remembering his own painful childhood, Ballinger never physically or psychologically punished his children for their transgressions. Because he was so loathe to chastise his children in any way, the onus of disciplining them fell upon Hally who, as he remarked, "is more inclined than I to take them to task for their behavior. I know I should discipline them when they misbehave or are sassy, but I just cannot bring myself to do it. They are such innocent little creatures at heart, & I spend so little time with them as it is, that I cannot bear having to punish them."[30]

In many respects a rather atypical father, Ballinger was traditional relative to society's more fundamental expectations. He considered himself solely responsible for earning the family's livelihood, a role he took so seriously that his exertions often drove him to physical and mental fatigue. Even after attaining significant professional and financial security, Ballinger still worried whether or not he was amply providing for his family, or that he was not earning enough to sustain his wife and children after his death. Although enjoying a companionate relationship with his wife, Ballinger nevertheless expected Hally to devote her life almost exclusively to domesticity. It was incumbent upon Hally to run an efficient and tidy household, provide an enriching and nurturing environment within the home, rear morally sound children, display the appropriate gentility on

"My life is now fulfilled"

A city view of Galveston, Texas's largest antebellum city, with an 1860 population of over seven thousand inhabitants. *Photograph by Shche and Potter, 1860–1861. Courtesy Rosenberg Library, Galveston, Texas.*

public occasions, and above all else, be a constant font of emotional support for her husband. Thanks largely to her abundant energy, force of personality, and devotion to her family, Hally Ballinger more than fulfilled her husband's expectations.

The Galveston of Ballinger's day was confined to the island's eastern end, the tip nearest the deep-water pass at Bolivar Point. The town's main thoroughfares ran parallel with the island's length, and were (in order) Water Street, the first street off the waterfront, Strand, Mechanic, Market, Post Office, and Church streets. The island's beaches were on the other side, facing the open sea, and access to the beach front ran along short streets, numbered from first to thirty-third. The town's layout comfortably accommodated a population of just over seven thousand inhabitants. It was a city small enough that one could easily walk to any destination in less than an hour.[31] Even so, Galveston's lawyers generally chose to live no more than a few blocks from the courthouse and had their offices as close to their homes as possible. Ballinger's office was on the Strand, only a fifteen to twenty minute walk from his home, and only two blocks from the courthouse. It was a perfect arrangement for a man driven by his work.

When not out of town, Galveston's geography defined his daily routine that mixed work and home. Ballinger was an early riser, up at sunrise, but no later than seven. He then walked to the market and returned with fresh produce, meat, and fish. Ballinger described his early morning sojourns as "the most pleasurable moments of my day—it was before the town came alive & the air was fresh & everything at the market always smelled so wonderful. It was the time when I would arrange my day in my mind." Ballinger so enjoyed his walk to the market, that he became the family's food shopper, rather than Hally or the servants. Nine o'clock found the Ballinger family at the breakfast table, the only meal during the day that Hally "insisted we all have together."[32] By ten Ballinger was either at his office or in court, where he remained until three or four in the afternoon. He then returned home for afternoon tea, frequently accompanied by friends and colleagues to enjoy conversations as wide-ranging as his table was ample. Around five-thirty, Ballinger returned to his office, where he labored through writs and court documents, answered his mail, but willingly stopped all such tedious work to discuss law with clerks or to chat with colleagues about literature, politics, history, and philosophy. One of Ballinger's most passionate office pastimes was his omnivorous reading of newspapers. Daily he read at least eight and sometimes ten cover to cover. He was especially fond of the larger Southern metropolitans such as the New Orleans *Picayune* and Mobile *Register*, and was overjoyed when he received week-old copies of either the New York *Herald* or *Tribune*. His reading of the papers kept him informed of the times and especially of current political events throughout the country. Often he would interrupt his reading to discuss or comment on a news item of interest. It would "remind him of something he had read in a book or had happened in Houston or somewhere else," Tom Jack noted. "That incident would lead to another and still another & an array of thoughts & lengthy discourse would follow until most of the afternoon was thus consumed. His lectures & ideas were so profoundly brilliant that they kept everyone in the office in complete attention & eager for him to go on." Yet, at other times, when no pressing issues or work claimed his attention, Ballinger retreated to his office and "for unknown reasons sat silently dripping with melancholy."[33]

By eight-thirty in the evening Ballinger was back at home to enjoy a quiet dinner with his wife—the children already fed and put to bed. Generally, by eleven o'clock, but frequently later, Ballinger went to bed. On average he slept only about five to six hours a night. He frequently suffered from insomnia and would "rise and read, sometimes for several hours," before falling asleep. Despite his restlessness, Ballinger believed he had a good life and one that he enjoyed. It was a life that perfectly suited his personality and temperament, for it was ordered, neat, and above all, predictable.[34]

By the end of the decade Ballinger had transformed his once miscellaneous practice into one almost exclusively devoted to realty and nascent corporate problems. Each spring and fall Ballinger traveled several hundred miles to attend the sessions of the district court at Brazoria and Matagorda, as well as the Texas Supreme Court at Tyler. While sometimes enduring the privations of the Texas hinterland, Ballinger was no itinerant country lawyer following a judge from one town to another, picking up clients wherever he could. From the moment he hung out his shingle, Ballinger's practice was urban-oriented, and his trips were not intended to attract new clients but were attempts to expand the scope of his principal Galveston practice.

Ballinger never lacked for private clients, even though he practiced in a city that boasted an unusually talented bar. During the 1850s, either alone or in conjunction with Tom Jack, he averaged fifteen appeals-court cases a year that were important enough to be officially recorded in printed court reports. More than half of them were probate cases involving wills, trusts, or other aspects of inheritance. At least a third were creditors' suits against debtors, in which Ballinger represented creditors suing to collect funds or competing with other creditors for a debtor's assets. Increasingly Ballinger, despite his role in debt cases, represented defendants more often than plaintiffs. As a result, he so frequently advised compromise that he often represented all parties to a dispute. The same preference for compromise and conciliation also marked his outgoing office correspondence, as time and again he advised clients to concede differences if they could, to seek arbitration rather than confrontation. Whether it was a family feud over inheritance or a disagreement between business partners, Ballinger's advice was the same. "Beaver" Williams (son of Samuel May Williams), who was studying law with Ballinger and Jack, described how Ballinger dealt with a prospective client. He would listen to the individual's story, "patiently & earnestly, occasionally interrupting the man as the story progressed by asking a question or two. The man would answer it and then he would proceed and end his story." After the interview, Ballinger would say, "I am not satisfied on some points—Come back to the office in a few hours & I will give you my opinion." When the client returned, Ballinger might say, "You are in the right," and the appropriate papers would be completed to bring suit. Ballinger might also tell the client: "You are in the wrong & I advise you to compromise. Do not bring suit for you will lose."[35] Ballinger's notoriety for arranging compromises extended beyond Texas. In 1860 he was called to New York by Samuel Colgate to arbitrate a dispute whose resolution cost a rival soap manufacturer twenty-five thousand dollars.[36]

Ballinger's unfailing courtesy and unusual combination of warmth and reserve drew people to him wherever he went; even casual acquaintances wanted to confide in him and win his approval. As a result, Ballinger was often overburdened. After a six-hour siege in his office by an out-of-town friend, Ballinger complained that "few people understand when it is appropriate to be sociable—most believe that their time & needs are all that matter & that no one else could possibly have anything more important to do but listen to their life story. I too often make the mistake of engaging such people by showing a little interest in their concerns. I must correct this fault before I go insane!"[37] The worst nuisances were garrulous clients who "sit by your side for hours & dwell away about their cases until you feel like sending them & their stories to the Devil." In desperation, Ballinger often locked his office door.[38]

By 1860 Ballinger's annual income ranged between six and ten thousand dollars. Only part of his yearly total was actually cash received for services rendered. Several of his settlements were similar to the one he recorded in his diary after winning an inheritance suit: "The property was valued at $21,000—our part being one-third—$7,000—We took Martin & Beall's indebtedness of $5,700; and the one-half block north of Atchinson's for which Potter is offered $5150—and $150 to be made up otherwise—That will do for a good fee."[39] The final amount Ballinger received depended upon his ability to secure favorable judgments from the court. Like most of his colleagues, Ballinger found it more lucrative to negotiate on a contingent fee basis. For example, for his services during the Flats Case, the Wharf Company in 1860 agreed to pay Ballinger "2,000—to be paid in four installments over the next 18 mos. & $4,000 contingent on success."[40]

Compared to today's inflated incomes in the legal profession, Ballinger's dollar earnings seem meager. Yet, it must be remembered that inflation was nonexistent in the antebellum period, and the cost of basic goods and services were ridiculously low and constant when matched to the present, fluctuating prices for the same commodities. The cost of living rose only 7 percent between 1850 and 1870, and less than 2 percent between 1850 and 1860. In 1860 a loaf of bread (one pound) cost about five cents; a pound of butter, ten cents; a dozen eggs, eight cents; ten pounds of potatoes, ten cents; and twenty-five cents for five pounds of sugar. Between 1856 and 1860 Ballinger rarely spent more than two hundred to three hundred dollars annually on food, and when he did, it was usually for imported luxuries such as Cuban cigars, Spanish port, French claret, or silk "that Hally insisted she must have." For such amenities Ballinger paid sixty dollars "extra" for the year 1858. In general, Ballinger's household expenditures on necessities were minimal, and thus an income of at least six thousand dollars could easily cover book-buying sprees, family vacations, private schools and tutors for his children, fashionable clothing for his wife, new carriages, eight slaves, and enough left over to dabble in land speculation.[41]

Without question Ballinger's earnings were substantial for his time. His annual income was fifteen to twenty times greater than the average skilled worker received during the antebellum period! Skilled laborers such as carpenters, painters, blacksmiths, machinists, and "engineers," were paid between $1.61 and $1.65 per day for a minimum of ten to twelve hours of work. Yearly incomes for such occupations ranged between $360 and $500. Unskilled workers in the South such as cotton weavers, spinners, and packers, made less than a dollar a day. The average wage paid to such individuals was about sixty-seven cents a day. Farm laborers in the United States earned a monthly average of $13.66 with board. In Texas, a farm hand received twelve dollars a month with board. When comparing Ballinger's income with what the majority of Americans earned during the antebellum period, the Galveston attorney was indeed doing very well. Even measured against the salaries of most present-day Americans, including many members of the legal profession, Ballinger's income was considerable. Translated into present dollars, Ballinger's 1860 yield of ten thousand dollars would be the equivalent of approximately $135,000.[42] Not bad remuneration after only six years of private practice.

How did Ballinger's earnings balance against those of his peers? Quite well, especially when matched with the compensation of many of his Texas colleagues. Although only scant information is available on antebellum lawyers' salaries, a good number of practitioners earned substantial, and occasionally very high incomes. Practices were particularly remunerative in the Northeast, and in the more developed urban centers of the South like New Orleans. For example, the New Orleans jurist Francois Xavier Martin wrote a friend that "A lawyer of Common talent makes from $4 to

$5000; several make $8 or $10,000. What is understood as a fee in ordinary parlance is $500. They call a good fee $1000 or $1500." Another Crescent City attorney, Judah P. Benjamin, was making between forty thousand to fifty thousand dollars a year by the late 1850s from a practice devoted almost exclusively to commercial affairs. At about the same time, William H. Seward's New York firm reported a net income of one hundred thousand dollars. Another prominent New Yorker, William M. Evarts, was making about seventy-five thousand dollars a year by the early 1850s. In Boston, Benjamin R. Curtis's professional receipts for the period 1857 to 1874 were estimated at $650,000.[43]

Although most attorneys made considerably less than a Seward or Benjamin, the national cost of living was low enough during the antebellum period to afford most practitioners a fairly affluent lifestyle on incomes of two to three thousand dollars annually. In Houston, for example, future district court judge Edward Albert Palmer felt "comfortably fixed" on a salary of only thirteen hundred dollars after two years of private practice. Despite his comparatively sparse earnings, Palmer was pleased, for his efforts at least allowed him to "support myself and little family (My dear wife and sweet little Boy). . . . It is a pleasing consolation to know that we are making our own living and every person who is able to do it should have a thankful heart."[44] As Palmer's existence confirmed, one could live very comfortably in antebellum Texas on an annual income of one thousand dollars. Indeed, with "that much money," one could not only build a fine home, but surround it as well with several hundred acres of good land.

As alluded earlier, by the time Ballinger began his practice, the Galveston bar was "crowded to the overflowing." Such a condition, combined with the all-out competition that characterized the profession in general in the late antebellum period, made the prospect for earning a decent living bleak for many beginning attorneys. "The bar offers but little prospect for profit, or even subsistence, to the host of greedy applicants who throng it," lamented one young jurist. Another disenchanted practitioner wrote, "Perhaps you have heard of Isbell's misfortune. He courted a bucksome lass near home—was discarded and following in the wake of Don Quixote, resolved to do pennance by starving, and in order to carry out his resolution most effectually has turned his attention to Law."[45] Beginning practitioners quickly learned that the struggle to establish and maintain a practice was only half the battle: one had also to keep his financial head above water. Compounding a lawyer's financial difficulties was the fact that many clients were reluctant to pay their bills, or simply could not when hit with hard times. Paying a legal fee would be the last priority for clients having "scarcely enough to go to market."[46] Such conditions easily "swallowed up" any lawyer not completely devoted to his practice. Only those, like Ballinger, who loved the law and possessed the tenacity and ambition to "stick with it" through the depressing periods of few clients and little income, would eventually rise to the top of their profession. Attorneys lacking these attributes were doomed to failure.

Young lawyers standing at the threshold of their careers confronted an intriguing paradox. While established attorneys touted the law as the only profession that could lead to honor, distinction, and financial success, novices found the daily grind of their vocation forbidding. For those ultimately succeeding in the law, even for those (such as Ballinger) having family, professional, or political connections to enhance their chances, the road to fame and fortune was nonetheless a difficult route to travel. Many, like Ballinger, took the risks, enduring all manner of personal trauma in order to some day attain the professional acclaim and financial success to which they had so long aspired.

An 1858 daguerreotype—Ballinger's first photographic likeness—showed a young man satisfied with himself. In his best suit Ballinger sat stiffly for the photographer, obviously proud of his tailor-made suit, which Tom Jack insisted he have for the sitting. After seeing the results of his efforts to get his partner to take the photograph, Jack wrote to his parents that "Will is not a pretty man—nor is he an ugly one. He is simply a homely looking man." At this time Ballinger weighed about 140 pounds, and he was so thin that he appeared even taller than six feet. Jack further described his brother-in-law as having a face "that was long—sallow—cadaverous—no matter how hard Will attempts to look different, he appears sorrowful & sad. I suppose this is just his disposition."[47] For all of Jack's recounting, he failed to capture the feeling conveyed by the daguerreotype. Sitters had to hold a pose for several seconds without moving, and thus it showed Ballinger's face as grave and unsmiling. Yet, upon more objective scrutiny, the image conveyed a sense of a man who had attained his goals. No longer was he attempting to impose the rule of reason upon impassioned emotions; no longer was he afflicted by mood swings that went from extreme euphoria to deep melancholy. He was at peace with himself.

When Ballinger turned thirty-five in 1860, he could look back with great satisfaction on his rapid rise in his profession. He could also feel secure about his status among Galveston's elite, of which he had become an integral member. His circle of friends not only included powerful merchant-financiers such as Robert Mills, but also the city's newspaper editors, Willard Richardson and Hamilton Stuart, as well clergymen such as Catholic Bishop John Marie Odin, and the Episcopalian Benjamin Eaton of Trinity Church. In an era of lavish dinner parties, the Ballingers were noted for their Sunday afternoon feasts, to which were invited visiting dignitaries as well as members of the elite. Ballinger owned a fine home and earned an income sufficient to support his expanding family. By decade's end, Ballinger had achieved all that he hoped he would when he came to Galveston seventeen years earlier. Had his political beliefs been confined to behind-the-scenes maneuvering, or his practice solely to making money, his life would illuminate little more than a prominent lawyer's life in nineteenth-century America. The years after 1860 would have been denouement; the story of a man simply growing old, unlikely to explore new ventures or play a significant role in the events of his time. Such, however, was not Ballinger's fate.

Chapter Six

"SECESSION IS REVOLUTION"

Like many white Southerners, Ballinger looked for a rational way to deal with the problems caused by the existence of slavery in a free American society. After the Mexican War this became especially true for the Galvestonian as the public controversy over slavery increasingly defined both national and Texas politics. As a slaveholder, Ballinger was as uncertain and insecure about slavery as most Southern whites, because of the fundamental paradox the institution forced them to confront: they were committed to human equality in principle but to human bondage in practice. For Ballinger, and probably for a large number of his slaveholding brethren, hypocrisy was no solution; the paradox presented him with a genuine dilemma, ultimately resolved by acceptance of the proslavery polemic. By embracing the racist rhetoric of the proslavery argument, which had reached its most doctrinaire level by the 1850s, Ballinger found the means of relieving the personal anxiety caused by his society's most glaring incongruity. Despite his commitment to the proslavery argument, in his personal involvement with both slaves and free blacks, Ballinger's conduct and attitude often contradicted his supposed "soundness" on the institution of black slavery.

The frequent ambiguities in Ballinger's responses to the peculiar institution in no way implied any public or even private condemnation of slavery. Indeed, by the time Ballinger purchased his first "house servant," a young girl named Elizabeth for twelve hundred dollars, he had come to accept black bondage as not only "a natural state for the African," but as "necessary to the development of this country [South] & elevating to the negro. Only under the constant guidance & care of the white race can the negro be appropriately civilized. They are our burden to assume & uplift, and each time we take a negro into our household we must fulfill that obligation to the highest degree."[1]

It is obvious from such remarks that Ballinger was as insistent as the majority of his fellow slaveholders in asserting the doctrine of inherent white superiority over blacks. The belief in white superiority allowed slaveholders to rationalize slavery while uniting all Southern whites in defense of a system of racial subordination in which all members of the dominant race had the same stake. Once associated with slavery, racial prejudice assumed a certain functional quality adding to both the strength and the brutality of slavery as an institution. In essence, racial prejudice and slavery symbiotically created an environment in the South in which the alleged inferiority of blacks was used to justify their enslavement, and their subordination as slaves was used to justify their supposed inferiority.[2] Though agreeing that the differences between races were greater than those between individuals within each race, and that the uncivilized were inferior to the civilized, Ballinger nonetheless believed that the inferior were "neither to be disdained or to be considered weak & incapable of rising above their present station." In an address before a Galveston lyceum gathering in 1859, Ballinger further asserted that what presently set black folk apart from white folk was their lack of knowledge, and that could be remedied by education, which would "humanize them and make them greater contributors to society for the betterment of both races."[3] Ballinger personally fulfilled his "obligation" to his slaves by providing them with rudimentary reading and writing skills. Indeed, he often assisted his wife and children during their "slave tutorials." Though Ballinger's ideas offend modern sensibilities, his message was far different from the widely accepted theories of George Fitzhugh, Josiah Nott, and other proslavery apologists who argued that the African and Caucasian races were unalterably different, distinct, and separate.

By 1860 Ballinger owned eight slaves. As a slaveholder, Ballinger displayed both the virtues and limitations of the "good master." He allowed his slave Josey to visit his wife virtually any time he desired, but was unwilling to buy that wife so the couple could live together because he already owned more household slaves than he needed. When his slaves were recalcitrant or disobedient, he did not automatically assume it was the slaves' "inherent nature." Yet, when behavior "modification" failed to correct their actions, Ballinger sanctioned flogging as an appropriate punishment. On numerous occasions Ballinger arranged emancipation for the slaves of others, legally when possible and illegally when that was the only option. In the "Murrow case," the owner of a slave family, a J. S. Murrow,

"Secession is Revolution"

freed the entire family (a mother and three children), but stipulated in their freedom papers that this "privilege' could be revoked at any time if they were unable to find "suitable enployment." Apparently no longer able to maintain the family, Murrow freed them out of financial necessity. However, he was confident in the near future his economic outlook would improve, and at that time he would want his property back. The family wasted little time seeking Ballinger's help. The attorney was so impressed by the family's "sincerity & stability, and devotion to each other," that he employed them in his own crowded household until he was able to find them jobs in the city amongst friends and relatives. Thanks to Ballinger's efforts, Murrow never reclaimed his "property," for he could never prove that the family was "incapable of sustaining themselves as a free people."[4]

Ballinger's most celebrated emancipation case involved a slave woman named Betsy Webster. What made the Webster affair such a controversial and emotionally charged experience for Ballinger, and for many slaveholders wishing to emancipate their slaves, was the public wrath they incurred. Their actions were perceived as direct challenges to the sanctity and security of the institution at a moment when white Southerners were already alarmed by the number of freedmen in their midst. Since by the 1850s, the defense of slavery had reached its most fervid level, the earlier spirit of manumission was being reversed by a renewed commitment to the institution's preservation. The spread of cotton culture across the Southwest, especially into Texas, created an increased demand for slaves, and in the process, previous misgivings about the efficacy and morality of black servility were buried by the proslavery rhetoric. Those daring to defy this trend were faced with hateful glares and ugly words—even ostracism. Bitter relatives, angry over the loss of their "inheritance," often went to court to deprive slaves of their promised freedom. The possibility of public disgrace often intimidated would-be emancipators and the attorneys assisting them in these matters.[5] Committed to the law as an instrument of justice, Ballinger nonetheless understood that this could be his fate for helping Betsy.

According to Webster's will, Betsy was to receive her former master's entire estate, which was to be held for her in a trust administered by a Mrs. E. J. Hardin of Columbus, Georgia. Though the inheritance was placed in the custody of Mrs. Hardin, Webster made it perfectly clear that his property was "to be disposed of at the pleasure and request of Betsy."[6] On May 12, 1856, four days after he had made his will, David Webster died.

Not long after the will was admitted to probate in the Galveston

County Court, it was contested by a Webster relative from New York. In April 1857 a Martha Greenwood, claiming to be a cousin and sole heir of Webster's estate, instituted suit in the Galveston District Court to contest the will's validity, particularly as it pertained to Betsy's freedom and property. Betsy quickly responded to the suit by seeking Ballinger's counsel. Aware that Betsy was "presently without money," Ballinger agreed to accept her case on a contingent-fee basis. In order to pay for Ballinger's advocacy, Betsy sold a portion of her inheritance, seven lots of city property with an estimated value of twenty-two thousand dollars. Ballinger received a down-payment of five thousand dollars from Betsy, but the remaining four thousand was "to be paid contingent upon success." When Greenwood's attorneys learned of Betsy's sale of a portion of the lots, they accused Ballinger of fraud and forgery, perpetrated against their client "by certain parties in conjunction with the defendant, for the purpose of fraudulently swindling Mrs. Greenwood out of her just, lawful, and equitable rights and property."[7]

Greenwood's attorneys hoped to nullify Betsy's freedom by seizing upon the trend toward reversing the rate of manumission by boldly declaring that a slaveowner's last will and testament was not to be considered a legally valid form of emancipation. This maneuver reflected the increasingly restrictive policies being enacted in most Southern state legislatures and sustained by most Southern courts in hopes of curbing or completely abolishing manumission laws. Blacks like Betsy, attempting to secure their freedom, often encountered new judicial obstacles. Local judges reinterpreted many of the more clement rules for freedom suits and liberal interpretations of manumission laws established in the previous decades. Texas courts, however, were noted for their liberality in a time of intense racial repression. Local courts tended to ignore the laws affecting a Texas slaveowner's right to emancipate his slaves, and unlike the majority of their counterparts in the Lower South, Lone Star courts continued to either grant or deny manumission on an individual basis.[8]

By insisting that Betsy was a slave as long as she remained in Texas, and to be considered a free person she must leave, Greenwood's attorneys were attempting to exploit local white fears and prejudices regarding the presence of free blacks. Comparable to the rest of the slave states by the 1850s, Texas too had enacted fairly stringent removal laws. Such decrees mandated that all emancipated blacks had to leave the state "voluntarily" within a certain period or they forfeited their freedom and could be clapped back into bondage.[9] Ballinger initially tried convincing Betsy to migrate but "She would not hear of it. She said that she was a free woman by the law & that she was determined to prove that in court which was her right as a free woman—that is why she has <u>employed</u> me."[10]

As the news of Ballinger's defense of Betsy circulated about the island, James Love warned his nephew that many Galvestonians would react "most strongly against your defending of a negress. Many of your friends & associates will believe you have betrayed your Southern principles & that you are no longer to be considered sound on the subject of slavery. You will be accused of all manner of wrongdoing & your honour and integrity as a gentleman will be assailed. May Providence help you in this present affair."[11]

Without question Ballinger's defense of Betsy aroused local racism. From the anonymous notes and letters he received, many Galvestonians did indeed believe Ballinger was no longer "sound" on slavery. Despite accusations of being a "nigger lover" and "disgrace to both your race & profession," Ballinger was determined to uphold the sanctity of the law and secure Betsy's rights under it. No degree of derision could deter him from that purpose. The more local bigotry attempted to vilify Ballinger, the more resolved he was in pursuing victory. He confided to his diary that he would "not permit the wretched thoughts & malevolent deeds of petty and dishonorable people prevent me from doing what I believe to be right. I <u>will</u> triumph!"[12]

Juridically, Ballinger focused Betsy's defense on the legitimacy of Webster's will. Accordingly, he asserted that wills, "over a succession of ages," had been accepted as "the legal disposition of a man's intentions to be performed after his death, and must be carried into effect." Any other interpretation not only would "be an infringement upon that liberty and prostrate the great landmarks of property" but also "would introduce a latitude of construction boundless in its range and pernicious in its consequences." Since Webster's will was legal, it was Betsy's title to freedom, regardless of her residence. Even Texas's extradition laws were not applicable to Betsy because she received her freedom by a "completely lawful document, one recognized by every court of law in this nation." Ballinger maintained that it was "utterly unfounded" to assume Betsy's nonremoval "continued her in the status and under all the disabilities of legal slavery." Ballinger then reminded the court that although Webster stated in his will that Betsy "should remove herself," he nevertheless left the final decision to migrate up to Betsy. Yet, that was not the central issue of the case—Betsy's freedom was, and since that was already "fixed and perfect by the will, it [removal] was a condition subsequent, not precedent. "[13]

Ballinger further convinced the court that Betsy was entitled to her freedom by shrewdly and dramatically portraying Betsy as an "exemplary" slave, and as a free woman determined "not to abandon the home [Galveston] where all her attachments centered. She has lived many years in this city in a home of comfort and taste—a white cottage embowered amid flowers and orange trees. All her affections clung to this island home, where she had lived with her former master, sustaining perhaps, relations to him not sanctioned by law, but sanctified by all the sentiments of her nature."[14]

In a peculiar way, Ballinger too was on trial. He had been accused by Stancel & Stancel of "base fraud and forgery" for not only accepting as payment property that was not Betsy's because of her alleged slave status at the time of transaction, but also for supposedly "hoodwinking" Mrs. Hardin into signing the papers conveying the property to him. Ballinger naturally considered these charges to be absurd and personally insulting. He responded to the incriminations by forcefully declaring that "Betsy was saved her freedom and her property—paying for it not oppressively, not as much as she would have willingly given to us; but paying for it at a rate which we felt that men of honor and justice would recognize that we had dealt fairly with Betsy Webster. And what was the wrong committed towards her? For what neglect or injury of her rights am I impeached? It is that I did not procure, or assist in her forcible extradition from Texas. . . . For the recovery of her rights my name is stigmatized with the vilest charges which malignity itself could fasten upon the basest character."[15]

After Ballinger's final plea, there was little doubt Betsy would keep her freedom. According to the court: "By the will of Webster the slave Betsy was made a free woman. Being a free woman she was so in toto, and legally vested with the property devised to her, to use it as she pleased. Being a free woman, and not being under any disabilities requiring a guardian, neither her former master nor the court has any right to divest her of her person or property."[16]

Justice Oran Roberts then surprised the court by declaring that he believed it was his duty "to make a few observations relative to another matter"—Ballinger's vindication both as an attorney and "gentleman of the highest honor & integrity." Roberts stated that the charges of fraud against Ballinger by Stancel and Stancel had "as little foundation to stand upon in the minds of those well acquainted with him, as in the facts disclosed in the record." Roberts then declared that only an individual with Ballinger's proven "legal ability and tact, influence in regulating and controlling public opinion, of political and moral standing in the community" could have won for Betsy her freedom in the face of "such public opposition to making slaves free."[17]

The justice's statement was the vindication Ballinger had hoped for. From the beginning Ballinger had been worried that his defense of Betsy would have serious professional repercussions, as many of his peers had openly criticized his efforts on Betsy's behalf. Now, before the state's highest court, Roberts had confirmed what Ballinger had maintained from the start: to deny Betsy her freedom would have been an egregious legal and moral error. Though committed to upholding the order and stability of a slave society, Ballinger nonetheless believed that African-Americans, slave or free, were entitled to fundamental human rights. The notion that slaveowners could do whatever they wanted with their slaves was contradictory to Ballinger's belief that his society was just and good. If blacks were to be kept dependent, they were vulnerable and needed special protection. To Ballinger this was especially true for free blacks, for they, more than slaves, needed "our greater attention & affection, for the moment they become free, they will incur all the public scorn & wrath that is attendant to their new status. Our obligation to care for them & protect them from the vileness of others must become even more vigilant for they no longer are entitled to that because they are not our slaves."[18] Ballinger believed that a paternalistic, master/white solicitude must continue even after emancipation.

Equally important to Ballinger as defending Betsy's human rights, was his perseverance in the face of public imputation. Had he taken his uncle's advice and quit the case out of fear of defeat or professional disgrace, he might have always wondered whether it was because he lacked the personal courage and confidence essential to endure such controversy. Beginning with the Webster case and continuing for the remainder of his life, Ballinger often took the high road on the sensitive issues of his time. Such displays of heroism were reflections of his desire to see justice prevail, regardless of personal or professional consequences. When a case such a Betsy's engaged his moral sense, his dynamic power of conviction and sincerity enabled him to overcome judge, jury, and even communal hostility to secure victory for his client. As Ballinger told James Love after the trial, "every lawyer, if he is worth his salt, needs to be challenged, legally, ethically, emotionally, & those who rise to meet those challenges at such levels, are truly to be considered lawyers in every sense of the word & profession. I consider myself to have earned that distinction."[19]

As committed as Ballinger was to protecting the rights of free blacks, and despite benign treatment of his own bondsmen, he nonetheless considered enslaved blacks to be property, and as such, he was bound by law and personal identification to preserve the sanctity of the peculiar institution. Throughout the slaveholding South, the status of slaves was that of property; a slave had no real human rights. Although most Southern statutes—including those of Texas—recognized the slave as a person for criminal purposes, and slaves were in fact more accountable for crimes than whites, they were in all other instances, a commodity, to be bought and sold at any time, like the cotton they picked. The slave was simply a capital asset who belonged to the land.[20] Ballinger did not challenge these legal constraints even when he attempted to circumvent them. Even his representation in cases of quasi-free blacks involved no challenges to public law. Indeed, during the 1850s Ballinger gave his legal assistance to numerous slaveholders, helping them to retain or recover chattels that had either run away, been stolen, or lost in personal disputes, probate, or other litigation. Ballinger's readiness to use his legal talent in this capacity proved to be a highly remunerative enterprise. More important, Ballinger's involvement in "slave catching," like his acts of redemption, was yet another manifestation of the dichotomous attitudes many slaveowners had regarding black bondage.[21]

Because of his professional success, hiring out contracts, and acting as executor for several mainland planters, Ballinger had numerous opportunities to purchase estates. He could have easily shifted his occupation from lawyer to planter, perhaps making even more money in the latter capacity. Ballinger, however, had no interest in being a planter, nor did he desire to own a vast retinue of slaves even though he could afford such purchases. For Ballinger, slaveholding was more than an additional source of income, or the appropriate trappings of the compleat Southern gentleman. To Ballinger and to the majority of his slaveholding brethren the peculiar institution was the cornerstone of Southern society, essential not only to his section's prosperity but to stability as well.

In many ways Ballinger's relationships with black folk, both slave and free, epitomized paternalism. Applying the concept to Ballinger is not to suggest that he was necessarily a "good" or even benign master. He was simply a slaveowner who took personal interest in his slaves' lives. He knew his slaves by name and interacted with them on a regular basis, not only directing their work but also looking after their welfare and intervening in their lives. He saw his slaves as his "people," inferior members of his extended household from whom he expected work and obedience but to whom he owed guidance and protection. Ballinger spoke frequently of his "love" for his slaves, and although such expressions contained much hyperbole, he also expressed the very real conviction that there was more to slaveowning than profit and loss.

Ballinger's roseate and often myopic perception of slavery probably resulted from his exposure to the interesting manifestations the institution assumed on the island. As one study has shown, Galveston's approximately seven hundred slaves had a rather privileged existence compared to their mainland brethren. An interesting competition developed among the city's slaveholding grandees to see whose slaves were better cared for and allowed the most liberties. This rivalry ranged from permitting "one's negroes to dine at the supper table with the entire [white] family, usually outside during the spring and summer months, so all would be visible to neighbors," to maintaining one's negroes in a style befitting their master's status." Since Galvestonians frowned on conspicuous consumption, the elite indulged their acquisitiveness by pampering their slaves with all manner of cast-off finery. On Sundays and holidays Galveston's black community displayed their owners' frippery with such flair that the spirit of it resembled a Mardi Gras celebration.[22] Every Sunday Ballinger let his entire "household" have the day off, allowing them the use of his carriage and horses for the day, as well as letting them put on and keep any clothes and jewelry his wife and children "no longer required." Ballinger wanted his bondsmen to "have a little cheer while they can. They all seem to love wearing our clothes &c. It is a harmless activity & seems to bring them much satisfaction to drive & walk about town & to associate with the other negroes. It has become a regular occurence that all look forward to."[23]

Though individual slaveowners such as Ballinger believed themselves "enlightened" in their treatment of slaves, their unstated assumptions contributed to the dehumanization to which African Americans were forced to adapt. Regardless of how solicitous the guise, in law, custom, ideology, and practice, slaveholders did their best to ignore their slaves' humanity. This in turn created irresolvable contradictions within their own existence, inconsistencies amplified by the master's aversion and inability to alter their behavior. No matter how benign or paternal the treatment and attitude, slaves remained little more than valuable property in their master's mind. Many slaveholders such as Ballinger were willing to answer their bondsmen's call for decent treatment and respect; yet, they could not respond to their bondsmen's most cherished request—freedom. From the black codes to the racist treatises pronouncing black inferiority, and to the supposed Biblical sanctification of slavery, nearly every Southern white man's vision of upward mobility depended on the presence of a large black population, but not on an understanding or association with them.

Immersed in an expanding law practice and in regular contact with Northern clients, Ballinger's economic interests, like his political Whiggism, made him an ardent Unionist. By 1860, however, Ballinger could no longer remain detached from the North-South crisis. Daily the issues seemed more ominous and personal. No other question perplexed him more than sectionalism, and ultimately it would force him to choose between a nation he cherished and a heritage he could not forsake.

In Texas, support of slavery did not necessarily preclude allegiance to the Union. Such were the sentiments of many ex-Whigs and "loyalist" Democratic slaveholders refusing to accept the notion of state sovereignty or any of the other manifestations of Southern radicalism. As the secession crises intensified, the burden was on this moderate faction to convince their fellow citizens of this argument and prevent the Lone Star state's withdrawal from the Union.[24] Ballinger was one Texan of such temperament. Like many Southern professionals he was in regular contact with his Northern clients, whom he did not perceive as a threat to his region. In fact, Ballinger and many other Texas businessmen—especially Galvestonians—actively promoted stronger commercial ties with the North, welcoming Yankee investment to help Texas develop more rapidly.[25] Ballinger believed that secessionist agitation was merely another facet of the decade's "spectacular" politics.

Few Texans were as determined as Ballinger to remain apolitical in a decade consumed by intense sectional partisanship. Only occasionally and strictly within the confines of his office amongst his closest friends, did Ballinger offer opinions on the volatile issues of slavery and sectionalism. Ballinger believed it was crucial that he and other "sane & responsible men" remain calm as sectional tensions intensified. "The wild talk of party heat" must not overcome the logic and dispassion necessary to defeat "the forces of recklessness" by which Southerners were "presently being guided." Any other conduct, Ballinger feared, would aid the fire-eaters who had already "so maddened the hearts & minds of the [Southern] people that we shall have serious dangers to our gov.t if not its disruption."[26]

Throughout the 1850s Ballinger contended that sectionalism was a constitutional problem to be resolved "within the framework of the existing Union." He believed the Constitution had a unique ability to produce national cohesion. As a nationalist Whig, Ballinger maintained that his party and its leaders (most notably Henry Clay, one of Ballinger's heroes) had always championed national rather than regional interests, and that the welfare and preservation of the Union was always foremost in the hearts and minds of party members. Indeed, membership in the Whig Party meant something more than issues to Ballinger. He believed passionately in the party's principles, which to him embodied the promise of American life. Economically, it stood for growth, development, and progress. He believed Clay's American System was "pure genius" because it created one vast interdependent economic web among the sections. When economic interests worked together, so would political interests, and sectional rivalries would be subsumed in a powerful American nationalism. Class tensions would also disappear, for this "just and equitable and prosperous system" would give all Americans "hope, energy, and progress."[27]

Ballinger's unionism was an inherent part of his essential conservatism. Though there was not in Ballinger's life the stuff of a systematic philosophy of conservatism, he nonetheless considered himself to be a conservative. His political and social outlook reflected his reading of Burke and Hamilton, and like most conservatives, he revered the historical past because he believed it held valuable lessons for the present and future. Ballinger considered democracy primarily a way of living. Of greater importance was the preservation of those institutions forged in history that mapped and stabilized democratic living. But preservation depended upon change. "The only true conservative," he told his brother-in-law, Guy Bryan, "is the man who resolutely sets his face toward the future."[28] Ballinger believed in change, but gradual change—change within established institutions, change obtained by adapting, managing, and administering. Moreover, change had to be directed from a position of power by men who appreciated what was and what had been. They had to be informed and, much more difficult, to be moral. Their morality had primarily to come from character, which in Ballinger's view, was a product of long seasons of hard work. To Ballinger, the uses of power had one common, revealing objective: stability.

Ballinger was aware that at any time social stability and order could be destroyed by the abuse of power, leading to social violence. To modulate the threatening conflict Ballinger relied upon personal morality as well as the "human bonds" history prepared: the accepted traditions of political and social behavior by which people imposed order on themselves. Yet these traditions had to be constantly reenforced and strengthened if they were to remain the bulwarks against chaos. To Ballinger, as always, the key to preventing disorder as well as controlling popular passions, was education. The government must provide the schools necessary to inculcate all citizens with the intellectual independence "essential to this Republic's survival." Without access to knowledge, individuals would lack the ability to challenge their government "rationally, with understanding of the complexities of Democracy & the individual responsiblities that are part of it." Only access to learning guaranteed the diversity that could withstand the forces of majoritarianism, which Ballinger believed "are as pernicious to the survival of Republican government & virtue as any dreaded epidemic."[29]

The increasing displays of civil disobedience, which offended Ballinger's sense of justice and order, were clear indications "that a general contempt & disregard for all authority has fastened itself upon the country." When the minds of the unthinking populace are "loosened from their attachment to traditional establishments & courses, they seem to grow giddy & are prone to run into anarchy." In such tumultuous times, if order and stability are to be restored, it was imperative that the nation's "political pilots employ their greatest skill to keep men steady & within proper bounds." Ballinger wondered, however, if the nation's political leaders, North or South, were capable of rising to such a challenge, or had they become "corrupted by their lust for power & property and design on government, that they are no longer able to harness such passions & make them subservient to the public good." If that was the case, then perhaps it was time for men like himself, devoted to the rule of law, order, and justice, but who had remained detached from the issues of the 1850s, to "plunge heart & soul into the present crisis & try to save this great Nation from destruction."[30]

As the critical year 1860 began, it became clear to Ballinger that he had underestimated the secessionist momentum. He had earlier denounced the secessionists as rabble rousers and demagogues out for political office and public notoriety, but as nothing more threatening than that. He now blamed himself for having allowed the secessionists to gain ascendancy, for had he and other "responsible citizens" come forth and vigorously opposed the fire-eaters, "the present calamity might have been avoided."[31] But for the moment, events accelerated faster than Ballinger's ability to respond. At the national level the Democratic Party met in Charleston in April, only to see delegations from eight states of the Lower South withdraw over the refusal of Stephen Douglas and his supporters to endorse a platform demanding federal protection of slavery in the territories. The remaining delegates proceeded to the selection of a candidate. Stephen Douglas led on every ballot but could not muster the two-thirds majority (of the original number of delegates) required by party rules. Finally the managers adjourned the convention to meet again in Baltimore in June. At the Baltimore session, most of the Southerners reappeared only to walk out again. Other Southerners, meanwhile, had assembled at Richmond. The decimated Baltimore convention nominated Douglas. The Southern bolters at Baltimore joined the Richmond Democrats to nominate John C. Breckenridge of Kentucky for the presidency. Sectionalism at last divided the Democratic Party.[32]

In early May 1860, the Constitutional Union Party met in Baltimore. Although the party posed as a new organization, the overwhelming majority of its members were former Whigs and Know-Nothings. At its convention the "Old Gentleman's Party" decided that the best way to avoid the calamity of disunion was to take no explicit stand on the issue of slavery expansion. Instead, the party's nominee, wealthy Unionist slaveholder John Bell of Tennessee, was to represent the spirit of sectional accommodation that had led to compromise in 1820 and 1850. The party's campaign slogan became, "The Constitution, the Union and the Enforcement of the Laws."[33]

Initially, the Bell-Everett combination aroused little enthusiasm in the Lone Star State. However, the news of Abraham Lincoln's nomination by the Republicans finally pushed Ballinger into joining the Constitutional Unionist camp. At this juncture in the crisis, Ballinger realized that defense of slavery had become an integral part of his conservatism. Since slavery to Ballinger was a way of life and not just an economic interest, he would naturally perceive any threats to the institution as direct assaults on his world's order and stability. Although embracing as a Whig nationalist the capitalist system, he nonetheless found himself increasingly identifying with the paternalistic ethos of his slaveholding brethren. As several studies have shown, paternalistic masters such as Ballinger were the South's most vocal Unionists. This was especially true for conservative Whig nationalists like Ballinger, who believed that abolitionists as well as Southern radicals, were the products of excessive democracy. They thus gravitated to the new party, hoping it would not only protect slaveowners' property rights, but check as well the excessive democracy that had unleashed not just the abolitionists, but the more dangerous secessionists as well. In short, the Constitutional Unionists based their opposition to secession on traditionally Whig principles:

nationalism to defend the Union, anti-democracy to attack secession.[34]

It was not until August, after "wasting mornings all summer long in political discussion which amounted to nothing" that Ballinger and his Unionist associates officially organized the Bell and Everett Club of Galveston of the Constitutional Union Party. By failing to capitalize on early momentum, Ballinger lamented that the party's weekly meetings were "rather slim affairs" at which members struggled to display "a good deal of enthusiasm."[35]

Because of paltry efforts throughout Texas, it was the Galveston Bell-Everett organization that eventually dominated, and island Whigs, led mainly by Ballinger, his Uncle James Love, and Oscar Farish, who set the party's agenda for the state. To Ballinger it was imperative that the party focus its efforts on developing a platform that would be the best alternative to Southern radicalism. Ballinger convinced his fellow party members of this plan, and on August 20, 1860, his resolutions were formally adopted by the party and published in the local papers the next day.[36]

Ballinger quickly established a reputation as one of the party's most popular and respected public speakers. He received numerous requests for his orations from Bell-Everett clubs around the state. In his speeches Ballinger called upon Texans to "remember we are all Americans first & that our foremost allegiance is to the national government created by the Constitution, written by our Forefathers. This is what the Constitutional Union Party stands for—nothing else."[37] In his speeches Ballinger was careful not to inflame public passions by directly accusing either the Democratic Party or any of its leaders of perpetrating the present crisis. But as the summer of 1860 progressed, it was apparent to Ballinger and other party members that despite their efforts to generate public support, too many Texans remained loyal to the Democratic Party. If that held true, then Southern secession was imminent. Ballinger was so disturbed by such an ominous prospect that he believed it was time for him to challenge head-on the secessionist impulse in Texas.

On the evening of August 23, 1860, over three hundred of Ballinger's fellow Galvestonians gathered to hear him deliver one of his most impassioned public addresses. Ballinger's "Secession Speech" reflected the pro-Union, conservative, and patriotic sentiments of his party while revealing the innermost thoughts of an individual who had refrained from all partisan politics for almost a decade. In his speech Ballinger argued that "every disunionist was in fact a revolutionary," and revolution was so dangerous that it should be pursued only after every legal remedy had failed. Ballinger

"Secession is Revolution"

The Custom House was the physical symbol of Galveston's antebellum commercial dominance as Texas's leading entrepot. Galvestonians such as Ballinger took great pride in their city's preeminence and personally did all they could to sustain it. *Sketch by Theodore R. Davis. From* Harper's Weekly, *October 27, 1866.*

pointed to the French Revolution as graphic testimony to what happens when a society loses "all respect for the laws and traditions which govern & protect the public from the vileness of others."[38]

Ballinger then presented his case against secession, charging that secessionist Democrats had willfully misled the South. Like the leaders of the Republican Party, the Southern fire-eaters had "senselessly perpetrated a crisis" for their own selfish reasons of power. Secessionists exaggerated sectional grievances to the point that Southerners believed they "had reached an inevitable crisis in their relations with the North." Such was not the case. Northerners were "not so totally unlike us—they are not degenerate from our national character—nor do they seek—the great mass of them—to do us fatal mischief and evils." Ballinger attributed the extremists' rise to power to their ability to "so madden and inflame the public mind—using every oratorial trick and form of deception they know." The majority of Southerners could not see that the insurgents' claims "of oppression & conspiracy to subvert the rights of the Southern people, were unnecessary, false, and delusive." The fire-eaters had portrayed themselves as "saviors" to the Southern people, determined to uphold "the bulwarks of the Constitution," as well as Southern honor and property rights against "fabricated" Northern encroachments "upon those liberties." The real purpose of the "seceders at Charleston" was not to protect Southerners' "peace and security" but to "fire" Southern hearts and minds into revolution. Secessionist arrogance had reached the point where "they believed they could easily deceive us, and lead us down the path of disunion and war."[39]

Ballinger then reminded his audience of the ties of race and history, and the emotional attachment all Americans shared "to a glorious and righteous past and equally fulfilling future." He insisted that the nation built by Hamilton, Madison, and Washington could not be destroyed by the "likes of [William Lowndes] Yancey, Jeff Davis and Barnwell Rhett." Ballinger maintained that subconscious loyalties created an indestructible bond between Northerners and Southerners that could not be broken by the sophistries of "designing and arrogant politicians." Even if Lincoln were elected, Ballinger was confident the Southern people would not be panicked into revolution by these "artful manipulators." Southerners would secure "Constitutional guarantees" for slavery's lasting protection rather than "take up arms against the gov't" for no other reason than having been "manipulated into such a senseless and destructive act by men who care not what happens to this great country."[40]

With lawyer-like arguments and invincible logic, simply, calmly and dispassionately, Ballinger had presented his case against the secessionists. He had arrayed his facts and historical data concerning the controversy. His listeners were a well-informed, intelligent people—fellow lawyers, clergymen, editors, and merchants. To them he had argued his cause as he often had before the Texas Supreme Court. He appealed to their reason rather than their emotions. He had devoted much time to research and preparation; and now, like a courtroom lawyer, well fortified with briefs and precedents, he had challenged in proper order each and every argument the secessionists were making against the North. Though his speech was a success—"the Unionists all seemed delighted"—Ballinger worried about the impression he had made. He confided to his diary that the position he had taken would probably be "injurious" to his practice and "reputation in the community." Despite his forebodings, Ballinger was proud he had committed himself to the "cause of the Union," and of alerting "the Southern people to the vile chicanery of the Secessionists."[41] Once again, despite the possibility of public imputation, even ostracism, Ballinger's indefatigable pursuit of the truth, his candor, and his fidelity to his convictions, prevailed over concern for his own personal or professional well-being.

Throughout the fall of 1860 Ballinger was optimistic. There was still enough moderate strength in the South for his party's candidate, John Bell, to garner enough votes among "responsible citizens" to win the election. He believed Bell's election essential if the Union was to be saved from "the awful spectre of secession and war."[42] As election day approached, even the most sanguine of Bell faithfuls realized a united North had enough electoral votes to give Lincoln the election and that a crisis was thus at hand. "If S.C. goes out of the Union either the Union must be acknowledged as so feeble as to be of no value or the effort to coerce her will lead to a gen'l disruption," Ballinger noted. "We have troublesome times ahead." The news of Lincoln's election reached Galveston on November 8, 1860, producing "a deep sensation in our midst. . . . Many of our wise & good men are in favor of immediate dissolution—Still it seems to me that much of the sentiment is the offspring of party heat & is not mature & well considered."[43]

Ballinger's illusion of reconciliation was shattered when in mid-November local insurgents called for an emergency meeting to mobilize public support for a secession convention. From around the state Ballinger received the alarming news that similar meetings were being held. Associate State Supreme Court justice James Bell wrote Ballinger that although his recent Union speech in Austin was well received, there was nevertheless "very great anxiety in the minds of conservative men here. I fear that if a convention assembles here, the existing state government will be overturned by it." From Houston came equally disheartening reports. Walter Botts told Ballinger Houstonians were "greatly frightened by Lincoln's election. There is now far more unanimity of sentiment for secession than I anticipated. Withdrawal of the state from the Union seems to be regarded by nearly everyone as the plan to be pursued and the only difference among the people is whether they should wait action of the Legislature or call the convention at once to decide the matter."[44]

Ballinger attended the Galveston gathering held on November 14, finding it the largest assemblage of Galvestonians he had ever witnessed. The secessionists commanded the meeting from the start; several moderates made speeches, but as Ballinger lamented, it was clear from the crowd's responses that Galvestonians had lost "their sensibilities" and were no longer "reasonable in their attitudes toward the Union." At one point Ballinger pushed toward the platform, intending to make one final plea for compromise, but the congestion of people and their hostility discouraged him, and he returned to the crowd. When he reached his home that night he could not sleep. He felt ashamed that his courage had failed him at that crucial moment during the public debate. In his diary he wrote: "I cannot disguise from myself the deep apprehension if not conviction that our

Govt. will be overthrown & the Union dissolved."[45] That evening Ballinger typically turned to his books, finding sad comfort and affirmation for his premonitions in Burke's *Reflections on the French Revolution.*

Throughout Texas, citizens were organizing "minute men" companies, and Lone Star and black flags were hung from public buildings "in token mourning of Lincoln's election." Some Texas newspapers were optimistic that once Northerners realized the seriousness of the crisis, they would decide "to retain the South in peace." The Galveston *News* maintained that for purely economic reasons the South's "constitutional rights" would be guaranteed. Northern capitalists, aware "the Union will lose its chief value when it shall lose the slave states," would force the Republican Party to compromise on the slavery issue. The paper was certain that "even before disunion is consummated," the obstruction of trade "will be sufficient to give a foretaste of what its final consequences will be."[46]

Despite fortifying broadsides, by mid-December 1860 there was no doubt Texas would secede. The only question was the manner in which the state would divorce itself from the Union. The majority of Texans were "cooperationists"—Southerners favoring a united withdrawal of the Southern states from the Union, and the establishment of a Confederacy. However, many Texans, including Gov. Sam Houston, believed that if secession was inevitable, Texas should restore her separate independence and stand alone against both the Union and the Confederacy. This position became known as the "Lone Star" movement. By playing on Texans' pride in their Lone Star heritage, Houston and others hoped to prevent Texas from aligning herself with a temporary Southern Confederacy.[47] Under the leadership of Oscar Farish, several Galvestonian moderates organized their own "Lone Star Association in favor of Texas standing alone—& against a Southern Confederacy." As Ballinger further noted, "They started out only opposing a Southn Confedcy in the event of disunion but now have declared for Texas resuming her independent nationality—No doubt most of them are Unionists at heart." Though somewhat sympathetic to the movement's Unionists, Ballinger refused to join the organization. His goal was still "for the preservation of the Union on principles which will secure our safety & peace." If, however, "the Union must be broken," then he was "for the greatest confederacy that can be formed. I am no Lone Star man," he wrote, "I think it a chimera."[48]

As the year 1860 moved through its last fateful days, those championing the old Union were resigned to its approaching demise. "This Govt will be overthrown & the Union destroyed," wrote Ballinger. "I hope for the best & it may be that public order & prosperity will not be weakened & that security will be given to the institution of slavery—But I have strong fears to the contrary, and my best judgment is that we are doing an unwise and fatal thing. I have no heart in the cause—Its responsibility & glory I leave to others." Former Unionist and "uncle" Thomas Harrison wrote Ballinger that "the children of those not in the front of the present secessionists would be ashamed of their fathers." Ballinger rather testily remarked that he was "willing to bide the test of time on that subject."[49]

Although believing the Republican Party "dangerous," especially to slavery, which the party hoped "to put under a ban & make odious," and that "experience has demonstrated the necessity of further guards against sectional majorities," Ballinger maintained that all such changes were "to be sought peacefully & within the Union." He considered "the disruption of the Union without such efforts . . . treason to humanity." Again he expressed regret that he lacked the courage at the public rally in November to give "strong testimony to my Union sentiments & to my conviction of the recklessness by which we are being guided." Ballinger felt "more than ever excommunicated from public affairs and politics." He decided to face the fact that "Secession is Revolution. I submit to it in preference to civil war, and shall do the part of a loyal citizen of the state. I put these words here on the record," he concluded, "for the eyes of my children in after times."[50]

Throughout the 1850s Ballinger maintained his staunch Whig unionism. But now in the midst of secession and impending civil war, Ballinger was forced to reevaluate his beliefs, and found himself ready to abandon his traditional perception of the nature and purpose of the Constitution and the federal union it created. Like most Texas Unionists from the Upper South, Ballinger believed the Union and the Constitution were sacrosanct, the genesis of the venerated founding fathers. These ideas Ballinger did not question until the secession crisis. The Union proved its value over time by providing all Americans with a common purpose and identity. Ballinger had also believed that the Union's functional qualities bound its people together as tightly as its ideological ones. Foremost of these functions was to provide law and stability. He regarded law as subservient to popular custom, believing in the force of informed public opinion to bring about meaningful social change. He feared any other course might destroy traditional behavior patterns protecting the commonweal from the excesses of individualism. Like a true Hamiltonian conservative, Ballinger possessed a pessimistic outlook, believing individuals inherently depraved and motivated by self-interest. If such passions were not constantly restrained by the appropriate institutions, rampant particularism would plunge the entire society into the abyss of violence and anarchy. In essence, Ballinger had always concluded that the Union provided institutional checks to maintain order, stability, and harmony in society. By the secession winter, there was no longer anything that Ballinger could identify that would help him reclaim his unionism. All of the old ideological and functional nationalist props sustaining his faith in the Union and the Constitution were swept away by the secession crisis.

The final blow to Ballinger's once uncompromising unionism came when he concluded that the majority of Texans had lost "all faith & confidence in the govt." What impressed Ballinger was the fact that Texans' loss of "allegiance" was genuine; they were not "merely activated by passion." They were willing to "risk the consequences" of war rather than "continue under the Old Union." When so many Texans decided that the Lincoln administration would attack Southerners' rights to own slaves, Ballinger re-lented, declaring the government should "never be a source of terror & apprehension in a people. When it comes to that it is time for Revolution."[51]

On deeper reflection, Ballinger discovered what he concluded was the real cause of the sectional crisis: blind adherence to the Constitution. Institutional checks devised by the Founding Fathers to protect minority rights, especially the property rights of Southern slaveholders had broken down, and by 1860 no longer existed. The American people failed to reform and maintain those safeguards. Ballinger found it ironic that from the beginning, Americans framed their political and legal system to accomodate changing interests and attitudes. Yet, as Ballinger lamented, no one, not even himself, accepted the view that the Constitution and the government of its founders "was not adequate to secure the allegiance of all their children. This is because of error in its structure—of features not adapted to these times & of features to be added to it." Incredulous now, Ballinger complained that even while the nation divided, no one admitted the Constitution was "imperfect & in need of constant revision." Instead, "every one North & South cried out 'the Constitution is perfect—only give us the Constitution', and forthwith one section proceeds to throw it off altogether and the other to regard it no more than if it was and is in existence." According to Ballinger, the people's and even his own sublime faith in the Constitution had become "a superstition & an absurdity," making disunion inevitable.[52]

Ballinger ultimately concluded his unionism had been a condition of his Southernism, and when confronted with the painful decision of having to choose between his ideals and his heritage, he realized he could not turn his energies against home and kin. Moreover, as a civic activist, he realized that Texas and the South needed his talents and experiences. His loyalty to the Southern cause was ultimately more genuine and forceful than those who never questioned the necessity or wisdom of secession; yet, the agony of his decision made Ballinger a determined rebel, fighting in the end for a cause he had not made.

As Ballinger moved closer to accepting the legitimacy of secession, he concluded the Southern people were doing something more momentous than simply severing their legal relationship with the federal government. He found ultimate justification for his conversion to the separatist cause in the idea that Southerners were liberating themselves from a tyrannical government violating its compact with the Southern people. Belief in such a rationale also provided him with the means to justify the righteousness of the Southern cause. Like so many other Southerners, Ballinger believed the South's struggle for independence was fundamentally the same political conflict his ancestors fought against the oppression of the British Empire. In 1861, only the players had changed. Instead of George III, Lord North, and Parliament, it was Abraham Lincoln and his "black Republicans" who conspired to destroy liberty. If the relationship between the federal government and the Southern people deteriorated to the same level that existed in 1776, then the same moral obligation confronted the Southern people to sever their contract with their government. In Ballinger's view, when Texas seceded from the Union by a popular referendum on February 23, 1861, Texans were reenacting "the same right of Revolution our Forefathers believed incumbent upon them in order to free themselves from a tyrannical Government. We are doing no less than that at this moment in history & hopefully, Providence willing, History will prove our cause to be equally as noble & glorious."[53]

Ballinger's acceptance of the legitimacy of secession did not represent the triumph of localism over nationalism. Like many former Unionists, Ballinger transferred his nationalism to the Confederacy, hoping to preserve the best of the old Union while evolving toward a new order that would eventually prove superior to the former association. Converts like Ballinger were convinced that "only as members of a large & stable nation can we continue to prosper, and Providence willing, secure our complete independence & fulfill our destiny." In short, Ballinger shared the hopes of many Texas Unionists that the Confederacy would be all the things the old Union was, and more. The new nation would protect individual liberties, guarantee law and stability, propagate the original American mission, and do so in harmony with slavery.[54]

Ballinger found overwhelming support for his conversion within his family. His Harrison and Jack relatives, who were rabid secessionists and "Southrons," were particularly pleased with his transformation. Uncle "Tommy" Harrison was especially elated, telling his nephew that he chose "the proper position & course in the recent change in our political relationship with the U.S." Harrison knew what an emotionally wrenching ordeal Ballinger endured before accepting the right of secession. He consoled Ballinger by respectfully acknowledging "no man had more patriotism in his heart for the U.S. than yourself, and that was never a wrong sentiment for one to possess." More important than Harrison's empathy was his affirmation for the reasons ulitmately leading Ballinger to support secession. Harrison agreed with Ballinger that the American people made the government "for certain purposes benefiting themselves & their posterity—the preservation of equality & liberty—the peaceful possession of property." When the government failed to accomplish or subverted "the purposes of its creation," then the people were no longer bound to give their respect and support to that government. Indeed, in Harrison's view the people had a "duty to themselves & to their children to demand that they alter or abolish that gov't."[55]

Even more important to Ballinger than family support for his conversion was the prospect of war. By late March 1861 Lincoln made it clear he would never accept secession. The prospect of the use of force to maintain the Union struck Ballinger as repugnant to the spirit of free government. He considered the use of coercion more odious that secession itself. Consequently, Ballinger's commitment to disunion intensified, and he resolved to share the fate of his fellow Southerners. Whatever Ballinger believed or hoped for was immaterial now. "The silver cord is loosed—the golden bowl is broken. . . . The national government may be re-established—The political union may be perpetuated—but if so, it will be by force and we will be practically a conquered vassal people." Though fearful "we will pay a horrible price for our freedom," Ballinger devoted himself to the cause of Southern independence.[56]

Chapter Seven

"WITH EVERY ENERGY OF THE BODY CONSECRATED"

To many former Unionists, the transfer of loyalty to the Confederacy resulted only after an agonizing emotional and intellectual readjustment of their perceptions of the nation. To these Confederate converts, ideology rather than peer persuasion was the principal motivation for supporting the separatist cause. These were men who never wavered in their loyalty to the United States until concluding that the federal government, under the domination of the Republican Party, directly threatened Southern institutions and security. By the spring of 1861, they united with the majority of Texans to resist federal coercion, and to uphold a new government dedicated to preserving Southern rights and principles. Ballinger was just such a case. Throughout the war Ballinger remained a loyal Confederate, working diligently to maintain the principles Southerners had cited as the basis of their nation.

Soon after Texas officially joined the Confederacy, Ballinger wrote a letter to Jefferson Davis, provisional president of the new nation, offering his "fullest devotion to the Revolution. You have only to designate the front and my whole heart, every faculty of mind, and every energy of the body shall be consecrated to the service." Despite lingering reservations about "the rightness of our present actions," Ballinger assured Davis that his observations were "born of a true Southerner," who was voicing such opinions "out of a heart totally committed to the happiness & greatness of the Southern people." Ballinger recognized that the only realistic chance Southerners had for success was for all to "plunge wholeheartedly into the Revolution for a separate national government. No one can feel more profoundly than I do, that once undertaken the Revolution must be made good; the issue for the Southern people is independence or Death. Subjugation is no alternative for us. We neither know nor can we ever learn to be a conquered, vassal race."[1]

As early as May 1861, Ballinger had expressed concern about his city's and state's defense. In a letter to Louis T. Wigfall, Confederate senator from Texas, Ballinger tried to impress upon Richmond authorities the importance of adequately defending not only Galveston but the entire Texas coast from Federal assaults. Galveston's defense was especially critical, for the Queen City was "the most important commercial point in Texas—so situated on the coast to be almost certain of attack in the event of a war of any duration." Implicit in Ballinger's letter to Wigfall was the fear that Texas would soon be relegated to secondary importance as far as the Confederacy's overall security was concerned. The Galvestonian sensed this possibility, wanting to ensure his city's and state's defenses immediately. If the war dragged on indefinitely Ballinger rightly worried that the state would be so drained of men and goods that even a token Federal force could seize a key port like Galveston if precautions were not taken early to fortify its defenses.[2]

Early proof of Ballinger's dedication to Confederate independence came in late July 1861 when Gov. Francis Lubbock asked him to go on a special mission to Richmond. Bearing a requisition from Gen. Earl Van Dorn, commander of Confederate troops in Texas, Ballinger was to procure several cannon for Galveston's defense from anticipated Union attacks. Accompanying Ballinger to Richmond were fellow Texans Henry Potter, William Ochiltree, and John Sydnor.[3]

Ballinger and his companions arrived in Richmond on August 4, ten days after leaving their Galveston homes. The next day Ballinger's party reported to the Confederate War Office. Initially only Ballinger was to meet with Sec. LeRoy Pope Walker, but he convinced the others that "we should all be present at that hour so as to make an imposing front." Walker was surprised to see the Texans, telling the delegation that he believed Texas forces were more than adequate to all exigencies. Ballinger was dismayed by Walker's comments, but after a few hours, he convinced the secretary to allow him to obtain the guns from the Ordnance Bureau. Walker also promised Ballinger an engineer to help prepare Galveston's defenses, and from the secretary of the navy, Stephen Mallory, he was assured "a good naval officer & gunners."[4]

Despite assurances, Ballinger was frustrated at continuous "paper shuffling" by Confederate officials and enraged when he was notified by the Ordnance Bureau that the guns he was to receive were to be of a smaller caliber than those he was promised previously. Ballinger had "harsh words & unpleasant exchanges" with personnel at the Ordnance Bureau and the situation remained muddled until after a long meeting with the bureau's director, Josiah Gorgas. As with Walker, Ballinger convinced Gorgas that Texas needed its original request filled. Gorgas agreed, signing authorization for Ballinger to receive the guns initially promised.[5]

Although pleased by Gorgas's compliance, Ballinger was told that only half his order was to be filled in Richmond. He had to obtain some artillery from the arsenal at Baton Rouge, along with gun carriages, which also had to be made in New Orleans. At this juncture, the Texans decided that Potter and Ballinger would leave for New Orleans immediately with the cannon that were available, and that Sydnor and Ochiltree would wait in Richmond until the rest of the order was filled.[6]

While in Richmond, Ballinger visited the Tredegar Iron Works, studying "the various stages in making cannons, shells &c," so he could promote the establishment of such industry back in Texas. "We can be of great help to the cause in this capacity," he believed; "We have all that is needed in Tx. to make such weapons." Ballinger also heard—much to his companions' delight—that Van Dorn had been relieved of his Texas command and that Brig. Gen. P. O. Hebert, a West Point valedictorian and former governor of Louisiana had been placed in command of Texas. Ballinger and other prominent Texans had urged Van Dorn's removal for some time because they believed the general "inadequate to the challenge of defending Tx."[7] At the time little did Ballinger or any other Texan know that Van Dorn's successor would become the most despised of all the state's Confederate commanders.

After spending ten days in the Confederate capital, Ballinger, on August 15, received his cannon, shot and shell, and made preparations immediately for the return to Galveston. He soon discovered, however, that the bureaucratic bumblings of Confederate officials were minor annoyances compared to the technological problems of the homeward trip. Despite military guarantees that his cargo would be shipped straight through to New Orleans, it took almost a week to transport the guns by rail to Bristol on the Virginia-Tennessee border; engines had a way of disappearing from lonely sidings without making scheduled connections; and Ballinger heard numerous reports of derailments and collisions during daylight runs. Exhausted from worry that the cannon would either be lost or destroyed, Ballinger finally reached New Orleans on September 1,

1861, with his own cargo still intact. The journey from Bristol to New Orleans, normally a three-day trip, had consumed twelve days and concluded the rail portion of his return, for no lines ran west to the Texas border.[8]

Relieved that his cannon had made it to New Orleans, Ballinger was confident that their transport the rest of the way would go more smoothly. He was soon disappointed. Again in New Orleans he experienced the bureaucratic snarls that seemed endemic throughout the Confederate system. Only after some "harsh words" with the local quartermaster was Ballinger allowed to move on with his cargo. Adding to Ballinger's frustration, the gun carriages, unavailable in Richmond, were not to be procured in New Orleans either. Ballinger could not delay the delivery of his cannon by the several additional weeks required to wait for New Orleans manufacturers to complete the carriages. At first he opted for sending the guns by water, but blockading Union gunboats ruled out that possibility. In desperation, he resolved to push on overland, taking part of the material with him in wagons and leaving fellow agent Henry Potter in New Orleans to follow with the rest as soon as the carriages were ready. From the beginning of his mission Ballinger had hoped to have his cannon safely in Galveston by early fall, avoiding the September torrential downpours that made the roads from New Orleans to the Texas border impassable quagmires. But now, due to administrative incompetence and obduracy, he had to contend with what became the most serious obstacle of his entire mission.[9]

Ballinger decided to take his cannon to Alexandria on the Red River then across to the Sabine and down to Niblett's Bluff. The drive from New Orleans to Alexandria went smoothly but from Alexandria to the Sabine River he faced increasing difficulties as he tried crossing the marshy bayou country of southwestern Louisiana. The predictable downpours slowed his progress but Ballinger persevered, reaching his destination—Niblett's Bluff on the Sabine—on October 3, 1861.[10]

While Ballinger proceeded successfully, his compatriot Potter fared less well, sending word to Ballinger on October 10 that his cannon were "bogged down—chains all broken & unable to get further—& he is utterly hopeless of getting thro. This is horrible!" Ballinger decided to send Potter on to Galveston, leaving to himself the responsibility of transporting both his and Potter's guns the rest of the way. Potter was to report the situation to Gen. Paul O. Hebert, the new Confederate commander of Texas. Meanwhile Ballinger tried to get Potter's cargo to Niblett's Bluff, but was unable to do so by the time help from Galveston arrived on October 13. A Maj. T. S. Moise, quartermaster to General Hebert, headed the rescue mission, and once again Ballinger was unimpressed with this latest representative of Confederate officialdom: "He [Moise] talked freely but wouldn't advise us of what should be done—had no understanding of our situation—an extremely uninspiring fellow possessed of unbounded arrogance." According to Moise, Hebert had ordered two gunboats, the *Jeff Davis* and the *Belle Sulphur*, to steam up the Sabine and rescue the attorney and his cannon, transporting the guns by water rather than overland. However, both vessels ran aground about halfway up the river, leaving Ballinger and his cargo still stranded at Niblett's Bluff. Ballinger now realized that if he hoped to see his guns delivered to Galveston, he would have to transport them himself by building his own flatboats there on the bluff to carry the guns down river.[11]

On October 22 the transports were completed and after testing their durability, Ballinger loaded his guns on them. On October 23, he watched his cannon float down the Sabine on their way to Galveston. The next day Ballinger boarded the *Belle Sulphur* which finally made its way to Niblett's Bluff. Ballinger arrived in Orange at four A.M. the next day and immediately boarded the train for Houston. After an overnight stay in Houston, Ballinger boarded the train for the island, finally reaching his home in the afternoon of October 25.[12]

Three days later Ballinger's cargo arrived in Galveston. All five cannon as well as their shells and shot were completely intact, to Ballinger's relief. Potter's guns did not arrive until early January 1862, and only after Ballinger bombarded Confederate officials in Texas, Louisiana, and Richmond protesting the delay. Had the attorney not unleashed such an intense letter campaign, he was convinced "the guns would have either remained in Louis.a or been sent elsewhere, & God only knows where that might have been. If there is a weakness within our Government, it is the inability to provide adequately for our defenses & other needs. I pray things will improve, but my instincts tell me that will not be the case."[13] Despite such forbodings, for the moment Ballinger was pleased with his effort. In a letter to his brother-in-law, Tom Jack, who had recently enlisted in the Confederate army as a private, Ballinger told of his ordeal and that he considered his mission to have been successful. But there was little time to celebrate. "I am afraid we will need the use of the guns soon," Ballinger concluded after hearing rumors that an "expedition of 16,000 men sailed from NY some time ago—likely headed for Texas. Enemy gun boats appear off the harbor every day & rounds are fired." At least Ballinger knew that Galvestonians felt more secure now that his guns were there.[14]

Unfortunately, Ballinger's valiant effort to secure his city's defense was never effectively appreciated by the Confederate command in Texas. Only three of the eight guns brought from Richmond were used to defend his beloved city. The rest were sent to Houston where Confederate officials relocated in the summer of 1862, deciding to abandon the island and make the Bayou City their place to stand against the Yankees. One year after Ballinger delivered his cannon to Confederate authorities, Galveston fell to a token Federal force, causing Ballinger "the greatest pain & anger—the likes of which I have not felt in many years." To Ballinger the seizure of his city represented one of the most unnecessary and dishonorable Confederate debacles of the entire war. Galveston should never have fallen into enemy hands, for Ballinger's trip to Richmond a year earlier was to procure cannon sufficient enough to protect the city from any Yankee assault. Yet, as the attorney observed on the day of the city's capture, "For many months there has been a foregone conclusion not to defend the place. Batteries were built and the guns removed, and they are now up here in the streets. With the guns we originally had—those I went to Richmond for—the present fleet could have been driven away. A better stand could have been made right at Galv.n than anywhere else."[15]

Several months before Galveston officially fell, Confederate commander P. O. Hebert, placed Galveston under martial law, ordering inhabitants to vacate the island as quickly as possible. Ballinger was incensed by Hebert's proclamation and refused to comply. The attorney and other loyal Galvestonians remained on the island only to watch their Queen City deteriorate under the duress of martial law. In a letter sent soon after martial law was declared, Ballinger warned Hebert that "the measure is wholly unnecessary & will result in the worst conditions imaginable. Most seriously affected will be the City's poor, who, if not provided for, will become most desperate and inclined to all manner of mischief & criminal activity. Robbery & sabotage will become commonplace, and order will only be restored when the people are allowed to return." Despite Ballinger's remonstrations, Hebert refused to retract his decree.[16] Once Galvestonians realized that the military was not going to defend the island, the exodus to the mainland began. Beginning soon after martial law was declared and into the early months of 1862, every train and steamboat for Houston was filled daily to capacity with Galvestonians and their belongings. After a

"*With every energy of the body consecrated*"

In October 1861, Ballinger's beloved city of Galveston fell to Federal forces, to remain in enemy hands for 15 months. Ballinger believed the Yankee capture of Galveston was one of the Confederacy's most senseless and humiliating defeats. "*A Sketch by an Officer.*" *From* Frank Leslie's Illustrated Newspaper, *February 7, 1863.*

visit to Houston, Ballinger told Hally, who, along with the children, had moved with his mother-in-law to Waco, that many former islanders were living in the Bayou City, some in "miserable shanties." He further lamented to his wife after returning to Galveston, that his beloved city "has the most abandoned & desloate appearance that can be conceived. I felt relieved to have gotten away even for a brief period. It was positively painful."[17]

Although Ballinger believed in "making a stand at Galveston," the Confederate high command felt otherwise. According to Col. Joseph J. Cook, commander of Confederate forces defending the city, the eight Yankee vessels blockading the island were "of such force" that it would have been "senseless to make a stand against them." Apparently, Cook had decided to abandon Galveston several days before the actual attack, and in fact made arrangements with the local railroad to be ready with transportation. It was Cook's decision to give up the island without a fight that so enraged Ballinger. According to Cook, supposedly in the middle of an attempted negotiation, the Yankees unleashed their superior firepower until they destroyed the Confederates' one ten-inch gun. Ballinger, however, maintained that "the gun was spiked without firing a shot & the men ordered to fire their barracks & leave their post without giving any resistance," and wondered how the military hoped "to hold the City if this is the manner of our soldier's behavior at the sight of the enemy." Largely as a result of his guns "not properly used," Galveston went "dishonored into the hands of the enemy to remain during this war. I feel deeply grieved & humiliated—much of my pride & interest in the place gone."[18] The city's surrender unleashed political repercussions in Richmond as well, causing Hebert's removal from his Texas command. Hebert's replacement, Gen. John Bankhead Magruder, seeking to vindicate his military reputation, which had been tarnished in recent campaigns in Virginia, decided to retake Galveston, which he accomplished in a surprise attack on "hungover" Yankee troops in the early morning hours of January 1, 1863.[19]

With his romantic spirit and earlier elan for military adventure, one might have expected Ballinger to enlist in the Confederate army. Why he chose not to serve in the Confederate military raises a perplexing issue, particularly when all around him, friends and relatives were enlisting without hesitation, believing it their "duty and honor" as Southern patriots and gentlemen to fight. Ballinger did not lack courage nor was he afraid of combat and being killed as a result. He had faced that prospect before at Monterrey, and during the heat of battle proved his mettle. Yet, as a result of his participation in the Mexican War, Ballinger no longer had any illusions about war, having witnessed firsthand its awful finality. Unlike many of his compatriots who had never experienced the horrors of battle, and momentarily were caught up in the euphoria of the martial spirit, Ballinger had no such delusions. At age thirty-six, Ballinger was a bit too old to fight, though because of his experience he would have received an officer's commission. Believing war to be a young man's crusade, Ballinger decided that he could best serve the Confederacy in some other capacity. Ballinger's asthma was also a factor in his decision to remain on the homefront. He was well aware of the physical hardships and emotional trauma caused by war, and how such constant stress and anxiety could precipitate serious attacks. If that was the case, Ballinger certainly would not want to become a liability to his fellow combatants. Moreover, Ballinger had a family and he undoubtedly feared for its welfare if he left to fight, especially in a war he often privately doubted the South would win. By 1861 he had five children, all under the age of eight. It would be characteristic of Ballinger to believe that his absence would jeopardize his family's well-being. This, in the final analysis, was more important to him than the cause he had sworn to uphold "with every energy of the body consecrated."

Instead, Ballinger accepted a position as receiver of alien enemy property. The position was an important one, though its occupants were likely to become unpopular. Two months before Ballinger received his commission, the Confederate Congress had passed a sequestration act calling for the confiscation of all enemy-held property in the South. As Ballinger told fellow Texans in a circular released the day after his appointment (October 29, 1861), the law's passage was the result of the United States government having "departed from the usages of civilized warfare in confiscating and destroying the property of the people of the Confederate States." Southerners' only protection against "such wrongs," he said, was to retaliate by passing the Sequestration Act. The measure not only would indemnify Southerners for their losses but restrain as well "the wanton excesses of our enemies."[20]

In his circular Ballinger wanted to reassure Texans that he would prevent "the oppression of any class of our own citizens," and respect "the private business affairs of merchants and others, dealing frankly and in good faith with the Receiver beyond the necessary ministers of the law." Ballinger also defined who was to be considered an "alien enemy" as anyone having "domicil in any of the United States, whether citizens or not," as well as the citizens of any foreign or neutral nations "carrying on business or traffic within the States at war with the Confederacy." In addition, the residents of the border states, as well as any of the trans-Mississippi and Indian territories, and the District of Columbia, were not to be regarded as alien enemies unless they committed "actual hostilities against the Confederate States, or aid or abet the United States in the existing war." All proceeds from the sale of expropriated property were to be collected in a special Confederate Treasury fund, which officials believed would eventually total $250 million in Confederate coffers.[21]

Enforcement of the decree centered in the new Confederate district courts, of which Texas had two—the Western District presided over by former state district judge Thomas J. Devine of San Antonio, and the Eastern District under Justice William Pinckney Hill, a lawyer from Marshall, Texas. Hill and Devine were empowered to appoint receivers to search out and confiscate all locally held enemy assets. The law required all citizens to report such property, and a failure to comply was punishable by a fine up to five thousand dollars and imprisonment for six months. The offender was also civilly liable for double the value of withheld property. Receivers had at their disposal a variety of legal controls by which they could obtain additional information regarding alien holdings. Two of the more common methods employed by receivers were grand jury probes and the "encouragement" of private denunciations. Rarely did Ballinger employ "informants," believing such tactics to be "unethical & arbitrary" to turn "neighbor against neighbor." While some receivers willingly resorted to such action, Ballinger instead preferred to serve writs of garnishment or ex parte sequestration judgments which would result in the sale by court order of perishable goods and other impounded property.[22]

Three types of sequestration cases were filed in either the Western or the Eastern District Courts. The most common cases filed in both courts involved debts owed by Southerners to Northern merchants. Like most antebellum Southern states, Texas was cash poor, forcing the majority of the state's merchants to operate on Northern credit. Receivers like Ballinger were aware of this, and thus sent out thousands of interrogatories to inquire from local merchants the amount they owed to their Northern counterparts. By the time the two district courts opened their January 1862 terms, receivers throughout the state had compiled a debt list of over two million dollars owed to Northern businesses. Ballinger reported over twenty thousand dollars owed by Galveston merchants to Northern clients, a figure he put together within the first three months of his receivership. After collecting this information, receivers then filed sequestration actions against these debts. If the creditor was an enemy alien—and in most instances he was—the court sequestered the debt, ordering the local merchant to pay it directly to the district receiver.[23]

Actions against the real and personal property of Northerners usually followed these suits. Northern speculators had invested heavily in Texas land, and by 1861 owned considerable acreage. For example, in Ballinger's four-county receivership district of Galveston, Liberty, Harris, and Chambers Counties, either Northern or foreign residents owned over two hundred fifty thousand acres; in the district just north of Ballinger's, the receiver reported over a hundred thousand acres owned by "enemy aliens." As Soon as Ballinger identified ownership, he sequestered the lands and sold them at auction at prices far below their actual value. Cattle, goats, horses, sheep, chickens, wagons, even furniture and slaves owned by Northerners eventually were seized and sold at auction. When the Confederate Treasury received the proceeds from such sales, the case was closed.[24]

Much to Ballinger's joy, Texans throughout his district responded favorably to his call for cooperation. Within a few weeks all sorts of items began pouring in, ranging from eight thousand head of cattle owned by a

Californian, to ten slaves owned by a New Yorker, to railroad iron, sawmill machinery, lumber, dry goods, and livestock. By December 1861, Ballinger found it necessary to rent a warehouse in Houston for the storage and sale of these acquisitions, most of which were either auctioned off, "fetching good prices," or donated to the government.[25]

The majority of Texans voluntarily reported their possession of enemy alien property and willingly turned it over. Ballinger knew, however, that many citizens were withholding alien property. One informant told the attorney that "a man named Terhune, now residing in New York, has lots of merchandize presently being stored at the home of a Mr. Weiss of Houston." Ballinger promptly investigated the allegation and discovered that the informant was correct. Weiss had hidden furniture, clothing, jewelry, and other valuables. Ballinger personally served Weiss with a writ from Judge Hill, and Weiss confessed that most of what Ballinger saw did indeed belong to Terhune. Ballinger decided not to seek an indictment against Weiss, concluding, "He has suffered much public dishonor—that is just punishment." After Ballinger inventoried the goods, Hill's court sequestered the merchandise and ordered it sold at auction for over four thousand dollars.[26]

By early January 1862, Ballinger had deposited $51,883.17 with James Sorley, special Confederate treasurer for Texas, and it seemed that money would soon be pouring into Confederate coffers. Such was not the case. Initially, Ballinger benefited from the patriotic euphoria sweeping across the South in the first year of the war, which helped him and other receivers take in substantial amounts of alien property. But proceeds at public sales seldom totaled the anticipated worth of the merchandise. As the original war fervor waned, Texans stopped reporting alien property. Hoarding became endemic and once Texas was cut off in 1863 from the rest of the South, its citizens were more inclined to violate the law because their isolation effectively removed them from the once-long arm of Richmond authorities. Ballinger complained about Texans' "lack of cooperation," and their "selfishness which will lead to more drastic measures taken to enforce the law." Some even had the "effrontery to openly denounce the law & impugn my authority as to its failure."[27]

The most promising source of revenue for the Confederacy came from another source: confiscation of the substantial indebtedness owed by Southerners to Northern alien enemies. Confederate authorities, however, had to be cautious in their approach toward this objective. Southern businessmen, already antagonized by the General Sequestration Act, were unwilling to sanction any further directives aimed at the confiscation of their property or financial resources. Confederate administrators, increasingly desperate for revenue, had no choice but to try to enforce the measure regardless of public ire. No sooner was the announcement made of the law's enactment than the predicted outcries were heard. Receivers in particular were aware of the business communties' denunciations, and as Ballinger soon discovered, most merchants refused to report their Northern debts. "A large no. of the city's [Galveston] population is opposed & distrustful of the recent laws. Those who have outstanding debts in U.S. & say they will not acknowledge them." Ballinger feared that such attitudes would soon "affect entire state & greatly damage our cause & alienate our people."[28]

So overwhelming was merchant protest that an official change of policy occurred on February 15, 1862. The amended law exempted from collection the principal on debts owed to alien enemies until "one year after peace should be secured." This moratorium on the principal remained in effect until the end of the war, leaving only interest payments to be made in the meantime. The new policy cut significantly into anticipated revenue but made Confederate regulations more compatible with the more liberal laws enacted by the individual states. Prior to passage of the new decree, many district judges and receivers had refused to enforce the provision of the original law, fearing their actions would only further arouse an already hostile business community.[29]

Ballinger wrote an editorial defending the Sequestration Act on the basis of the Confederate government's constitutional right to confiscate alien enemy property "as necessary for the common good of the nation and the security of all its citizens." Ballinger hoped his article would bolster fledgling public support for the measure, arguing that "the confiscated property of alien enemies belongs to the Confederate States of America, to be used to obtain the necessary funds to fight this war," and that confiscated property does not belong to the states. Ballinger reminded his readers that the act's passage was in retaliation to the Union's similar decree which "has lately resulted in the wanton confiscation of Southern property, especially our slave property, by the Union armies presently invading our nation." He believed the Confederate government in passing the act was "exercising the main business of fighting a war—to assail and injure the enemy and repay him for injuries of like kind," and to indemnify those Southerners who had suffered from the enemy's "wicked spoliations."[30]

Despite several more broadsides and public exhortations to get Texans to comply with the laws by the fall of 1863 Ballinger had become so disillusioned with the entire confiscation program that he believed a massive revamping was in order. In his frustration he now considered the sequestration laws impolitic, and the funds they produced "a mere drop in the bucket." He believed immediate payment out of sequestration funds of all debts owed by Northerners to Southerners should be implemented. He also believed that those Southerners who reported or turned over Northern property should be given the proceeds from the sale of those goods. Such a policy would "increase the liberality of many, & make <u>Patriots</u>, otherwise indifferent."[31] Ballinger's proposals for revamping were incorporated into a bill that Texas representative Peter W. Gray tried pushing through the Confederate Congress in 1863. Though Gray was unsuccessful, a majority of the House Judiciary Committee approved the measure. Congress's rejection, however, was offset by a modest victory in Texas. Due to Ballinger's constant agitation, Texas courts agreed in October 1863 to allow the sale of confiscated property whenever receivers believed it essential.[32]

With all its flaws, sequestration probably brought in over twelve million dollars. Ballinger estimated that by June 1864, "at least $2 million" had passed through his Eastern District receivership. Since acting as a depository for the entire district, Ballinger was responsible for keeping accounts as accurately as possible. The scattered receipts found among his papers testified to the substantial sums he transfered to James Sorley. Sorley continued receiving deposits from Ballinger until early May 1865.[33]

During the war years Ballinger's legal practice was largely confined to his duties as receiver; his official position provided by far the lion's share of his income and took most of his time. In addition to his regular salary, he received an annual commission of several hundred dollars for his responsibilites as depository. Ballinger's income seems impressive on paper but the constant devaluation of Confederate currency compounded by increasing family expenses made most of his gains deceptive. The majority of Ballinger's legal cases involved war-related issues ranging from the defense of clients accused of desertion and mutiny to the assault of an officer, to securing the discharge of individuals from military service.

Ballinger's most controversial wartime case was his defense of a family friend facing court-martial for desertion. While pleading on behalf of Capt. John Murray, Ballinger found himself on the wrong side of popular opinion. Not since defending Betsy Webster had he incurred such public scorn for his stand. Family members as well criticized his defense of

Murray, believing he had betrayed both his profession and the Southern cause.

It was during the Confederate assault on Fort Butler at Donaldsonville, Louisiana, in June 1863, that Murray had allegedly deserted his command. Fort Butler was a heavily fortified installation on the west bank of the Mississippi. Not only was it well defended by Union troops but Yankee gunboats on the river augmented Federal strength. Confederate Brig. Gen. Tom Green, with a cavalry force of over five thousand men, nonetheless attempted to take the fort. Green had been sent to Donaldsonville by Gen. Richard Taylor, commander of the District of Louisiana, to regain a foothold on the lower portion of the Mississippi. No sooner did Green order the charge than the gunboats opened fire, killing or wounding scores of Rebel cavalrymen in the first few minutes of battle. It was then that Captain Murray supposedly deserted. What apparently happened was this: seeing the futility of any more assaults, Murray countermanded his superior's order and withdrew his regiment from the battle. Unfortunately, few officers or men heard his call for retreat. Maj. Robert McWaters, the immediate superior whose orders Murray had countermanded, was furious. McWaters and Murray had exchanged harsh words before this battle and afterwards McWaters "publicly denounced Murray as a coward & deserter, and had him taken away in chains in front of his entire regimt." A court-martial was in order for Murray for desertion. Rather than suffer this indignity, Murray fled from his captivity and returned home. If found guilty, Murray faced certain imprisonment, perhaps even execution.[34]

After a conversation with Murray, Ballinger knew the captain was innocent. "Can I allow this to happen to a dear friend whom I know in my heart is a most courageous & honorable man, a soldier, as brave as any we have? "queried Ballinger to Tom Jack. "I can not believe he has committed these acts without there being just cause." Despite "the odium that will be attached to my defense," Ballinger took on his case. Murray finally came to trial in October 1864. For several months Ballinger gathered evidence and obtained affidavits from the survivors of Murray's regiment. All testified that Murray did order a retreat contrary to McWaters's orders, but "all were glad he did. He saved many more from a cruel & senseless slaughter."[35]

It was Ballinger's questioning of McWaters that ultimately won his client's acquittal. Ballinger lambasted McWaters for being "so far removed from the scene of battle that he could not see what was happening to the regiment. A good commanding officer should be in the thick of battle with his men—leading them on & knowing when to advance or retreat so as to save the lives of his men. This is precisely what Capt. Murray did." Ballinger also accused McWaters of "petty jealousy & vindictiveness," and of undermining Murray's standing and reputation by accusing him "unjustly of cowardice & desertion—to inflict such infamy that soon all would turn against him." Ballinger paraded witness after witness to the stand, all testifying that "everyone knew of the Maj's hatred for Capt. Murray." McWaters finally confessed that he indeed hated Murray and wanted him thrown out of the regiment. He also admitted that he hoped the charge on the fort would have killed Murray.[36] Ballinger contended that Murray's desertion after his arrest was "natural" for Murray possessed a "high sense of honor & loyalty to his family," and thus would not want "to inflict the shame of such an indignity [court-martial] upon them." On October 24, 1864, all charges against Murray were dropped, and he was allowed to return to his command. The court also ordered McWaters relieved of duty and discharged from Confederate service.[37]

Throughout the proceedings Ballinger feared his client would not receive a fair hearing because "the general hostility among our citizenry toward any person suspected of desertion is presently so great, that I am fearful of the consequences." Ballinger worried that even while awaiting trial, his client could become "the victim of wanton acts of reprisal by our citizens." Ballinger was anxious for his own safety as well. During the proceedings he received several anonymous notes and threats from "loyal citizens" expressing outrage that "a reputable attorney as yourself has willingly come to the defence of a known deserter, coward and traitor to our cause. . . . We hope that is not the case, but if it is, which your present actions imply, then we wish you and the traitor to the Devil."[38]

So concerned was Ballinger for Murray's security that before the trial began he wrote a rather insolent letter to Col. William Bates, the presiding justice of the military court, holding Bates accountable for the safety of Murray's life. Ballinger further told the colonel that because "the public has become so maddened over desertion" he did not want his client "to be thrown to the wolves—to be the sacrificial lamb to calm the prejudices & fears of the masses as if these were the days of the Roman Empire."[39]

Soon after the trial began, Ballinger received a letter from his Uncle James Love, reproaching him for having sent "such an objectionable letter to Col. Bates." Never one even to momentarily empathize with his more sentient nephew, Love was incensed by Ballinger's display "of overreaching sympathy for this man which has affected your judgment on this matter." What concerned Love was the impression his nephew had made not only upon Bates and the court, but upon the public as well. Love feared Ballinger had "disgraced" himself by letting his personal feelings for a client get the better of him. Nothing was as guaranteed to arouse Love's ire than for an attorney to let sentimentality or passion overrule his professionalism. Love knew Ballinger had such a weakness, especially when it involved friends or causes he cared about. Yet the judge was determined to protect his nephew from "this most juvenile & high-minded penchant which I fear will someday be your undoing." Though admitting he knew very little about the case, Love nonetheless maintained he could "scarcely imagine an excuse for an officer possessing the character and high qualities you attribute to him, for desertion. Not only that, but leaving his command at the time of battle." To James Love, the whole matter was simple: whether Murray was innocent or guilty was moot; he must be punished "to arrest the already too high desertion of our men."[40]

Love's letter astounded Ballinger. Did his venerated uncle no longer care about justice, of individual rights and liberties? Because of the war and the strains it had placed upon Southern society, was the rule of law to be discarded? Did "examples" have to be made of individuals in order to maintain public morale? These were the questions Ballinger put to his uncle in his response. Despite their ethical differences when it came to the law, James Love was one of the most respected men in Ballinger's life. Love's letter despaired Ballinger but he understood his uncle's position. He knew that Love's principal concern was for Ballinger's personal and professional welfare. Ballinger thus took "no offence" at his uncle's letter, reassuring Love that "All will be well. I have been vindicated and so has my client. I do not believe any damage to my career or standing in the State or Gov.t has resulted."[41] Ballinger was right: within a few months of Murray's acquittal, few Texans cared or even remembered that William Pitt Ballinger defended a "deserter." They had much more urgent crises to deal with by the beginning of 1865. More important to Ballinger than whether the public would remember the Murray controversy was his commitment to see truth and justice prevail regardless of personal consequences. This was something Ballinger wrestled with throughout his long career. As he demonstrated in the Webster case, when confronted with having to decide between professional success or maintaining his integrity, Ballinger consistently chose the latter.

Ballinger's strong support of the Richmond government's policies frequently caused him to become enmeshed in some of the most bitter and divisive issues affecting the Confederacy throughout its short history. One such controversy was conscription. From the moment the Confederate Congress passed the first national conscription law in American history in the spring of 1862, opposition to the act emerged throughout the South, including Texas. Southerners resisted the measure for a variety of reasons. The draft law was poorly conceived and executed. It was discriminatory and filled with loopholes. Officeholders, even minor ones, were exempt, as well as individuals considered "indispensable" to maintaining the home front. Exemptions for doctors and skilled craftsmen made sense, but substitution was permitted and abused. As in the North, a wealthy man could hire a poor one to go in his place. Finally, in Texas, the law became particularly hated because virtually any man of substantial wealth or prominence was dismissed.[42]

Resistance to the law was immediate. Thousands of Texans protested it on principle but Gen. Paul Octave Hebert, Confederate commander of Texas, reacted swiftly, silencing opposition by putting all of Texas under martial law in May 1862. The decree was sustained by both Gov. Francis Lubbock and the state supreme court. Ballinger too supported conscription, believing "all our men, found to be of sound body & mind, are subject to military duty—to the exigencies of the defence & preservation of the country. The success of our struggle involves as I believe everything worth living or dying for, and it is incumbent upon all to bear and forbear." Since the Southern people were at war, the central government had the right in the name of "public interest and private rights" to conscript troops." Moreover, since the Confederate government was created by popular consent, the government had the right to demand compulsory military service from its citizens. Though supporting conscription, Ballinger believed only those Southern males "of appropriate age & physical ability shd be put into our army. We must be careful to send to the front only the most able-bodied. This will ensure our armies' well-being & prevent further criticism that the Govt is taking all men regardless of their condition."[43]

Initially anxious about martial law, Ballinger accepted its premise, asserting that "the rebellious nature of our citizenry concerning the latest acts of Congress relative to conscription, has made such a declaration essential for the public safety." He denied it was "a wanton exercise of power," but necessary under present circumstances.[44]

Ballinger also supported restrictions on habeas corpus. Soon after the war began, some Confederate military commanders, like their Union counterparts, began arresting civilians for alleged disloyal activities, refusing to surrender them to civil authorities when presented with writs of habeas corpus. In February 1862, the Confederate Congress empowered President Davis to suspend the writ in areas in danger of Union attack. Davis thereupon declared martial law in several parts of the Confederacy. Rebel generals like Hebert promptly did the same on their own authority in their respective districts. Davis revoked their actions, but the crisis of invasion and battle in the West allowed Hebert and others to continue military rule until the "crisis" had passed. Cries of protest were heard from Texas to Virgina as Southerners feared that a military despotism would soon be established, destroying the constitutional liberties they were fighting for.[45]

In an editorial for the Houston *Telegraph* Ballinger outlined his reasons for supporting suspension. He asserted that the constitutions of the United States, the Confederate states, and Texas all sanctioned the suspension of habeas corpus "in cases of rebellion or invasion as the public safety may require it." Admitting that "the urgency of the act" might have been premature in the trans-Mississippi, especially in Texas, he nonetheless believed "the proportions of present invasion are as gigantic and the dangers of our overthrow as menacing" as they were in the eastern states of the Confederacy. Moreover, Ballinger was convinced that in all the states there were "traitors and disloyal factions" plotting the Confederacy's overthrow. Such threats to Texas's security demanded harsh measures. Yet Ballinger did not mean to justify even the slightest usurpation of power by the military. He reassured his readers that though civil authority had lost some of its effectiveness as a result of the strains of war, it never "ceases in its supremacy over military authority." Finally, Ballinger feared that without the right of suspension, "unorganized, irresponsible mob patriotism" would "inflame the peoples' passions," bringing about the end of the legitimate, orderly functioning of the law.[46]

Ballinger frequently found that the best way to generate popular support for Confederate authority was to express such an imperative in editorials. Journalism had always appealed to Ballinger, and privately he agreed with friends who claimed that by becoming a lawyer he had "spoiled a good editor." Ballinger initially wrote only sporadically at the outset of the war or "as the situation demanded" on a variety of war-related matters for Gulf Coast newspapers. However, as the conflict intensified he realized there was an ever increasing need not only to continue to promote adherence to government policies but to bolster morale was well. Thus, in the fall of 1864, he contracted with E. H. Cushing of the Houston *Telegraph* to write two to three editorials each week for $12.50 a month.[47]

Ballinger believed his duty as a journalist was to do more than inform: he had a responsibility to the national cause. He had long since transferred his allegiance from the United States to the Confederacy. All that remained was to help others become dedicated patriots. When secession transformed sectionalism into nationalism, Ballinger embraced in toto the new political structure. Ballinger, perhaps more than most Southerners, understood the true nature of the South's war. In his mind it was a struggle for national independence, and to this end he devoted his energies.

In one of his first editorials for the *Telegraph*, titled "On the Greek Revolt Against Turkey," Ballinger wanted to boost his compatriots' morale by historically validating the cause for Southern independence. Through the use of dramatic analogies and impassioned rhetoric, which became the essence of his style, Ballinger hoped to show Southerners how their plight resembled that of Greek patriots in the early 1820s, fighting to free themselves from the oppression of the Ottoman Empire. The Greeks, like the Confederates, believed "no fate more degrading than bondage" to a hostile nation and thus "took up arms to liberate themselves, knowing that they were engaging an enemy twenty times their superior." Because of overwhelming odds against them, the Greeks realized the need for unity and "complete devotion to the cause, without which they would never have won their independence." Ballinger also warned his readers that the Yankees, like the Turks, have proved "their determination to crush us. Though their [Turkish] power had gone much to decay, there was no people more valorous and proud, so susceptible of intense national and religious enthusiasm, of fierce, vindictive resentment and hate than the Turks." Ballinger's readers knew he was also describing the South's present foe.[48]

Ballinger's patriotism did not render him blind to reality. Although intially believing recognition by France and England was "only a matter of time," Ballinger's reasons were not founded in the "absurdity of King Cotton," but rather in the concepts of *real politik*. Ballinger did not want Southerners to delude themselves into thinking that British and French policy was guided by anything but "clear and enlightened convictions of their own interests." Ballinger counseled his readers to be patient and resolved "to carry on our struggle with all we presently possess." Ultimate victory would come from "the will and determination of the Southern people," not from foreign assistance.[49]

Ballinger was convinced the issue of slavery had little to do with foreign recognition. Though believing Southerners were fighting for self-government and not slavery, Ballinger admitted that "the great issue which drove us to assert our rights grew mainly out of the slavery question." Yet, he was certain no nation that befriended the South would "commit the illogical absurdity as the condition of its friendship on that issue!"[50]

In another essay, Ballinger argued that intervention would occur when the European powers "feel it necessary to prevent the Confederacy from being reunited with the U.S." In France's case, reunification would threaten the security of Emperor Louis Napoleon's puppet regime in Mexico. But as long as the war lasted, Maximilian would not "have any practical trouble with Lincoln or from the Monroe Doctrine, nor any serious dispute with the Confederate States of America." In short, Ballinger was convinced that Louis Napoleon's ambitious imperialism was one of the Confederacy's best guarantees of French intervention.[51]

Throughout most of 1862 and the spring of 1863, Confederate armies appeared to have the Yankees on the run, particularly in the eastern theater, and as long as "we suffer no signal disaster" European recognition was a certainty according to Ballinger's uncle Thomas Harrison, who had just returned from Richmond with "the latest news regarding our negotiations with Great Britain & France." Harrison had been assured by Confederate authorities that "it [recognition] will come because they [Britain and France] are hitherto subsisting on the goods in store and the surplus cotton on hand—all of which is due to run out soon. Once that is gone, then they will need our cotton once again and the price will be high! Once they realize how desperately they need our cotton in the future, they will not hesitate to recognize us."[52]

To a certain degree Harrison was right: the Confederate cotton embargo was having some effect in Europe but not enough to force either Britain or France into an alliance. Moreover, by mid-summer 1863, the fortunes of war turned against the South, and with major defeats on both fronts the hopes for intervention dissipated. The battle of Gettysburg and the fall of Vicksburg in July of that year proved to be the coup de grace to Southern expectations, especially in Great Britain. Although the mercurial Napoleon III continued dangling the carrot of French recognition in front of Confederate leaders, he too would soon abandon such pretense as well.[53]

In his next editorial, Ballinger told his readers that "There is nothing yet transpired giving any guarantee that any such intervention will be attempted," and returned to his theme that Southerners should not rely on foreign help. "We should continue to act as if we had to fight the war out alone and allow no relaxation and spare no exertion to prosecute it to a successful and glorious end. If foreign aid comes well and good; if not it should make no difference with us."[54]

Ballinger noted that European manufacturers were no longer dependent on Confederate cotton; "They have developed and fostered cotton fields in other parts of the world that produce as good a cotton as our best upland or short staple. Nay my friends, our belief in 'King Cotton' has been a curse, not a blessing."[55] As a student of history, Ballinger knew from the outset that diplomatic success rested upon military success. For all the major European powers, foreign policy was dictated by results of battles.

After the "absurdity of King Cotton" had been exposed, Ballinger urged his compatriots to turn their attention to manufacturing. In an editorial written soon after the cotton embargo was lifted, signifying the failure of King Cotton diplomacy, Ballinger reminded Texans that "years before secession we urged the building up of all sorts of industry—the production of everything of necessity to civilized life within our borders. Had these counsels been heeded, how much better would our condition be."[56]

To Ballinger, the most sensible and expedient way for the South to overcome its industrial backwardness was for the state to provide the initial impetus. Thus, in a letter to Texas governor Francis Lubbock, Ballinger urged Lubbock to "put the entire resources of the state—public lands, money, credit, all if need be—toward the establishment of foundries &.c to manufacture our own cannon & arms."[57] Ballinger was advocating a state-run economy based on the nationalization of local industry. An industrial sector had to emerge capable of rapidly securing and producing the essentials of modern warfare. If the Confederacy depended for its life upon victories on the battlefields then it was imperative that it have the means of producing the hardware necessary for those victories, Then and only then could the ultimate victory of independence become reality.

All of Ballinger's hopes of a decisive battle, foreign recognition, and the end of the war with Southern independence secured, were eclipsed in the few months following Lee's defeat at Gettysburg and the simultaneous fall of Vicksburg in early July 1863. "Our prospects ahead indeed look to me very gloomy," wrote Ballinger, "the strength of the enemy increasing every day, whilst ours is becoming exhausted. No prospect before us now but war to the knife, & from the knife to the hilt."[58]

Like many Southerners looking for a scapegoat, Ballinger's irascible uncle, James Love, blamed Jefferson Davis for "the calamities that have fallen upon us. He has allowed the Yankees to go where they please, defeat after defeat he has caused." Love's criticism did not stop at Davis. Equally culpable was Davis's cabinet whom Love charged as being "mostly inadequate to the burden upon us." Despite his uncle's rebukes of the Davis government, Ballinger supported the president and his policies. Yet, after the setbacks of July 1863, he realized the war would go on indefinitely, and that Southerners needed to brace themselves for protraction. It was time for "honest & sober reflection on the realities of this conflict." Southerners must be made to feel "the full shock of our disasters," in order to regain "the fire in their spirit necessary to recoil from defeat & press on to victory." Ballinger was upset with Texas editors who wrote "delusive articles in which Lee was to dictate peace from Phila. Such only exaggerate the hopes of our people & will have disastrous effect on their morale when they find out that events were otherwise."[59]

Ballinger's changed conception of the war was reflected in an editorial written soon after the fall of Vicksburg. Conspicuously absent from the article was the buoyant prose and confidence of his earlier pieces. His tone was more somber and deliberate. He no longer wanted his readers to delude themselves, as he had personally, into thinking that with only a few more Confederate victories the North would sue for peace. Ballinger now told his readers that "There will be no decisive battle." Admitting that he and others had been wrong in predicting that a particular engagement would win the war, he concluded, "If we are left to work out our earthly salvation it must be done by hard knocks, long continued against an inveterate foe, determined on our enslavement."[60]

Ballinger's importance as a Confederate nationalist rested primarily on his unwavering support of the Richmond government. In this role Ballinger proved more a devoted Confederate than political theorist, pledging to sustain the central government's authority even if it meant the sacrificing of personal liberties and local sovereignty so dear to his compatriots in 1860. Not all Southerners, however, were as willing to abandon the states' rights ideology associated with the Confederacy's origin. Every Confederate state, including Texas, contained anti-administration spokesmen.

Within the first year of the war, Lone Star senator Louis T. Wigfall emerged as one of the administration's most severe critics, railing against every attempt by the Davis government to impose greater uniformity and centralization upon the Southern war effort. Though Wigfall certainly made life difficult for Jefferson Davis, it was not until Pendleton Murrah's election as the governor of Texas in 1863 that Lone Star provincialism more directly affected the Confederate war effort. Like his counterparts in the East, Murrah constantly criticized Jefferson Davis's "dictatorial power." A political maverick, Murrah disliked the Richmond government's centralizing war measures, which, by 1864, drove him to obstructive resistance. Murrah believed it was his duty to uphold both the people's rights and those of the state, which he was convinced were being violated in the name of the war effort. To a large degree, the governor was correct; the Confederacy, desperately staving off defeat and oblivion, showed increasing disregard for legality. Murrah accused the Richmond government of "national encroachment" upon Texas, urging Texans to be wary of subsequent Confederate policies designed to subjugate the state further.[61]

In 1863 the Confederate government announced what soon became one of its most unpopular initiatives: the induction of state militias and other forms of state troops into its regular armies. No sooner did the promulgation of the new mandate reach Texas than Pendleton Murrah responded. He hurriedly pushed a frontier defense act through the state legislature exempting all Texans serving against the Indians in western local defense units from conscription. Although the act continued the policy of sending men to camps for training, it required that those transferred into the Confederate service be stationed only inside the state. In 1864 Murrah further antagonized Confederate officialdom by refusing to turn over Texas conscripts for service outside the state. In the early spring of that year, Gen. Edmund Kirby Smith, commander of the Trans-Mississippi Military Department, was in desperate need of men to fight Union movements in Louisiana. He ordered the dispatch of Texas state forces to Louisiana, but Murrah quickly countermanded Kirby Smith by ordering the state units not to cross the Sabine River. Murrah equivocated on technicalities until the crisis passed; the Texas forces never reached the front.[62]

Ballinger, the Confederate nationalist, believed Murrah had no "claim on the conscripts as against Confedt authority. It has no foundation in law or Constitution, or in good policy." Ballinger never acknowledged the Confederacy as an association of sovereign states. He believed the Confederate Constitution, modeled after the United States Constitution, created a strong central government, capable of positive action and not just negative obstructionism. Moreover, the authority and needs of the central government, based on the Constitution's "necessary and proper clause," superseded those of the individual states especially during a time of national crisis. This was precisely why Ballinger had such difficulty understanding Murrah's position. Though acknowledging that each state had a "limited sovereignty" that was recognized and protected by the constitution, no state, according to Ballinger, could pass any laws contravening "the right of the central government to call into service any person to perform his duty to protect the country from invasion." In the Galvestonian's view, once Texas joined the Confederacy her people "entrusted to the Confederate government the paramount command of their military resources & direction of all military operations." Thus, only with Congressional consent could the states "keep troops in time of war."[63]

Disturbing Ballinger most was the fact that by the spring of 1864 the Confederacy was trying desperately to stave off defeat and oblivion. To deprive the government of much needed troops at this crucial time was an egregious act of betrayal by Murrah and other state officials. Ballinger found absurd and "horribly distressing and subversive" the idea that Southerners may "owe military service to the state but not to their Country." To the attorney, such a position was a blatant "usurpation of power by the Govr. & the Legislature," as well as a display of "a most unpatriotic & irresponsible attitude."[64]

Much to Ballinger's dismay Murrah was not swayed by his editorials or public exhortations to uphold Confederate decrees. Ballinger thus decided to innundate Murrah's office with "frank" letters, directly telling the governor that his military policy was "without equivocation outside the law." He also told Murrah that the Confederate military was trying to avoid conflict, but if the governor persisted in his policies, Ballinger feared, Confederate authorities would use force to take the men they needed.[65]

Initially concerned that Murrah might take his views "unkindly," Ballinger soon discovered that the governor refused to take the bait. Murrah had no intention of debating Ballinger. Frustrated by Murrah's obstinance and miffed by the governor's refusal to acknowledge his entreaties, Ballinger believed he had no other recourse but to take the issue directly to the people. In an editorial written soon after the crisis had passed, Ballinger hoped to convince Texans that future attempts by the governor to withhold state troops from Confederate service would "not only endanger the security of our State," but also convince other states that the Texas government was lacking in its devotion to the national cause.[66]

Largely as a result of Ballinger's and other Confederate Texans' editorials and entreaties to Murrah, the governor eventually was forced to cooperate with the Confederate military. On May 28, 1864, the legislature revised the law to allow the transfer of state troops into Confederate service. In his official report, Magruder told a much-relieved Kirby Smith that Murrah's compliance had been "prompted by the loftiest patriotism."[67]

The second great rift between Murrah and Confederate officials involved the cotton trade. To raise needed state funds, the governor set up his own organization in competition with the Confederate Cotton Bureau, which had been created by Gen. Kirby Smith in the fall of 1863 in reaction to the impregnable Federal blockade. The bureau, empowered to impress cotton, was to haul bales to Mexico under government supervision, there to be sold for war material only. Texas planters objected to impressment and became even more angry when they were paid in worthless Confederate bonds for one-half their cotton.[68]

The flaws of the Confederate system were obvious, especially to Murrah. He allowed the Texas military board, responsible for the state's war procurement since its creation in 1862, to go into the cotton business. The board also bought up one-half the production of individual planters for state bonds—but under Murrah's scheme, the board transported all the contracting planter's cotton to Matamoros. There the planter, or other holder, could do with his half as he pleased, selling it for gold or for trade goods. The planter or speculator could make enormous profits at no risk. The state plan was soon driving the Confederate Cotton Bureau out of business.[69] Since many Texans were already wary of the Richmond government's centralization policies, the creation of the Cotton Bureau represented one more attempt by Confederate authorities to assert national hegemony. Consequently, Confederate Texans soon found themselves in the thick of another "test of wills" between Pendleton Murrah and the officials of the Trans-Mississippi Department of the Confederate States of America.

Ballinger knew the only way the government could procure enough cotton to exchange for badly needed supplies was through impressment. He thus defended the decree "as the only means we presently have of supplying our soldiers." Since the Confederate Constitution, Congress, President Davis, and even the United States Supreme Court had all sanctioned the impressment of private property provided compensation was given, Ballinger found it "very strange" that Murrah could deny this right. Ballinger criticized the Murrah administration for "setting its will above the law," and of "evincing a wanton disregard for the needs of our soldiers." He warned that if Murrah did not stop his activities, the Confederate government would be "rendered impotent in its present condition and in this crisis, and we shall cease to be free men."[70]

Despite Ballinger's personal crusade to villify Murrah, the governor remained calm and determined to pursue his initiatives. In his correspondence with Ballinger, Murrah tried to disarm his opponent by dissembling his own animosity with bland politeness. In one of his replies Murrah defused Ballinger's antagonism by praising the attorney's "unselfish devotion to the People of Texas" and his "forthright & prudent understanding of the problems presently affecting our State. If all intelligent citizens would deal with equal candor it would be better for the public interest."[71]

Ballinger was not mollified by Murrah's blandishments, and in fact strongly insisted that the two should meet and settle their differences over present policy. Ballinger saw himself as a sort of mediator between the two camps, hoping to convince the governor to cooperate with the cotton office and Kirby Smith. Ballinger and Murrah finally met on Friday June 22, 1864, and for several hours the Galvestonian gave his "views fully & with candor." Despite repeated attempts to find a compromise, Ballinger realized Murrah was "resolute in his own course." The Galvestonian found Murrah's obstinancy rooted in ambition "to do good by the State, but also to gain reputation." As Ballinger later told Guy Bryan, Murrah believed his actions were lawful and beneficial to Texas, for he believed his policies were preventing a "military despotism from being fastened upon the state." Ballinger feared force would be applied to end the impasse.[72]

Kirby Smith had been reading Ballinger's editorials supporting impressment and was aware of the attorney's exchanges with Murrah. Months of personal entreaties and the sending of several emissaries had failed to stop Murrah's operations. An exasperated Kirby Smith, knowing he was headed for another showdown with Pendleton Murrah on the issue of states' rights, turned to Ballinger for counsel. So confident was Smith of Ballinger's interpretation that he decided if it did not clearly sanction his authority to impress cotton, he would cease the Cotton Bureau's operation.[73]

Ballinger immediately responded to the general's letter. In his seven-page reply, he expanded his editorial arguments, reassuring Kirby Smith that he thought "it unquestionable that the right of the Government does exist to take cotton in order to provide supplies for its armies on making compensation to the owner." Ballinger told Kirby Smith that it seemed strange to him that in peacetime people accepted the right of impressment for such purposes as road construction and canals, yet they were refusing to "extend that power in time of war to clothe an army, supplying it with ordnance &c." Ballinger believed such "public disposition" illogical.[74]

Murrah and his supporters had claimed the right of eminent domain in order to challenge the legality of impressment; that is, only the state government, not the Confederate government, had the right to take private property with compensation. Ballinger believed Murrah's interpretation of eminent domain to be a desperate and unconstitutional maneuver to vindicate states' rights. True to his Whiggish heritage, Ballinger maintained that in the final analysis the "political community"—which he interpreted as the Confederacy—was "the true and ultimate possessor of power." Consequently, Ballinger saw Murrah's proclamation of eminent domain over Texas cotton as "a specious contrivance" designed to "enhance the power of the state to the injury of the national Government."[75]

Fortified by Ballinger's interpretation, Smith confidently asserted that as commander of Confederate forces he had the right to order the impressment of cotton. Murrah was warned that if he refused to abandon his "present course," Smith would "not hesitate to order full impressment, for I cannot in duty and conscience allow your policies to affect our soldiers in such a harmful manner." Murrah, confident he could exact another compromise from Kirby Smith, called for a conference in Houston in early July 1864. This time, however, the Confederacy's condition was too critical for the general to allow another capitulation. Smith was unwilling to negotiate on the cotton issue or yield on his right of impressment or on any other wartime prerogatives. As a result, from their July meeting until the end of the war Murrah abandoned all further attempts to pursue a separate Texas policy, cooperating fully in most things with Confederate authorities. But despite the best efforts of Ballinger and Kirby Smith, it was now far too late for the export of cotton to materially affect the war's outcome.[76]

Though sustaining itself in the first two years of the war, by early 1863 the Confederate economy was in shambles, and "King Cotton diplomacy" had failed to create European allies. By the fall of 1864 Union offensives in both theaters had so weakened the Confederacy that further resistance was appearing more and more senseless. The Confederacy was simply collapsing. Even Texans, far from the bloody battlefields, were aware that the war's climax was fast approaching. Daily it seemed local newspapers had nothing to report but the latest Union victory and the terrible losses of life and property.[77] After the fall of Atlanta in September

1864, even the most devoted of Rebels realized the end was near. As Ballinger confided to his diary, Sherman's taking of Atlanta demonstrated "the immense superiority of force they [the North] now have South & is a more decided manifestation of their superior strength than ever." Ballinger now predicted the South would be overrun and slavery ended. "God help us—all looks dark."[78]

Despite private lamentations, Ballinger, ever the loyal Confederate, continued to publicly exhort his Southern brethren to press on, writing in the last six months of the war some of his most spirited and patriotic editorials. Worrying Ballinger most was whether the Southern people could sustain a "spirit of endurance" in the face of so many demoralizing and devastating defeats. Soon after reports of Atlanta's destruction reached Texas, Ballinger hoped to stir outrage toward the invaders that would "forge irrevocable bonds" among Southerners, inciting them "to resist to the very end." Though hoping for "final victory," Ballinger warned his readers that history proved only a virtuous people could expect deliverance from an enemy's "enslavement." Using the French Revolution as his example, Ballinger asserted even that movement's "genius," Rousseau, "recoiled from its consummation" when he realized "the virtue of the French people was not equal to the stern and arduous undertaking before them." According to Ballinger, as the French became consumed by self-interest and love of power, their revolution rapidly degenerated into "the most awful display of wanton depravity, violence, and fanaticism." Fearing that too many Southerners had already abandoned the South's "Revolution" for "the love of money, property, and gains" Ballinger implored his compatriots "not to forsake our glorious cause at this critical hour in our history." If Southerners maintained their public virtue, then no degree of Yankee barbarity could prevent them from "achieving the most glorious independence ever won by any people."[79]

Ballinger's commitment to the Confederate cause was perhaps a result of his tragic personal life during the war. In four short years he saw many friends and relatives and three of his children, including his only son, William Pitt Jr., become casualties of war. Because of his own childhood affliction, Ballinger could not bear to watch his progeny suffer even the mildest physical discomfort. At the slightest indication of illness, Ballinger would immediately call for the doctor, for he did not want his children "to endure any pain or suffering if it can be helped. I want them to live long & healthy lives, & I will do all that is necessary, regardless of the cost, to ensure that."[80] A serious or prolonged ailment and subsequent death plunged Ballinger into the depths of depression. Ballinger blamed himself for his children's passing, believing that his extended absences had somehow contributed to their illnesses and deaths. He was separated from his family for most of the war because of his official duties, and because of the potential danger to them of living in Galveston, he early in the war sent Hally and the children to his in-laws in Waco where they remained for the duration.

Ballinger's guilt over his absences in such trying times seemed to intensify his devotion to the Confederacy, stirring in him a yearning for the success of the cause for which he had sacrificed so much. In the private recesses of his study, Ballinger confided to the pages of his diary his sense of loss and despair. He was particularly despondent after the death of his two-year-old daughter Ann in the summer of 1863. She was the second child in less than a year he had lost to a yellow fever epidemic. In his personal eulogy, Ballinger mourned his most recent child's loss as well as reflecting on his feelings of guilt for having been away from his family for the past several months. He blamed himself for his child's passing, believing for the first time since the war began that he had neglected his family, sacrificing their well-being "for the Revolution." Ballinger was not a deeply religious man but believed God was punishing him for having forsaken his family for a cause that was not as righteous as he had believed. "What will become of my other children if I continue on this most reckless course? I must stop here & now—take stock of what is most important & keep all other concerns in proper proportion. I pledge this upon the graves of my departed children. May God forgive me & give me the strength to endure these most painful times."[81] Despite his pledge, Ballinger could not abandon the cause of Southern independence, even if it resulted in several more years of personal anguish.

In the midst of his private suffering, Ballinger struggled to understand the circumstances that underlay it. Throughout the war he was torn between an intellectual commitment to the Union and a deep, emotional identification with the South. The interaction of the two frequently caused him to have conflicting assessments of the Confederacy and the War Between the States. Once he embraced the idea that secession was revolution and that the Southern people had the right to form their own government, Ballinger realized he could no longer function as a citizen of the United states. Yet, he remained devoted to the principles underlying the old Union: constitutional restraint, the division of sovereignty, and the internal balances that checked governmental power and popular passions.

But with the North and South at war, such principles seemed increasingly irrelevant, and continued adherence to them little more than loyalty to a past long gone.

As Ballinger labored to rally Confederates to fight to the end, he was stunned to learn late in 1864 of the swelling desire for a negotiated peace. Not only was such a policy being urged by Congressmen, but by members of the administration as well. To the Galvestonian even "a momentary contemplation" of a negotiated peace with the Lincoln government was "absurd & delusive." As he further told Guy Bryan, once the war for Southern independence began, Southerners pledged themselves "before mankind that we w.d maintain it at all costs. The issue was single and plain. It was uncomplicated and admitted of no compromise." Ballinger believed that it was "impossible" for Southerners to consent to a return to the Union, for to do so would only "disgrace us in the eyes of the world & ultimately result in a peace of submission & dishonor."[82]

Ballinger also opposed the idea of Texas seceding from the Confederacy, which was popular not only among states' rights advocates, but among loyalists as well, such as Galveston District Court judge Peter W. Gray. In a conversation with Ballinger in early 1865, Gray made a case for Texas to separate from the dying Confederacy. The judge argued that Texas ought to "approach foreign govts. to ascertain whether we could get separate protection in the last resort." Ballinger opposed the scheme, countering that "No govt. w.d entertain such a proposition & the moral & political effect w.d be bad on the general cause."[83]

More alarming to Ballinger than a friend's speculations were the more serious considerations of Pendleton Murrah to have Texas become a French protectorate. In early January 1865, Ballinger received a letter from Murrah asking his opinion on whether or not it would be wise to open negotiations with the French in case of Union victory.[84] Though earlier differences over conscription and impressment had caused antagonisms, during the last few months of the war Ballinger and the governor became close correspondents, openly and candidly discussing their respective views on Texas's future. Despite Ballinger's attacks on his administration for its states' rights policies, Murrah respected Ballinger and knew he would be hard-pressed to find anyone more experienced in the art of mediation than the Galveston attorney.

Ballinger opposed the governor's scheme, telling Murrah that Texans would interpret his actions as an admission that their cause was hopeless. To Ballinger, Murrah's most important task "at this dark hour of our

Revolution" was to maintain "the moral firmness of the people." Ballinger convinced Murrah to postpone sending an agent to France "until events proved it more prudent to do so."[85] But time was running out for the Confederacy, Texas, and for French schemes in the New World. With each passing day the prospects of Texas becoming a French protectorate dwindled. Already Louis Napoleon's puppet regime in Mexico was collapsing. No sooner had the Austrian archduke Maximilian arrived in 1864 to become emperor than ex-president Benito Juarez declared a war of national liberation upon the beleaguered monarch and his Francophile supporters. In addition, the Lincoln administration, invoking the Monroe Doctrine, strongly intimated that as soon as the rebellion was over, it would send troops to Mexico to help liberate that nation from foreign occupation. With such challenges before him in America, it is highly doubtful Napoleon would have been willing to make Texas a protectorate. Criticized at home and scoffed at in Europe among the major powers for his New World adventurism, the last thing Napoleon needed was war with the United States. Though torn apart by four years of bloody civil strife, the United States, with a combat-hardened Union army, would have presented the emperor with a very formidable adversary.[86] If Texas became a French protectorate, and war broke out as a result, in all likelihood Texas would become a major battleground. After escaping the ravages of civil war, it seems unlikely Murrah or any Texas official would want to inflict such a condition upon Texas. Perhaps this was the scenario Ballinger envisioned. If so, he surely would want to dissuade Murrah or anyone else from pursuing a policy of separation and annexation.

Ballinger also believed that any arrangement between Texas and France was destined to be short-lived. Ballinger understood that of all Anglo-Americans, both North and South, none were as chauvinistic or as enthnocentric as Anglo-Texans. Scornful of Mexicans, Indians, African Americans, and even Yankees for their supposed cultural and political deficiencies, it is unlikely Anglo-Texans would have accepted French rule as readily as Murrah or others might have wished. It would not have taken Texans very long to associate Napoleon's centralized Catholic autocracy and "effete" culture with the authoritarianism and equally "degenerate" customs of his hated Mexican predecessors. As a result of Mexican rule and war with the North, an intense and potentially virulent nativism had emerged in most white Texans, causing open hostility toward any people or nation that threatened their unique existence. In the final analysis, Ballinger believed it would be better in the long run for Texas to endure the humiliation of defeat and Union occupation than to see the Lone Star State suffer the devastation of protracted war or revolution.

With most of her territory under Yankee control, her armies dwindling away, and her economy in complete shambles, the Confederacy by March 1865 was clearly doomed. However, President Jefferson Davis, with support from his commander-in-chief, Robert E. Lee, still had one card to play in a desperate attempt to stave off the inevitable: the conscription of slaves into the Rebel army. Without question, of all the wartime measures proposed by the Richmond government, the idea of arming slaves aroused the most controversy.

With the North's increasing use of black soldiers, by the summer of 1863 voices throughout the Confederacy began lobbying in newspapers and letters to Richmond and state officials that the South should more effectively utilize its adult male slave population. One of the first Confederates to actively promote the wider use of Southern slaves was Ballinger. As early as the summer of 1862, far sooner than most fellow Texans, Ballinger suggested that not only should the construction of "entrenched camps in different parts of the State" be done by slave labor, but in order "to save them [the slaves] from the enemy" they should be made part of our army, & armed with musket."[87] Friends and relatives rebuffed Ballinger's "curious ideas." Yet he continued agitating for the arming of slaves, and by the fall of 1865 he was no longer a lone voice on the issue. Summer setbacks and manpower shortages convinced even more Southerners to consider the use of blacks in grey.

To a Rebel nationalist like Ballinger, the Confederate government had the right to virtually all forms of Southern property, including slaves. This was especially true if the government considered the property essential "to protect society or save itself." Ballinger also believed that slaveowners were not entitled to compensation, for their slaves were not being taken for "public use," but rather for the "exigencies of the defence & preservation of the country." Ballinger reminded Texans that while Southerners sat around debating the issue of compensation, the Yankees were taking slaves and "converting them into instruments of war against us."[88]

Ballinger, like many antebellum slaveowners, displayed conflicting attitudes toward African Americans. Such ambiguity perhaps made it easier for him to embrace the idea of blacks in uniform. An avowed racist, Ballinger nonetheless believed slaves were human beings first and property second; persons, who were, like their white counterparts in time of national crisis, just as "subject to military service in defence of the country." Since the Confederate Constitution gave the government unlimited wartime powers, it had the right to call upon "the services of all capable of bearing arms & fighting in the cause."[89]

Despite a willingness to recognize the slaves' humanity, Ballinger never once intimated during the war that slavery should be abolished or that those blacks who served or fought for the Confederacy should be rewarded with their freedom. To the Texan the freeing of slave soldiers would "revolutionize our whole society—it would impoverish the country and be a dire calamity to both the negro and white race." Ballinger was still convinced of slavery's "beneficences" and thus believed slaves would "gladly fight to help preserve a way of life which has proven itself as beneficial to them as it has to the white man." For Ballinger and for the majority of Southern whites, the war against the North was fundamentally a white man's conflict; a struggle for independence or liberty, which included the right to own slave property.[90]

The movement to arm the slaves—with or without emancipation—received a great boon in early March 1865, when Commander-in-Chief Robert E. Lee publicly announced his support of the idea. The Virginian had never been a strong proponent of slavery, so few Southerners were surprised by his advocacy. Lee, however, unlike Ballinger, believed that slaves indeed would fight for their country but only if emancipated. Once the revered General Lee threw his support for arming the slaves, Ballinger was certain it would not be long before the idea became official war policy. He thus exhorted Texans to press their legislature to pass a resolution recommending the measure to Congress. Ballinger believed there was still time for Southerners "to avail" themselves "of this crucial option for our independence." The Confederate Congress on March 13, 1865, grudgingly and narrowly passed a bill to enlist black troops.[91] Whether Southern blacks would have fought for the Confederacy with or without the promise of freedom remained a moot question. Before any regiments were organized the war was over.

On April 1, 1865, Grant finally defeated Lee's rag-tag army near Petersburg, Virginia. Realizing he could no longer defend Richmond, Lee moved west with his remnant army in the forlorn hope of finding a way to avoid Union forces to his south. The news of Lee's abandonment of Petersburg caused the final collapse of Southern morale. On April 2 Confederate officials began fleeing Richmond to avoid capture. Lee realized that further bloodshed was futile, and asked Grant for surrender terms on April 7. On Sunday, April 9, the two leaders met in the McLean House at the crossroads hamlet of Appomattox Courthouse. Twenty-five thousand Rebels laid down their arms; in military terms, at least, the long war was now over.[92]

The news of Lee's surrender saddened Texans, yet they made a desperate effort to maintain a bold front. Governor Murrah and Generals Kirby Smith and Magruder exhorted the people and soldiers to fight on; editors argued that it would be at least a year before the Yankees could invade Texas and that meanwhile help could be secured from abroad. Throughout the state Texans held public meetings, pledging never to submit to Yankee oppression.[93] Ballinger too believed there was still hope for the Confederacy. Only five days after the Army of Northern Virginia capitulated, President Abraham Lincoln was assassinated. Upon hearing the news of Lincoln's death, Ballinger initially condemned John Wilkes Booth's action, declaring that he "abhorred assassination. The act is one not to be justified or excused." He also acknowledged that "If our fate is subjugation," Lincoln "would have more laxity toward us than most of his party."[94]

Upon reconsidering Lincoln's attempt to subdue the South, Ballinger concluded that Lincoln's fate was deserved after all, for the president's actions had "every quality of tyranny." Ballinger labeled Lincoln a "fanatic" and the "most formidable of all our oppressors. I am writing an article on his death which I hope will excite our people & create in them a desire to continue our struggle against the North." Ever the die-hard Rebel, Ballinger declared in his editorial that he had "never felt a greater sense of exaltation." Apparently assassination was the miracle he and other hardcore Confederates had long hoped for that would save the South. Ballinger was certain that with Lincoln gone Northerners would lose their "passion for the war, lay down their arms, and return to their homes to mourn the loss of their leader." While Northerners grieved, Southerners would regain their earlier elan and drive the Yankee invaders from the South. In what was his most impassioned broadside of the war, Ballinger reflected upon Lincoln's death, inviting his readers to share in his perverse joy. He conceded that Lincoln had been a great leader, but "once fully embarked in the war," he allowed "ambition and fanaticism to obtain control of him." Such passion transformed Lincoln into "the grimmest monster history has ever produced." Ballinger maintained that Lincoln became so obsessed with the Confederacy's destruction that he resorted not only to the use of "foreign mercenaries from every land" but "by the arms of our

"With every energy of the body consecrated"

own domestic slaves" as well. Ballinger concluded his editorial by calling upon Southerners to rejoice, to allow themselves "to feel the thrill electric, divine at this sudden fall in his own blood of the chief of our oppressors.... Whoever would impose the fate of servitude and slavery on these Confederate states, whatever fatal Providence of God shall lay him low, we say, and say it gladly, God's will be done."[95]

But the time for heroism had passed, and with it the dream of Southern independence. No amount of emotionally charged broadsides could sustain the the Southern people any longer. Even as Ballinger wrote, Confederate armies east of the Mississippi were surrendering, leaving only westerners under Kirby Smith to oppose the Yankees.

Chapter Eight

"THE SPIRIT OF THE PEOPLE ARE READY FOR SUBMISSION"

As Ballinger pondered the Confederacy's defeat, he feared he too would soon be destroyed. His greatest anxiety was that he would be prosecuted for treason for his activities as a Confederate official, or at least have to contend with a barrage of civil suits that would ruin him financially. Even if neither of these two calamities occurred, he was uncertain whether he could secure a presidential pardon, which would restore his civil rights. However, over the next nine years Ballinger successfully surmounted or avoided these and other obstacles to both his personal and professional life. Beginning in late May 1865, with his trip to New Orleans to negotiate Texas's surrender, to the advent and demise of Radical rule, Ballinger looked for ways to overcome the trauma of Reconstruction. Above all else, Ballinger's Reconstruction activities demonstrated his ability to cope not only with the shock of defeat, but with the social and cultural changes resulting from four years of bloody civil strife.

Civil government in Texas collapsed totally between May and June 1865. Although Generals Kirby Smith and Magruder, backed by Gov. Pendleton Murrah urged Texans to continue the war in the West, their entreaties fell on deaf ears. Texans knew the war was over, and everyone but the die-hards were desperately thankful it was.[1] Ballinger was one such grateful Texan. Though for several weeks after Lee's surrender he exhorted his compatriots to fight a guerrilla action "from the hills, swamps, forests, from wherever we must, for as long as we must, until we have won our independence," by May 1865 Ballinger finally accepted defeat. He was now convinced that further military resistance would be both futile and dangerous. Texas troops were thoroughly demoralized; feeling "hopeless—

& if a campaign is attempted they will throw down their arms." Even the most devoted Rebels had to accept that "the spirit of the people are ready for submission to the power of the U.S." and that "the political situation dictates there shd be no further protraction of the war—no useless sufferings should be demanded of our people or soldiers."[2]

Within a week of officially ending hostilities, Murrah sent for Ballinger to discuss the feasibility of appointing a special civilian peace mission that would negotiate with the triumphant Union commanders in New Orleans. Many Texans were surprised by Murrah's call upon his old nemesis for advice. However, when Ballinger arrived at the governor's office, he found their views to be "very much in accord on the subject of surrender," and that Murrah had told him that "if he sent anyone to N.O. he wished me to go."[3] As Murrah had realized earlier when contemplating a separate peace with France, he would be hard-pressed to find a more skilled, veteran negotiator than Ballinger. By the end of the war, Ballinger had emerged as one of Texas's most respected and powerful individuals, whose devotion to the Confederacy and Texas he proved throughout the war. Moreover, Ballinger possessed credentials the Yankees would respect: a well-educated, successful, urban professional, familiar with the "Northern temperament"; officer in the Mexican War; Confederate official; and member of a powerful local elite. Murrah and Magruder were confident that if anyone could convince the Yankees not to invade and militarily occupy Texas, it was Ballinger.

Ballinger was initially reluctant to accept the appointment but after further deliberation agreed, believing it would be better for Texas to negotiate terms with the Union generals than "with Andy Johnson who I have no doubt wd tell us we were all traitors who were to be punished and admonish us in advance of our fate." Ballinger insisted there should be two Texas emissaries to New Orleans. Murrah concurred. For his fellow negotiator, Ballinger requested the veteran Texas diplomat Ashbel Smith, whom he believed to be "one of the most sincere & practical men I know. I shall defer to him as his experience & reputation renders proper."[4]

Before leaving for New Orleans Ballinger was instructed by Murrah and Magruder to negotiate an armistice with the commander of the Union fleet presently anchored off Galveston harbor. The Union commander, Capt. Benjamin F. Sands, agreed to meet with Ballinger on his flagship the *Fort Jackson*. The captain was willing to transport the Galvestonian to New Orleans and in the meantime he assured Ballinger that he would not commit any act of aggression. The commander also told the lawyer that since he had been at Galveston he had observed a quasi-armistice, even though he had been tempted to bombard the island, which would have "gratified the ardent adventurous young men in his fleet & get his own name in the papers." Much to Ballinger's relief, Sands, like most Americans, North and South, was anxious to end the war and reunite the country. Ballinger and Ashbel Smith, carrying a letter of recommendation from Sands, boarded the U.S. gunboat *Antona*, which sailed for New Orleans on May 27, 1865.[5]

Ballinger and Asbel Smith were determined "to prevent any invasion or occupation of Texas by U.S. troops—or appointment of military govt." In his best courtroom demeanor, Ballinger tried convincing the generals a military occupation of Texas was unnecessary because Texans had laid down their arms and gone home in peace. Let the normal legal process take its course, he pleaded; regular elections were scheduled to take place automatically in August and the election was "in no degree dependent upon those who at present exercise state authority." Ballinger assured Union officials that secessionist influence was dead in Texas, claiming that Texans were "ready in sincere faith to return to their relations to the gov't of the U.S." Ballinger also told the generals that Texans would comply with any loyalty test they might administer to voters, ensuring that only those who had remained loyal to the Union participated in the election. Ballinger guaranteed Texans would elect a governor and legislature fully able to enforce the policy of the United States government.[6]

Ballinger's mission had two goals: to prevent Federal occupation while ensuring white Texans close control of black labor. Ballinger told his hosts "immense evils would result from any circumstances which should at once cause a dislocation of the labor of this state." Because Texas produced more cotton than all other states, the loss of only a few weeks' labor would be catastrophic. Ballinger maintained that until "the status of the negro population is fixed, and regulations for their government completely enforced" Union officials should keep blacks from leaving their plantations. This, the Galvestonian urged, was the only alternative the new regime had if they hoped to prevent the failure of the current cotton crop and the state's economic ruin.[7]

Although Gen. Edward R. S. Canby, Ballinger's principal Union contact, made "no assumptions," and listened "politely," he along with Gen. Philip H. Sheridan, Canby's superior, turned down practically all of the attorney's proposals. The generals told the Texans that the sending of troops to the Lone Star State was inevitable. Ballinger and Smith were assured that troops were not being ordered to Texas "for any hostile or unfriendly purpose but to secure order." Ballinger probably was more than a bit incredulous when Canby further stated that he "was certain the people would prefer the presence of the troops to keep law & order" rather than counting on local authorities to keep the peace. Canby's determined stance rendered it futile for Ballinger to pursue that issue any further. Though failing to achieve his mission's principal objective, Ballinger was not totally disheartened. He was able to extract from Canby and Sheridan a promise that the occupying army would do its best in limiting black mobility. Ballinger was also assured that the army would assist white employers in promoting and maintaining labor contracts, thereby ensuring a secure black work force on Texas plantations and farms. Canby reassured the Texans that although there might be "commotion a little while," he was certain "the negroes wd not be permitted to follow the Army or be idle." Before leaving for Mobile, the general reiterated that he would see to it that Texas freedmen "would be required to remain at their homes [plantations] until their condition was finally settled."[8]

Ballinger was advised that if Texans hoped to receive any political concessions, it would be necessary for him and Smith to go to Washington and present their case to President Andrew Johnson, for only he could grant such exemptions. The generals warned the attorney however, that even if Johnson was receptive to their proposals, Congressional radicals, already antagonized by the President's leniency, were in no mood to yield any further allowances. Ballinger was aware of the radicals' growing power but believed that regardless of their "influence over policy" he would try to "present the Texas position." No sooner had Ballinger made arrangements to go to Washington than Canby notified the jurist he was having difficulty obtaining the necessary paperwork. Despite daily assurances that Ballinger's credentials were on their way, Canby finally admitted that he could not secure the appropriate papers because he was being pressured by Texas radical Unionists not to let Ballinger go. In the radicals' view, Ballinger's trip "portended evil—they opposed me representing Texas for I had been engaged in the most odious work of the rebellion—confiscating their property whilst they were fighting for the Union." After hearing Canby's admission Ballinger decided to postpone his mission to Washington. Without a letter from Canby, the Galvestonian would "have no standing from which to be heard." A dejected Ballinger now rationalized that a journey to Washington at this juncture "would effect nothing—the policy as to Texas already has been determined."[9]

Before leaving New Orleans, Ballinger wrote to Andrew Johnson "so

"The spirit of the people are ready for submission"

as to present the subject of my mission [to New Orleans] fully before him." The attorney worried that Johnson might interpret his meeting as an usurpation of presidential authority. Most Southerners, including Ballinger, considered Johnson a vindictive turncoat. Yet, like it or not, he was now president of the United States and Ballinger sensed that in the future Johnson might become the South's best ally against the radicals. Ballinger also had a personal stake in currying the new president's favor. On May 29, 1865, Johnson issued a general amnesty absolving most Confederates for their illegal wartime activities. However, there were several classes of ex-Confederates to whom Johnson had forbidden a general pardon. Ballinger fell within two of these: as receiver of alien enemy property he was considered an official of the Confederate government, and his assets, despite the war, were still above the twenty thousand dollar mark. Only upon direct petition to the president could former insurgents in Ballinger's classification receive a pardon.[10]

In his letter Ballinger never apologized for supporting secession nor recanted his service to the Confederacy. He nonetheless did not want Johnson to consider him a secessionist and told the president that to the very end, he not only opposed secession, but until the war had begun, he did not "waiver in hope or in readiness to struggle for the restoration of the Union." Even after the war had intensified and he had become a devoted Confederate, he still believed secession "unwise and fatal to Southern interests," and "never indulged sanguine or even cheerful hopes of the future of a Southern Confederacy." Ballinger then declared that if at any time during the war he could have "restored the status quo, undone secession, and brought back a harmonious Union," he would have gladly given his life for that end. Ballinger concluded his letter by reassuring Johnson that his presence in New Orleans was "not calculated to usurp or denigrate the authority of your office."[11] Though his letter was intended only as an introduction, Ballinger knew this gesture was essential if he hoped to obtain a presidential pardon in the future.

On June 19, 1865, five days after Ballinger's return from New Orleans, Gen. Gordon Granger arrived in Galveston with eight hundred troops to begin the Federal occupation of Texas. On that day Granger read Lincoln's Emancipation Proclamation, and since that moment "Juneteenth" has been regularly celebrated by black Texans. Reactions to Granger's decree varied widely depending on the individual slave and his experience in bondage. The news of freedom prompted many slaves to leave their mainland plantations, reflecting an obvious negative view of slavery under that particular owner. Even the most "pampered" of urban slaves, such as Ballinger's, found the call of freedom too exhilarating to resist. The attorney was dismayed when three of his most "privileged" bondsmen, Sally, Lucy, and 'old Henry'—"up & left one night upon hearing the news of their emancipation. I did not know of their flight until the next day when young Ellick told me. I believed they would never leave our household—they were always provided for in the kindest & most generous manner & I would continue to do so even now. I am saddened by their running but there is nothing I can do."[12]

Two weeks later, much to Ballinger's relief Henry returned "home." He apologized for having left and "Said he was too old for his new status & wanted to live the rest of his life with us if he could." Ballinger's ex-slaves had managed to procure a small boat which they used to cross the bay to the mainland. They then walked to Houston. Henry reported that after arriving in the Bayou City, he "didn't know what to do after a few days" so he decided to return to the island. Sally and Lucy however, met "some young bucks" and they all decided to try to make their way to New Orleans. Henry told them that would be foolish, but they refused to come to Galveston with him. Hally was upset when she heard the news and wanted Ballinger to go after them, but as the attorney told his family, "They were free to do as they pleased—the law was with them. I don't believe anyone, even our negroes truly understand what it [freedom] all means."[13]

Regardless of how particular slaves responded to emancipation, all freedmen soon discovered there were strings attached to their freedom. Granger advised freedmen to remain with their former masters and work for their wages. He also warned blacks that they would not be allowed to congregate at army posts nor would they receive government support. Only the most destitute or ill would receive relief; others would not receive any assistance. He backed his order by treating idle and footloose blacks as vagrants subject to arrest. Even when traveling on highways, Texas freedmen were to have passes from their employers.[14] Ballinger was pleased with Granger's dictum and with the federal authorities' execution of most labor contracts.

Unlike many white Texans, Ballinger accepted both the end of slavery and the need to provide freedmen with "special, extraordinary, active guardianship & protection." Such assistance, Ballinger insisted, was not to be afforded by the Freedmen's Bureau but by the state. To Ballinger, local solicitude was morally responsible, economically sound, and politically strategic. If white Texans hoped to soon rid themselves of the Bureau's supposed encroachments upon their "relations with the freed peoples," then it was essential that each "community frame wise, benevolent regulations to help uplift our negroes. They are entitled to our good faith efforts & to all that our government [local and state] can accomplish to make freedom do the most & best for them. It is in their best interest & ours."[15]

Ballinger was careful to distinguish his state system of guardianship from the Black Codes being enacted in other Southern states. As Southern whites regained political control they quickly enacted laws to keep freedmen in "their place," especially as a secure labor force. These decrees were nothing other than modified versions of the antebellum Slave Codes. Ballinger condemned the codes as "intended to establish a quasi slave system wholly inconsistent with their [the freedmen's] freedom." As Ballinger rightly predicted, freedmen rebelled against the codes, making it impossible for Southern whites to have a reliable labor force. It was essential, Ballinger argued, to treat freedmen in a way "in which confidence & self-reliance should be implanted in them." He believed it imperative that white Texans showed that they were the freedmen's "true guardians & friends" and not "some Northern stranger or fanatic who will dupe them & betray them."[16]

To most Unionists, giving the state authority over the freedmen would result in the virtual reenslavement of most African Americans. To most of Ballinger's compatriots, whether they were ex-slaveholders or not, that was exactly what "home rule" implied, and thus they eagerly awaited the opportunity to reestablish racial supremacy. As Ballinger admitted to John Hancock there was still "a conviction with many [whites] so strong in the belief that servitude is their [the freedmen's] normal & best condition." Ballinger assured Hancock that he did not share such sentiments. He asserted, however, that only those "familiar with negro behaviour—their dependence & ignorance," could fully provide for them. The "strangers" of the Freedmen's Bureau, did not understand ex-slaves. Like most white Southerners, Ballinger believed the Bureau represented an effort by vengeful Unionists to "mortify, degrade, & punish the whites & not merely to protect the blacks." He considered its agents "aliens, bigots & fanatics who have prejudices & hostilities to carve & intervene between us and our negroes. They only use our negroes to promote their own power."[17]

Ballinger's concern for African Americans' welfare seems blatantly disingenuous for an ex-slaveholder. He nonetheless helped many freedmen adjust to the vagaries of their new status. "We owe them that much for the years of faithful service they have rendered to us." Whether Ballinger was motivated by guilt, an accustomed paternalism, or by purely economic and political considerations to aid local blacks in obtaining decent treatment and opportunity, is difficult to determine. For the remainder of his life, he helped his own ex-slaves as well as many other freedmen with money, food and shelter, employment, or whatever else was needed.[18] Unfortunately, not included in his commitment to helping black Texans was an acceptance of equality. To the end of his life Ballinger remained a racist, telling Guy Bryan three months before his death that he still believed "The African or negro race will never become the equal in any capacity to the white race. They simply do not have the faculties of mind, the disposition, the character, to rise much above their present condition."[19]

Soon after the Federal occupation of Texas began, the Seventy-sixth Illinois Regiment established its camp along the northern fence line of Ballinger's property. "They get water from our cistern," he grumbled, and "steal our chickens & are a very troublesome lot. They distract the ladies by their depredations & interfere with the negro women."[20] Ballinger ignored these irritations to devote his full energy to securing a presidential pardon for himself and his friends and relatives. For the attorney, a presidential pardon was an immediate necessity. Since he fell within two of the general amnesty's exception catagories, he had to be pardoned personally by the president. Until that occurred he remained subject to criminal charges under the 1862 treason act for his activities as Confederate receiver. Under the same law, his real estate, cash assets, and stocks could be confiscated, and he could neither purchase nor sell property—a crippling restriction for a lawyer heavily involved in real estate transactions and who frequently accepted property as payment for his professional services.[21]

Ballinger was painfully aware of his circumstances, and on the eve of his departure from Galveston he observed that he felt he had "no rights and was not my own master until I get my pardon." Ballinger was fortunate that his prewar unionism was still remembered, especially by Provisional Governor Andrew Jackson Hamilton who promptly reviewed his case. Hamilton recommended Ballinger's pardon "very kindly & promptly and in strong terms." Soon after receiving Hamilton's endorsement the Galvestonian was inundated by requests from local businessmen wanting to retain him to carry their petitions along with his own to Washington for presidential approval. Before leaving Galveston Ballinger had the petitions of "Uncle Jimmy, Uncle Tommy, T. R. McMahan, Allen

Lewis, R. J. Hutchings & T. W. House." Hamilton also recommended other prominent Galvestonians and they agreed to pay all of Ballinger's expenses "for coming on to attend to their cases." As Ballinger further noted, if he was successful in obtaining his compatriots' pardons, he would "realize something considerable & most acceptable at this low ebb in my fortunes."[22]

Ballinger also received from Hamilton the useful information that his uncle, Green Adams, a prominent Kentucky Unionist, had developed a close relationship with Andrew Johnson while serving as a Treasury Department cotton agent in Nashville during the war. At that time Johnson was provisional governor of Tennessee. Ballinger learned that Adams was already in Washington, hoping Johnson would remember his wartime services and appoint him to a lucrative government post. Over the next several months Ballinger relied heavily on Adams's contacts but he owed his own pardon to the influence of another relative: his brother-in-law, Samuel F. Miller, associate justice of the United States Supreme Court.

Miller, a staunch Whig-Republican, had been appointed to the Supreme Court by Abraham Lincoln. Miller and Ballinger had been close friends since their youth, and despite often heated arguments over political differences, they remained close even through the war years. Much to Ballinger's surprise, the war had tempered significantly his brother-in-law's social conservatism. Miller voted to sustain much of the radical agenda, especially the radicals' concern for the freedmen's welfare. The Court, insisted Miller, should be particularly supportive of those congressional measures that "place the negro on an equality with the white man in all his civil rights." In Miller's view, the Supreme Court had a moral obligation to protect freedmen from white reprisals.[23]

Though sympathetic with the radicals' social policies, Miller disagreed with those Republicans who believed Reconstruction was a congressional rather than a presidential responsibility. These "ultra impracticables," Miller charged, had little faith in Johnson, and wanted "to precipitate a rupture" with the president rather than try to work with him, which the justice believed essential for the nation's welfare. Much to Ballinger's relief, Miller believed it "wholly unwise & mischievous" for the radicals to pursue a policy of revenge "upon the whole of the Southern people." To Miller, the radicals' purpose was "to punish & degrade the Southern people," while establishing themselves "as special friends of the President and his policy, in order that they may monopolise the executive patronage."

Since the executive-legislative conflict did not yet require the vindication of any constitutional provisions, the Court should act "prudently" and not challenge Congress on key Reconstruction issues.[24]

Miller agreed with Ballinger that the majority of Southerners should be treated with "liberality & forgiveness." The justice, however, insisted that before a restoration of civil rights could occur, white Southerners had to "abandon their former leaders and evince a sincere intention to yield slavery, and give a true and loyal support to the federal government." Miller was convinced that Ballinger and his compatriots desired "a reunion on terms as pleasing to the rebels as can be obtained." Miller was especially disturbed by Ballinger's inference that those Southerners who had rebelled against the federal government, no matter "how prominently," should be exempted from "personal guilt." To Miller, such a claim was a "complete absurdity." Miller stunned Ballinger when he raised the question of whether the Galvestonian and his fellow Confederates should be charged with treason. The justice was convinced that examples had to be made of those Southerners whose actions against the federal government were blatantly traitorous. Though favoring the death penalty, Miller did not believe it should be applied en masse. Much to Ballinger's relief, the justice "would limit it to a half dozen of the most prominent and most wicked." Miller was certain these individuals "were governed by ambition to become the leaders of a Southern aristocracy." Even more egregious to Miller than these individuals' supposed desire for power was their "manifest disregard for their constitutional obligations to the Union." To Miller, this was their most unpardonable crime, for in the process their "wanton actions" inflicted upon the nation "misery and horror incapable of description."[25]

Ballinger naturally wondered whether his esteemed brother-in-law considered him a traitor as well for his actions as receiver. Much to his chagrin, Miller did indeed charge him with disloyalty, confessing that "reason dictated that in some way you should be punished." Miller also admitted that if Ballinger had been "one of the most eminent in guilt of all the rebels," he should then "suffer the highest punishment which the law provides for all."[26]

Ballinger was shaken by his brother-in-law's chastisement. In a letter to Hally, he related Miller's conclusion that "if I were anyone else, he wd not hesitate to see me swing from the gallows." However, five days after receiving his scolding, Ballinger heard that Miller had supplied him with letters of introduction to both President Johnson and Secretary of State William Seward. In his endorsements the justice stated that he had known

"The spirit of the people are ready for submission"

Ballinger "since he was ten years old intimately & I have never known a man whose integrity I would rely on more confidently." Ballinger was relieved by his brother-in-law's change of heart. As Miller later told Ballinger that even though he believed him guilty of treason, his actions "had not in the least affected my estimate of your character for honor & truthfulness, nor diminish my affection for you." Thanks to Miller, within a week of his arrival in the capital, Ballinger's pardon was granted—at Seward's personal request. Recording his receipt of pardon on August 25, 1865, Ballinger acknowledged that Miller's letters were largely responsible. "A Godsend," he remarked. "There is no one in the world I respect more highly than Miller or outside of my own direct family am more attached to. He is as much like a brother as I could desire. I love him most warmly & devotedly."[27]

Andrew Johnson might have been less inclined to grant Ballinger's pardon had he known of the jurist's opinion of him four months earlier. In the editorial columns of the Houston *Telegraph*, Ballinger wrote, "Of all the partisans, Andrew Johnson has ever been the most unscrupulous, the most extreme, and the most vindictive. He is the vilest of all demagogues and is known by all men to lack integrity, to lack justice, to lack honor, to lack humanity . . . it is our sincere belief, that no man is less fit to bind together, to sustain, to guide."[28] But circumstances alter perceptions, and with his pardon in hand Ballinger, despite lingering reservations, had little choice but to "sustain him against the other wing [the radicals] of the Republican party."[29]

Ballinger's success in obtaining his own pardon proved impossible to duplicate for his clients. By the time of Ballinger's pardon, Johnson's initial policy of excluding Confederate leaders and other disloyalists from political affairs had unraveled completely. By August 1865 thousands of Southerners, the majority of whom had been barred from the general amnesty because of their income, had filed for individual pardons. At first the president cautiously granted amnesty, but by September 1865 they were being issued by the several hundreds per week. By early 1866 over seven thousand Southerners excluded from amnesty under the twenty-thousand-dollar clause had received clemency. By the spring of 1866 Johnson had granted 13,500 pardons out of about fifteen thousand applicants.[30] Ballinger thus was not surprised when he heard from a variety of sources that "the North was complaining of too many pardons—many Republicans are alarmed at the great number of pardons being granted & are vigorously protesting to Seward and are looking to him for its correction." He also heard from

Seward that a special Executive Bureau was being organized to screen all applications because Johnson was supposedly "overwhelmed with personal solicitations." Apparently his information was correct, for the number of pardons granted dropped "from about twenty to two a day."[31]

In obtaining his fellow Texans' pardons, Ballinger used a two-pronged approach, engaging first in personal appeals to Johnson, Seward, and Attorney General James Speed. In his entreaties Ballinger emphasized not only his clients' character but also their "desire to once again become Citizens of the United States, in complete fidelity to the Government." He then argued that geographical and economic factors required their full membership in society if Texas's prewar commercial prosperity was to be restored. They were businessmen, he declared, most of whom were "not criminated in secession—useful to the community in the restoration of business—that in a commercial town [Galveston] for its businessmen to be under disability prevented its future development." Ballinger also reminded government officials that Texas needed "a little special attention" because the number of pardons granted to its citizens was "behind hand" compared to the other former Confederate states.[32]

Despite an endorsement from Samuel Miller who told Johnson, "You may rely implicitly on any statement of Mr. Ballinger as to matter of fact. I think he would not recommend the pardon to your Excellency of any person whom he believed would use his liberty to the injury of the federal government," the Texan still was having difficulty getting the president to examine his clients' cases. Only his brother-in-law's, Guy Bryan's, was "on the Pres.ts table. Things are in confusion. I seem as far from my objective as at the beginning—don't know what to do next." After several more days of inaction, Ballinger realized that an intermediary was essential if he hoped to obtain amnesty for his clients. Ballinger was fortunate in that he did not have to look very hard to find someone with inside connections. At his disposal was his wily uncle, Green Adams, whom Ballinger was certain was on the most intimate terms with the president. Once Ballinger engaged Adams as his pardon agent, the president's docket, which the Texan had been told was "cluttered & chaotic," miraculously cleared up.[33]

Three days after enlisting his uncle's assistance, Ballinger was granted a personal audience with the president, which had been arranged by Adams. On September 1, 1865, Ballinger met with the seventeenth president of the United States. Johnson received the attorney "most courteously," and before they discussed the business at hand, the jurist thanked the president for granting his pardon. He then assured Johnson he would do all in his

"The spirit of the people are ready for submission"

power "to contribute to the restoration of govt & order in Texas." Ballinger then told Johnson that his was the only pardon so far from Texas and that he had brought many applications recommended by Provisional Governor Hamilton. Ballinger hoped Texas's "remoteness and the no. of pardons granted from other States," would prompt Johnson "to give greater attention to the Texas cases." The president asked Ballinger to leave a list of applicants and to call again the next day. That evening in his hotel room, Ballinger confided to his diary his impressions of Andrew Johnson. "He is a rather good looking man—tho' how far from prejudice I dont know. He has a good deal of dignity of person—though not much ease of manner. I think he enjoys the importunities of the rebels, and thinks it right to force them to humiliate themselves all in his power."[34]

With Adams acting as his pardon broker, and within a few weeks of his meeting with the president, Ballinger secured the pardons of forty fellow Texans. For his services his uncle received thirty-five hundred dollars. Ballinger too profited from the venture. His net receipts totaled approximately five thousand dollars, exclusive of the payment to Adams, and he obtained further fees of twenty-five hundred dollars on his return home, in cash, land, and gold.[35]

Ballinger could not return to Galveston without first stopping in Kentucky to visit his parents and relatives. When he showed up in Barbourvile, he provided a pleasant surprise for his family. Ballinger wondered, however, if James Franklin would disapprove of his support for the Confederacy. The elder Ballinger and many other members of the Ballinger clan had remained loyal to the Union during the war and were now, according to Ballinger, displaying a "proscriptive vindictive Unionism" toward those kinsmen who had supported the Confederacy. Much to Ballinger's relief, James Franklin accepted his wartime activities "as being a matter of patriotism & devotion to principle." Ballinger's stepmother, Elizabeth, "sympathized with the South throughout" and told her son she could not have "aided in any way war against her own children."[36]

Much to Ballinger's dismay, his father had been sick for several months, but upon seeing his son, "he jumped from his chair and rushed with open arms to greet me. He said my coming invigorated him." According to Ballinger's mother, until their son's arrival, James Franklin "just sat around filled with despair over the war." Ballinger discovered his father's grief was only partly the result of war. James Franklin was broke financially but being the proud patriarch, could never admit his condition to his son. Only after hearing from his mother of his parents' hard times, was Ballinger aware that life had not gone well for the Kentucky Ballingers for quite some time.[37]

Ballinger was so disturbed by his parents' penury that he vowed the moment he was back in Texas he would sell property in Houston and use the money to bring his parents to Galveston. The attorney believed his Houston property would yield five thousand dollars, which would be enough to build his parents "a comfortable home of their own." Ballinger was certain that moving his family to Texas was "best for their happiness" as well as his own, for "Nothing would gratify me so much as to see father and mother united with their children for the remainder of their lives—& happily situated."[38] In the summer of 1867, James and Elizabeth Ballinger moved from Kentucky, into their new home on Galveston Island.

As in the past, Ballinger found a trip to Kentucky to be exhilarating, rekindling in him a desire "to put forth all my energy & devote myself as fully as is possible to my career & not let other interests or passions distract me from what is most important—my family & practice." Ballinger returned to Galveston on November 25, 1865, ready "to do nothing but the Law."[39]

No sooner was Ballinger home in Galveston than he and Tom Jack immersed themselves into resurrecting their lucrative prewar practice. Now that he had assumed responsibility for his parents' security, Ballinger was especially eager to regenerate his antebellum business. By the early months of 1866 the firm was employed in over one hundred suits on the District Court level alone. "We take lunch in a basket and do not come home to dinner," Ballinger remarked. "I have never in my life however, been more indefatigably industrious—Our business prospects seem to be excellent."[40]

In many ways Ballinger's practice resembled other law firms in post–Civil War Texas. However, because of their kinship, the partnership of Ballinger and Jack was much more intimate than most of their associates' arrangements. The two shared equally all work, expenses, and income. Most other establishments had two or three partners, usually unrelated, carrying on their individual work while sharing overhead expenses in a common office. Yet, like their colleagues, Ballinger and Tom Jack occasionally used clerks—apprentices studying the law under the tutelage of one of the partners—to help perform routine legal tasks around the office. Those "reading the law" in such an office were being trained for the bar, but not necessarily to become a member of the firm. Before the war Ballinger and Jack had emerged as one of the premier firms in realty law.

Thomas M. Jack, WPB's brother-in-law, and law partner from 1854 to 1880.
Photograph courtesy Rosenberg Library, Galveston, Texas.

However, the disruption of the war and its immediate aftermath for awhile forced Ballinger and Jack to become a more traditional establishment. Like most of their peers, they too accepted work in a variety of areas ranging from divorce to probate, personal injury, and debt collection. Individual attorneys established their reputations either by erudtion or theatrics in the courtroom—for Ballinger it was clearly the former. Firms' reputations depended on their most distinguished partners, and the leading ones often included individuals such as Ballinger who gained notoriety outside as well as inside the halls of justice.[41]

Though Ballinger had long since become the more celebrated jurist, Tom Jack was no second-rate attorney. Jack was a more than capable lawyer who quite possibly would have emerged on his own as one of his brother-in-law's more noted rivals. He was a confident, hard-working yet relaxed partner, who carried his load. An omniverous and rapid reader, Jack made it his job in each case to go through all the relevant decisions he could locate, either in the firm's library or in other libraries around the state, as well as in the usual legal reference works and dictionaries. Because so many litigation subjects were repetitious, he compiled a kind of legal index in a large book where he recorded the precedents he discovered on a wide variety of topics. As Ballinger and Jack increasingly dealt with "business" firms, especially railroad companies, Jack prepared a separate, smaller notebook entitled "Corporations." In addition, he drew up briefs for many individual cases, outlining the principal issues and precedents. For his part, Ballinger did virtually all the paperwork involved in cases, preparing even the most formal and routine documents in his own hand. Ballinger recognized the contribution Jack's research made to his courtroom victories, and thus fees from cases were divided equally. On many cases the partners worked together, with Jack doing the research and bookwork while Ballinger dealt with clients and the courts. Ballinger and Jack handled many cases independently, or with other attorneys. In a rough division of labor, Jack managed the office and supervised the students who were reading law with the firm, while Ballinger more often appeared in court. Perhaps the most important role Jack played was in keeping his brother-in-law from becoming obsessed with his work. It was always Jack who urged Ballinger to slow down, take a vacation, or to go home after putting in a fifteen-hour day at the office. On many occasions Jack literally would have to physically force a stubborn Ballinger out of the office. If not, Ballinger would have remained at his office, asleep at his desk, which he frequently did anyway. Because he was not as compulsive or as driven by feelings of insecurity as Ballinger, Tom Jack was content being the "junior partner."[42]

The majority of Ballinger's postwar cases involved debt collection, for which he usually charged 10 percent of the amount recovered plus costs. It is difficult to determine how many cases were settled short of a lawsuit; nevertheless, records indicated that a substantial portion of Ballinger's cases were resolved in court. Of approximately 190 cases filed in the Galveston District Court between October 21, 1865, and November 21, 1867, in which either Ballinger or Tom Jack appeared as counsel, 146 either involved debts, failure to honor a contract, or were an effort to enforce a judgment by attaching the defendant's property or by garnishing his wages. Many of these cases resulted in default judgments after the defendant failed to appear in court. Also a number of Ballinger's cases were dismissed on the plaintiff's motion, probably after an out-of-court settlement had been reached.[43]

Late 1865 and early 1866 saw a number of inquiries from Ballinger's old Northern clients wanting to know the status of their prewar collections and the prospects of recovering them. Ballinger too was interested in reviving his "Northern connections," which had been one of the firm's more lucrative prewar enterprises. Much to Ballinger's joy, many of his former clients were eager to retain him as their collection agent and immediately began sending him new business. Apparently, these clients did not hold the Texan's actions as Confederate receiver against him. In fact, A. Blum and Company of Boston, which had lost considerable merchandise in confiscation sales presided over by Ballinger, not only engaged the Galvestonian as their advocate but referred new business to the firm as well.[44]

Fear of suit, his clients' welfare, and possible federal pressure prompted Ballinger into learning the whereabouts of confiscated property and notes. Beginning in the late fall of 1865 he started sending letters of inquiry to former Texas receivers to whom he had forwarded Northern-owned notes. However, by February 1866 he was still unable to account for 159 claims of 67 Northern creditors. Ballinger was sued only once for losses arising from his activities as receiver, and settled out of court for an unknown sum. He was fortunate for in such suits his pardon would not have protected him since it applied only to federal prosecution. Ultimately, the United States Supreme Court ruled that acts committed under Confederate law were not immune from private civil suits.[45]

Ballinger was also anxious to resume his role as administrator for a number of estates—a lucrative duty requiring little effort and meshing nicely with his and Jack's ongoing side business of land and timber speculation. For a minimal amount of work, largely confined to writing letters and drafting titles of conveyance, Ballinger derived a steady income, usually ranging between two and three thousand dollars annually. Those amounts were based on a commission for tracts of land sold, usually 10 percent but sometimes as much as 15 percent.[46]

A rather costly real estate adventure engaged in by Ballinger during this period indicated how quickly he was able to rejuvenate his practice. In the summer of 1866 Ballinger and Tom Jack purchased half a block of downtown Galveston for ten thousand dollars in gold. The jurist not only built office buildings on the property, spending seven thousand on construction costs, but over the next three years spent another twenty thousand building his firm's new three-storied office to accommodate an expanding practice. The new office was designed to house both their firm and rental offices for other island attorneys.[47] It appeared Ballinger was attempting to centralize Galveston's legal services under his auspices while establishing his firm as Texas's most complete legal resource center.

Ballinger's was a very ambitious and expensive goal. He realized that only the most thorough library would attract reputable jurists. Thus, while in Washington securing his pardon he began building his future athenaeum by purchasing a complete set of reports for every state as well as the English reports. Prices were not cheap nor were the books easily obtained. Even readily available sets sold for five dollars per volume and none were quoted for less than $4.50 by Baker & Voorhis, Ballinger's New York dealer. Ballinger spent over a thousand dollars on the library while in Washington and budgeted at least that much yearly until his library was as exemplary as he intended. Offering to sell the library to the Texas Supreme Court in 1874, Ballinger boasted to Chief Justice Oran Roberts that "The law book sellers who come to Texas say that our library is the best in the South—public or private."[48]

One of Ballinger's more professionally fulfilling postwar endeavors was his political and financial assistance in George Paschal's effort to codify Texas's laws. Ballinger and Paschal had been friends and colleagues since the early 1850s. During that troubled decade they became especially close, collaborating on numerous projects to promote the professionalization of the Texas bar. They also united on other issues ranging from railroad construction and the election of judges, to trying to prevent their state's secession. Once Texas seceded and joined the Confederacy, Ballinger became the passionate rebel while Paschal remained an ardent

Unionist. Despite taking different sides, the jurists' respect for each other prevented philosophical differences from destroying their friendship. Throughout the war years they remained close friends, communicating regularly and candidly discussing their disparate views about the "Revolution in a friendly spirit."[49]

Like Ballinger, Paschal adhered to the same professional ethos when it came to law and politics; both agreed that nothing discredited the profession more than lawyers-turned-ambitious office seekers. Like his Galveston colleague, Paschal never sought or accepted any political office. Though a Jacksonian, Paschal was not an antebellum populist agitator, a "have-not" with grievances against the planter oligarchy or other elites. Like Ballinger, Paschal's faith in popular government was tempered by a conservative conviction that the purpose of the law was not to enforce freedom but to protect property.[50] Because Ballinger and Paschal shared such devotion to the rule of law, it was only natural for them to join forces after the war and produce one of the nation's most complete legal reviews: *A Digest of the Laws of Texas*.

Paschal actually began his digest during the war, spurred on by his own arrest in 1863 for disloyalty. The charges brought against the Austin jurist were so specious that even the judge-advocate at his military trial later remarked that the nature of Paschal's recreancy was "so peculiarly and completely within the province of civil authorities," that there was no case for the action of the military tribunal. Even Ballinger, the loyal Confederate, was outraged that his friend had been hauled before "this illegal convening. I deplore this latest action of the Military & will do my utmost to see this injustice undone."[51]

Ballinger felt "bound by honor & loyalty to a dear friend" to do all he could to get Paschal released. Unleashing a wave of protests to Confederate officials from top to bottom, Ballinger was determined to "stop this usurpation of civil authority." Ballinger viewed Paschal's arrest as "that extreme example when the power of the military usurps proper civil authority and abuses those who had entrusted to them such power, believing that it would never turn on the People." Despite Ballinger's entreaties and public criticism, Confederate authorites refused to drop the charges of disloyalty against Paschal. Ballinger's relentless effort, however, forced the military court to reconsider its original accusations. Ultimately all the commission could prove was that Paschal was guilty of neglecting to render his property for assessment and consequent failure to pay the Confederate war tax. For this "crime" Paschal suffered the penalty of the law which required the confiscation and sale of all property and the imposition of a double tax.[52]

More than ever both men came to realize that Paschal's ordeal was largely the result of chaotic legal conditions. Not only were civil courts closed, but publication of all court reports had ceased. "It was hard enough," Paschal told Ballinger, "to keep the Court within bounds when the decisions were reported. What we shall have when they are dependent upon memories and upon records, subject to be expunged, Heaven knows."[53] Soon after the war's end Paschal turned to Ballinger for assistance. His most immediate needs were money and his friend's moral and political support, without which he knew he would have difficulty getting his digest published and circulated. By the summer of 1865 Paschal had run out of funds to finish the first volume. Beginning in August 1865 Ballinger loaned Paschal close to a thousand dollars over the next year so he could complete his undertaking "in a timely & thorough manner." As Ballinger further told Paschal, "You have labored too long & hard over the past years & have overcome great obstacles to allow this great enterprise to fail now. I pledge I will do all I can to see this through to the end." Paschal knew it would be some time before he would be able to generate enough revenue from the book's sale to repay Ballinger. In the meantime, as an act of good faith, Paschal turned over to Ballinger several cases which he hoped would be "ample compensation for all you have done." Ballinger gladly agreed to the arrangement and over the next year made substantially more money off Paschal's cases than he had loaned to the Austin jurist. In one settlement case alone Ballinger made over four thousand dollars. Not a bad return for giving an old friend a helping hand.[54]

Perhaps more important than his financial assistance was Ballinger's willingness to help Paschal politically. Because of his wartime unionism and subsequent support of the radical agenda, Paschal feared his unpopularity would hamper his work's acceptance. Paschal was also convinced that without the signet of "the legal fraternity," of which Ballinger was its "greatest luminary," his digest would have little public appeal. Paschal believed all his apprehensions would be relieved if Ballinger would write letters to the state's leading newspapers "with the weight of your name boldly attached to them." Paschal was certain that if Ballinger did this his work would be well received throughout the state.[55] Once again Ballinger agreed to help his friend, spending the summer months of 1866 writing countless letters to the state's most respected journals recommending Paschal's digest. By the time of the first volume's release Ballinger had secured public endorsements from some of Texas's most widely circulated publications. Thanks to Ballinger, Paschal could count on the advocacy of the Houston *Telegraph*, both the Galveston *News* and *Civilian*, the Austin *State Gazette*, the Dallas *Herald*, and even the intensely partisan and rabidly secessionist Clarksville *Standard*—a feat Ballinger confessed, requiring his "utmost skills as a lawyer" in cajolery and browbeating.[56]

Thanks to Ballinger's unrelenting support, the *Digest*'s first volume finally appeared in October 1866, and was hailed by the Galveston *News* as "an accomplishment of massive proportions." Paschal was immensely proud of his efforts, and never one to sell himself short, he proclaimed to Ballinger it was "unlike any law book ever printed in America. It will live as long as Texas laws survive. It is the most complete production ever published—every section has all the labor that is necessary—it is beautiful." In many ways Paschal's work was indeed "unlike any other" legal text in the country. Its uniqueness was its arrangement of all the state laws: laws in force, repealed laws, and any notes concerning changes in judicial construction were all placed side by side. "The object," Paschal declared, "has been at all times to give the old law the mischief and the remedy in the same view." Beginning with an annotated United States Constitution, Paschal also appended annotated versions of the Constitution of the Republic of Texas, the Articles of Annexation, the Constitution of 1845, the Ordinances of Secession, and both the provisional and permanent Confederate Constitutions. To this he added the recently adopted state ordinances and the subsequent Constitution of 1866. All of this preceded the codification of statutes.[57]

Despite endorsements from leading journalists, attorneys, and politicians, the legislature refused subscription. The lawmakers' rejection was partially, if not wholly, political. It seemed that from the beginning of his effort, Paschal's politics kept getting in the way of the digest's success. Too many Texans still had axes to grind with the Austin jurist for his wartime unionism. Ballinger was as distressed as Paschal by the legislature's rejection, for he too had invested much money and time in the *Digest*'s completion. Although understanding "the people's resentment of Paschal for his Unionism," Ballinger believed it was wrong for them to continue "to bear such animus toward him. The war is over—it is time to forgive & forget, for reconciliation. Paschal has proven himself with his work to be a noble & honest man—devoted to the Law which should stand above all else."[58]

In a letter written soon after the legislature's veto, Ballinger tried consoling a distraught Paschal. Ballinger too felt "the same deep sense of betrayal & anger," for as he reminded his friend, he had been for some time as "intimately connected with the project as its author." Ballinger was equally disdainful of "the little minds that have blocked your success." Ballinger counseled patience, for "The present does not matter—it is what we leave behind for posterity, for our children & their children, is what matters most. You must find solace in knowing you have assembled a great masterpiece of the Law & that the law lives on forever."[59]

Not surprisingly the digest was well received nationally, especially in the Northeast, where Paschal secured over a hundred prepaid subscribers in New York even before the book's release in Texas. He also received orders from another hundred customers in Philadelphia and Boston and dozens more from Baltimore. By 1875 the digest had been through five editions, each containing the necessary revisions covering Reconstruction through the promulgation of the 1875 state constitution. In fact, when the constitutional convention of that year met to draft Texas's present document, the delegates were provided a copy of Paschal's digest. Ballinger's prediction that Paschal's work would someday become "one of the Law's great masterpieces" clearly came true.[60] Paschal, with Ballinger's help, succeeded in bringing order to Texas laws at a time when the state was immersed in its greatest political and legal turmoil. In a deeper sense, the digest was testimony to both Ballinger's and Paschal's commitment to the rule of law; ensuring that the "long, heroic struggle" of John Marshall and Joseph Story would not be foresaken on the Texas frontier.

Chapter Nine

"TO FILL THE FULL MEASURE OF MY AMBITIONS"

Despite a pledge to refrain from "all political causes & devote all my energies to my practice & family," Ballinger found that no matter how hard he tried he could not suppress his passion for politics and at least "offer some opinions" on the various issues affecting Reconstruction Texas. For example, though he did not attend the gathering, Ballinger was keenly interested in the proceedings of the convention for the 1866 constitution, which was drafted under federal mandate and became the state's new charter.[1]

Ballinger was particularly concerned with the discussion of changing the structure and function of the Texas Supreme Court. In letters to Oran M. Roberts, chairman of the judiciary committee, former governor Elisha M. Pease, and delegate John Hancock, Ballinger outlined a number of interesting proposals. To Roberts he revealed that his political thinking was still fundamentally Hamiltonian. The war had little effect on Ballinger's conservatism, especially when it came to safeguarding the legal system from democratic excesses. As he explained, "the justices of the Court should be appointed by those possessing the highest knowledge of the Law and the legal system—from among the ranks of the State's most able lawyers & members of the Bar with the <u>highest</u> <u>reputation</u>. It is imperative that once chosen, these men sh.d be removed as much as is possible from partisan politics. To elect judges <u>en</u> <u>masse</u> leads to a popularity contest which brings to the forefront not the most qualified but only the most popular and usually the least able lawyer."[2]

Ballinger realized his suggestion of an appointed judiciary was unpopular. The Texas democratic tradition was too entrenched to propose that important officers would no longer be subject to popular approval. As George Paschal reminded Ballinger, though justices were "never entirely free of political influences—we cannot guard against human imperfection," an elected judiciary was an "essential component of a democratic government—an almost universal rule that cannot be changed."[3]

Ballinger also proposed that the high court's justices be elected for longer terms and that the chief justice be elected indirectly, being either the candidate receiving the most votes, or the one chosen by the justices from among themselves. Ballinger was certain his provisions were necessary to avoid "the waste of talent" that resulted when several well-qualified candidates ran for the office of chief justice. He also urged that the number of justices be expanded from three to five, for in Ballinger's opinion most justices were "not in the most robust health. I have not seen a consecutive week when at least one of the judges was not absent, or not in working order from indisposition of himself or family, or from an accidental cause." Ballinger concluded that three judges could not do "the manual labor" necessary to carry out the functions "of this most vital department of the Gov.t."[4]

Finally, he suggested a legislative advisory role for the Supreme Court under which magistrates might recommend laws to the legislature. Though his last proposition fell on deaf ears, many of Ballinger's urgings were adopted. The court was expanded from three to five justices and the chief justice was made a nonelective official chosen by his fellow justices. Also, the terms of the court's justices were increased from four years to ten, an idea even a democrat like George Paschal approved as being "excellent in keeping good judges."[5]

Though initially hostile to Andrew Johnson, whom he feared would have "a natural & infinitude of revenges to satisfy," Ballinger's opinion of the president changed considerably after Johnson pardoned him. Ballinger's abrupt change of attitude reflcted his realization that Johnson's Reconstruction policies, especially when compared with those of the radicals, were by far the most favorable to the South. After modifying Lincoln's "ten percent" proposal, Johnson, like his predecessor, expected Southern whites to take the lead in establishing new state governments loyal to the Union.[6]

Ballinger never extended his approval beyond the president to the Northern wing of the Democratic Party. He was convinced the majority were as determined as their Republican counterparts "to degrade & punish the South." Despite his suspicion of Northern Democrats, Ballinger was willing to give Andrew Johnson more than just verbal support. Along with other local conservatives Ballinger helped form a Galveston-based Johnson-Union club through which the president's Reconstruction program was actively promoted. Similar organizations, emerged throughout Texas, and it was decided to hold a statewide convention in July 1866 in Navasota to elect delegates to attend the National Union Convention in Philadelphia that summer. The gathering was to be a rally of the president's supporters from across the nation. Ballinger was chosen as a member of the Galveston delegation to attend the Navasota convention.[7]

Much to Ballinger's disappointment, the Navasota convention initially degenerated into a gathering of Lost Cause extremists who had little if any intention of allying with Northern Democrats. The majority of the delegates harbored "great feelings of animosity & suspicion" toward all Northerners, whether they were Democrats or even copperheads. According to Ballinger, the sole purpose of these "hot enthusiasts" was "to unite all the Secessionists here, go to Philadelphia en masse and there display their devotion to the Rebellion. They expect the others [Northern Democrats] to accept their platform without any compromises or concessions." The Galvestonian feared such a display of arrogance would prove disastrous for Johnson and Presidential Reconstruction.[8]

Fortunately Ballinger and other more temperate men ultimately gained control of the proceedings. Ballinger was chosen chairman of the resolutions committee, and after "dismissing the hotheads" from his committee, decided to personally frame the convention's declarations. Many voiced disapproval of Ballinger's draft because it denied the right of secession. Despite inflammatory speeches and personal insults, Ballinger remained calm, determined not "to let the mindless fanatics have their way—to impose on us a platform that is divisive & will only lead to further degradation & despair." The attorney replied to one particularly annoying secessionist that Texans had settled the question of secession, "that the right did not exist—that all argum.t on the subject had been closed by the results of the war. The question of honor was were we truthful in that declaration or did we speak to deceive others if not ourselves." Ballinger then warned the convention that if Texans continued to advocate the legality of secession, then the radicals' accusations and actions against white Texans were well founded. Ballinger's argument apparently was convincing, for his resolutions were adopted even though many delegates still felt "that disclaims of secession touch our honor & sensibility."[9]

Ballinger was chosen as one of the Texas delegates to attend the

Philadelphia convention but refused, citing personal and family commitments. Soon after his return to Galveston, the attorney received a message from Ashbel Smith, beseeching him to reconsider going to Philadelphia. Smith and others were upset with Ballinger's alternate, a man named William Sellers from Montgomery County. Smith was certain that once the "secessionist fanatics" discovered that Ballinger had declined, they quickly replaced him in "a wholly arbitrary procedure, without consultation with other delegates." Smith was convinced Sellers "was not a good choice. He is arrogant and will do our cause at Philadelphia more mischief than good." Smith's entreaties could not convince Ballinger to change his mind. He confessed to Smith that though he was still "hopeful of some success," he was "never sanguine that our ultimate purpose w.d be attained. The secessionist mind is still too prevalent among our citizenry to effect any positive changes. I have grave doubts that the meeting at Philadelphia will bring forth much good."[10]

On August 14, 1866, the new party's delegates from both North and South met at Philadelphia. They quickly drafted a platform calling for the immediate readmission of the Southern states. To symbolize party solidarity and sectional harmony, South Carolina's massive Governor James L. Orr marched into the hall locked arm-in-arm with the diminutive Gen. Darius N. Crouch of Massachusetts. When Andrew Johnson learned of this gesture he was so overcome with emotion that he pronounced the convention more important than any that had met since 1787. Despite dramatic displays of unity, behind the scenes dissension reigned. In the end the convention did not try to establish a new national party, but merely called for the election of pro-Johnson congressmen. In this they failed utterly. Despite all manner of oratory and maneuvering to sway voters, the November election results showed that the president had lost control of the nation. Even the most confident Republicans were astonished by their easy victory. The Grand Old Party retained its three-to-one majority in both houses of Congress and gained ascendancy in every Northern state as well as in West Virginia, Missouri, and Tennessee.[11]

Ballinger was not surprised by the Republican landslide. He doubted from the start that the new party would have much success. "I warned [Ashbel] Smith, [Guy] Bryan, & the others of this, but they remained sanguine thro to the end that the President's policies would prevail. No man who was called 'radical' had any trouble being elected. I believe it is time for further adjustments—to do what is most practical & wise, even compromise with the radicals if necessary. I do not believe they are all devils out for revenge. The great mass of them are reasonable, honest men who want what's best for the State. I will encourage others to establish relations with them & try to reach agreements."[12]

Conservatives' fears that a massive radical takeover of Texas was impending were momentarily allayed by ex-Confederate James W. Throckmorton's victory over the Unionist-Republican nominee Elisha M. Pease in the 1866 gubernatorial race. With Throckmorton's victory, white Texans made it clear that they endorsed the Democratic Party's opposition to black suffrage and supported Presidential Reconstruction. Like most conservative regimes throughout the old Confederacy, Throckmorton instituted only the most minimal changes in black-white relations, and displayed a magnanimity toward former rebels that drove the radicals to distraction. By his admininstration's second year Throckmorton was beset with a multitude of problems he seemed unable to handle.[13]

The conservatives' arrogance infuriated Unionist George Paschal. He not only condemned their "insolence" but Andrew Johnson as well for having abandoned the freedmen to the mercy of whites. Paschal found Johnson's actions "illogical," for after demanding compliance with the Thirteenth Amendment he then turned his back on black citizens, knowing they "would soon become a forgotten & oppressed people." The Austin jurist then warned Ballinger that if the freedmen's condition did not improve, and that if white Texans continued their "unrepentant ways those associating with such individuals will simply be overwhelmed."[14]

Paschal's forebodings strongly affected Ballinger. He began urging fellow Texans to accept both the Thirteenth and Fourteenth Amendments and to get back into the Union as quickly as possible. Ever the pragmatist, Ballinger realized that only by "extending to the negro a restrictive or minimal franchisement" as well as other basic rights, could white Southerners hope to avoid radical reprisals. From the beginning Ballinger had opposed the Black Codes, "strongly protesting their passage as unwise & harsh, but only a few heeded my advice. They have come back to haunt us." As he further told Guy Bryan, "We are running out of time—the storm is gathering and a worse fate is before us. We can no longer deceive ourselves—We must self-reconstruct."[15]

Unfortunately, Ballinger's admonishments went unheeded. The majority of white Texans refused to acknowledge either amendment. Thus, in the eyes of radicals both at home and in Washington, Texans had not learned their lesson; the election of so many former rebels was an insult to the Union. By the spring of 1867 Northern public opinion had

had enough of the South's unrepentant behavior. The radicals, now in complete command of Congress, responded by passing the Military Reconstruction Act of 1867 that abrogated civil authority in Texas and soon placed the state under the absolute control of Gen. Philip Sheridan, commanding the Fifth Military District of Louisiana and Texas. Within a few weeks of assuming command, General Sheridan removed James Throckmorton from office. The general then declared the 1866 constitution null and void and appointed Elisha Pease interim governor. Pease purged the state government of all ex-Confederates, replacing them with loyal Unionists. One of the many individuals removed from office was Ballinger's uncle James Love, criminal court justice for Galveston and Harris Counties.[16]

Ballinger was outraged by Love's removal. After putting together petitions signed by numerous Galveston and Houston attorneys, attesting to the judge's competency, Ballinger then sent scathing letters to both Sheridan and interim governor Pease, protesting "this most vile & unwarranted act of turpitude ever perpetrated upon a citizen of this State." Ballinger felt especially betrayed by Pease, whom he had considered to be "an honest & fair man, incapable of committing such an ignominious deed." Ballinger eventually discovered that it was not Pease who ordered the removal of ex-Confederates but the state's military commander, Gen. Joseph J. Reynolds. Prompted by complaints and editorials protesting Reynolds's purges, Winfield S. Hancock, the new Fifth Military District commander, ordered Reynolds to cease the removal of any further state officials. Hancock's reprimand had little effect on Reynolds. The general was determined to ensure a radical victory in the forthcoming 1869 elections under the recently revised state constitution.[17]

Just before the election, Pease resigned as governor, disgusted by Hancock's refusal to minimize the military's presence in the state, and by Reynolds's continued high-handedness. Pease had never liked being governor and had reluctantly assumed the job "to aid in carrying out the laws of Congress for equal rights for all." After resigning in September 1869, Pease wrote Ballinger apologizing for having "associated with such vile & unscrupulous men." He also apologized for having caused Ballinger and his family such "senseless grief & insult."[18] Never one to harbor a grudge or vendetta, Ballinger forgave Pease for his "misguided acts of passion." Within a few months of Pease's abdication, Ballinger and the Connecticut Yankee reconciled their differences and resumed their former friendship.[19]

In the 1869 gubernatorial race, the Reynolds-backed radical Edmund

"*To fill the full measure of my ambitions*"

J. Davis defeated the moderate Republican, former provisional governor Andrew Jackson Hamilton. Ballinger voted for Hamilton, believing him to be "the best alternative to radicalism." In early January 1870, the victorious radicals assumed their offices, and on February 8, the state legislature, also controlled by the radicals, convened and ratified the Fourteenth and Fifteenth Amendments. On March 30, 1870, President Grant approved the act of Congress permitting the Texas delegation to take their seats. On April 16, General Reynolds formally terminated military rule in Texas, thus bringing Reconstruction to an end in the Lone Star State.[20]

Ballinger's response to the election results was probably typical of most conservative Texans who had hoped to secure a moderate victory. He was certain "the Radicals will never be able to establish themselves here without military force. Their manipulation & control of the negro will turn the people against them. It will only be a matter of time before the people will rise up and turn them out."[21] Time eventually proved Ballinger's assessment correct. Until then Texans would witness yet another phase of Reconstruction that began on January 11, 1870, when the first Republican governor of Texas, E. J. Davis, took office.

After the election Ballinger returned to his prewar reserve, vowing yet again that he would "end once and for all, here & now, my involvement in political affairs. To the Devil with all those who constantly take me away from my family & practice. To the Devil with all politics." Moreover, a decade of intense political activism proved physically too much for the attorney. Though his asthma had subsided significantly, Ballinger still suffered from a variety of other afflictions. The most serious was chronic diarrhea, which by this point in his life was causing him greater discomfort than his asthma. In the past, Ballinger simply endured the ailment until it passed. A long bout with this malady in the spring of 1871 caused him to lose ten pounds in three days. Hally refused to call Ballinger's usual physician, telling her husband that it was time to try a specialist. It is unlikely the doctor Hally called even remotely approximated a gastroenterologist. Medicine was still years away from the professionalization and specialization that would produce such an individual. Nonetheless, Hally believed the new physician on the island, a Dr. Wiley, fresh from Harvard, was the man for her husband.[22]

Wiley was sent for and even the skeptical Ballinger admitted being impressed. Wiley diagnosed Ballinger as having "chronic irritation or inflamation of the upper intestines & that I require strict and close treatment for their cure which shd be certain & not difficult." All of Ballinger's previous doctor's treatments were discarded by Wiley, who told his patient that their remedies had done more harm than good. Wiley gave Ballinger a new prescription of drugs which, according to the good doctor, were the result of the most recent research and experimentation. Ballinger was probably apprehensive about taking new drugs but agreed to take "a tonic pill & a prescription to act on the liver—and various other medical suggestions—with rules as to diet &c." As far as Ballinger's diet was concerned, Wiley interestingly prescribed milk, oatmeal porridge, mutton, and beef—foods most of today's physicians would tell patients with chronic diarrhea to most definitely avoid. Above all else, Wiley told Ballinger "rest, quiet, and the avoidance of fatigue was essential."[23]

Ballinger agreed that the doctor's assessment of his condition was accurate. However, he did not agree with Wiley that he needed a month's rest at home. After spending only a week recuperating he was back at work. "We have a very heavy docket & I cannot allow Tom to handle all the cases alone. I feel as strong as ever & capable of constant work." Ballinger was deceiving himself. No sooner was he back at his desk than he suffered a relapse, and this time his illness was more serious than fatigue or diarrhea. On April 11, 1871, Wiley informed Ballinger that part of his right lung had collapsed and that long and complete rest was essential if he expected to regain his former health.[24]

Halley and Dr. Wiley knew that the only way Ballinger would get the rest he needed was if he took an extended trip away from Galveston and his practice for as long as possible. After considerable procrastination, Ballinger finally succumbed to his wife's insistence to go to the North and Canada as soon as possible. As the attorney remarked in his diary, he had "never seen Hally so obsessed with an idea—she is perfectly rabid about our going."[25] On June 12, 1871, Ballinger left Galveston accompanied by his wife and two oldest daughters, Lucy and Betty.

From his "Family Notebook" as well as from recollections from Betty his second-oldest daughter, it appeared that Ballinger's two oldest progeny received the greatest share of paternal attention, particularly after the death of his only son, William Pitt Jr., in 1863. Not until after his second son was born (Thomas Jack was born in 1866) did any of the other Ballinger children receive as much fatherly solicitude as Betty and Lucy. Schooled in Galveston until she was thirteen, Betty was then sent off to New Orleans to attend one of the South's most presitigious schools for young ladies, Miss Hull's French School. There she excelled academically and by the end of her first year, was first in her class. Betty credited her father for having prepared her for the rigors of academic study, especially in history and English. Perhaps most impressive was Betty's rapid learning of French, which Ballinger boasted she spoke "more eloquently and beautifully than most Frenchmen." He was proud that his daughter was "very clever & wins the praise of all who meet her." Betty "studied" at Miss Hull's for two years, but by her third year she had had enough of Hull's "constant scolding and general mean temperament." Ballinger wanted his daughter to finish her education at Miss Hull's, but Betty was as high-spirited as her mother and homesick as well. She later told her nephew that New Orleans was "a most horrible place—crowded, dirty, noisy, and most unfriendly all of the time." One month before Ballinger left for the North, Betty returned home. Betty remained at home until she was sixteen. She was then sent to Baltimore to attend the Southern Home School, where she "graduated" in 1873. She returned to Galveston where she taught school for a number of years, while becoming one of Galveston's and Texas's most noted civic and social reformers. She was also the cofounder of the Daughters of the Republic of Texas.[26]

Ballinger's oldest daughter Lucy, by contrast, was not a very serious student. She attended Miss Hull's French School in New Orleans where she "established herself in her own right." Lucy did well enough to satisfy both her parents and her teachers, and after completing her education, she too returned to Galveston. Unlike Betty, who could care less about the Galveston social scene, Lucy became quite the Galveston belle. Her coming of age to be courted was celebrated by an elaborate eighteenth birthday party, where she reportedly outshone all others. Lucy also established a reputation for being somewhat a coquette, enticing many a gentleman caller, yet repeatedly rejecting the young swains who tried to woo her to marriage. Unlike Betty who never married, Lucy eventually married the oldest son of Robert Mills, Andrew G. Mills, with whom she lived happily for forty years.[27]

A "grand tour" of the North beginning with a trip up the Mississippi was an especially exciting sojourn for Ballinger's daughters. Except for attending school in New Orleans, neither Betty or Lucy had traveled much beyond the Gulf Coast, nor had they ever been on a steamboat on the great river. Ballinger believed such mode of travel would be "an exhilarating experience" for his children, allowing them "to see the beauty & majesty of that Grand Old River & the serenity & charm of the surrounding countryside & its people." Ballinger was also certain such travel would be of great educational value as well. As the boat wound its way up the river, he never failed to point out all the historical points of interest. From the site of the battle of Vicksburg to the great plantations that "once stood out like Cathedrals" Ballinger filled his daughters' minds with the images of antebellum Southern life. Like most adolescents, Ballinger's daughters found their father's romantic musings incredibly boring. Years later Betty told her nephew Ballinger Mills, Ballinger's great-grandson, that she was indeed "often bored to tears by Papa's ramblings about this place or that. But he was so excited to tell us about all the history or quaintness of a certain place. We just listened politely, all the while hoping he would soon stop. I remember all we wanted to do was run about the boat, making nuisances of ourselves with the other passengers, and flirt with the cabin boys and the other young gentlemen on board."[28]

The Ballingers spent the summer months traveling and sightseeing in the Northern United States and throughout eastern Canada, eventually going as far as Quebec City. Hally, especially, was excited about their holiday, for it had been fifteen years since she was last "at the North." No sooner did they reach St. Paul, Minnesota, the terminus of their trip up the Mississippi, than Hally "sprang to life. She seems to be in the best health & condition I have seen her in quite some time. Every thing is new to her—the beauty of the scenery—fine farms & cattle & the busy stir of industry interest & charm her."[29]

From St. Paul, Ballinger traveled east and then southeast by train to Chicago, where he stayed only a few days because of "the awful smell of the packing houses & incessant noise." Yet, he found Chicago to be a "very industrious place," with "many nice avenues and fine homes. Took a drive thru' the city away from the main center of town, and found it to be much more pleasant than first meets the eye. I think in a few more years, it will become a very magnificent place." Ballinger found the rest of his trip through the heartland to be "delightful. The crops are luxuriant standing in the fields—and every body we saw & conversed with was friendly & looked prosperous."[30]

The Ballingers found Canada especially "wonderful this time of year—the face of the country is very beautiful. The weather is very fine cool & bracing and I feel decidedly stronger & better tho' I would not want to live here during the winter." Ballinger and his family were particularly enchanted by Canada's natural beauty which the jurist believed surpassed "all I have seen in our country. Its [Canada's] expanse defies the imagination. We traveled for hours by train & coach & saw only a few people, farms, & towns. I have never seen such a sparsely settled environment."[31]

"*To fill the full measure of my ambitions*"

After spending a few days in Toronto the Ballingers moved on to Montreal and then Quebec City, places "so rich with history, culture, & charm," that they decided to stay in Canada an extra two weeks. Besides visiting churches, monuments, museums, and gardens, Ballinger also took the time in Montreal to go "to the Court House, & stayed some time listening to proceedings in the Police Court." After getting a personal tour of the courthouse which included the library, the Texan remarked that he was "umimpressed" with the collection, believing his own library "to be much more complete." Ballinger was also certain that his Texas legal brethren would be uncomfortable with the formality of Canada's courts, especially the wearing "of gowns & a particular dress. I don't think Texas lawyers would find such requisites at all to their liking."[32]

On one of their excursions from Quebec City, the Ballingers stopped for lunch at a small tavern "owned by a Mr. Hall, a black negro man." The fact that the place was owned by a "negro" did not bother Ballinger, for as he remarked in his diary, "such was becoming more common place even in the U.S." Ballinger's daughters, however, were surprised at seeing "a negro this far North—they could not comprehend negroes outside of the U.S., or even the South for that matter." As the Ballingers were about to order, a white woman appeared, whom Hall introduced as his wife. The Ballingers were undone by this revelation. Though certainly no stranger to black-white relations (many of Ballinger's prewar clients had black mistresses), the jurist nonetheless was unwilling to accept a black man with a white woman. Apparently even the most educated and cosmopolitan Southern white males believed that inherent in all black men was an insatiable desire for white women. Ballinger was repulsed by this razing of one of his culture's most fundamental tenets. Yet, ever the Southern gentleman, he politely told Hall his children were not feeling well and that he needed to return to his hotel. Later that evening, he recorded in his diary that though the "woman seemed to be contented & if she is so, I have no right to be otherwise—but it is very repulsive to all my interests. I pray such relations will not occur in our country now that the negro is free."[33]

Despite the Hall episode, Ballinger and his family found the rest of their stay in Quebec enjoyable. By September the Ballingers were back in the United States and on September 25 Ballinger celebrated his forty-sixth birthday in New York City at the Astor Hotel, "My favorite place for lodging and dining in all of New York. After a superb meal Hally told the waiter it was my birthday and all sang 'Happy Birthday' to me & the children had gifts—a memorable celebration." Ballinger remained in New York until October 3 and then traveled to Washington, D.C., where he "took the children out every day to see our glorious Capitol and other monuments & museums around the city." After spending ten days in the nation's capital, Ballinger finally left for Galveston, arriving there on October 22, 1871, "fully restored to my former health & eager to return to work."[34]

Upon returning to Galveston, Ballinger plunged into his work with renewed vigor. However, within a few months of his return and despite a resolve not to let his penchant for civic affairs "to reign free over me again," Ballinger found he could not resist the allure of Texas politics. Always the patient pragmatist and devotee of peaceful, orderly change, Ballinger was especially alarmed by the increasing animosity of white Texans toward the radicals as well as by the white terrorism unleashed on black Texans. Though certainly no supporter of the Davis administration, Ballinger nonetheless believed the governor to be inherently "an honest & decent man who means to do good for the State." Unfortunately, Davis was "easily influenced by others" and thus had been "led down the wrong path." As he further told Fletcher Stockdale, "the Governor no longer has the capacity to retrieve the administration from the disasters which have been brought upon it by the corrupt & power-mad individuals who have had his confidence since the inauguration."[35]

Though supportive of the opposition, Ballinger remained suspicious of the Democrats and their "tendency to resort to perversity & dishonorable tactics" in order to bring down the radicals. Like many Southern conservatives, whether they were ex-Whigs or Democrats, Ballinger realized white Southerners had to convince Northerners that their movement to overthrow the radicals represented something other than a return to the old order. It was time to put the issues of Civil War and Reconstruction to rest and move forward to a new agenda of "convergence." An integral component of convergence was a willingness amongst its advocates to adapt to the reality of African Americans voting and holding office. These proponents of what became known as the New Departure argued that the Democratic Party could return to power only by promising to implement policies of moderation and accommodation, especially toward black Southerners.[36]

Like most convergence advocates, Ballinger saw himself occupying an ideological middle-ground between the doctrinaire Negrophile of the left and the fanatical Negrophobe on the right. On the the left were the radicals, the freedmen's false friends. In Ballinger's mind, the radicals were responsible for bringing about the freedmen's downfall because they pushed African Americans ahead of themselves and elevated them beyond their proper station in life as alleged subordinates. More serious to the attorney than the radicals' error of judgment was their baseness of motive. They had used their pretended friendship for political and private aggrandizement. At the other end were the Negrophobe fanatics who were not satisfied with "Home Rule" but wanted to wage aggressive war on the freedman, strip him of his basic Constituional rights, ostracize him, humiliate him, and rob him of elemental human dignity.[37]

Ballinger had always believed that every properly regulated society had superiors and subordinates, with each class acknowledging its responsibilities and obligations. Yet, each should be guaranteed its status and protected in its rights. Though believing blacks were inferior and belonged in subordinate roles, Ballinger denied that they had to be ostracized, segregated or publicly humiliated. In Ballinger's mind African American degradation was not a necessary corollary of white supremacy. As the jurist told Guy Bryan, though freedmen were "in our power," whites, particularly those of Ballinger's class, were their "custodians. We should extend to them as far as possible, all the civil rights that will help them be decent and self respecting, law-abiding & intelligent citizens. If we do not help elevate them, they will surely bring us down."[38] As can be seen from Ballinger's statement, convergence ideology was clearly an aristocratic philosophy of paternalism and noblesse oblige.

In editorials reflecting the New Departure agenda, Ballinger avoided white-supremacist appeals and Lost Cause histrionics. Instead, he called upon fellow white Texans to "gracefully and magnanimously acquiesce in accomplished facts," by "acknowledging the negro's legal status" and accepting them as "full citizens." By downplaying the issue of race, Ballinger hoped convergence would attract black votes, for African Americans would realize that their true "guardians" were patricians like himself and not the radicals. He also hoped to win the support of moderate and conservative white Republicans once they became convinced that most Democrats sincerely accepted "the accomplished facts of the War." As Ballinger further told Guy Bryan, it was time for white Southerners "to bury the past & move forward." White Texans had to accept "the fact of the negro's right to vote," and thus their acts of "intimidation & violence" toward freedmen must end.[39]

Unfortunately, Ballinger's pleas for moderation and accommodation went unheard. Like most white Southerners, few white Texans embraced the legitimacy of Reconstruction or the permanence of black suffrage.

Even among its supporters, the New Departure was less of a genuine commitment to the democratic revolution manifested in Reconstruction, than a strategy for mollifying Northerners about the Democratic Party's intentions. Most Northern whites knew that in their hearts few of their Southern brethren accepted black civil and political equality. As a Mississippi editorial declared in 1871, "We are led to this course, not through choice, but by necessity—by the stern logic of events."[40]

Ballinger found a receptive forum for the New Departure in Gulf Coast newspapers. Unfortunately, few of the state's other journals supported the plan. More reflective of white Texans' temperament than Ballinger's call for moderation, were the strident, racist editorials of the Austin *Democratic Statesman*. Beginning with its inaugural issues in July 1871, the paper consistently denounced the "despotism" of the Davis regime, calling on loyal Southerners to rise up against the Republican program which had "belabor[ed] the South with outrages and indignities of its brutal soldiery, with political disabilities, with defamation and contumely, with violence to their social life, with the mockery of republican government without representation, and with the horrid rule of a service race instructed in demoniac oppression by the basest scurf and offscourings of its myrmions." In another editorial, the *Democratic Statesman* accused any white Texan who supported "the principles of the 'new departure'" as "traitors to the white race and the Democratic Party."[41]

Ballinger was greatly disturbed by the *Democratic Statesman*'s inflammatory editorials. To the jurist, such rhetoric was "perverse in nature" and a "distortion of facts for partisan purposes." More alarming to Ballinger was the harm the *Statesman*'s comments would have on "our present cause for unity among Democrats & Republicans, black and white." As Ballinger further told Fletcher Stockdale, if white Texans hoped to throw off radical rule, it was essential to "rally to our cause the negro—they must be convinced of our sincerity to protect their rights under the Constitution." Ballinger feared that the tirades of papers like the *Statesman* would drive Texas freedmen deeper into the Radical camp. The radicals then would be able to "use the negro vote, as they have in the past, to sustain themselves in power." Ballinger also despaired that white-line bombast would alienate moderate Republicans as well, for "they too would believe they could not trust us & that we had only wanted union with them until we had driven the Radicals & negroes from office."[42]

If the New Departure's principal objective was to "redeem" the South from radical rule, then all of Ballinger's concerns that white-line politics would prevent this proved unwarranted. Indeed, even as accommodationists such as Ballinger searched for a middle ground, the majority of Southern Democrats were abandoning the centrist rhetoric of the New Departure, favoring a return to the open racism of early Reconstruction. Since the New Departure failed to attract black votes, and since the majority of white Southerners never accepted the movement, the cry of white supremacy proved to be the best tactic for mobilizing rank-and-file Democrats and even winning over scalawags. The Democrat's victory in the October Congressional elections marked the beginning of the end of radical Reconstruction in the Lone Star State.[43]

Texas "redeemers" began to reclaim their state from radical rule in the fall of 1872. Since Reconstruction in Texas had formally ended a year earlier, previously disfranchised Democrats could now vote, thus ensuring a Democratic victory. In the November elections the Democrats easily regained control of both houses of the state legislature. In the congressional elections, the party captured all five House seats, but Republicans James W. Flanagan and Morgan C. Hamilton, retained their seats in the Senate. Though the governorship was not at stake, E. J. Davis must have known his days in the governor's mansion were now numbered.[44]

Ballinger was pleased by the conservatives' resounding victory. He was optimistic the legislature would be able to repeal most if not all of the radical agenda. Yet, he feared that if the legislature moved "too boldly—with vengeful & extreme actions," then President Grant might come to Davis's rescue by reimposing military rule. Ballinger was disturbed by rumors calling for Davis's impeachment. According to his sources, Davis had declared publicly he "w.d do all he could to thwart the Legislature—& had asked military aid from the President." Ballinger was certain the Grant administration would send troops if Davis was "touched." Thus, he opposed any sort of impeachment maneuver even though friends assured him they had the voting strength necessary to accomplish such action. Typically, Ballinger counseled restraint, believing, "Events will reveal what is to be our next course of action."[45]

In August 1873 the Republicans renominated Edmund Davis for the governorship. The Democrats, meeting in Austin one month later, nominated Richard Coke of Waco, a former secessionist and captain in the Confederate army. Though Davis could claim a number of successes such as his aid to small farmers and businessmen, education programs, and full civil rights for all Texans, his defeat was inevitable. Coke and the Democrats focused their campaign on condemning the "Obnoxious Acts" of the

Twelfth Legislature while championing states' rights and their devotion to the Confederacy.[46]

During the campaign Ballinger had numerous opportunities to confer privately with Coke on a variety of issues. Coke impressed the attorney as being "a man of great integrity & straightforward manner. He is cool sensible fair & strong—he does not exhibit temper or passion." Much to Ballinger's relief, Coke showed little antipathy towards Davis and the radicals. Ballinger hoped Coke was "strong enough to resist any such notions. Many around him are urging revenge. It is time for reconciliation—for peace and harmony, unity amongst all our People—I have urged this most earnestly upon Judge Coke."[47]

Without question, the December 1873 elections were some of the most scurrilous and corrupt in Texas political history as both parties bluntly declared that power would be won depending upon who outfrauded whom. No practice was ignored. Black Texans were especially vulnerable to bullying, for their votes were essential for a Republican victory. Democratic Party thugs rode through black townships brandishing their revolvers or repeating rifles, swearing they would kill any black man who even came close to a polling booth. As a result of terrorism and fraud, few white Texans were surprised that Richard Coke was elected the state's sixteenth governor by a two-to-one margin—Coke received 85,549 popular votes to Davis's 42,663. At every level of state and county government the Democrats were victorious. Despite an attempt by the Davis administration to invalidate the election on a constitutional technicality, the Democrats refused to be denied the fruits of their victory.[48]

Over the next several weeks Davis appealed to President Grant for assistance, requesting the support of federal troops to keep him in office. Grant rejected each of Davis's requests, ultimately forcing Davis to relinquish his office on January 17, 1874. Two days before Davis left Austin, the newly elected legislature had assembled and inaugurated Richard Coke the new governor. Upon hearing the news of Davis's departure and Coke's inauguration, Ballinger confided to his diary that he never felt "more sanguine" about "the political news which is more satisfactory than at any previous time in our recent history. I feel extremely relieved & happy that no violence has taken place & that all difficulties shall be settled peaceably."[49]

Shortly after his inauguration Coke asked to see Ballinger "on a matter of upmost urgency." The attorney's meeting with Coke on the afternoon of January 23, 1874, proved to be one of the most important encounters of

"To fill the full measure of my ambitions"

Guy Morrison Bryan, Ballinger's brother-in-law and close friend, and one of Texas's most prominent 19th-century political figures. *Photograph by J. H. Rose, Galveston. Courtesy Prints and Photographs Collection, CN10513, Center for American History, University of Texas at Austin.*

his career. After an exchange of pleasantries, Coke changed the topic of conversation, telling Ballinger that as soon as the new government was stabilized, his first priority was to organize a new state supreme court and appoint Ballinger to the bench. Ballinger was overwhelmed by Coke's offer. But after some "fluttering" he regained his composure, thanked the governor "for his good opinion," and then politely told Coke that because his "pecuniary cond.n" was still "uncertain," and until he felt more solvent, he could not accept the governor's offer. Coke hoped Ballinger would change his mind, for he would realize that "the People of Texas, as well as this office, would be greatly honored by your presence on the Bench. There would be no greater service that you could perform for the People of this State."[50]

Ballinger's friends and relatives were determined to see him on the bench. From his position as Speaker of the House of the Texas legislature, Ballinger's omnipresent brother-in-law, Guy Bryan, pressured the governor to nominate Ballinger regardless of the attorney's desire to remain a private citizen. Bryan assured Coke that Ballinger would not reject the offer if the governor made it "a matter of civic duty." Thus, in another entreaty to the Galvestonian, Coke declared that "Justice to the People of Texas" demanded that Ballinger "make any ordinary sacrifice" to accept the Texas Senate's official confirmation "as an Associate Justice of the Supreme Court.[51]

The Senate's confirmation pushed Ballinger toward a crucial career decision. He now admitted that he was "drifting towards" accepting the appointment, for "it w.d be entirely to my taste—it would fill to the full the measure of my ambitions." If he waited until he felt financially solvent, "such a position might not come then. This is the very point in time for useful service to the State." Despite pressure from Coke, Bryan, and a host of others to accept his confirmation, Ballinger knew in his heart that there was only one person who could help him through his present dilemma: Hally. After twenty-four years of marriage, Hally, without question, had become her husband's closest friend and confidant. As a result of their companionate relationship, Ballinger rarely made any important family decisions without first consulting his wife.[52]

For several days Ballinger and Hally discussed "the matter of the judgeship." Sometimes their conversations lasted "all night long & into the early morning hours," until finally, after three days of intense debate, Hally prevailed, convincing her husband that his acceptance would "place a great financial burden upon our family—its future security and even present well-being." As Ballinger confided to his diary, when it came "to the test of our family's welfare Hally was invincibly opposed to my acceptance—and I have made up my mind in consultation with her fixedly not to accept the Judgeship."[53]

On the surface, Hally's desire for family security appeared to transcend all other considerations. However, years later, in a letter to Guy Bryan, Ballinger revealed "the whole truth." It was not Hally's practical nature but rather her "heart and affections secretly revolted against the idea." Yet, Hally had most "dutifully & delicately" concealed her opposition from Ballinger and he never would have known her true feelings "but for an accident." He awoke one night "from sleeplessness from this ordeal" and found Hally crying. After much pleading, he "drew from her the truth." Hally's distress was "from the idea of such a distant & most probably prolonged separation from me—that the children w.d long for my presence & our home would become a very empty & lonely place." Ballinger then confessed that it was this "discovery and the manner of it made it certain in my mind that I could not accept nomination."[54]

"To fill the full measure of my ambitions"

In a letter to Richard Coke, the attorney told the governor that he could not accept the position because of "present professional obligations." Though Hally's personal distress was the main reason for his withdrawing, Ballinger did not disclose such intimacy to the governor. He then told Coke that a supreme court justice's salary would "not afford me that exemption from pecuniary embarrassment which should be the condition, above all men, of a judge upon the bench." Not wanting to appear mercenary, Ballinger assured the governor his withdrawal was "not a question with me of gain, but of adequate support of my family." Despite Coke's recommendation for an increase in the salaries of supreme court justices, Ballinger could not be persuaded to accept appointment. On February 4, 1874, Coke regretfully complied with Ballinger's request to rescind the attorney's name from nomination.[55]

Ballinger's decision was lamented throughout the state. In the Austin *Statesman*'s opinion, there was "no more eminent jurist in this State for whose great abilities we have entertained a higher respect, or for whose private character we have cherished a kindlier or more cordial appreciation than for Judge Ballinger." The *Statesman* expressed "great regret" that Ballinger had resigned, for there were "very few men in Texas" who had his "requisite virtues for a position on the Supreme Bench, a position which, we feel assured he would have adorned." In a similar vein, the Dallas *Herald* supported Ballinger's decision not to accept the justiceship, for "no individual with as distinguished and as lucrative a practice as Mr. Ballinger would willingly accept a salary of $4,500, which is about the compensation of a first-class clerk. Few men who are worthy of the position earn less than $8,000 to $12,000 per annum, and it is as unnecessary as it is absurd to assume the greatest responsibilities of the State at a personal sacrifice and possible personal embarrassment."[56]

With the justiceship now behind him, Ballinger hoped he would be able to focus exclusively on his practice. He was certain his absence from Ballinger & Jack while preoccupied with his appointment to the bench had caused his practice to suffer. However, whether or not Ballinger was hard at work during his crisis, his presence still would not have been enough to prevent his firm from feeling the effects of the Panic of 1873, one of the nation's most prolonged economic contractions. Indeed, until the downturn of the 1930s, the Panic of 1873 was considered the Great Depression, lasting, with intermittent periods of recovery, to nearly the end of the century.

The exhilarating yet frenzied economic expansion of the immediate postwar years came to a wrenching halt in the fall of 1873. In September, Jay Cooke and Company, the cornerstone of the nation's banking system, went under after being unable to market millions of dollars of bonds of the Northern Pacific Railroad, a line that was to provide the country's second transcontinental system. The failure of Cooke's company precipitated a national financial panic as hundreds of banks and brokerage houses failed as well. So intertwined was the stock market with railroad speculation that it temporarily suspended operation while investors attempted to recoup losses and "rally" the market back to health. Factories throughout the country laid off thousands of workers as a result of the railroad industry's collapse. Of the nation's 364 railroads, eighty-nine went into bankruptcy by the end of the panic's first year. Eighteen thousand related businesses failed in two years. Unemployment rose to 14 percent by 1876 as hard times settled across the land like a pall.[57]

Even through the tumultuous period of Reconstruction, Ballinger's firm flourished, recording some of its highest annual income during the years 1870–1873. In fact, in the late-spring of 1873, only four months before the House of Cooke went under, Ballinger recorded his highest monthly gross income ever: $5,500. At the close of 1872, he likewise noted that his total professional revenue was "the best I have ever received in all my days at the law. Our business for the year was at $39,565—this represents our best income since we began. I hope we are able to continue in such a fashion." Unfortunately, over 30 percent of the firm's receipts were from out-of-state clients, mostly Northeastern businesses for which Ballinger and Jack served as collection agents and local counsel. By 1874 Ballinger's earnings had dropped to less than a thousand dollars monthly over a four-month span. Most of his Northern patrons had either stopped sending him business or had gone out of operation all together. Indeed, as Ballinger bemoaned to Guy Bryan, he had "never known things so perfectly flat in the law before. We are not getting any money—not $100, now where we got $1,000 last year. These are the worse times I have known since I began my career. Tom & I are full of despair & wonder daily what is to be the outcome. Until things get better at the North, I believe recovery will be long & hard."[58]

No doubt Ballinger's dramatic loss of income because of the national depression caused him great concern. However, always the resourceful attorney and provider, Ballinger found other ways to offset his loss of Northern business. At home, he began diversifying his clientele, shrewdly offering his services to the booming cattle industry of South and West

Texas, and to the railroad barons who, despite the downturn, were still building lines across the Lone Star State. As will be seen, Ballinger rather quickly bounced back from the hard times by becoming one of the state's leading railroad attorneys. By the end of the decade, thanks largely to his cultivation of this business, Ballinger's annual income surpassed even his "most exotic expectations of earning a livelihood in this profession."[59]

Within a few months of his supposed retirement from public service, Ballinger was unanimously elected by his fellow Galvestonians to go to Austin to help write a new state constitution. The convention was to assemble on the first Monday of September 1875. Ballinger had hoped to distance himself from political involvement, particularly at a time when his practice was at such a low ebb. However, once again, he found himself unable to resist this latest appeal to his sense of civic responsibility. Ballinger was deeply concerned about his forthcoming role at the convention. Soon after his election he revealed his anxiety to Guy Bryan, confessing that he felt "totally unprepared for my purpose. I have never felt so uncertain about what I am about to do or hope to accomplish. I do not possess sufficient knowledge on the subject of constitutions." Ever the consummate scholar, Ballinger compensated for his unfamiliarity with constitutional history by immersing himself in the subject. He read countless numbers of treatises and essays, ranging from some of the earliest documents ever written on the subject of constitutional government to the discourses of his favorite philosopher, Edmund Burke. Ballinger also scoured the more recent "debates of the Kentucky convention of '49, as well as those of the Constitutional Convention of 1787, the Texas Convention of 1845, and the Virginia Convention of 1832—all produced sound documents which contain much valuable information that will assist me in preparing for our convention." After several weeks of intense study, Ballinger felt confident that he had "prepared adequately for my duty & intend to carry it all forth to the best of my ability."[60]

Arriving in Austin on September 5, 1875, Ballinger quickly found himself immersed in the convention's business. The first few days were devoted to the appointment of committees and the meeting's general format. Of special concern to the attendants were the topics of delegate compensation and whether or not the debates should be published. It was finally decided that convention members should receive five dollars per diem and twenty cents a mile in travel allowance for their efforts. Much to Ballinger's disappointment, the motion to allow the printing of the debates was voted down. As the jurist told his wife, "We are here to represent the

People of this State, yet it has been decided that they are not to be informed firsthand of what is to transpire in this hall." Ballinger protested this "absurd notion," concluding that "a political convention is not a body to shed light or to instruct our successors. If I say anything I think has value I will try to have it sent to my constituents and preserved."[61]

It was during these first few days, while the convention wasted "valuable time & energy discussing trivial matters," that Ballinger remarked that though "the delegates are generally favorable as to disposition, they are not very strong as to ability. A good deal of ambition prevails in certain quarters. I hope both can be curbed, for if not, we are headed for some very difficult times." On the convention's fourth day the standing committees were announced and Ballinger was appointed chairman of the Committee on the Executive Department and was named second on the Judiciary Committee, which, according to the jurist, "many generally expected me to head—altho John Reagan is a fine choice." Despite being somewhat miffed at not being selected for the Judiciary Committee, Ballinger noted that he was generally pleased with the committee assignments and that he had been treated "with proper considerations."[62]

On September 20, the gathering's fifteenth day, an interesting controversy emerged—election postponement, which became one of the most bitterly contested convention issues. Perhaps more important, the postponement dispute marked the first time Ballinger spoke at length at the convention, and by the end of the debates, he had clearly emerged as one of the gathering's most cogent speakers. Convention historian Seth Shepard McKay proclaimed Ballinger to have been "one of the most capable men, if not the most capable, at the convention. It is a matter of great regret that his speeches were not printed in full by any of the newspapers."[63]

The issue on which Ballinger made his first of many lasting impressions was whether or not an ordinance should be passed postponing the state election until after the new constitution had been ratified. Under the existing charter (the 1868 document) elections were to be held in December 1875. A special committee, of which Ballinger was a member, was appointed to study the resolution. The majority report favored postponement until the constitution had been popularly accepted. The report further declared that since the delegates had been chosen by popular consent the convention had the right to postpone the election. Suspension would not only save "confusion and embarrassment" but "an unnecessary expense" of three hundred thousand dollars.[64]

Ballinger disagreed with the majority report, maintaining that the convention could not pass any legislative decrees because its authority was restricted "to framing a new Constitution for the State and of submitting the same to the People for adoption or rejection." Once the convention finished the constitution and submitted it to the people, "it [the convention] had no power of sovereignty left, either executive, legislative, or judicial." Ballinger then asked, "Where did the convention get the power to put in force a measure like the one recommended by the majority report?" Regardless of the plan's "economy," the convention could not postpone the election. Only the present legislature had that power and it had refused to postpone the election. Ballinger warned delegates that "If the convention could suspend a general election and prolong the terms of officers, they did not see what the convention could not do."[65]

After a two-day moratorium on the election debate, the question was raised again on September 23. Ballinger reiterated that the convention did not have the right to pass the ordinance, and that the resolution could be put into effect only if it was submitted to the people. Ballinger reminded delegates that they had been sent to Austin "to make a constitution, not to pass ordinances to suit their own fancy. The people did not for a moment suppose that this body would arrogate to themselves the power to make the results of their labors a finality."[66]

Ballinger was so disturbed by the election issue that he went to see Gov. Richard Coke, hoping to convince him to block "this most egregious breech by the Convention." Much to his initial relief, Coke agreed, reassuring the jurist that "he wd be glad to see no election—he wanted what was right done. He said he had been examining the subject & distrusted the power of the Convention in the matter." However, over the next three days Ballinger heard that several members of the majority group had visited the governor, and as a result, he was no longer certain Coke would "stand firm on the issue." The night before the final vote was to be taken, Ballinger met with Coke and confided to his diary that "the Gov. is not as determined as before to prevent the Conv.n from passing the ordinance. He is most anxious to avoid collision with the convention, and I think will submit to it if adopted."[67]

Loss of Coke's support made it all but impossible for Ballinger to muster enough delegates to vote against the majority report, which was adopted on September 24. Though his argument was defeated, local newspapers praised Ballinger's "brilliant effort on behalf of the minority opinion. Judge Ballinger's erudition left little doubt that the minority report was legally and technically accurate in its assumption on the issue of postponing the election. However, we must also acknowledge that for the purposes of expediency and economy, the approval of the majority report will better serve the interests of the State."[68]

Ballinger was involved in another heated controversy, one that addressed the issue of constitutional amendments. The Legislative Committee had proposed that the legislature at any regular session could, by a two-thirds vote, propose amendments. The amendments then would be submitted to the general electorate for ratification but would not become law until two-thirds of the members of the next legislature had approved the changes. The committee's report inspired bitter debate over the amendment issue; Ballinger recommended that the clause calling for subsequent legislative acceptance be removed. In a stinging rebuttal, Ballinger labeled the approval requirement as "anomalous to the whole legislative process. There is no need for the legislature, once an amendment has been approved by the people, to resubmit the measure to that body. I see no good reason for such action unless the 120 men comprising the legislature, induced by outside influences, wish to act in opposition to the will of the people."[69]

As the debate continued, Ballinger, exasperated, decided to suggest a simple alternative to the amendment process: all proposed amendments, once accepted by a majority of the electorate, should "automatically without any further legislative action, become law." Ballinger believed his plan would "enable the people, with utmost facility to amend the constitution. The constitution should at all times be under the active and careful supervision of the people, and they alone ought to be able to change it with reasonable facility." Despite attempts by several hardcore Redeemer factions to intimidate Ballinger into modifying his proposal, his alternative was accepted in toto by the convention and made part of the new constitution. Soon after his resolution's adoption, a buoyant Ballinger confided to his diary that he was "perfectly indifferent" to the charges of the "reactionaries" against him. "I think they are of service to me as they war on the majority of the Convention."[70]

No other subject at the convention seemed to generate as much reaction as the question of executive authority. The "Obnoxious Acts" were still fresh in the delegates' memories and they were especially hostile to those measures of the 1868 Constitution that had granted the governor unprecedented appointive power. Delegates were determined to curtail executive privileges as well as shorten terms of office and reduce salaries for all government officials. Ballinger opposed the Executive Committee's resolutions and as chairman sought to soften the committee's demands. He was successful in obtaining concessions in all areas but one: that of restricting the governor's appointive power. On this issue the Democratic and Granger majority was adamant. The committee voted overwhelmingly to reduce the governor's prerogatives. The previously assigned offices of comptroller, treasurer, land commissioner, and attorney general were now to be elected offices. The governor's right to declare martial law was limited, as well as his use of the veto.[71]

A reduction of the governor's salary was also on the agenda, and on this question, too, Ballinger protested. In his minority report the attorney caustically remarked that he had "no idea the governor's office was sought for profit. A salary of $5,000 annually will surely attract the most qualified individuals. The amount is not even equal to the payment of his actual expenses. What a disgrace to our State that our leading official must be called upon to maintain his office out of his private income."[72] Ballinger's excoriations failed to persuade his committee on the importance of adequate salaries. The convention accepted unanimously the committee's resolution to pay the governor an annual salary of four thousand dollars.

Ballinger next found himself embroiled in the poll tax controversy. The ordinance called for the imposition of a poll tax as a voting prerequisite, with the proceeeds being used for educational purposes. The issue became one of the most protracted disputes at the convention as delegates split into east and west factions, with those from East Texas unanimous in their support for such a law because of their desire to disfranchise black Texans, most of whom could not afford to pay a poll tax. Interestingly, in order to defeat the measure, Ballinger and other independents had to combine with Republicans and Grangers. Had he been unwilling to join forces with the "agricultural element," the resolution more than likely would have passed.[73]

It was obvious the poll tax clause was a blatant attempt by white-line Democrats to disfranchise African Americans. Yet, advocates insisted the proposal did not restrict suffrage on the basis of race, color, or previous condition of servitude. Moreover, they claimed that even the new constitution of Pennsylvania contained such a clause, "and Congress had not interfered with them." In short, poll tax supporters rather disingenuously claimed that such a law was a "righteous principle between the citizen and the state, by which the former contributes to the support of the government which protects him."[74]

Ballinger admitted such a tax could be levied legally. He opposed the measure, however, on the grounds that it was a blatant restriction of suffrage—"the denial of which is too great for the neglect or inability to pay tax." Moreover, Ballinger reminded the convention that proceeds from the poll tax were to be used for public education. Yet, only one-tenth of the income derived from the tax was being used to promote public education. Thus, Ballinger could not, "in good conscience, when asked by the people for the great blessing of education, give them a stone instead of bread." Had the convention been willing to earmark more money from the poll tax for education, as well as adding a property tax "to establish a system of free education for all the children of the State," Ballinger declared he would have supported the measure. For then in "clear & honest conscience," he could have said "to the poor white man and to the colored man, this matter is to secure in the highest degree the happiness of your children and good government, and you must contribute to it in order that you may derive the benefit, and you shall take no part in the government unless you contribute to it."[75]

Ballinger closed his argument against the poll tax by telling delegates that if such a measure passed, it would violate the Congressional act readmitting Texas into the Union, in which it was explicitly stated that no class of citizens should be disfranchised except for crime. No matter what the supposed justification, it would be only a matter of time before the federal government "would say to Texas you have broken the conditions on which you were admitted to the Union, and it becomes our duty to determine what the punishment shall be and what condition shall be imposed." If Texans hoped to avoid federal reprisals, such as a reduction in the state's Congressional representation, then it was essential "to eliminate this most foolish proposal from our constitution. How can we compel a man to go to war, serve as juror, work the roads, and all manner of other obligations, and yet deprive him of his suffrage because he did not have a dollar to pay his poll tax." Ballinger also accused the bill's sponsors of devising a "scheme not to preserve schools but to restrict the suffrage, especially the colored vote." Echoing his earlier convergence position on African American political rights, Ballinger again called for "accommodation." Since the Fourteenth Amendment granted African Americans citizenship, they were thus "entitled to the fullest security and protection under the laws, and included in that right of citizenship is the right to vote without any impairment."[76]

Thanks largely to Ballinger's strenuous opposition and Granger and

Republican support of his arguments, the poll tax proposal was defeated by a vote of sixty-one to twenty. Flush with victory, the coalition then went on to strike down voter registration and to deny to women, but not to aliens, the right to vote.[77] Though unwilling to grant Texas women political rights, the new constitution at least upheld on paper the Jacksonian concept of universal manhood suffrage by extending the franchise to all male Texans regardless of color.

Ballinger was one of the strongest supporters of free public education at the convention. In perhaps what was his most impassioned speech at the gathering, he declared that "it was among the clearest powers and the most imperative duties of the State to give the benefits of free common school education to all the children of the State. This not only had been accepted, but treasured in all the American states." Ballinger then accused the supposed "friends of free schools" of duplicity and betrayal of the idea because of their insistence that the system be created "only when the means provided would do it throughout the whole state for a period of four months every year. Yet not one cent of taxation was made imperative and taxation was limited to one-tenth of the State revenue. This is notorious!"[78]

Ballinger then pointed out that the rest of the country, most notably the North, had made the establishment of public education a priority. They had at least laid the foundation and "when economy allowed, built upon it." He then asked whether Texas "alone was unable to do even that? If we say we are too poor to levy taxes, will we forever be too poor to establish free schools?" The Galvestonian then challenged the excuse that Texans presently were too impoverished because of the upheavals of Reconstruction to support a public school system. He found it hard to believe that Texas "with her boundless territory, her genial sun, her immense capacity for production, with population teeming into her soil, would be unable to establish free schools." Ballinger's and others' pleas for an increase in the public school fund fell on deaf ears. The convention refused to appropriate more money for education. Once again, Democratic reaction to supposed Republican excesses rather than careful analysis of the issue proved to be the principal reason for the measure's defeat. According to the final article, the legislature could appropriate only one-fourth of the general revenue for the support of public schools.[79]

Ballinger was so enraged by the final education bill that he charged the Democrats with being "reactionaries directed toward ignorance." The Galvestonian was not alone in his indictment of the Democrats and Grangers for their failure to establish a sufficiently funded public school system. Gulf Coast newspapers supported Ballinger's position. The Houston *Telegraph* declared Texas would not "recover for a century from the disgrace of the archaic and senseless attitude towards the education of Texas children displayed by the convention." The Galveston *News* lamented that "the convention, after decreeing universal suffrage, has now also decreed universal ignorance."[80]

Ballinger was involved in other constitutional issues ranging from judiciary reform to the disposal of public lands to the question of internal improvements. In most instances he opposed the final resolutions on these matters. He was especially upset with the changes made in the judicial system, which decreed that all court judges from justice of the peace to the Supreme Court were to be elected and that the number of courts was to be reduced. The Judiciary Committee also established a dual system for criminal and civil proceedings at the appellate level. Equally disturbing to Ballinger was the convention's call for a decrease in the salaries of Supreme Court justices from four thousand dollars to three thousand. The Galvestonian contended that such a reduction was "an insult to the Supreme Court" and would "induce the Bar of the State to vote against the Constitution. No document that would pull down the judiciary would receive the support of any member of the Bar. No lawyer of the requisite attainments would take such a position at the salary offered." Ballinger was appalled when he heard the amendment's supporters stating that "these judges were gentlemen who had acquired competency and do not expect to save anything. If they had not acquired a competency at the age at which they usually reach the Supreme bench, they could not have earned any higher salary than it was proposed to give them!"[81] Despite Ballinger's strong opposition, the judicial reforms were adopted and made part of the constitution.

As reflected in the Texas Constitution, the late nineteenth century was not a time of much innovation in judicial organization. Like Texas, most states had a pyramid system of courts, poorly manned and badly paid, especially at the bottom tier. Because of the demand for public parsimony, it was unthinkable to "waste" money to create any sort of administrative position to better control and coordinate the system. Beyond some changes at the federal level, politicians had little interest in making court organization more rational. Judges were not shifted about as needed nor was litigation monitored or rules set up to tell courts how to "behave." Though higher courts controlled lower courts through the power to reverse decisions, such ascendancy could be exercised only through the appeals process. As a result, numerous cases were ensnarled, in overlapping jurisdiction. To correct such a muddled system, Ballinger and other judicial reformers advocated strengthening the powers of the chief justice, but in most states, including Texas, lawmakers prevented any possibility of judicial leadership by downgrading the office of chief justice. Indeed, so fearful were Texans of even the slightest hint of concentrated or centralized power, even in the judiciary, that in the name of the sacred Jacksonian concept of rotation in office, all justices were to be elected—even clerks of the court, which was an absurdity from the standpoint of administrative effectiveness. In short, Texas magistrates were not only poorly paid but were reduced in authority as well, to an embarrassing level of subservience to popular will. As Ballinger and others lamented, such a court system could not possibly meet the full needs and demands of a nation and state experiencing rapid socioeconomic change.[82]

By late November 1875 the work of the convention was complete. On November 22 an ordinance of submission to a vote of the people was presented, stipulating that as soon as the new document was popularly ratified it would go into effect on the third Tuesday of April 1876. The resolution also provided that general elections should be held simultaneously for all state, county, and district officials. Ballinger expressed disapproval as soon as the declaration was read, maintaining that "the constitution should be submitted alone, separate from any elections. It should be allowed to sink or swim on its own merits, free from partisan influences which the general election would invite." After "duly noting" Ballinger's protest, the remaining delegates voted his proposal down.[83]

On November 24 the convention met for the last time. Various delegates, encouraged by Ballinger, who had become opposition leader, entered their protests against the new charter. Ballinger's dissatisfaction with the completed document earned the jurist an interesting legacy of dissent. Few delegates would have predicted that by convention's end the usually restrained Ballinger would have emerged as one of the gathering's most vociferous critics. Throughout the proceedings Ballinger consistently protested against the excessive and partisan reactions of the Democratic majority to the last vestiges of Reconstruction. Though he had opposed radicalism, Ballinger was more judicious in his assessment of the Davis administration than his Democratic cohorts. Indeed, there were moments during the convention when a disgusted Ballinger denounced his fellow delegates for their "petty desires for revenge—such a disposition will make a mockery of this document & be a curse upon our body politic for decades to come." Privately in letters and diary entries he confessed that at times he had greater antipathy toward the Democrats than he ever felt toward the radicals. Ballinger, disillusioned with what was taking place at the capital, remarked that his compatriots were "no more suitable to framing a constitution than the roughest butcher to perform the most delicate surgical operation."[84]

Ballinger's disaffection with the new document stemmed more from his opposition to the Democrats' reactionary policies than from any real philosophical disagreement with the convention's purpose. Because of his belief in human frailty and his deeply rooted fears of disorder, Ballinger believed the new constitution would fasten upon Texas a demogogic majoritarian democracy. Throughout his adult life Ballinger held that informed reason was the best means to control individual passions. In his political world, well-educated leaders informed a populous ready, like good juries devoid of prejudice, to hear and assess the evidence and vote accordingly. Neither leaders nor the rank and file could be safely trusted with power if unchecked by the other. Though necessary to protect individual rights and maintain legality, power must always be restrained. Ballinger thus deplored the governmental structure created by the new constitution, for there were few, if any, legitimate executive or judicial checks on legislative power. As he had in the antebellum period, Ballinger would continue to look to the federal Constitution as the sole protection against the unrestrained power of the Texas legislature. Equally alarming to Ballinger was his detection that the Borbons would use the document to smother the development of a two-party system, casting those like himself committed to Texas's economic development, as threats to the established order. The document was clearly in spirit and letter an instrument of the antebellum, agrarian South. With such feelings toward the convention and the constitution, few Texans were surprised when Ballinger spoke out publicly against the new charter. In a series of editorials written for both the Galveston *News* and the Houston *Telegraph*, Ballinger challenged the legitimacy of the new constitution. He summoned its leading proponents "to amend the present document and make it fit to become the organic laws of the State." Though the *News* provided Ballinger with an open forum, he was disturbed by the journal's blatantly racist condemnation of the constitution's failure to mandate a poll tax—an issue Ballinger vehemently fought against at the convention. He could not convince the paper's editor, Willard Richardson, to stop the "inflammatory speeches on the poll tax & negro issue. You must cease this kind of discussion—the issue is dead—continued agitation will hurt all our People. The negro must be allowed his rights—to deny him what he is entitled to by law will only bring down the entire State and we will be condemned by others as liars and hypocrites."[85]

Unfortunately, Richardson refused his friend's counsel and continued publishing white-line editorials that declared Texas would soon have a "Senegambia" on the Gulf Coast, for "from fifteen to eighteen counties on and near the coast would be given over completely to negro rule. Ratification would deliver over the counties of the 'Black Belt' [Brazoria, Colorado, Fort Bend, Harrison, Matagorda, Washington, and Waller] hopelessly, irredeemably to African misrule." Richardson further warned that whites living in these counties would be "put completely under the control of their former slaves. Negro judges will be elected, and soon the entire coast will suffer from negro immigration and white emigration." Despite Richardson's refusal to refrain from white-line bombast on the poll tax issue, he agreed with Ballinger on the other major issues, allowing the jurist "all the space you might need to prevent ratification."[86]

In one series of articles for the *Telegraph* Ballinger attacked both the postponement issue and "the absurd and excessive election process" that had been established. "The convention had claimed to save the State $300,000 by postponing the fall election, yet at the same time ordered twice as many elections as had been held formerly. . . . Within a decade we will be forced to elect every official from the lowliest clerk to the governor at an expense presently unimaginable." Echoing his convention protests, Ballinger reminded his readers the delegates' "only power" had been "to frame a constitution and submit it to the people. They had no legal power to take such action as to propose the postponement of the election. To allow the postponement of the election to take place would be high moral treason against the People of Texas."[87]

Ballinger also condemned the convention's failure to levy sufficient taxes, "even a poll tax if necessary of $2.00," which would have brought "into the school fund the sum of $400,000 annually, sufficient to employ a thousand teachers for eight months in the year." Although opposing the poll tax at the convention, Ballinger reversed himself by the time of ratification. It appeared his desire for the creation of a decent public school system outweighed his previous objections, and in his subsequent releases he voiced approval for a poll tax, "provided the tax measure be used for the purpose of raising funds for the education of all our children, black and white." Ballinger had not changed his mind on black suffrage. He was as determined as before "to insure the negroe's right to vote. This tax <u>must not</u> be used to restrain the negro from voting. He has been lawfully granted citizenship and the right to vote, and cannot and should not be deprived of that right."[88]

Despite vigorous attempts to vilify the constitution, neither Ballinger nor the Republican and Democratic state conventions, which also had rejected the document, could persuade the public to do likewise. Yet, only a week before the election, Ballinger was optimistic that after talking "with lawyers in and about the office & town [Galveston] about the Constitution &c," he found "opinion very much against the Instrument & expect it will be defeated. They say the News the Railroads and the Radicals will all oppose it, besides a large no of independent voters. I am confident it will go down in defeat."[89] Much to Ballinger's subsequent chagrin, Texans on February 18, 1876, overwhelmingly endorsed the constitution by a margin of 136,606 to 56,652.

As Ballinger repeatedly declared at the convention and throughout the ratification campaign, the 1876 Constitution was no noble declaration of principles and organic law but a cumbersome piece of reactionary legislation and repressive thinking. Its adoption was accomplished by men devoted to an idyllic past that no longer existed. In viewing the constitution and ratification in such a way, Ballinger would cut himself off from Texas politics during the last decade of his life. Though remaining professionally ambitious, he became increasingly indifferent to public opinion, especially when it came to politics. He was neither able nor willing to compromise his personal beliefs to fit a popular political style. Interestingly, his unwillingness to refashion the conservatism he had shaped largely in jurisprudential terms made him a dissenter in a society most of whose values he shared.

Chapter Ten

"THE LAWYER OF TEXAS"

As soon as the hustings of ratification were over, a disappointed though resigned Ballinger returned to his practice, swearing "that the next time the Public separates me from my family & practice it will be by sending me to Devilsville—nothing else."[1] However, as so often in the past, Ballinger soon found himself thrust into the political limelight. Eighteen seventy-six was a national election year, and in one of the most controversial presidential contests in the country's history, haunted by the legacy of Reconstruction, the Republicans, despite accusations of fraud and corruption, triumphed again. Though victorious, the Republicans were forced to compromise with their Democratic adversaries in order to retain the White House.[2] Despite the dubious nature of the Republican succession, their retention of national power portended well for Ballinger.

As soon as the "Compromise of 1877" was accepted by North and South,[3] the new president, Rutherford B. Hayes, announced that a thorough reform of the federal bureaucracy would take place, and that new appointments would not be awarded for partisan service nor would they reflect any sectional favoritism. Southerners were hopeful that as a conciliatory move, the new president would appoint a number of prominent Southern Democrats to key public offices. Texans in particular were heartened by the president's gesture, for Hayes had some very strong Texas connections, which certainly could be used to political advantage. If the president was true to his word, then it was only a matter of time before some of the state's more illustrious native sons would be on their way to Washington to fill important government positions. This possibility was presented to Ballinger in the early months of Hayes's tenure when Supreme Court justice David Davis entered the Senate, creating a vacancy on the bench.

When approached by friends and relatives regarding his possible nomination to the Court, Ballinger confessed he was "very favorably disposed to the idea of serving on the Bench—I must admit that I had no more thought of myself in connexion with the Supreme Bench than with the Roman papacy. I will accept the office if conferred upon me—Hally agrees to it completely & believes I wd make a very good justice." Yet Ballinger believed there were Southerners "of higher qualifications" and that he would be acting "selfishly & wrong if I assented to accept."[4]

With the possibility of a Texas appointment before them, the state's congressional delegation wasted little time in preparing the way. Within days of Hayes's inauguration, Texans began lobbying for Ballinger's appointment. They came armed with recommendations from Governor Coke and the present Texas Supreme Court justices, as well as letters from leading Texas Republicans, most notably ex-governors Elisha M. Pease, Edmund Davis, and A. J. Hamilton.[5] Few individuals however, were more persistent champions of Ballinger's nomination than his two brothers-in-law, Guy Bryan and Samuel F. Miller.

As early as 1874, Miller disclosed his hope that his Texas kinsman would soon be appointed to the federal Supreme Court. Soon after Ballinger resigned from the Texas Supreme Court, Miller wrote his brother-in-law expressing support for his decision as well as telling him that he hoped "to yet see you in our Court." Miller was certain Ballinger was destined for an appointment because he clearly was "the most eminent and respected jurist in the State, if not in all the South." Moreover, Miller believed the new administration "must recognise the right of the South to representation on our bench." The vacancy also had to be filled by someone having the "knowledge of that peculiar system of local law of which Louisiana and Texas are the principal examples." In Miller's mind Ballinger was the perfect candidate, and he was willing to use all the means at his disposal to convince the president of that.[6]

Joining Miller on Ballinger's behalf was Guy Bryan, who perhaps could be of even greater service to Ballinger because of his close, personal relationship with Hayes. Bryan and Hayes had been classmates at Kenyon College in Ohio (class of '42) and during their time together there they developed a deep and lasting friendship that withstood even the strains of Civil War. Indeed, down to his death Hayes referred to Bryan as "my best friend."[7]

After finishing college, Bryan returned to Texas to read law under William Jack, Ballinger's father-in-law. After Jack's death from yellow fever in 1844, Bryan put his legal career "on hold," and instead took up politics and a variety of other enterprises. Bryan, like Ballinger, was smitten by one of the Jack girls, Laura, Hally's younger sister, whom he married in 1852.[8] Before the war, Hayes would spend several weeks and sometimes months with Bryan in Texas, touring the state and getting acquainted with many other up-and-coming young Texans. In 1859 Hayes heard Ballinger give a rare political speech, after which he remarked that he had "rarely heard such erudition & force—Mr. Ballinger is no doubt a brilliant lawyer & a fine political orator who should give serious thought to a career in politics."[9] Since Bryan and Hayes corresponded regularly and knew each other's lives intimately, when Ballinger's name came up as a candidate for the Supreme Court it was not that of a stranger to "Rud" Hayes.

Ballinger forbade Bryan to mention his name to the president. Bryan, however, was as determined as Miller was to secure Ballinger's nomination. In a series of letters to his old college classmate, Bryan began promoting Ballinger's candidacy. Typical of Bryan's entreaties was one sent on March 13, 1877, only a week after Hayes entered the Oval Office. "Dear Rud: I have seen it stated that you will not appoint Democrats, South. If such be your action, you are wrong. Appoint as many Democrats as you can well do, the more the better. Adhere to your resolution in regard to the Su-preme Bench from Texas; the one we spoke of is your man above all others. Texas is opening her mind and heart to you; no appointment that you could make would commend you more to the judgment of both parties here, than that of Ballinger." A week later Bryan wrote "Rud" again, reminding Hayes that Ballinger was "recognized as the Lawyer of Texas, the peer in learning and character of any man whose claims can be considered by the President, and is eminently qualified to be Judge Davis' successor."[10]

Ex-governor Elisha Pease also wrote on Ballinger's behalf, declaring that the jurist's legal reputation was "not to be excelled by any lawyer in the State. I think him in every way qualified and believe that he would do honor to the position." Interestingly, as the endorsements began flooding Hayes's office, Ballinger began having second thoughts, and was especially opposed to Bryan's "most insistent conversations with the President." Ballinger appreciated his brother-in-law's "kind feelings" but did not want him to "exert the slightest influence upon the President." Ballinger believed Bryan's lobbying would be interpreted by Hayes as "great presumption on my part."[11]

A few days later Ballinger received a letter from Miller, to which he replied that he "was not the right man to appoint—I am not qualified to assume such an important position." Ballinger then told Miller to try to put John A. Campbell, who resigned from the Court in 1861 in order to serve the Confederacy, "back on the bench." Ballinger was certain Campbell's reappointment would "electrify the South—nothing in history would be handsomer."[12]

Miller promptly responded to Ballinger's letter, telling his brother-in-law that after reading it over again, he found Ballinger's "fear of want of capacity for the place a little nonsensical." In Miller's view, Ballinger's professional success was "clear proof" that he was qualified for the position, and that he would be "the peer of your brothers and in usefulness the superior of many." After scolding Ballinger for his penchant for self-deprecation, Miller then addressed his brother-in-law's belief that John Campbell was the best man for the job. In Miller's opinion, Campbell was not only too old (he was sixty-six at the time) but more important, he was not as "pure" as the Texan believed him to be, for he had not absolved himself of "the spirit of rebellion." Indeed, in Miller's view, there was no one "more saturated with its spirit" than Campbell unless it was "old [Robert] Toombs." More disturbing to Miller than Campbell's participation in the rebellion was "the persistency with which he continues the fight when all good men ought to seek to forget it as much as possible." Though Ballinger had been a Confederate, Miller assured him that his past record would have little effect on his appointment because he had done "nothing to promote secession" nor "have you shown any disposition to foster the animosities of the late war."[13] In short, Ballinger's strong opposition to secession and his support of convergence during Reconstruction would go a long way towards convincing Hayes and other Republicans that he, unlike Campbell, was willing to accept defeat and reconciliation.

Guy Bryan was as optimistic as Miller regarding Ballinger's appointment. After a meeting with Hayes, Bryan, through Miller, informed Ballinger of "the very positive progress" being made with his candidacy. According to Miller, Hayes told Bryan unequivocally "that his present purpose was to appoint a real Southern man—that it seemed wrong that so large a part of the Union should be without a representative in the Court." Bryan then naturally suggested Ballinger "as the proper man." Bryan then gave the president his brother-in-law's political history, emphasizing the "prominence" of Ballinger's conservatism and "ancient affection for the whig party." Hayes reminded Bryan that he was already familiar with Ballinger's politics, having heard him make an "impressive speech in Galveston many years ago on the Wilmot Proviso." Bryan and Hayes concluded their conversation with "Rud" assuring his old classmate that at this point only Ballinger and New Orleans lawyer William H. Hunt were being considered for nomination. After Bryan's meeting with Hayes, he and Miller met for drinks celebrating (prematurely) Ballinger's "certain" nomination with "good Champaign [sic] with great energy."[14]

As the nomination process became more competitive and political, Ballinger's desire began to wane. Initially the leading contender, by the early summer of 1877, he was no longer the front-runner, as several more aspirants had emerged, most of them Southern born and Unionists. Besides Campbell, there was the Alabama carpetbagger William B. Woods, federal circuit judge for the Fifth Circuit; William H. Hunt of New Orleans; Kentuckians John Marshall Harlan and Benjamin H. Bristow; Missourians Samuel Miller Breckenridge and Henry Hitchcock; and Georgian Herschel V. Johnson. These were all men whom Ballinger characterized as "good lawyers & judges with much experience in the administration of the Law & are much better connected politically to the President—all were Unionists and such loyalty will surely become an issue. I no longer believe my name shd be considered & will tell Bryan & Miller to cease at once their advocacy."[15]

Ballinger's assessment that his Confederate past would "work hard against" him was correct. He knew it was politically impossible for Hayes to nominate any ex-Confederate regardless of qualifications or willingness to "renounce the past." No doubt Ballinger sensed this early on, and since he had "great respect & affection" for both Miller and Bryan, he felt he could "no longer proceed with the nomination." He could not pursue his own "ambitions knowing that I had embarrassed or crippled my two dearest brothers." Ballinger thus informed Bryan, Miller, and his other sponsors that he "presently felt unqualified to meet the requirements of serving on the Supreme Court." He only intimated in his letters that his Confederate past was a factor in withdrawing his name from nomination. Rather, he insisted to the end that he simply felt unqualified. Surely Miller and Bryan both knew at the time that their brother-in-law's reasons were deeper than supposed feelings of inferiority, even though they knew of Ballinger's penchant for excessive humility, especially when the potential for public acclaim was dangling before him. Years later, Ballinger confirmed his kinsmen's suspicions, freely admitting "with feelings of great turpitude" that he indeed had "thrown them a ruse," designed to save them from "disappointment and a rupture in your relations with the President, which at the time I was convinced would occur if you continued to press for my nomination."[16]

After deciding to withdraw, Ballinger first notified Bryan of his decision. He told his brother-in-law that even if he accepted nomination and was appointed, his lack of "judicial reputation and experience" would have relegated him to being "a third or fourth rate Judge, which does not greatly attract me." Since his "place" at the Texas bar was "among the highest of any lawyer in the State, it would be folly to take a position on the Supreme Bench." Ballinger confessed "to a jealousy against the political element" that seemed to be controlling the selection process. Yet, he was confident that in the end "the President for the Bench would give weight, and weight alone, to legal qualifications." Ballinger closed his letter by reminding Bryan that when he "declined going on our own Supreme Bench, it was with a very fixed feeling that I should adhere throughout to the pursuit of my profession and to private life as an independent gentleman and wholly a non-office-seeker."[17]

In October 1877 Hayes nominated John Marshall Harlan of Kentucky to fill the vacancy. When the news of Harlan's nomination reached Texas, local newspapers and politicians accused the president of "attitudes and policies not congenial to the prevailing political predilection of Texas, and as a result an opposition has sprung up that is presently too strong for even combined endorsement of an entire state."[18] Such partisan responses, though gratifying to Ballinger, were unwarranted. He had withdrawn his name from nomination and thus Harlan's appointment was not the result of slight or political maneuvering by Hayes. True to his word, Hayes did appoint a Southerner, and, as Ballinger knew, it had to be someone with a clean political past—one untainted by secession and support of the Confederacy. In Miller's own words, Harlan's background was "impeccable on both accounts." To the very end of the selection process Ballinger favored John Campbell, but after Harlan's nomination he too saw "the wisdom in the President's choice" and believed his fellow Kentuckian was "the best possible choice given the President's political restraints. Judge Harlan is no doubt a man of great integrity, an eminent jurist, who has all the judicial elements well mixed in him. He will serve the Bench honorably and faithfully." Ballinger assuaged Texans' disgruntlement with Hayes when he publicly announced "that the President, upon my request and honoring my wishes to withdraw my name from nomination, graciously complied."[19] On November 26, 1877, the Senate confirmed John Marshall Harlan's nomination. He lived to serve almost thirty-four years on the Court, becoming one of its most distinguished members.

Over the course of the next six years Miller tried to secure Ballinger's appointment to several more federal judgeships, ranging from a position on the Court of Claims to two other vacancies on the Supreme Court as well as an appointment to a federal district judgeship at Galveston during Chester Alan Arthur's administration. Much to Miller's dismay Ballinger was not interested in any of the positions, telling his brother-in-law in 1883 that a federal appointment "this late in life [Ballinger was fifty-eight at the time] was supremely foolish from a practical & financial standpoint. The pecuniary needs of my family prevent me from accepting it [the federal district judgeship]. A salary of $5,000 annually is impossible for my needs. Tho' I am eternally in your debt for the kindness you have shown me over the past years, please cease all efforts on my behalf." Miller was disappointed by Ballinger's refusal "to rise above your present station." Yet, he did not let his frustration with Ballinger's seeming lack of ambition ruin their relationship. The two men remained close friends and confidants for the rest of their lives.[20]

The constant distractions of possible judicial appointments did not cause Ballinger's practice to suffer. Indeed, by the beginning of the 1880s, Ballinger & Jack had become one of the most reputable and profitable firms in Texas. Ballinger realized, as did many other attorneys in the post-war years, that the coming of the railroads to the Lone Star State had ushered in a new era in the practice of law. As rail lines stretched across the vast Texas hinterland connecting scattered towns and nascent cities, the Texas economy was dramatically reordered. By the 1880s Texas was no longer an isolated, little-developed region of small farmers. Ambitious railroad construction transformed the state into one of the fastest-growing commercial economies in the country.[21]

Unlike traditional businesses, railroads would require more capital and more sophisticated levels of coordination, thus raising a host of new legal issues in the areas of finance and corporate organization. Also, as interstate enterprises railroads would generate new regulatory questions. Law firms responding to railroads' legal needs soon found their establishments moving rapidly away from a traditional to a more specialized operation. In short, railroads stimulated the growth of corporate law, which in the prewar years, particularly in Texas, was virtually nonexistent. In this sense, railroads transformed Ballinger's practice as they reshaped the Texas economy.[22]

At first, Ballinger served his railroad clients much as he did his other patrons. Railroad owners were just one more group of local businessmen easily added to his ongoing client list with problems in real estate, probate, collection, and other matters. However, railroads did not long remain like other businesses. Beginning in the 1870s the powerful eastern railroad barons came to Texas, searching for local lines to buy in order to further consolidate their national networks. As the Panic of 1873 swept across the Lone Star State, one by one the small, undercapitalized railways running through eastern Texas fell into receivership. As Texas roads fell into the hands of the "robber barons" they came to symbolize the power "foreigners" had over the local economy.[23]

As state governments became more determined to end the railroads' abuses, the lines' owners increasingly looked to local attorneys for counsel. It fell to lawyers to interpret the new laws and resolve the many complex issues stemming from broadly worded regulations. This sort of work, combined with the new areas of corporate finance and organization, made railroads an ambitious lawyer's most important clients. Ballinger saw this great potential for his practice. Long an advocate of improved transportation as the key to economic development, Ballinger admonished himself to become "more thorough in Railroad law. Our State will soon be covered with lines & there will arise a no. of legal matters which we must be able to answer. RR's are the wave of the future & I must be prepared for their business."[24]

Equally important to Ballinger as the potential profitability of railroad clients was his belief that railroads would revolutionize transportation and become the most important manifestation of the burgeoning industrial order. Their social impact would be unprecedented. However, it was the greater possibility of serving justice by making the law fit new circumstances that drew Ballinger so insistently toward corporate law. Because of his devotion to power and order, it was essential that those with power—such as himself—use it to impose order. Only then, Ballinger believed, could there be morality. In the past, accepted traditions of political and social behavior imposed order on individuals and society. Yet these traditions, he recognized, depended heavily on material conditions which were changing rapidly in the late nineteenth century. Ballinger welcomed the change, and foresaw more strength than danger in the new industrial order. But it demanded concomitant legal changes whose contours tradition could not draw. Strong laws could be used to define and enforce the resolution of socioeconomic conflicts in an orderly manner. Social relations had changed "far more rapidly since the end of war than in the preceding two centuries." As Ballinger further told Guy Bryan, "the chief breakdown is in dealing with the new relations that have arisen from the economic changes of our time. Every new social relation begets a new type of wrong-doing—of sin, to use an old-fashioned word—and years pass by before society is able to consider this sin a crime which can be effectively punished by law."[25]

Such beliefs as Ballinger's create dilemmas for the practicing attorney, whose primary responsibility is to protect his client's interests. Ever the pragmatist, Ballinger realized he could serve few clients if he was limited to serving his own ideal justice. As he told a young colleague, despite the young man's ability to unravel complex issues and weigh precedents, he never would become a respected lawyer if he made "equity, justice, law, and morality all on your side before you will take a case."[26] Reconciling the inherent conflict between the pursuit of ideal justice and the obligation to defend clients' interests made Ballinger open to change—as long as it was gradual rather than abrupt, evolutionary rather than revolutionary. Ballinger thus hoped his work would help create a legal environment favorable to industry while simultaneously prescribing the rules for its operation. Ballinger also strongly supported industrial combination, which he believed demonstrated "the almost limitless possibilities of power and productivity. Such progress should never be arrested. If it ever was, our nation would never rise to the greatness for which it is destined."[27] Industrial combinations such as railroads, susceptible as they were to the temptations of unbridled power, had to be made responsible through law to the whole people.

In order to prepare his firm for the influx of railroad business, Ballinger hired a new partner, thirty-year-old Marcus Mott, in November 1867. Mott, a native Louisianan, moved to Galveston when he was eight years old. Mott's early education was desultory at best but he did manage to study law while serving as district deputy clerk. He was admitted to the bar in 1859 and until the outbreak of war worked as an associate with the Galveston firm of Thompson and Goldthwaite. He joined the Confederate service in 1861, becoming a captain in the Eighth Texas Cavalry Regiment, better known as Terry's Texas Rangers, which eventually came under the command of Ballinger's uncle, Thomas Harrison. It was through "Uncle Tommy" that Ballinger first became acquainted with Mott, and after several letters from Harrison endorsing Mott as "a first-rate young attorney," Ballinger asked Mott to join his firm. No doubt the lure of practicing law in the emerging railroad industry of the Lone Star State helped attract Mott to Ballinger and Jack.[28] Though not the scholar or methodical thinker Ballinger was, Mott proved to be a devoted, diligent, and practical colleague who assumed, along with Tom Jack, the responsibility for the

Marcus F. Mott, a partner in Ballinger's law firm from 1872 to 1894. After Tom Jack's death in 1880, Mott assumed Jack's role as Ballinger's closest professional confidant. *Photograph courtesy Mills, Shirley, Eckel & Bassett, L.L.P., of Galveston, Texas.*

partnership's more routine business such as collection, probate, and realty matters which were still quite extensive.

During the 1870s Ballinger's railroad work was primarily confined to handling issues for smaller Texas lines. He acted as general attorney for two of the state's earliest roads, the Galveston, Houston & Henderson (GH&H) Railroad, an important line in southeastern Texas, and the Galveston, Harrisburg & San Antonio, a railroad linking Galveston to San Antonio, which would hopefully bring hinterland trade to the island rather than to the Queen City's archrival Houston. A good portion of these roads' legal problems included the sensitive issue of disposing of land grants, which the state legislature decreed be sold quickly. More routine matters however, consumed the bulk of Ballinger's time, especially suits by shippers against the lines for failure to deliver freight on time, alleged charging of higher rates for short hauls and lower rates for longer hauls, spoilage of goods, and other questions of common carrier law.[29] Ballinger's most controversial and protracted cases involved the new body of judge-made law of torts, which before the industrial revolution were virtually nonexistent. In the antebellum period common law had little to say about personal injury actions based on the negligence of another. As the nation industrialized in the postwar years, it was that area of tort law that witnessed the most rapid changes.

By the late nineteenth century, few Americans doubted that the railroad was the key to economic development. Yet, trains were like wild beasts, rampaging through the countryside, killing livestock, pedestrians, and innocent children as they played near the roadbed, setting fire to crops, smashing freight, and belching black smoke and shaking homes to their foundations as they roared through crowded urban neighborhoods at all hours of the day. In a sense, tort law and railroad law "grew up" together, becoming symbiotic by the late nineteenth century.

The key link between tort and railroad law was that they were both interpreted as laws of negligence, of carelessness—the inflicting of harm, not intentionally, but because of some lapse in diligence or judgment. Liability for negligence was not absolute; it was based on fault. As tort-railroad law evolved, fault meant a breach of duty to the public, meaning that the defendant—the railroad—had not done what was considered reasonable to protect the public welfare. Though public hostility toward the excesses of industrial capitalism was on the rise by the late nineteenth century, the legal system typically avoided any extremist position toward the new order. If key enterprises such as railroads had to pay for all damage done by "accident," lawsuits would soon drain them of their economic blood. Thus prudence and caution became the order of the day as judges carefully limited damages to some moderate measure. In short, the prevailing attitude of the judicial system was to protect capital as much as was possible from popular outrage while allowing the people a modicum of redress for the harm done them by the plutocracy's machines.[30]

During his two decades of railroad work, Ballinger spent the majority of his time defending his clients for alleged negligence. Suits against the lines ranged from damage to passengers' baggage, transporters' cotton, cattle, lumber, crates of melons, and barrels of apples, to engine sparks setting fire to grass and pasture land, to the construction of bridges, water-towers and stations that encroached upon or destroyed private property, to locomotives that killed cattle and horses as well as children and other pedestrians or bystanders, to employees suing for injuries sustained while at work, and finally to urban homeowners and businessmen complaining of noise, smoke, dirt, and fire from engine sparks as trains roared through busy downtown areas.[31]

From Ballinger's legal files it appeared that in the early, formative years of tort law, railroads rarely hesitated to pay damages. Railroad owners were no different than their industrial counterparts in that they too wanted to avoid litigation. If suits against the lines could be kept out of the courts, companies would not only be saved money, but more important, precedents would not be established. Regardless of the type or degree of harm inflicted, most lines instructed their attorneys either to pay the full amount sued for, or try to reach an out-of-court settlement. As Oscar G. Murray, general freight and passenger agent of the Galveston, Houston and Henderson Railroad, informed Ballinger in 1878, it was the line's "desire to avoid all litigation, and to adjust, by agreement of parties, all legal liabilities without trouble, or expense of claimants." Ballinger was to go to court only if "you have evidence established on the most thorough investigation, that claimant was completely in the fault." If Ballinger did go to trial and then lost, he could appeal only if he was certain the judgment against the company was "erroneous, or amount of recovery can be reduced on appeal." Based on these specific instructions, Ballinger usually recommended to Murray that the GH&H "pay out at once."[32]

On many occasions claimants refused settlement, forcing Ballinger to trial. Much to his employer's satisfaction, he was usually successful in getting judges to at least lower the original amount demanded. For example, over the three-month period of July–September 1878, ten claims totaling twenty thousand dollars were brought against the newly formed Gulf Colorado and Santa Fe, for which Ballinger was general counsel. Unfortunately for the new line, Ballinger was able to negotiate a settlement in only four of the cases, reducing the total amount of the claims by only five hundred dollars. The remaining six cases went to court and were decided in the plaintiffs' favor. However, much to the company's delight, Ballinger was successful in placing a significant degree of "reasonable doubt" in the court's mind, and thus in their awarding of damages, the judges cut the amounts of the original claims by as much as one-half.[33]

Though Ballinger handled a variety of claims for his railroad clients, over 50 percent of his cases involved the killing or maiming of livestock. For example, in the year 1877–1878, Ballinger paid out over five thousand dollars in settlements to stock owners whose cattle were killed by the railroad. On many occasions Ballinger wanted to contest the claim, believing he could prove negligence on behalf of the stock owner. The company, however, instructed him to either pay the claim in full or negotiate a settlement. All that changed in late 1878 when a Georgia court ruled in *Uriah Bartley v. The Georgia Railroad and Banking Company* that henceforth Georgia railroads were no longer liable for stock killed or injured on the track "when there is no carelessness or neglect on the part of the employes [sic]." As Judge Paul Gibson of the Superior Court of Richmond County, Georgia, further decreed, "When it is conceded that there was no neglect on the part of the employes [sic] of the roads, and every diligence used to prevent the damage or injury, I cannot conceive of how it can be possible for the courts of justice to give damages for injuries to stock on the roads."[34] This was the precedent Ballinger and other railroad attorneys had long been anticipating. For several years railroad companies had been paying out thousands of dollars annually to the owners of injured or killed stock, believing they were at fault. Now, with one simple ruling, the burden of negligence shifted dramatically from defendant to plaintiff, giving attorneys much more room to negotiate, or contest outright, claims against their railroad clients.

Upon hearing of the Georgia court's ruling, J. H. Crowley, master of transportation for the GH&H notified Ballinger "to cease <u>at once</u> all payment to individuals who have claims against the road for injured or killed livestock. Begin thorough investigation of all such claims to ensure they are legitimate. Contest any you believe are not & prepare for court if necessary."[35] Stock owners were not pleased by the Georgia precedent. Within six months of receiving Crowley's bulletin, Ballinger's immediate pay-out rate fell by 70 percent. Only in the most blatant of circumstances was he willing to settle, and even then the amount paid was significantly less than the original claim. Perhaps more important, Ballinger's willingness to go to trial, particularly when claims exceeded the two-hundred-dollar mark, increased dramatically. Even if the court ruled in the plaintiff's favor, Ballinger was confident he could at least win a drastic reduction in the final judgment. Consequently, his court appearances on his railroad client's behalf increased by almost 50 percent within six months of the Georgia court's decision.[36] As more and more state courts followed the Georgia precedent, it became apparent that the judicial system was more enterprise-minded than business owners and attorneys originally thought. Indeed, from the late 1870s on, courts invented new and more cunning traps for the injured plaintiffs. One of these traps—implicit in the Georgia decision—was the concept of contributory negligence. Another was the fellow-servant rule and the concomitant assumption of risk.

As the number of railroad accidents proliferated, judges throughout the land became alarmed by juries' tendency to almost automatically find for the plaintiff. This was especially true when individuals were either maimed or killed by trains. Judges then used contributory negligence as a sort of "brake" on such popular "excesses." The fundamental idea of contributory negligence was simple: if it could be proven that the plaintiff was even remotely negligent himself, then damages could not be recovered from defendant.[37]

The doctrine of assumption of risk was almost as devastating a blow to personal-injury victims as contributory negligence. Plaintiffs could not recover if they willingly put themselves in positions of danger. Employers found assumption of risk especially applicable in cases of injured workmen; miners, railroad men, and factory workers could be said to assume the ordinary risks of employment merely by accepting their jobs, and thus could not recover damages from their employer for injury received while performing their work.[38]

The fellow-servant rule evolved simultaneously with assumption of risk. According to this doctrine, an employee (servant) could not sue his employer (master) for injuries caused by another employee. He could recover from his employer if it could be proven that the employer's negligence had caused the harm through "negligent misconduct." However, this right meant nothing in a factory or railroad yard. The employer was a rich entrepreneur or a soulless corporation. In a coupling, turntable, or switching accident, it was a fellow servant who was negligent, if anybody. According to the law, the fellow servant was of course liable; but it would have been utterly senseless for one poor worker to sue another, equally impoverished. Combined with the assumption of risk, the fellow-servant rule left injured workmen with little legal recourse.[39]

Armed with such an arsenal of new legal weapons, Ballinger and other railroad attorneys were now capable of defeating virtually any suit against their clients. The new doctrines of contributory negligence and assumption of risk made even protracted trials worth it, for in the end Ballinger knew that most judges would either dismiss the case or at the very least lower considerably the amount awarded. Even appeals were worth Ballinger's effort, for higher court judges were more likely than their lower court counterparts to invoke contributory negligence and either reverse the lower court's decision or throw it out altogether.[40]

By the 1880s Ballinger's use of contributory negligence, assumption of risk, and the fellow-servant rule had become very effective. Much to the relief of both the Galveston, Houston & Henderson and the Gulf, Colorado & Santa Fe, the majority of the lines' personal-injury cases involving employees or private citizens were reversed or dismissed altogether on the basis of these doctrines. Knowing most courts to be on the side of railroads, fewer and fewer individuals were willing to take their cases to trial, thus allowing Ballinger the upper hand in negotiated settlements. In only about 30 percent of his cases did he have to pay claims in full. In all the rest he convinced claimants to accept compensation that frequently lowered their original charge by as much as 60 percent.[41]

There were of course cases Ballinger could not settle, or win by going to trial, or on appeal. Ballinger's legal files and court records indicate that there were certain types of personal-injury cases which tugged at the heart-strings of even the most conservative judges. Even the most persistent and cleverest of lawyers had difficulty reversing or getting dismissed cases involving the death or maiming of children by trains. Plaintiffs even refused Ballinger's settlement offers which sometimes were significantly more than the original claim. When it came to the death or crippling of their children, parents were determined to have the fullest redress of their grievances against the railroads.

In the Nixon (*Houston & Texas Central R.R. Co. v. J. A. Nixon and Wife*) and Dickson (*Galveston, Houston & Henderson Railway Co. v. Anne Dickson*) cases, both sets of parents were suing the railroads for causing the deaths of their children. In the Nixon case plaintiffs were asking for damages of thirty-six thousand dollars as a result of the train having run over their daughter Sarah, whom they claimed never saw the train as she crossed the track. The Nixons claimed "that the bell was not rung, the whistle sounded, nor other warning given." After a thorough investigation Ballinger found that the railroad was at fault and offered to settle out of court for the sum of twenty-five thousand dollars. The Nixons refused his offer, forcing Ballinger to trial. During the trial Ballinger tried to convince the court that the child's parents were "contributory negligents" for allowing their daughter to play so close to the track, and that when she attempted to cross the track she "contributed by her own negligence to such injury," for according to Ballinger "being on a railroad track is prima facie evidence of negligence." The jury disagreed with Ballinger and voted unanimously for the Nixons to recover full damages. Ballinger used the same arguments in the Dickson case, but again the jury found for the plaintiff awarding Anne Dickson full recovery in the amount of thirty thousand dollars for the death of her son John, who was also killed at a railroad crossing because of defendant's negligence.[42]

In the Hanagar and Douglas cases, employees of the Galveston, Houston & Henderson on two different occasions claimed they were severely injured as a result of "gross negligence by the Company." Walter Hanagar and Malcolm Douglas were both brakemen on the line's freight trains and were suing the road for thirty-six thousand and thirty thousand dollars respectively for loss of limb (Hanagar lost his right arm, and Douglas had to have his left leg amputated). Both men were claiming their accidents were the result of the company's "failure to furnish safe and proper brakes & brake chains." As Ballinger further told J. H. Crowley, plaintiffs were asserting that the chain causing their injuries "gave way because it was rotten," and that the company knew the chains were defective. If Hanagar and Douglas were correct, that the chains were indeed of poor quality, the company could be found liable for having used unsafe and dangerous equipment. Ballinger believed he could relieve the company of possible negligence by showing that the manufacturer of the chains rather than the company was responsible for the accidents by having sold the GH&H defective equipment. Ballinger thus asked Crowley for detailed information pertaining to "where was the car manufactured that was involved in accident, how long in use? Were the brake chains made in company's own shops, or were they purchased, if so, from whom? What was the character of defect in chain, if chain made by Co. were skillful & competent people used? If ordinary caution and care used, could character of defect been discovered by such reasonable inspection?"[43]

Unfortunately for the Galveston, Houston & Henderson, the chain was made in one of the company's shops, and according to Crowley, was not properly inspected before leaving the factory. Since the chain was defective, Ballinger decided that it would be in the company's best interest to try to settle. Crowley agreed, authorizing Ballinger to go as high as twenty-five thousand dollars in both cases. Neither plaintiff, however, was "willing to accept a penny less than their full recovery." Ballinger was thus forced to trial, warning Crowley that the court probably would decide against the company. In his defense Ballinger invoked both the assumption-of-risk and fellow-servant rules, hoping to show that as brakemen, both Hanagar's and Douglas's "injuries had resulted from the negligence of a fellow servant, and also by an accident in the regular course of [their] employment, the risks of which [they] had assumed in accepting the employment and entering the service." Ballinger also contended that the chains should not have been used until they were "first checked for reliability by someone knowledgeable as to their capacity and safety." By using the phrase "someone knowledgeable as to their capacity and safety," Ballinger was shrewdly attempting to shift negligence from the company to a fellow servant, which he hoped would make another employee rather than the GH&H liable for damages. Ballinger's scapegoat was a man named Sutcliffe, who at the time of both accidents was the master mechanic in charge of the yard, and thus should have checked the chains for their reliability and safety. If he could convince the court that it was Sutcliffe's "negligent misconduct" and not the company's, then it would be futile for either of the plaintiffs to sue an equally poor fellow employee. Ballinger put together a sound defense, one that was usually effective. The court, however, thought otherwise. In both cases, the court ruled against the GH&H, declaring that the line should have "excercised greater care in the procuring of equipment, and use thereof," and thus the GH&H, not one of its employees (Sutcliffe), was guilty of negligent misconduct. Much to Ballinger's chagrin, in a period of six months his client was ordered to pay a combined total of sixty-six thousand dollars in damages.[44]

Throughout his long career Ballinger prided himself on his devotion to truth, justice, and doing what was morally right regardless of personal consequences. However, Ballinger's "railroad work," as he liked to refer to his employment by the lines, slowly forced him to inure himself to the abuse his clients often inflicted on individuals. Ballinger was aware that his railroad employers were "a troublesome lot." Nonetheless, he believed it was his "duty to find out what the law was & tell my client what rule of life to follow. That was my job. If the rules changed, well & good, but until they did, I served my client to the best of my abilities & ensured his best interest."[45] Such a callous statement seemed contrary to Ballinger's inherently ethical, protective nature. No doubt, at a personal level, Ballinger remained a principled man. However, after twenty years of railroad work, his professional persona had changed; he had become a realist—shrewd, practical, matter of fact. He was still wanting to right a wrong whenever it was in his power to do so, but he did not go out of his way in search of cases of injustice to combat. Nor did he unduly defend the weak and oppressed from the ruthlessness of the powerful. Yet, it was often hard for Ballinger to suppress his compassion. In 1883 he represented the Missouri Pacific against an old family friend who sued to prevent tracks being laid six feet from his kitchen door. "Poor old fellow," Ballinger wrote, "its a hard sort of law at the best that a railroad corporation can carve right through someone's property. I confess I am having great difficulty presenting a very vigorous showing [defense]." A few months later, he felt "very distressed" when the same line insisted he force the sale of a widow's property under the terms of an earlier, unfavorable agreement. Ballinger's sensitivity and fairness usually enabled him to escape ill will: out of his own pocket he paid the widow "just compensation for her land," which ended up being almost twice as much as the railroad had intended giving her. Despite atoning for his client's indifference, Ballinger brooded, "The lawyer must steel himself like the surgeon to think of the subject before him & not the pain his knife may cause."[46]

As Texas roads came under the control of national networks, the lines' attorneys soon found themselves involved in the machinations of the railroad giants. Working for the Galveston, Houston & Henderson and the Gulf, Colorado & Santa Fe put Ballinger in contact with the most famous railroad magnate of the postwar era, Jay Gould. For nearly thirty years Gould was perhaps the most excoriated man in America. He was perceived by many, even those engaged in the same nefarious activities, as the archvillain, epitomizing the worst excesses of that wanton era we have come to call the Gilded Age. Every phase of Gould's business career was fraught with controversy. In his business dealings and ethical standards Gould was no more extraordinary than the rest of his peers. He simply was more brilliant and unwilling to conceal his activities behand a façade of social respectability or moral hypocrisy. He knew the game better than most and never deceived himself or others about it.[47]

By the time Gould's empire extended into the Lone Star State, he had already emerged in the East as the master of financial and corporate manipulation, especially when it came to railroads. For a time he controlled the Union Pacific, Wabash, Kansas Pacific and numerous other, smaller Eastern trunk lines. But the infamous financier also had ambitions as a builder. In Texas his objective was to integrate some of the state's more important roads into the national system he was building. One of the first lines Gould was interested in acquiring was the Galveston, Houston & Henderson, in which, as a result of Ballinger's counsel, he acquired controlling interest in 1881.[48]

Soon after taking over the GH&H, Gould acquired the much more important Texas & Pacific Railroad (T&P), incorporating it into his new line, the International & Great Northern Railroad Company (I&GN). Control of this road would provide him with an essential link in Texas for his growing transportation empire in the middle of the nation to the

Pacific. But the T&P would be of little value to Gould's grand design if its most important trunk line, the Houston Tap & Brazoria (HT&B) did not come with it. Command of this road would allow Gould access to the rich timber and ore deposits of East Texas all the way to the Red River. Acquisition of the Houston Tap proved to be more difficult than either the GH&H or the T&P, for the road was originally the brainchild of one of Texas's most dogged railroad entrepreneurs, Houstonian Paul Bremond. Bremond was the builder of many of the state's early lines, but like most of his associates ran out of money to finish his projects. As a result, the roads became easy prey for the consolidation schemes of Eastern magnates like Gould. Yet Bremond was determined to prevent his line's takeover. He accused Gould and the directors of the I&GN of the "unauthorized and wrongful appropriation" of the company's stock, and that once the lines were consolidated, "the directors by breach of trust" reneged on their agreement with Bremond to buy him out for one hundred thousand dollars. Instead, Bremond received only forty-three thousand, which Gould's directors said his stock, franchises, and property in the line were now worth because of the road having to be "reorganized."[49]

Bremond's claim of having been denied his just compensation was probably accurate. He sought to win his company back by challenging Gould's right to acquire the Houston Tap in the first place. Like most builders, Bremond knew that the state constitution explicitly prohibited outside control of Texas-chartered lines. Throughout the court battle, Bremond and his attorneys (Hutcheson & Carrington of Houston) attempted to invalidate the takeover by invoking the constitutonal decrees against such occurrences.

As Gould acquired various Texas lines, he hired the Houston firm of Baker & Botts as his general Texas counsel. After Baker & Botts lost the Bremond case at the trial court level in 1879, Gould became anxious and wanted Ballinger "to rescue the situation" by "coming to their assistance in this matter." Gould also wanted his principal New York attorneys, the firm of Shearman & Sterling, on the case as well. As the battle between Gould and Bremond dragged on, Ballinger emerged as lead counselor, with Baker & Botts assisting yet deferring to his opinions. Jay Gould ordered this new arrangement through Shearman & Sterling who told Ballinger that "Mr. Gould, our largest stock holders in New York, as well as our purchasing committee all feel that there is presently no better trial lawyer in Texas, whose record in winning appeals is more successful than yourself." Gould was confident Ballinger could "put together a most vigorous and elaborate argument on our behalf."⁵⁰

Ballinger knew the only way his client would be able to keep the T&P was to validate the act of consolidation. He needed to prove that Bremond had not only approved of the merger despite his assertions to the contrary, but since the consolidation took place in May 1873, three years before the constitution made such incorporation unlawful, the acquisition of the Houston Tap by the Great Northern was a legal transaction under Texas laws at the time. To substantiate his argument, Ballinger showed that the HT&B's original charter not only contained a provision authorizing its consolidation with another company, but all that was required to effect such a merger was a vote by two-thirds of the stockholders. Ballinger then pointed out that at a stockholders' meeting in February 1872, the stockholders all agreed to the consolidation and that Bremond knew of this decision and agreed to it as well.⁵¹

Perhaps most damaging to Bremond's position was Ballinger's evidence that Bremond deliberately stayed away from stockholders' meetings and thus his claim that he dissented from the consolidation with the I&GN, was false. As Ballinger further told Shearman & Sterling, Bremond did "know what was going on at the meetings." Ballinger's "star witness" was a Major Tipton, who not only kept Bremond informed of all transactions, but to whom the Houstonian also sent "letters of protest." According to Ballinger, Bremond's letters only contested his compensation for selling his line to the I&GN, but not the two roads' merger. Ballinger was confident that his possession "of very strong affirmative evidence" would show Bremond's "consent to and approval of consolidation."⁵²

Shearman & Sterling were pleased with Ballinger's "clear and full apprehension of all the points of this case. Your quick mastery of the main points will no doubt bring success." Shearman & Sterling's confidence in Ballinger did not prove unwarranted. After his presentation of the Tipton letters, Bremond's attorneys had little to say. They half-heartedly attempted to nullify the legislative act of May 1873 sanctioning the merger by claiming the legislature "had no power to effect a consolidation till plaintiff had consented, or been paid the value of his interest in the company." But as Ballinger reminded the court, Bremond had been paid his interest to the amount of forty-three thousand dollars. Moreover, the Tipton letters clearly proved Bremond had agreed to the consolidation. Ballinger then invoked a statute of limitations, asserting that Bremond's delay for three years "to bring any suit is a bar to his claim. Mere protests, however continuous, will not suffice." Finally, in conjunction with the three-year statute of limitations, Ballinger cited the relatively new doctrine of *ultra vires*, which he contended made it illegal for the I&GN's directors "to refund moneys" to Bremond. According to Ballinger, if the I&GN paid Bremond after a "lapse of three years more than he originally was entitled," the company would be "acting beyond the scope of its powers of incorporation [ultra vires] as defined by its charter."[53]

The Texas Supreme Court believed Ballinger's arguments were sound and thus ruled to reverse the lower court's decision against the I&GN and remand the cause. Though not an outright victory, Ballinger at least persuaded the court to send the case back to the trial court where he hoped he would be more effective than his predecessors. According to Associate Justice Gould (no relation to Jay), the lower court had erred in its decision against the I&GN by precluding the Tipton letters which, if "properly considered," might have led to a "different opinion all together on the subject of consolidation." The letters, Gould believed, proved Bremond authorized the merger. Moreover, even if Bremond had not sanctioned the merger, it was still valid because the majority of stockholders had wanted it. Gould also supported Ballinger's contention that since the consolidation had legislative approval, and since there was no constitutional ban on such acquisitions at the time, the transaction was lawful. Gould was not convinced, however, that Bremond received "equitable relief" from the I&GN for his interests in the HT&B. Gould was certain Bremond had been shortchanged by the I&GN, finding a peculiar discrepancy in the company's published reports showing the true value of the HT&B assets and the actual amount paid to Bremond. The justice believed this finding further supported his decision for remandment. He strongly suggested that the trial court "inquire fully as to the real value of Bremond's equitable interest in the Houston Tap, or the real value of his stock at the time the consolidation was practically effected."[54]

A little over a year later, the trial court, after "reexamining all the new evidence & testimony" Ballinger had brought before the state Supreme Court, awarded Gould the HT&B. Ballinger never doubted that would be the outcome, for as he told Marcus Mott, "the decisions of the [Texas] Supreme Bench relative to railroads, corporations &.c have become fiat—no lower courts will dare oppose them, for if they do they will be considered great nuisances & obstructions to the advance of progress & popular as well as legal opinion will turn against them." The lower court, however, did order I&GN to pay Bremond an additional seven thousand dollars as a result of "further inquiry into the amount of compensation originally awarded to Mr. Bremond when he sold the HT&B." Ballinger did not argue the amount awarded, for as he told Jay Gould, "It is a mere drop in the bucket when compared with the amount of business profit you will make on the merger once the lines have become fully operational." Gould agreed with his Texas counselor, and once again praised Ballinger for his "most expeditious & adroit handling of my affairs."[55]

Upon hearing the court's decision, Shearman & Sterling congratulated Ballinger, declaring he had "fulfilled" his reputation as one of Texas's premier trial lawyers. Ballinger found Shearman & Sterling's present effusiveness toward him to be disingenuous. From the moment Gould insisted on Ballinger as his main counselor, Shearman & Sterling "displayed much reluctance at accepting my opinions." As the jurist further confided to Marcus Mott, the New Yorkers wanted "detailed accounts of all the proceedings, which take up much valuable time. They do not seem to trust my judgment or to have the fullest confidence in my abilities. I hope their apprehension will soon end." Much to Ballinger's annoyance, they also flooded his office with their own briefs and opinions, insisting he use them rather than his own, which they were certain were "much less complete as to information and theory." Even after acknowledging Ballinger's "mastering of all the main points," they refused him full credit for his effort, reminding him "the argument on your side was first framed in New York."[56] It appeared Ballinger's New York brethren were having difficulty accepting the possibility that there might exist a lawyer, outside of their rarefied Wall Street environment, equal to them in skill and knowledge.

Like many well-established Northeastern firms, Shearman & Sterling had little respect for jurists and judges west of the Mississippi. To them, Western as well as Southern lawyers were still buckskin-clad, barely educated itinerants who entered the profession simply to make as much money as possible or to enhance political ambitions. To be sure, many Southern and Western practitioners still fit that description, even by the 1880s. However, by the late Gilded Age, the Western and Southern bars, like many other regional professions, were being transformed by the dynamics of industrial change. As railroads and other industries developed, these practitioners found themselves confronted by new challenges and demands. Even amid such profound change, the West and South still provided one with enough "space" to remain a simple country lawyer. But if one had greater ambitions as well as a desire for greater remuneration, then the buckskin, horse, and Lincolnian wit and rustic charm had to go. Those choosing the path of the corporate lawyer had little choice but to shed their rural personalities and attitudes and assume a more "dignified" and acceptable behavior. The nature of their work and clientele required such a metamorphosis. From the very beginning of his career Ballinger never even remotely resembled such a barrister; yet his Eastern counterparts thought otherwise. Thus, Ballinger's victory in the Bremond case not only vindicated his own reputation and image, but those of the majority of his Texas colleagues as well.

By the 1880s Ballinger's work for his railroad clients had become so consuming that he rarely accepted new business. The firm continued its work in debt collection and real estate but the demands of railroad law forced the partners to subordinate much of their general practice. For awhile, Marcus Mott and Tom Jack handled much of the firm's routine business, but Ballinger soon found that he could not do justice to his railroad clients without their assistance. Thus he delegated the routine matters to young clerks whom he hired or who were willing to volunteer their services in exchange for the privilege of reading law under one of Texas's premier lawyers. The files of Ballinger & Jack are full of letters from young aspirants such as J. E. Poole of Weimar, Texas, who told Ballinger that there was "no other lawyer in the State to whom I would find it a greater honour & privilege to read law under than yourself. Your reputation as one of the profession's greatest advocates & learned scholars is greater than you can imagine."[57] By the 1880s Ballinger usually had four to five such employees at a time working for the firm.

Despite the magnitude and complexity of railroad work, Ballinger & Jack remained a three-to-four-person partnership, and unlike many establishments, the alliances were not temporary; all of Ballinger's partners remained with the firm until death or retirement. Ballinger also never developed any sort of associate system for recruiting and promoting young lawyers with promise to full partnerships. Unlike Baker & Botts of Houston, who also had become railroad and corporate law specialists, and had expanded into one of the state's largest establishments, Ballinger insisted on keeping his firm small, believing it would "allow for greater intimacy in our working relations."[58] While firms like Baker & Botts were evolving into a more corporate type of arrangement, Ballinger shied away from such reorganization. Perhaps he feared that if his practice became more institutional, he would lose touch with it. After his family, nothing was as important to Ballinger as the law. Consequently, his practice was more than just a job or career—it was an extension of his very self—something he had devoted his entire life to seeing succeed, often at his family's expense.

John Wharton Terry, a partner in Ballinger's law firm from 1882 to 1928. Though practicing with Ballinger for only six years, Terry was, Ballinger believed, "a first rate lawyer & of great value to our firm." *Photograph courtesy Mills, Shirley, Eckel & Bassett, L.L.P., of Galveston, Texas.*

Ballinger could not bring himself to do anything that might minimize his personal involvement in his firm's daily operations.

Ballinger was no autocrat, however, insisting that everything be done his way. He allowed his associates great latitude in their work, wanting them to have "the fullest measure of success & contentment in their careers."[59] Ballinger liked having a close working relationship with his colleagues, for they were more than just fellow jurists—they were friends as well. Indeed, Ballinger was so concerned about keeping his office environment one of camaraderie and harmony that all prospective new associates or staff were screened for both their knowledge of the law and their personal compatibility. In short, Ballinger was content to keep Ballinger & Jack a small, personal, and directly managed establishment. Its founder simply would not have been comfortable in any other type of working environment.

Ballinger was briefly tempted to transform his practice into a more institutional arrangement. A trip to New York in 1880, however, convinced him to keep Ballinger & Jack the way it was. After visiting Shearman & Sterling as well as Cravath, Swaine & Moore, two of Wall Street's largest and most prestigious firms, the Texan remarked that though "they seem to be very efficiently run & are capable of vast amounts of work, and no doubt employ the finest attorneys," he found both offices "to be very cold & impersonal places. There is not much conversing among the lawyers—everyone seems to be constantly preoccupied with their own affairs. I don't think I w.d be happy in such a place or capable of much good work. The faces & gen.l temperament here seems to me to indicate that few find their work enjoyable."[60]

Ballinger's unwillingness to transform his practice into a more corporate arrangement did not prevent his firm from enjoying national recognition as one of Texas's premier establishments. As a specialist on the laws of Texas and railroads, Ballinger developed strong correspondent ties with influential corporate law practices in New York and other Northeastern cities. Indeed, by the early 1880s Ballinger had gained quite a reputation on Wall Street as one of the nation's top railroad attorneys. The Texan received letters from a number of prominent New York firms, praising his arguments in a variety of different railroad cases. George Sullivan of New York's Sullivan & Cromwell told Ballinger that he had "just read all the briefs in the [Shirley] case and found yours particularly very forcibly and ably presented. I was so much taken with it that I showed it to another attorney in one of the ablest law firms in New York [Dillaway, Davenport & Leeds] who also spoke in the very highest terms and thought the case had been placed in excellent hands."[61]

Ballinger's reputation for scholarship was also well known in the Northeast. The publishing house of Edward Thompson was putting together an encyclopdia of the most important railroad and corporation cases to date and wanted to hire Ballinger as their "general editor, with a free hand to revise, criticize, and suggest as to any improvement on our plan to present the whole law in the form and arrangement of an encyclopedia." Thompson was especially interested in Ballinger's knowledge of "matters of local practice and local statutory provisions, which you believe to be novel or valuable points of law and should thus be included." Ballinger agreed to help edit the encyclopedia and for his services received a quarterly fee of one thousand dollars until the work was finished.[62]

Though remaining a traditional establishment in organization and attitude, Ballinger & Jack became quite modern in its use of the latest office technology and personnel. In 1881 Ballinger hired his first secretary, a young man named William Bennett, who "henceforth shall be responsible for all our correspondence &c. & the general managing of the office. He has agreed to work for $25 a month." Two years later Ballinger rented his practice's first phone for five dollars a month from the Southwestern Telephone and Telegraph Company. Ballinger initially wanted only to try it out for six months, for he was "uncertain of its practicality." Three months later the jurist remarked that though he was still having difficulty justifying "its practical use here in the office," he and his partners as well as their families were having "great fun using this most magnificent invention. We seem to be calling everyone we know who has one just to hear the strange sound of their voices over the line."[63]

Ballinger's railroad work entailed more than just settling claims and lawsuits. In addition to his trial work, he had to keep the Santa Fe's general manager for Texas, J. H. Crowley, informed of all suits, settlements, compromises, judgments, and suits pending on court dockets on a quarterly basis. Such correspondence alone would more than justify Ballinger's hiring of a full-time secretary and purchase of a typewriter. Ballinger was also responsible for examining all the company's contractual arrangements, ranging from those made between the Santa Fe and its employees, and those between the line and its customers and shippers as well as the suppliers of its equipment. Suffice it to say Ballinger acquired a knowledge of the actual railroad industry beyond anything he initially envisioned. Being the consummate student, Ballinger enjoyed learning all of the industry's ins and outs, and did not mind when he was called upon to "look over" some new rolling stock or locomotive to make sure they were properly made and durable enough to withstand constant use.[64]

Ballinger was more than adequately compensated for all his work. Indeed, by the mid-1880s, over 60 percent of Ballinger & Jack's total revenue was generated by its railroad practice. Ballinger's annual retainer from the Santa Fe as the road's general counsel had reached twelve thousand dollars by 1885. He also received seven thousand per year for representing two other Texas lines—the Galveston, Harrisburg & San Antonio and the Galveston, Houston & Henderson. In addition, Ballinger was paid two thousand dollars annually by Baker & Botts of Houston for handling litigation in Galveston County as local counsel for the Missouri Pacific. By 1887 Ballinger's total professional income had reached forty thousand annually. That amount would be comparable to approximately $251,740 in current value. Ballinger also owned over fifty thousand acres of land scattered throughout the state which he had been accumulating since the mid-1850s. The value of his land was estimated at $343,000 by his land agent,

"The Lawyer of Texas"

H. M. Truehart, of Truehart and Company, a Galveston-based firm reputed to have been the largest real estate agency in the state at the time. Besides his salary from his respective clients, Ballinger was also given "free use of the wires" for all personal as well as business transactions, and free passes on the lines "for travel anywhere, at anytime" for both himself and his family. Even hospitalization and an insurance policy was provided for $4.50 per year. Not bad remuneration especially when compared with the annual wage of an industrial worker, which at the time, depending upon skill level, ranged between two hundred and three hundred dollars.[65]

As the major lines acquired more Texas roads, incorporating them into their national networks, their legal needs expanded commensurately. The companies soon realized that their general counselors could not possibly handle all the litigation and settlement of claims without local assistance. Consequently, by the 1880s, the majority of the larger roads had developed a hierarchy of lawyers, delegating different responsibilities to each tier so as to have the most extensive legal network as was possible in each region or state where their lines operated. Thus, one of Ballinger's chief responsibilities for the Santa Fe included hiring lawyers capable of handling the company's legal work throughout the state. Besides selecting and retaining good counsel, it was also incumbent upon Ballinger to make sure his retainees understood at all times the Santa Fe's policies and procedures, and that they did not deviate from those standards.[66]

The extensive system of local counsel used by the Santa Fe forced Ballinger into a role he was rather uncomfortable with—that of being a manager and of having to adopt a more corporate, impersonal relationship with his colleagues. Like most Texas attorneys Ballinger was used to the more informal and personal working arrangements that had existed before the advent of railroads. Prior to the 1870s most interaction between firms was the result of lawyers having worked directly and closely together on different cases. References from mutual acquaintances as well as political and social contacts also fostered closer ties within the legal community. However, with the coming of railroad-corporate law, the more personal and informal ties among lawyers of the pre-railroad era was replaced by a more formal and structured system. In short, railroad attorneys became less autonomous in conducting their practice, as they were now bound by the policies and procedures of a bureaucracy that labeled them as "company employees." Such impersonal relationships were foreign to most Lone Star attorneys. It was particularly difficult for independent-minded jurists like Ballinger who refused to transform their practices into a more corporate environment. Yet, he gradually adjusted to this more systematic way of "doing the law." No doubt Ballinger's less than sanguine feelings toward being an employee and supervisor were soothed away by the financial and professional benefits to be accrued from representing one of the largest corporations active in his state. Moreover, until 1886 when the Gulf, Colorado & Santa Fe merged with the Atchison, Topeka & Santa Fe, Ballinger, along with a handful of other Galvestonians, was directly involved in formulating the company's policies and procedures, as well as the legal standards to be adhered to by all levels of attorneys.[67]

Ballinger's primary contacts were the division attorneys in major Texas cities such as Fort Worth, San Antonio, Waco, and, much to Galvestonians' chagrin, Houston by 1884. Most of the division attorneys hired by Ballinger tended to be partners in well-established firms, such as Jones & Garrett and Davis & Beall of Houston, and Deberry & Smith of Cleburne, and Hefley & Wallace of Waco. All four practices had strong reputations for railroad work in their respective areas. Division attorneys handled a variety of legal work for the line, ranging from filing documents, overseeing the road's vast landholdings, paying taxes, and, of course, litigation and the settling of claims. Ballinger was allowed to determine the fee scale for division attorneys, and he in turn allowed more reputable firms to submit their own "bid" for their work. For example, after some haggling, Ballinger accepted proposals from Deberry & Smith and Hefley & Wallace to work for the line for one thousand and fifteen hundred dollars respectively per year. Ballinger believed Hefley & Wallace were entitled to more than Deberry & Smith because as he told Santa Fe president George Sealy, "Tarrant County [Fort Worth] is a growing place and no doubt our attorneys there will see much work come their way." The same was true for both Jones & Garrett and Davis & Beall, who received fifteen hundred dollars annually because of "the amount of work they must attend to in Harris and Ft. Bend Counties, which at present [July 1884] is the most extensive in the State." In addition to their retainer fees, the partners and their families received free annual travel passes as well as "free use of the wires for all business connected with litigation."[68]

Under the division attorneys were the local attorneys in the smaller towns who took care of the innumerable claims and damage suits occurring in the course of daily railroad operations. Most local attorneys were generally just beginning their legal careers, and despite their inexperience, if Ballinger believed them capable, as he did the second-year firm of Mathews, Wilkes & Wood of Lampasas, he would employ them with a starting salary of around five hundred dollars a year to handle "very routine matters requiring the most rudimentary knowledge of [railroad] law." By 1885 Ballinger was supervising fourteen firms at both the divisional and local levels at a cost to the Santa Fe of approximately twenty thousand dollars annually.[69]

Ballinger allowed his lawyers at all levels the autonomy to settle claims or try cases as they saw fit. He made sure, however, that at all times, the company's as well as his own policies and procedures were adhered to. In his quarterly circulars, Ballinger reminded his attorneys that it was "the desire of the Santa Fe Railway to avoid all litigation, and to adjust by agreement of all parties, all legal liabilities without trouble or expense to claimants." At all times attorneys were to help "promote good feelings between the Company and the people." Every effort was to be made "to create public sentiment favorable to the Company." Ballinger then outlined "points of observance" for when his attorneys should go to trial, which he emphasized was to be "a mode of last resort." Typically, Ballinger encouraged negotiated settlements to avoid the costs and tensions raised by jury trials. He thus advised his attorneys that "if you find upon your investigation that you cannot make a successful defence you are authorized to make the best compromise in your power. If however, you find success can be made it will be well to quash the service in order to get time to make your defence available." If losing at trial, appeals were to be made only if attorneys were certain the judgment was "erroneous and can be thus reversed, or amount of recovery can be reduced."[70]

Ballinger's autonomy within the Santa Fe's legal network ended abruptly in the spring of 1886. In April of that year, the line's merger with the Atchison, Topeka & Santa Fe (AT&SF) was finalized. The consolidation momentarily caused Ballinger some professional anxiety, for he was uncertain what his role, if any, would be under the new regime. The AT&SF was a major national network with an already established legal hierarchy manned by experienced attorneys. Within two weeks of the merger, Ballinger's fear of possibly being "let go" was allayed. He was notified by company headquarters that he was to be retained as general Texas counsel with an annual salary of seventeen thousand dollars.[71] From the beginning, Ballinger had little to worry about. The directors of the new company were not about to let a reputable, veteran attorney like Ballinger go, especially when he could easily find comparable employment with a competing road. Ballinger was pleased with his position and salary, but as he soon realized, he was no longer free to handle the line's legal business as he saw fit. He had become part of a modern corporation with a chain of command within which he was expected to operate at all times.

The Santa Fe's new legal structure was essentially a four-tiered pyramid, similar to those established by most of the other major lines to handle their extensive legal needs. At the top of the system were the lawyers and traffic managers headquartered in the company's main offices in Boston and New York. Now these men, rather than Ballinger or Sealy, set policies and procedures for the road's daily operation as well as the legal standards to be adhered to by all levels of attorneys. Within weeks of the merger, Ballinger received letters from George Peck, the corporation's general solicitor, outlining in great detail the new organization and standards "to be put into effect immediately." Ballinger was instructed to "have your arrangements with local attorneys conform to those which have been made on the Atchison system." Most important was Peck's announcement that henceforth all final decisions regarding the company's legal business were "to be made through the office of the General Solicitor." It was now clear to Ballinger that instructions from above rather than his own judgment dictated the strategy to be taken in the courthouse.[72]

Although initially rankled by his loss of autonomy, Ballinger understood the rationale for the new policy. As he told Marcus Mott after attending a meeting in Boston of all the line's regional counselors, "At first I felt very affronted by the new policies, but upon more dispassionate & rational examination, I have concluded them to be based on sound deliberation. Times have changed, my dear friend—the practice of law is going forward at such a rate that those who do not accept these changes will be left behind."[73]

In effecting the new policies, Ballinger found that he was expected to become more of a supervisor and advisor to the attorneys in his charge rather than doing the actual law himself. Instead of being directly involved in resolving claims and suits, he supplied legal advice to division attorneys handling such matters and assisted them in preparing briefs when matters went to court. At the same time, local attorneys became more accountable to the division attorneys, performing such services as monitoring juries and keeping track of individuals suspected of "harboring resentments & antagonisms toward the railroad." Ballinger also directed local lawyers to get to know every person on the jury panels and "bring every legitimate influence to bear to overcome any local prejudice which may exist against the Company."[74]

Ballinger had little difficulty implementing most of the Santa Fe's policies. However, there were some that caused recurrent problems. One of the most persistent issues generating tensions between corporate headquarters and its legal employees was the question of compensation. While general counsel for the Gulf, Colorado & Santa Fe, Ballinger set fees and retainers according to the experience of and a sense of fairness to individual attorneys. That policy changed, however, under the new corporate structure. Fees and salaries were now mandated by corporate officials and were to be enforced by Ballinger within Texas. Any changes in the new fee schedule had to be approved by the general solicitor. The Santa Fe's legal department did away with annual retainers, placing virtually all of its attorneys at both the divisional and local level on a contingency-fee basis. The amount of compensation for those attorneys remaining on salary was now determined by the number and types of cases they handled rather than by experience or equity.[75]

Ballinger was very limited in his discretion to depart from these standards. Consequently, his office was routinely flooded with complaints from the network's attorneys over fees and retainers. Seldom could he grant requests for increased payments, and when he believed one of his attorneys was being unfairly compensated for his work, he was forced to spend copious amounts of time compiling detailed statistical evidence to justify to corporate officials why this particular attorney was entitled to a raise. More often than not Ballinger's entreaties fell on deaf ears, for the Santa Fe seldom made changes in its fee schedules. Ballinger was disturbed by this "unpleasant policy," but there was little he could do but explain to his attorneys that his "hands were tied in this matter" by corporate policies.[76] Despite the tension over pay, most of Ballinger's network attorneys remained with the Santa Fe. The steady income, prestige, and client referrals resulting from their work for the line went a long way toward soothing egos and pocketbooks.

When Ballinger started his practice in 1854, the common man's lawyer still dominated the profession. However, over the span of his career Ballinger witnessed the great transformations in American jurisprudence and their impact upon the bar. In most respects Ballinger was the epitome of the Tocquevillian elitist. Yet he always seemed to have one foot astride the portals of his more rustic peers. Ballinger was thus an interesting combination of privilege tempered by a pragmatic acceptance of the democratic realities of his time. Though by the end of his career he had transformed his practice into a more corporate-oriented business, Ballinger was never completely comfortable with the new ethos. His refusal to adopt a more corporate and aloof image reflected his distaste for such an environment. No doubt the invectives hurled against corporate lawyers and their firms affected Ballinger. Like many of his contemporaries, he was distressed by the growing number of metropolitan firms, which had emerged even in Texas by the 1880s. To Ballinger, no other institution reflected so accurately the altered contours of professional and economic life in late-nineteenth-century America. With nostalgic fervor Ballinger frequently harked back to an earlier day of presumed professional esteem when his clients were his friends, acquaintances, and townsmen. At times he had difficulty comprehending those colleagues who preferred counseling corporations rather than people. Early in his career Ballinger joined the ranks of the American aristocracy by servicing the legal needs of nascent commercial and industrial capitalism. Yet he simultaneously provided counsel to all comers, often charging minimal fees or accepting simple gifts in exchange for his time. He moved easily between his casual, cluttered office, where informality nurtured trust and loyalty, and the courtroom, where his skill as an advocate earned him local renown. Self-reliant and persevering, Ballinger was every bit as much the country lawyer as he was part of the legal establishment.

Perhaps most disturbing to Ballinger and others of his era was their slow estrangement from their old, natural haunt, the courtroom. Lawyers still went to court—but the corporate lawyer, who rarely, if ever spoke to a judge except socially, made more money and had more prestige than any other lawyer. The corporation lawyer was a dramatic new figure at the bar but he did not chase others out of business. Most, like Ballinger, adapted, modifying their practices enough to be competitive. Thanks to the resiliency of "old time" practitioners like Ballinger, the corporate lawyer merely supplemented the traditionalist, superimposing yet another layer on an already multi-layered occupation. Before the Civil War, the most prominent, famous lawyers were lawyer-statesmen, who argued great cases before great courts, who went into politics, and above all, were skilled in the arts of advocacy. This kind of lawyer never became extinct, and this is the kind of lawyer Ballinger believed he had remained even amid the stresses of a changing professional role in a rapidly changing society.

Chapter Eleven

"AS A GENTLEMAN, CITIZEN, AND LAWYER"

I n the summer of 1885, late in his sixtieth year, Ballinger suffered a severe asthma attack, forcing him once again to "take a long & much needed rest. Hally & Dr. Smith feel I sh.d take a vacation to the North—visit friends & relatives, hunt & fish—maybe it is a good idea." Ballinger did not contest his physician's or his wife's admonishments, for he wanted to spend some time with his only son, Thomas Jack, born in 1866. Tom had just graduated from the University of Michigan, and as a sort of graduation present, Ballinger was going to take his son with him to the North. For the first time Ballinger would be traveling on pleasure without Hally, and as he confessed in his diary "the prospect of leaving on such an extended trip without my dear wife feels very peculiar—but she is adamant that only Tom and I are to go."[1]

In early July 1886, the Ballinger men headed for a two-month trek to the upper middle west, hunting, fishing, and visiting friends and relatives in Michigan, Wisconsin, Minnesota, and Iowa. Most important to Ballinger was his time with his son, whose birth twenty years earlier he had proclaimed as "an event that gratifies me more than any other." Yet, on that "most glorious day" he also confessed that he had not made "it an object of desire to have a boy born to us fearing disappointment." Only three years earlier Ballinger had watched his first son, William Pitt Ballinger Jr. die of yellow fever, which plunged him into prolonged depression. Thomas Jack's growth into a strong young man went a long way toward helping Ballinger ameliorate the trauma of having earlier lost young Willie. Perhaps more important, Thomas Jack came to personify all of Ballinger's hopes for the next generation. Tom symbolized the best of the Ballinger family heritage. In a letter to Hally, Ballinger talked about how pleased he was to finally have the time to enjoy his family, particularly his son. "We visited the Barkers and Lathrops & Tom impressed them favorably. All seemed delighted that we had come together. I have never had a deeper sense of thankfulness. This trip gratifies me more than any other. Tom has told me on several occasions that he never thought such a wonderful adventure was possible & that he hoped just he and I could do it again very soon. He connects me more with the future and increases my interest in it."[2]

Ballinger's "connection with the future" was more imminent than he anticipated in relation to his son. In the fall of 1886 Thomas Jack began reading law under his father's tutelage. A year and a half later, he was admitted to the Texas bar and in the fall of 1887, he became the junior partner in his father's firm. On Thomas Jack's first day as a member of Ballinger, Jack, Mott, Terry & Ballinger, its founder remarked in his diary that "today is one of the most joyous in my life. My son began work as a lawyer & nothing has filled me with greater pride & exaltation than to have him by my side doing the law. I hope we will enjoy a long, fulfilling & prosperous relationship."[3]

Unfortunately, Ballinger's working relationship with his son was short-lived. In early January 1888, after working with his son for only three months, Ballinger suffered another severe asthma attack, forcing him to his bed to try to recuperate. However, instead of improving, he got progressively worse, contracting pneumonia on January 17, 1888. The doctors were called but there was little they could do. After years of battling asthma, his body was simply too weak to fight off the ravages of the pneumonia. Ballinger was dying. On January 20, 1888, "the Nestor of the Texas Bar," was summoned to his final judgment.

Newspapers throughout the state published the news of Ballinger's death with expressions of "deep regret" and "the tremendous respect he held both as a lawyer and devoted citizen of the State, from all who knew him." The Galveston *News* was especially grieved by the loss of its favorite son, referring to Ballinger as "one of the most brilliant lights known to the present age of jurisprudence and a man the state could ill afford to lose, his very name being a tower of strength with the bench and bar."[4]

Hally was flooded with letters of condolence from lawyers from around the country, expressing their "great sadness" upon hearing of Ballinger's death. A week after the Texan's passing, senior partner John S. Davenport of the Wall Street firm of Dillaway, Davenport & Leeds, wrote

Thomas Jack Ballinger. *Photograph courtesy Mills, Shirley, Eckel & Bassett, L.L.P., of Galveston, Texas.*

that "In all my experience I never met a lawyer at whose feet I was so willing to sit and receive the law with perfect confidence in his wisdom and his full grasp of the subject. I think I may say with perfect conscientiousness, that I never saw a man who filled my idea of a lawyer in the best and largest sense so completely." Ballinger's partner, Marcus Mott, received a similar testimony from George Sullivan, senior partner of yet another prominent New York establishment, Sullivan & Cromwell. Sullivan referred to the Galvestonian as "One of the grandest men I ever knew. I treasure as one of the most precious experiences of my life the acquaintance and kindly friendship of this man."[5]

Of the countless professional eulogies Ballinger received, none perhaps was more appropriate and would have pleased him more than the compliment he received from Justice Oran M. Roberts of the Texas Supreme Court. In a memorial address given before the Texas Bar Association, of which Ballinger had been a charter member, Roberts expressed a sentiment that undoubtedly was shared by many of those attending the service. "The two greatest lawyers who have appeared before the Supreme Court in my time were William G. Hale and W. P. Ballinger. William G. Hale was an orator, W. P. Ballinger was not. When Hale finished his argument the Court thought it knew the law; when Ballinger finished his the Court knew it knew the law!"[6]

One of the more personal homages Ballinger received was given before the Galveston bar by James A. Baker, senior partner of the Houston firm, Baker & Botts. As Baker declared in his address, he believed he was the right man to reflect upon Ballinger's life because he had known the Galvestonian both personally and professionally "on a most intimate basis" for thirty-five years. In the Houstonian's estimation, what made Ballinger an outstanding lawyer was his incisive mind and "ingenious arguments," which were "always convincing. He was, without exception, the most painstaking and laborious man I ever knew in the practice." It was Ballinger's laborious investigation" that by "common consent" placed him in the forefront of the Texas bar.[7]

Baker also praised his friend's courtroom demeanor, certain that it too would be remembered as "one of the great hallmarks of his illustrious career." According to Baker, Ballinger was the most disciplined lawyer he had ever known. He never became "excited in the trial of a case" but always remained calm, courteous, and most important, dignified. There were few things more professionally inspiring than to hear Ballinger "illustrate by argument, a principle of the ancient common law," for his rendering was "as refreshing as the coming forth of a living spring from stagnant waters." Baker then lauded Ballinger's "public virtue." Ballinger was presented as an individual "always alive to the political condition of the country, and the political issues of the day." Though always deeply interested in political affairs, Ballinger nonetheless was "independent in thought and action," and "whatever his convictions, they resulted from the mature deliberation of a just and conservative mind and an honest heart."[8]

Finally, Baker extolled Ballinger's private life as "one in which he was beloved by all who knew him." Baker's assessment of Ballinger's character was uncannily accurate; the reflections of someone who did indeed know the jurist intimately. As Baker correctly noted, Ballinger was "simple in his habits and tastes, strong in his friendships, tender and devoted in his family relations, generous and charitable in nature, firm and unyielding in his convictions of duty." The Houstonian also rightly declared that Ballinger respected "candor and sincerity above everything else." Baker proclaimed Ballinger to be "one of the few men of his merit, attainments, and reputation who seemed satisfied with the position they earn and attain in private life." Baker then told the convocation that in one of their last correspondences, Ballinger had told him that foremost in his life had been "Contentment with my lot and surroundings in life; and as a gentleman, citizen and lawyer is the reputation I hope my friends, who know me, will attribute to me." Baker closed his oration by proclaiming to the gathering that "These, my dear sirs, are among the noblest aims in life, and Judge Ballinger achieved them all."[9]

According to Thomas Jack Ballinger, who attended the Galveston bar's ceremony in his father's honor, "When Judge Baker finished his speech, everyone stood up immediately, shouting 'huzzahs' in loud voices. As I looked around the room I saw men I had known since my childhood, whose reputations were among the highest in the state, with tears streaming down their faces." James Baker then called upon the attendants "to appoint suitable persons to send resolutions to the several courts in session in this city [Galveston], and the United States courts when in session" throughout Texas to declare a "state of mourning on the 5th day of March, 1888, and adjourn for the day in respect to the memory of our deceased friend and brother." The Galveston bar's decree was circulated throughout the state and "unanimously accepted." The city of Galveston decreed March 5 "a full day of mourning," closing all state offices, schools, banks, and places of business "so as to honor the memory of one of this City's most honored and respected citizens." But perhaps the words that would have pleased Ballinger most, were the simple ones whispered by his beloved Hally to James Baker at the funeral: "To live forever in the hearts we leave behind is not to die."[10]

Happiness was a word Ballinger rarely used when speaking of himself, and almost never when referring to other people. Throughout his life Ballinger concerned himself not with happiness but with hard work, duty, power, and order. To Ballinger these conditions were not prerequisites for ultimate happiness but ends in themselves. All interrelated, they blanketed myriad specifics. Hard work involved an identity with task, whether practicing law or civic responsibility; it was part of duty and a preliminary of order. Duty demanded alike service to country, productive labor, and devotion to family. It also demanded intellectual courage, honesty, and constancy. These qualities can produce obstacles to personal happiness.

Perpetually haunted by the conviction that he could have accomplished more had he put forth all he was capable of, Ballinger frequently drove himself to exhaustion as his undertakings became personal fixations. Even after his efforts brought victory and acclaim, Ballinger was unfulfilled: preoccupied with his penchant to digress from what he considered central in his life, he repeatedly admonished himself for having "no constancy." Yet, ironically, there was a constant in Ballinger's life—his belief in power, order, and justice. An institutionalist, a gradualist, and a moralist, Ballinger developed large plans for the uses of power. These had one common, revealing objective: stability. Through the exercise of his professional power Ballinger hoped to help provide order both for himself and for the well-being of the larger society in which he lived and worked.

Typical of his time, Ballinger rejected the idea that any classes and any permanent forms of privilege divided American society. On the one hand Ballinger believed that ambitious individuals like himself, who take full advantage of their opportunities were rewarded by society with a better material life. This he pursued, not for himself, but for his family's security. On the other hand, Ballinger believed the ambitious individual must present himself as a good citizen, one who defends images of moral probity and ethical integrity, whose character was unblemished by license and intolerance. Ballinger was an organizer: punctual, industrious, mathematical, and professionally impersonal. He sharpened his mind into an analytical knife. He sought accurate information, and acted with the "coldest logic and prudence," in hopes of establishing universal standards for moral and civil behavior. Ballinger also hoped his work would help build a better institutional order than had ever been known, an order that permitted meritorious individuals to realize their inner selves by means of publicly recognized status, power, and material security.

Though not an orthodox Christian and priding himself on his rationalism, Ballinger was somewhat of a fatalist, believing that his ultimate destiny was controlled by some larger force, some Higher Power. From his fatalism derived some of his most laudable traits: his compassion, his tolerance, his willingness to overlook mistakes. His sense of fatalism also helped him buffer the many reverses he experienced, and enabled him to continue a strenuous life of aspiration.

Ballinger was cautious when it came to political participation and endorsement. Personally attracted to the excitement and passion of political discourse, he abstained as much as possible from such affairs, fearing his political inclinations, if not constantly kept in check, would obtrude upon his larger concerns of family and practice. By the late 1850s, his apoliticism was swayed only by the conviction that the Union's preservation required that he throw off his restraint. His commitment led him to invest his reputation in trying to save the nation from dissolution and war. When that failed, he determinedly offered his services and allegiance to his new country—the Confederate States of America.

Above all else, Ballinger was a nineteenth-century man who shared many of the same experiences, disappointments, and tribulations of his contemporaries. Simple physical survival, rather than the performance of romantic and grandiose deeds, was the utmost concern for the majority of nineteenth-century Americans, including Ballinger. Yet, at the same time, individuals like Ballinger persevered, overcoming great physical debilities and accomplishing more than even themselves believed they were capable. Ballinger's motivation to rise above daily survival is particularly dramatic when set against the backdrop of the many historic events and crises, and social and economic changes from which he could not be separated. Torn between his self-imposed personal responsibilities and his intense motivation to reckon with the events of his time, William Pitt Ballinger accomplished more than the ordinary run of humanity.

Selected Bibliography

I. Archival and Manuscript Collections
Austin History Center, Austin Public Library, Austin, Texas.
    Austin Chronological File
    Frank Brown, "Annals of Travis County and the City of Austin (from Earliest Times to the Close of 1875)"
    E. M. Pease Papers
    Lucadia Pease Papers
    Pease-Graham-Niles Family Papers
Houston Metropolitan Research Center, Houston, Texas
    William Pitt Ballinger Papers
    Thomas M. Jack Papers
    Marcus Mott Papers
Rosenberg Library, Archives, Galveston, Texas
    Betty Ballinger Papers
    William Pitt Ballinger Diary
    William Pitt Ballinger Papers
    Gail Borden Papers
    Joseph Osterman Dyer, "History of Galveston"
    Ferdinand Flake, "Register of 1864 of the Male and Female Inhabitants of Galveston City"
    Peter W. Grayson Papers
    William Jack Family Papers
    Thomas M. League Papers
    James Love Papers
    Ephraim McClean, "My Connexion With the Mexican War"
    Samuel May Williams Papers
    Lorenzo Sherwood Papers and a collection of newspaper and magazine writings
    Ben C. Stuart, "Brief Chronology"; "Galveston's Early Military Companies"; "History of Galveston"; "Necrology"; "Scrapbook"
Center for American History, University of Texas at Austin
    J. Walker Austin Papers
    William Pitt Ballinger Diary and Papers
    Charles Besser Civil War Biographical File
    John Henry Brown Papers
    Guy M. Bryan Papers
    Benjamin H. Epperson Papers
    John Salmon Ford, "The Memoirs of John Salmon Ford"
    Andrew Jackson Hamilton Papers
    T. W. House Papers
    Thomas F. McKinney Biographical File
    Robert Mills Papers
    James P. Newcomb Papers
    John Henniger Reagan Papers
    O. M. Roberts Papers
    Ashbel Smith Papers
    George W. Smyth Papers
    Alexander W. Terrell Papers
    James Webb Throckmorton Papers and Letter Book
Texas State Library, Archives Division, Austin, Texas
    John S. Ford Papers
    "Galveston Sketches," Typescript Collection

WILLIAM PITT BALLINGER

Governor's Records
   Edward Clark Papers
   Richard Coke Papers
   Edmund J. Davis Papers
   Andrew Jackson Hamilton Papers
   Sam Houston Papers
   Francis R. Lubbock Papers
   Pendleton Murrah Papers
   Hardin R. Runnels Papers
   Elisha M. Pease Papers
   James W. Throckmorton Papers
Oscar Hass Collection
Texas Constitution of 1876
John Hancock Diary
Texas. Records of the Secretary of State. Election Returns
Texas. Tax records of Texas counties
Philip C. Tucker, "History of Galveston, 1543–1869"
United States Census
   Manuscript returns for 1850 and 1860
   Seventh Census of the United States, 1850
   Eighth Census of the United States, 1860
University of Texas at Austin Library
   Andrew Johnson Papers, Presidential Papers Microfilm

II. Newspapers

Austin *Democratic Statesman*
Austin *Weekly Southern Intelligencer*
Austin *State Gazette*
Bastrop *Texas Advertiser*
Brownsville *American Flag*
Clarksville *Standard*
Dallas *Herald*
Flake's Weekly Bulletin
Galveston *Civilian*
Galveston *News*
Houston *Telegraph*
Marshall *Texas Republican*
Harrison *Flag*
New York *Times*
New York *Tribune*
San Antonio *Alamo Express*
San Antonio *Express*
San Antonio *Herald*
San Antonio *News*

III. Public Documents

Abstract of all Original Texas Land Titles Comprising Grants and Locations to August 31, 1941. Austin: General Land Office, 1941.

Confederate States of America, Journal of the Congress, 1861–1865. 7 vols. Washington, D.C., Government Printing Office, 1904.

Day, James M., ed. *House Journal of the Ninth Legislature.* Austin: Texas State Library, 1964.

———, ed. *House Journal of the Ninth Legislature, First Called Session.* Austin: Texas State Library, 1965.

———, ed. *Senate and House Journal of the Tenth Legislature, Second Called Session.* Austin: Texas State Library, 1966.

District Court of Galveston, *Minutes, 1856–1880.* Galveston County Court House, Galveston, Texas.

Galveston County Commissioner's Court, *Minutes, 1856–1880.* Galveston County Court House.

Gammel, H. P. N. *The Laws of Texas, 1822–1897.* 10 vols. Austin: The Gammel Book Co., 1898.

Historical Statistics of the United States: Colonial Times to the Present. New York: Basic Books, 1970.

Hartley, Oliver C. *A Digest of the Laws of Texas.* Philadelphia: Thomas Coperthwait and Co., 1850.

General Records of the Department of State. Record Group 59. National Archives. Microfilm.

Inaugural Address and Message of Gov. Edmund J. Davis, to the Legislature, State of Texas, with Accompanying Documents, April 28, 1870. Austin: Tracy, Siemering and Co., 1870.

Journal of the Constitutional Convention of 1875. Galveston: Galveston *News*, 1905.

Journal of [Texas] Reconstruction Convention. Austin: State Printer, 1870.

Letters of Application and

Selected Bibliography

Recommendation During the Administrations of James Polk, Zachary Taylor, Millard Fillmore, and Franklin Pierce, 1845–1854. Record Group 59. National Archives.

Manning, William R., ed. *Diplomatic Correspondence of the United States: InterAmerican Affairs, 1831–1860.* 12 vols. Washington, D.C.: Carnegie Endowment for International Peace, 1932–1939.

Matamoros Consular Dispatches. Ramsdell Microfilm Collection. Center for American History.

Mathews, James M., ed. *Public Laws of the Confederate States of America.* Richmond: R. M. Smith, Printer to Congress, 1864.

———. *The Statutes at Large of the Provisional Government of the Confederate States of America.* Richmond: R. M. Smith, Printer to Congress, 1864.

McIlwaine, John S. *A Annotated Pocket Digest of Texas Laws.* Houston: Cumming & Sons, 1907.

Official Records of the Union and Confederate Navies in the War of the Rebellion. 30 vols. Washington, D.C.: Government Printing Office, 1894–1922.

Oldham, William S. and George White. *A Digest of the General Statute Laws of the State of Texas, [to which are subjoined the repealed laws of the Republic and State of Texas, by, through, or under which rights have accrued; also the colonization laws of Mexico, Coahuila, and Texas, which were in force before the declaration of independence by Texas].* Austin: John Marshall & Co., 1859.

Paschal, George. *A Digest of the Laws of Texas: Containing the Laws in Force, and the Repealed Laws on Which Rights Rest.* 5 editions, Washington, D.C.: W. H. and O. H. Morrison, 1866–1875.

———. *A Digest of Decisions [upon Texas law, of force and repealed, with references to all the civil, Spanish, and common law of decisions and authorities cited.]* 3 vols. Washington, D.C.: W. H. and O. H. Morrison, 1872–1875.

"Registered Reports of Operations and Conditions." Records of the Assistant Commissioner for the State of Texas. Bureau of Refugees, Freedmen, and Abandoned Lands, 1865–1869. Record Group 105. National Archives. Microfilm.

Richardson, James D., comp. *Messages and Papers of the Confederacy.* 2 vols. Nashville: United States Publishing Co., 1906.

———. *Messages and Papers of the Presidents.* 10 vols. New York: Bureau of National Literature and Art, 1908.

Robards, Charles L. *Synopses of the Decisions of the Supreme Court of Texas.* Austin: Brown and Foster, 1865.

State of Texas. *Journal of the House of Representatives, Eighth Legislature.* Austin: State Printer, 1866.

———. *Journal of the Eleventh Legislature.* Austin: State Printer, 1866.

———. *Journal of the Senate, Eighth Legislature.* Austin: State Printer, 1860.

The Supreme Court of Texas on the Constitutionality of the Concsript Laws. Houston: Telegraph Book and Job Establishment, 1863

Texas Legislature. *Resolutions of the State of Texas Concerning Peace, Reconstruction, and Independence.* Austin: State Printer, 1865.

United States Bureau of the Census. *Population of the United States in 1860: Compiled from the Original Returns of the Eighth Census.* Washington, D.C.: Government Printing Office, 1864.

United States Congress. *Congressional Globe, Containing Debates and Proceedings, 1833–1873.* 46 vols. in 109. Washington, D.C.: The *Globe* Office, 1834–1873.

———. House. Communication from

Governor Pease of Texas Relative to the Troubles in that State. 40th Cong., 2d. session, 1868. H. Misc. Doc. 127.

———. 36th Cong., 1st sess., 1859–1860. H. Exec. Doc. 57. Serial 1050.

———. *The Impeachment of Judge Watrous.* 34th Cong., 3d. sess., 1856–1857. H. Rept. 175. Serial 913.

———. *Report of the Joint Committee on Reconstruction.* 39th Cong., 1st sess., 1866. H. Rept. 30.

War of the Rebellion: A Compilation of the Official Records of the Union and Confederate Armies. 70 vols. in 128. Washington, D.C.: Government Printing Office, 1880–1901.

Winkler, Ernest W., ed. *Journal of the Secession Convention of Texas, 1861.* Austin: Austin Printing Co., 1912.

———. *Platforms of the Political Parties in Texas.* Austin: University of Texas Press, 1916.

IV. Pamphlets, Broadsides, and Public Addresses and Speeches

A Brief History of the Galveston Wharf Company. Galveston: Galveston Wharf Co., 1927.

Bryan, Guy M. *Galveston Committee of Safety and Correspondence: An Address to the State of Texas.* Galveston: n.p., 1860.

By-laws of the Galveston, Houston, and Henderson Railroad Company. Galveston: Civilian Book and Job Establishment, 1860.

Carnes, J. E. *Address on the Duty of the Slave States in the Present Crisis: Delivered in Galveston, December 12, 1860, by Special Invitation of the Committee of Safety and Correspondence, and Many of the Oldest Citizens of Galveston.* Galveston: News Book and Job Office, 1860.

Charter and Bylaws of the Galveston Wharf Company. Galveston: Civilian Book and Job Printing Office, 1861.

The Constitutional Union Party of Texas: Address of the Union Executive Committee to the People of Texas. Austin, n.p., 1860.

Gray, Peter W. "Address to the Citizens of Houston on the African Slave Trade." Houston: Houston Telegraph and Printing Co., 1859.

Haynes, John L., et al. "Address to the People of Texas." Austin: *State Gazette*, 1861.

O'Reilly, Henry. *The Slave Aristocracy Against the Democracy: Statements Addressed to Loyal Men of All Parties; Antagonistic Principles Involved in the Rebellion.* New York: Baker and Goodwin, Printers, 1862.

Oldham, Williamson Simpson. *Speech on the Resolution of the State of Texas.* Galveston: Civilian Job Press, 1861.

Proceedings of the Democratic State Convention of Texas Held in Galveston, April 2, 1860. Galveston: News Book and Job Establishment, 1860.

Proceedings of the State Convention of the Democratic Party of the State of Texas, Which Assembled at Waco, Monday, May 4th, 1857. Austin: John Marshall and Co., State Printers, 1857.

A Report and Treatise on Slavery. Austin: John Marshall and Co., State Printers, 1857.

Sherwood, Lorenzo. *Memorial to Congress, January 3rd, 1866: As Regards the New Railroad to be Constructed from Galveston to Kansas.* Galveston: Thomas Ewbank, Esq. and Others, 1866.

———. [Broadside issued by Sherwood explaining to the Citizens of Galveston why he would not deliver a scheduled address on the railroad question.] Galveston: Civilian Press, 1856.

Texas Convention, 1861. "A Declaration of the Causes which Impel the State of Texas to Secede from the Federal

Selected Bibliography

Union." Austin, 1861.

V. Source Material Extracted From Federal and Texas Courts of Law

James Baldridge v. Robert and D. G. Mills, District Court of Galveston, Mar. 31, 1857.

Warren W. Buel v. Galveston, Houston, and Henderson Railroad, District Court of Galveston, June 21, 1859.

William Cook v. Wilard Richardson, District Court of Galveston, November 23, 1860.

The Galveston Wharf Company v. Laurence Frosh, District Court of Galveston, January 2, 1861.

The Mayor, Aldermen, and Inhabitants of the City of Galveston v. Michel B. Menard, 23 Texas Reports, 350–395.

International & Great Northern Railroad Co., Moses Taylor et.al. v. Paul Bremond, 47 Texas Reports, 95–125.

Malcolm G. Douglas v. Galveston, Houston, & Henderson Railway Company, 55 Texas Reports, 564–567.

Robert Mills and another v. Fletcher C. Howeth, 19 Texas Reports, 257–259.

Robert Mills v. Alexander S. Johnston and another, 23 Texas Reports, 309–331.

Robert Mills v. John Nooman, District Court of Galveston, January 2, 1857.

Robert Mills and others v. the State, 23 Texas Reports, 295–308.

Robert Mills and another v. Thomas J. Walton, 19 Texas Reports, 271–273.

Robert Pulsford v. Galveston, Houston & Henderson Railroad, District Court of Galveston, June 30, 1859.

State of Texas v. Theophilus Freeman, District Court of Galveston, January 6, 1857.

State of Texas v. Robert Mills, et al., District Court of Galveston, January 12, 1857.

State of Texas v. Robert Mills, John W. Jockusch, and David G. Mills, District Court of Galveston, January 12, 1857.

State of Texas v. Thomas B. Chubb, District Court of Galveston, January 24, 1857.

State of Texas v. Samuel May Williams and others, 8 Texas Reports, 255–267.

State of Texas v. Samuel May Williams, et al., District Court of Galveston, January 20, 1857.

S. H. Summers v. Robert Mills and others, 21 Texas Reports, 78–92.

Betsy Webster v. T. J. Heard, 32 Texas Reports, 686–712.

Samuel May Williams and others v. The State, 23 Texas Reports, 264–292.

VI. Published Primary Sources

Archer, Branch T. "Texas and Her Resources." *De Bow's Review*, 19 (July 1855), 22–29.

Anderson, Charles. *Texas Before and on the Eve of the Rebellion.* Cincinnati: Peter G. Thompson, 1884.

Barr, Alwyn, ed. "Records of the Confederate Military Commission in San Antonio, July 2–October 10, 1862. *Southwestern Historical Quarterly*, 70 (July 1966), (Oct. 1966), (Apr. 1967); 71 (Oct. 1967); 73 (July 1969), (Oct. 1969).

Barrett, Thomas. *The Great Hanging at Gainesville, Cooke County, Texas, October A.D. 1862.* Austin: Texas State Historical Association, 1961.

Bell, James H. *Speech of Hon. James H. Bell, of the Texas Supreme Court, Delivered at the Capitol on Saturday, December 1st, 1860.* Austin: Intelligencer Book Office.

Bentley and Pilgrim. *Texas Legal Directory for 1876–1877.* Austin: Democratic Statesman Office.

Brown, John Henry. *History of Texas, 1685–1892.* 2 vols. St. Louis: L. E. Daniell, 1892–1893.

Burnham, W. Dean. *Presidential Ballots, 1836–1892.* Baltimore: Johns Hopkins University Press, 1955.

"The City of Galveston," *De Bow's Review*, 3 (Apr. 1847), 348–349. Written by an unidentified European traveler.

Culberson, Charles A. "General Sam Houston and Secession." *Scribner's Magazine*, 39 (May 1906), 584–591.

Davenport, J. H. *The History of the Supreme*

Court of the State of Texas. Austin: The Southern Press, 1917.

De Cordova, Jacob. *Texas: Her Resources and Her Public Men.* Philadelphia: E. Crozet, 1858.

De Lono, A. *Galveston Directory for 1856–57.* Galveston: Galveston News, 1856.

Degener, Edward. *The Minority Report in Favor of Extending the Right of Suffrage, With Certain Limitations to All Men Without Distinction of Race or Color.* Austin: Southern Intelligencer Office, 1866.

Devine, Thomas J., and Alexander W. Terrell. *Speeches Delivered on the 17th January 1862, in the Representative Hall, Austin, Texas.* Austin: John Marshall and Co., 1862.

Drake, Richard. *Revelations of a Slave Smuggler: Being the Autobiography of Capt. Richard Drake, an African Trader for Fifty Years, from 1807–1857.* New York: R. M. DeWitt, 1860.

Foote, Henry S. *The Bench and Bar of the South and Southwest.* St. Louis: Soule, Thomas, and Wentworth, 1876.

Ford, John Salmon. *Rip Ford's Texas.* Edited by Stephen B. Oates. Austin: University of Texas Press, 1963.

Hamilton, Andrew Jackson. *An Address on Suffrage and Reconstruction: The Duty of the People, the President, and Congress.* Boston: Impartial Suffrage League, 1866.

———. *Speech of Gen. A. J. Hamilton of Texas at the War Meeting at Faneuil Hall.* Boston: T. R. Marvin and Son, 1863.

———. *Speech of Hon. Andrew J. Hamilton of Texas, on the State of the Union.* Washington, D.C.: Lemuel Towers, 1861.

Hayes, Rutherford Birchard. *Diary and Letters of Rutherford Birchard Hayes.* Edited by Charles Richard Williams. Columbus: Ohio State Archeological and Historical Society, 1922.

History of Texas together with a Biographical History of the Cities of Houston and Galveston. Chicago: Lewis Publishing Co., 1895.

Houston, Sam. *The Writings of Sam Houston, 1813–1863.* Edited by Amelia W. Williams and Eugene C. Barker. 8 vols. Austin: University of Texas Press, 1938–1943.

Hurd, John C. "Theories of Reconstruction." *American Law Review,* 1 (Jan. 1867), 238–264.

Iglehart, Asa. "Is the Bar Unpopular.?" *American Law Register,* 17 (Nov. 1878), 681–688.

King, Edward. *Texas, 1874: An Eyewitness Account of Conditions in Post-Reconstruction Texas.* Edited by Robert S. Gray. Houston: Cordovan Press, 1974.

Lawrence, William. "The Constitution and the War Power." *American Law Register,* 13 (May 1874), 265–284; 14 (Feb. 1875), 65–73.

Leonard, W. A., comp. *Houston City Directory for 1866.* Houston: Gray, Strickland, and Co., 1866

Lubbock, Francis Richard. *Six Decades in Texas; or, Memoirs of Francis Richard Lubbock, Governor of Texas in War Time, 1861–1863: A Personal Experience in Business, War, and Politics.* Edited by C. W. Raines. Austin: Ben C. Jones & Co., 1900.

Lynch, James D. *The Bench and Bar of Texas.* St. Louis: Nixon-Jones Printing Co., 1885.

Marten, James, ed. "The Lamentations of a Whig: James Throckmorton Writes a Letter." *Civil War History,* 31 (June 1985), 163–170.

Morphis, J. M. *History of Texas.* New York: United States Publishing Co., 1874.

Newcomb, James P. *Sketch of Secession Times in Texas and Journal of Travel from Texas Through Mexico to California, including a History of the "Box Colony."* San Francisco, printed by author, 1863.

Olmsted, Frederick Law. *A Journey Through Texas: Or a Saddle-trip on the Southwestern Frontier*. New York: Dix, Edwards & Co., 1857.

Paschal, George W. "The Last Years of Sam Houston." *Harper's Magazine*, 32 (Apr. 1866), 630–635.

Patrick, Rembert W., ed. *The Opinions of the Confederate Attorneys General, 1861-1865*. Buffalo, N.Y.: Dennis and Co., 1950.

Phillips, Edwin. *Texas and Its Late Military Occupation and Evacuation*. New York: Van Nostrand, 1862.

Proceedings of the Tax Payer's Convention of the State of Texas. Galveston: News Steam Book and Job Office, 1871.

Rankin, Melinda. *Texas in 1850*. Waco: Texian Press, 1966.

Reagan, John H. *Memoirs, with Special Reference to Secession and the Civil War*. Austin and New York: Pemberton Press, 1965.

———. "A Conversation with Governor Houston." *Quarterly of the Texas State Historical Association*, 3 (Apr. 1900), 279–281.

Richardson, Willard. *Galveston Directory for 1859-60, with a Brief History of the Island*. Galveston: Galveston News, 1859.

———. *Galveston Directory, 1856-1857*. Galveston: Galveston News, Book and Job Office, 1857.

———. *Texas Almanac*. Galveston: Richardson & Co., 1859–1860.

Schmitz, Joseph, ed. "Impressions of Texas in 1860." *Southwestern Historical Quarterly*, 42 (Apr. 1939), 334–350.

Sherwood, Lorenzo. "Agencies to be Depended upon in Constructing Internal Improvements, No. 1 Statesmanship—What is it?" *De Bow's Review*, 19 (July year?), 81–88.

———. "Agencies to be Depended on in the Construction of Internal Improvements with Reference to Texas, by a Texan, No. 2." *De Bow's Review*, 19 (Aug. 1855), 201–205.

———. "Texas Railroads." *De Bow's Review*, 13 (Oct. 1852), 523–525.

A Sketch of the Life of the Hon. James H. Bell: Memorial Proceedings in the Supreme Court of Texas in Respect to the Memory of Hon. James H. Bell. Austin: n.p., 1893.

Spaight, A. W. *The Resources, Soil, and Climate of Texas*. Galveston: A. H. Belo & Co., 1882.

Sprague, John T. *The Treachery in Texas, the Secession of Texas and the Arrest of United States Officers and Soldiers Serving in Texas*. New York: Rebellion Record, 1862.

Strom, Steven, ed. "Cotton and Profits Across the Border: William Marsh Rice in Mexico, 1863-1865." *Houston Review*, 8 (1986), 89–96.

Terrell, Alexander W. "Recollections of Sam Houston." *Southwestern Historical Quarterly*, 16 (Oct. 1912), 113–136.

"Texas." *De Bow's Review*, 23 (Aug. 1867), 113–132.

Thrall, Homer S. *Pictorial History of Texas*. St. Louis: N. D. Thompson & Co., 1879.

Tocqueville, Alexis de. *Democracy in America*. Edited by Richard D. Heffner. New York: New American Library, 1956.

Townes, John C. "Sketch of the Development of the Judicial System of Texas." *Southwestern Historival Quarterly*, 2 (July 1898), 29–53, 134–151.

"Trials of a Filibuster." *Harper's Weekly*, 1 (Jan. 10, 1857), 23–34.

Walker, William *The War in Nicaragua*. Mobile, Alabama, and New York: S. H. Goetzel and Co., 1860.

VII. Secondary Sources: Books and Articles

Abbot, Richard H. *The Republican Party and the South, 1855-1877*. Chapel Hill: University of North Carolina Press, 1986.

Adams, Ephraim. *British Interests and Activities in Texas.* Baltimore: Johns Hopkins Press, 1912.

Addington, Wendell G. "Slave Insurrections in Texas." *Journal of Negro History,* 35 (Oct. 1950), 408-434.

Alexander, Thomas B. "Persistent Whiggery in the Confederate South, 1860-1877." *Journal of Southern History,* 27 (Aug. 1961), 305-329.

Ambrose, Stephen E. "Yeoman Discontent in the Confederacy." *Civil War History,* 8 (1962), 259-268.

Amlund, Curtis Arthur. *Federalism in the Southern Confederacy.* Washington, D.C.: Public Affairs Press, 1966.

Andrews, J. Cutler. *The South Reports the War.* Princeton: Princeton University Press, 1970.

———. "The Confederate Press and Public Morale." *Journal of Southern History,* 23 (Nov. 1966), 445-465.

Aptheker, Herbert. *American Negro Slave Revolts.* New York: Columbia University Press, 1943.

———. *The Negro in the Civil War.* New York: Columbia University Press, 1943.

Armstrong, A. B. "Origins of the Texas and Pacific Railway." *Southwestern Historical Quarterly,* 56 (Apr. 1953), 489-497.

Ashburn, Karl E. "Slavery and Cotton Production in Texas." *Southwest Social Science Quarterly,* 57 (July 1953), 257-271.

Avilo, Philip J., Jr. "Phantom Radicals": Texas Republicans in Congress, 1870-1873." *Southwestern Historical Quarterly,* 77 (Apr. 1974), 431-444.

———. "John H. Reagan: Unionist or Secessionist?" *East Texas Historical Journal,* 13 (Spring 1975), 23-33.

Baenziger, Ann Patton. "The Texas State Police During Reconstruction: A Reexamination." *Southwestern Historical Quarterly,* 72 (Apr. 1969), 471-491.

Baggett, James A. "Beginnings of Radical Rule in Texas: The Special Legislative Session of 1870." *Southwestern Journal of Social Education,* 2 (Spring-Summer, 1972), 27-35.

———. "Birth of the Texas Republican Party." *Southwestern Historical Quarterly,* 78 (July 1974), 1-20.

———. "The Constitutional Union Party in Texas." *Southwestern Historical Quarterly,* 82 (Jan. 1979), 233-264.

———. "Origins of the Early Texas Republican Party Leadership." *Journal of Southern History,* 40 (Aug. 1974), 441-454.

Barker, Eugene C. "The Annexation of Texas." *Southwestern Historical Quarterly,* 50 (Jan. 1946), 48-74.

———. "The African Slave Trade in Texas." *Quarterly of the Texas State Historical Association,* 6 (Oct. 1902).

Barney, William L. *Flawed Victory: A New Perspective on the Civil War.* New York: Praeger, 1975.

———. *The Road to Secession: A New Perspective on the Old South.* New York: Praeger, 1972.

Barr, Alwyn. "Texas Coastal Defense, 1861-1865." *Southwestern Historical Quarterly,* 65 (July 1961), 1-31.

———, ed. "Records of the Confederate Military Commission in San Antonio, July 2-Oct. 10, 1862." *Southwestern Historical Quarterly,* 70 (July 1966), 94-95.

———. *Black Texans: A History of Negroes in Texas, 1528-1971.* Austin: Jenkins Publishing Co., 1973.

———. *Reconstruction to Reform: Texas Politics, 1876-1906.* Austin: University of Texas Press, 1971.

Bartlett, Irving H. *The American Mind at Mid-Nineteenth Century.* New York: Thomas Crowell Co., 1967.

Beringer, Richard E., Herman Hattaway, Archer Jones, and William N. Still Jr. *Why the South Lost the Civil War.* Athens: University of Georgia Press, 1986.

Selected Bibliography

Berlin, Ira. *Slaves Without Masters: The Free Negro in the Antebellum South.* New York: Random House, 1974.

Bestor, Arthur. "The American Civil War as a Constitutional Crisis." *American Historical Review,* 69 (Jan. 1964), 327–352.

Billington, Ray Allen. *The Far Western Frontier.* New York: Harper & Row, 1956.

———. *The Protestant Crusade, 1800–1860: A Study of the Origins of American Nativism.* New York: Holt, Rinehart, and Winston, 1938.

Blackburn, J. K. P. "Reminiscences of Terry's Rangers." *Southwestern Historical Quarterly,* 22 (July–Oct., 1918), 38–77, 143–179.

Blackerby, H. C. *Blacks in Blue and Gray: Afro-American Service in the Civil War.* Tuscaloosa: University of Alabama Press, 1979.

Blassingame, John W. *The Slave Community.* New York: Oxford University Press, 1972.

Bloomfield, Maxwell. "Law vs. Politics: The Self-Image of the American Bar, 1830–1860." *American Journal of Legal History,* 12 (Oct. 1968), 306–323.

———. *American Lawyers in a Changing Society, 1776–1876.* Cambridge: Harvard University Press, 1976.

Bluementhal, Henry. "Confederate Diplomacy: Popular Notions and International Realities." *Journal of Southern History,* 32 (May 1966), 151–171.

Boles, John B. *Black Southerners, 1619–1869.* Lexington: The University Press of Kentucky, 1984.

———. *Religion in Antebellum Kentucky.* Lexington: The University Press of Kentucky, 1976.

Bowen, Nancy H. "A Political Labyrinth: Texas and the Civil War." *East Texas Historical Journal,* 11 (Fall 1973), 3–11.

Bridges, C. A. "The Knights of the Golden Circle: A Filibustering Fantasy." *Southwestern Historical Quarterly,* 44 (Jan. 1941), 287–302.

Brock, W. R. *An American Crisis: Congress and Reconstruction, 1865–1867.* New York: Harper and Row, 1963.

Brown, Charles H. *Agents of Manifest Destiny: The Lives and Times of the Filibusters.* Chapel Hill: University of North Carolina Press, 1980.

Buenger, Walter L. *Secession and the Union in Texas.* Austin: University of Texas Press, 1984.

———. "Texas and the Riddle of Secession." *Southwestern Historical Quarterly,* 87 (Oct. 1983), 151–182.

Burton, Margaret Sealy. *The History of Galveston, Texas.* Galveston, privately printed, 1937.

Butte, George C. "Early Development of Law and Equity in Texas." *Yale Law Journal,* 26 (June 1917), 699–709.

Callahan, J. M. *The Diplomatic History of the Southern Confederation.* Baltimore: Johns Hopkins University Press, 1901.

Campbell, Randolph B. "Carpetbagger Rule in Texas: An Enduring Myth." *Southwestern Historical Quarterly,* 97 (Apr. 1994), 587–598.

———. "The District Judges of Texas, 1866–1867: An Episode in the Failure of Presidential Reconstruction." *Southwestern Historical Quarterly,* 93 (1990), 360–364.

———. *An Empire for Slavery: The Peculiar Institution in Texas.* Baton Rouge: Louisiana State University Press, 1989.

———. *Grassroots Reconstruction in Texas, 1865–1880.* Baton Rouge: Louisiana State University Press, 1997.

———. "Scalawag District Judges: The E. J. Davis Appointees." *Houston Review,* 14 (1992), 75–88.

———. "The Whig Party of Texas in the Elections of 1848 and 1852." *Southwestern Historical Quarterly,* 73 (July 1969), 17–34.

——— and Richard G. Lowe. *Wealth and Power in Antebellum Texas*. College Station: Texas A&M University Press, 1977.

Cantrell, Gregg. "Racial Violence and Reconstruction Politics in Texas, 1867–1868." *Southwestern Historical Quarterly*, 93 (Jan. 1990), 333–356.

Carnathan, W. J. "The Proposal to Reopen the African Slave Trade in the South, 1854–1860." *South Atlantic Quarterly*, 25 (Oct. 1926), 410–429.

Carroll, John M. *Galveston and the Gulf, Colorado and Santa Fe Railroad*. Galveston: Center for Transportation and Commerce, 1985.

Carter, Dan T. *When the War Was Over: The Failure of Self-Reconstruction in the South, 1865–1867*. Baton Rouge: Louisiana State University Press, 1985.

Casdorph, Paul. *A History of the Republican Party in Texas, 1865–1965*. Austin: Pemberton Press, 1965.

Case, Lynn M. and Warren F. Spencer. *The United States and France: Civil War Diplomacy*. Philadelphia: University of Pennsylvania Press, 1970.

Cash, Wilbur J. *The Mind of the South*. New York: Alfred A. Knopf, 1941.

Chapin, Bradley. *Early America*. New York: Jerome S. Ozer, Publisher; revised edition, 1984.

Clark, Ira G. *Then Came the Railroads*. Norman: University of Oklahoma Press, 1958.

Clark, Thomas D. *A History of Kentucky*. Lexington: University of Kentucky Press, 1950.

Cole, Arthur C. *The Irrepressible Conflict*. New York: Macmillan, 1934.

———. *The Whig Party in the South*. Washington, D.C.: American Historical Association, 1914; Gloucester, Mass: Peter Smith, 1962.

Connor, Seymour V. *Adventures in Glory*. Austin: Steck-Vaughn, 1965.

Cooper, William J., Jr. *Liberty and Slavery: Southern Politics to 1860*. New York: Alfred Knopf, 1983.

Cotham, Edward T., Jr. *Battle on the Bay: The Civil War Struggle for Galveston*. Austin: University of Texas Press, 1998.

Craven, Avery. *The Coming of the Civil War*. Second Edition. Chicago: University of Chicago Press, 1957.

———. *The Growth of Southern Nationalism, 1848–1861*. Baton Rouge: Louisiana State University Press, 1953.

Cremin, Lawrence A. *American Education: The National Experience, 1783–1876*. New York: Harper & Row, 1980.

Crenshaw, Ollinger. *The Slave States in the Presidential Election of 1860*. Baltimore: Johns Hopkins University Press, 1845.

Crouch, Barry A., and L. J. Schultz. "Crisis in Color: Racial Separation in Texas During Reconstruction." *Civil War History*, 16 (Mar. 1969), 37–49.

———. "Unmanacling Texas Reconstruction: A Twenty Year Perspective." *Southwestern Historical Quarterly*, 93 (Jan. 1990), 275–302.

———. "All the Vile Passions: The Texas Black Code of 1866." *Southwestern Historical Quarterly*, 97 (July 1993), 13–34.

———. "A Spirit of Lawlessness: White Violence, Texas Blacks, 1865–1868." *Journal of Social History*, 18 (1984), 217–232.

Cumberland, Charles. "The Confederate Loss and Recapture of Galveston, 1862–1863." *Southwestern Historical Quarterly*, 51 (Oct. 1947), 109–130.

Cunliffe, Marcus. *Soldiers and Civilians: The Martial Spirit in America, 1775–1865*. New York: Free Press, 1968.

Curran, Francis X. "The Jesuits in Kentucky, 1831–1846." *Mid-America*, 35 (Oct. 1953), 223–246.

Cutrer, Thomas W. *Ben McCulloch and the Frontier Military Tradition*. Chapel

Selected Bibliography

Hill: University of North Carolina Press, 1993.

Daddysman, James W. *The Matamoros Trade: Confederate Commerce, Diplomacy and Intrigue.* Newark, Del.: University of Delaware Press, 1984.

Darst, Maury. "Artillery Defenses of Galveston, 1863." *Military History of Texas and the Southwest*, 12, no. 1 (1975), 63–67.

Davis, Glen. *Childhood and History in America.* New York: The Psycho History Press, 1976.

Davis, David Brion. "The American Family and Boundaries in Historical Perspective." In *From Homicide to Slavery: Studies in American Culture.* New York: Oxford University Press, 1986.

Day, James. *Jacob de Cordova: Land Merchant of Texas.* Waco: Texian Press, 1962.

Degler, Carl N. *The Other South: Southern Dissenters in the Nineteenth Century.* New York: Harper and Row, 1974.

———. *At Odds: Women and the Family in America from the Revolution to the Present.* New York: Oxford University Press, 1980.

Delaney, Robert W. "Matamoros, Port for Texas During the Civil War." *Southwestern Historical Quarterly*, 58 (Apr. 1955), 473–485.

De Leon, Arnoldo. *The Tejano Community, 1836–1900.* Albuquerque: University of New Mexico Press, 1982.

———. *They Called Them Greasers: Anglo Attitudes Towards Mexicans in Texas, 1821–1900.* Austin: University of Texas Press, 1983.

Deussen, Alexander. "The Beginnings of the Texas Railroad System." *Transactions of the Texas Academy of Science*, 9 (1906), 42–74.

DeShields, James T. *They Sat in High Places.* San Antonio: The Naylor Press, 1940.

Doherty, Herbert J., Jr. "Union Nationalism in Georgia." *Georgia State Historical Quarterly*, 37 (Mar. 1953), 18–38.

Dolan, Jay P. *The American Catholic Experience: A History from Colonial Times to the Present.* Garden City, N.Y.: Image Books, 1985.

Donald, David. *The Politics of Reconstruction, 1863–1867.* Baton Rouge: Louisiana State University Press, 1965.

Dorris, Jonathan T. *Pardon and Amnesty Under Lincoln and Johnson: The Restoration of Confederates to Their Rights and Privileges, 1861–1898.* Chapel Hill: University of North Carolina Press, 1953.

———. "Pardon Seekers and Brokers: A Sequel of Appomattox." *Journal of Southern History*, 1 (Aug. 1935), 276–292.

Dowd, Gregory. *A Spirited Resistance: The North American Indian Struggle for Unity, 1745–1815.* Baltimore: Johns Hopkins University Press, 1992.

Doyle, James A. *The Male Experience.* Dubuque, Iowa: William C. Brown Co., 1983.

Dufour, Charles L. *Gentle Tiger: The Gallant Life of Roberdeau Wheat.* Baton Rouge: Louisiana State University Press, 1957.

Duncan, Richard R. "Catholics and the Church in the Antebellum Upper South." In Randall M. Miller and Jon L. Wakelyn, eds., *Catholics in the Old South.* Macon, Ga.: Mercer University Press, 1983.

Dunn, Roy Sylvan. "The KGC in Texas, 1860–1861." *Southwestern Historical Quarterly*, 70 (Apr. 1967), 543–573.

Dumond, Dwight Lowell. *The Secession Movement, 1860–1861.* New York: Macmillan, 1931.

Durden, Robert F. *The Gray and the Black: The Confederate Debate on Emancipation.* Baton Rouge: Louisiana State University Press, 1972.

———. *The Self-Inflicted Wound: Southern*

Politics in the Nineteenth Century. Lexington: University Press of Kentucky, 1985.

Eaton, Clement. *The Growth of Southern Civilization, 1780–1860.* New York: Harper and Row, 1961.

———. *A History of the Southern Confederacy.* New York: Free Press, 1965.

Ericson, John E. "The Delegates to the Convention of 1875: A Reappraisal." *Southwestern Historical Quarterly,* 67 (July 1963), 22–27.

Eisenhower, John D. *So Far From God: The United States War With Mexico, 1846–1848.* New York: Random House, 1989.

Elliot, Claude. "The Freedmen's Bureau in Texas." *Southwestern Historical Quarterly,* 56 (July 1952), 1–24.

———. *Leathercoat: The Life of a Texas Patriot.* San Antonio: Standard Printing Co., 1938.

———. "Union Sentiment in Texas, 1861–1865." *Southwestern Historical Quarterly,* 50 (Apr. 1947), 448–477.

Escott, Paul D. *After Secession: Jefferson Davis and the Failure of Confederate Nationalism.* Baton Rouge: Louisiana State University Press, 1978.

Fairman, Charles F. *Mr. Justice Miller and the Supreme Court, 1862–1890.* New York: Russell and Russell, 1939.

Faust, Drew Gilpin. *The Creation of Confederate Nationalism: Ideology and Identity in the Civil War South.* Baton Rouge: Louisiana State University Press, 1988.

Feherenbach, T. R. *Lone Star: A History of Texas and Texans.* New York: Macmillan, 1968.

Foner, Eric. *Reconstruction: America's Unfinished Revolution, 1863–1877.* New York: Harper and Row, 1988.

Fornell, Earl Wesley. *The Galveston Era: The Texas Crescent on the Eve of Secession.* Austin: University of Texas Press, 1961.

Framo, James L. *Explorations of Marital and Family Therapy: Selected Papers.* New York: Springer Press, 1982. Especially helpful in understanding the Ballinger family dynamics was his 1970 essay, "Symptons from a Family Transactional Viewpoint."

Franklin, John Hope. *A Southern Odyssey: Travelers in the Antebellum North.* Baton Rouge: Louisiana State University Press, 1975.

———. *Reconstruction After the Civil War.* Chicago: University of Chicago Press, 1961.

Fredrickson, George M. *The Black Image in the White Mind: The Debate on the Afro-American Character and Destiny.* Reprint; New York: Wesleyan University Press, 1987.

Friedman, Lawrence M. *A History of American Law.* New York: Simon and Schuster, 1973.

Friend, Llerena B. *Sam Houston: The Great Designer.* Austin: University of Texas Press, 1954.

Gage, Larry Jay. "The Texas Road to Secession and War: John Marshall and the *Texas State Gazette,* 1860–1861." *Southwestern Historical Quarterly,* 62 (Oct. 1958), 119–126.

Garrison, George P. "Guy Morrison Bryan." *Quarterly of the Texas State Historical Association,* 5 (Oct. 1901), 121–136.

Gaston, Paul M. *The New South Creed: A Study in Southern Mythmaking.* New York: Alfred Knopf, 1970.

Graebner, Norman. *The Foundations of American Foreign Policy.* New York: Harlan Davidson, 1985.

Greaser, Galen D. and Jesus de la Teja. "Quieting Titles to Spanish and Mexican Land Grants in the Trans-Nueces: The Bourland and Miller Commission, 1850–1852." *Southwestern Historical Quarterly,* (Apr. 1992), 445–460.

Green, Michael Robert. "'. . . So Illy

Selected Bibliography

Provided . . .' Events Leading to the Creation of the Texas Military Board." *Military History of Texas and the Southwest*, 10, no. 2 (1975), 115–125.

Griffin, Roger A. "Antebellum Texas: Railroad Fever in a New State." In Ben H. Procter and Archie P. MacDonald, eds., *The Texas Heritage*. St. Louis: Forum Press, 1980.

Grodzins, Morton. *The Loyal and the Disloyal: Social Boundaries of Patriotism and Treason*. Chicago: University of Chicago Press, 1956.

Havins, T. R. "The Administration of the Sequestration Act in the Confederate District Court for the Western District of Texas, 1862–1865." *Southwestern Historical Quarterly*, 43 (Jan. 1940), 295–322.

Hansen, James C. and Luciano L'Abate. *Approaches to Family Therapy*. New York: Macmillan, 1982.

Hicks, Jimmie. "Texas and Separate Independence, 1860–1861." *East Texas Historical Journal*, 4 (Oct. 1966), 85–106.

Hietala, Thomas R. *Manifest Design: American Aggrandizement in Late Jacksonian America*. New York: Cornell University Press, 1985.

Holden, W. C. "Frontier Defense in Texas During the Civil War." *West Texas Historical Association Yearbook*, 4 (June 1928), 16–31.

Holt, Michael. *The Rise and Fall of the American Whig Party: Jacksonian Politics and the Onset of the Civil War*. New York: Oxford University Press, 1999.

———. "The Politics of Impatience: The Origins of Know-Nothingism." *Journal of American History*, 60 (Sept. 1973), 309–331.

Horsmen, Reginald. *Expansion and American Indian Policy, 1783–1812*. Norman: University of Oklahoma Press, 1992.

———. *Race and Manifest Destiny: The Origins of American Racial Anglo-Saxonism*. East Lansing: Michigan State University Press, 1981.

Hornsby, Alton, Jr. "The Freedmen's Bureau Schools in Texas, 1865–1870." *Southwestern Historical Quarterly*, 77 (Apr. 1973), 397–417.

Howe, Daniel Walker. *The Political Culture of American Whigs*. Chicago: University of Chicago Press, 1979.

Hughes, W. J. *Rebellious Ranger: Rip Ford and the Old Southwest*. Norman: University of Oklahoma Press, 1964.

Hyman, Harold M. *A More Perfect Union: The Impact of the Civil War and Reconstruction on the Constitution*. New York: Alfred A. Knopf, 1973.

———. *To Try Men's Souls: Loyalty Tests in American History*. Berkely: University of California Press, 1959.

Jager, Ronald B. "Houston, Texas, Fights the Civil War." *Texana*, 11, no. 1 (1973), 30–51.

Kerby, Robert L. *Kirby Smith's Confederacy: The Trans-Mississippi South, 1863–1865*. New York: Columbia University Press, 1972.

King, Alvy L. *Louis T. Wigfall, Southern Fire-eater*. Baton Rouge: Louisiana State University Press, 1970.

Kirk, Jeffrey. "The Family as Utopian Retreat from the City." *Soundings*, 55 (1972), 21–41.

Kohn, Richard. *Eagle and Sword: The Federalists and the Creation of the Military Establishment in America, 1783–1802*. New York: Free Press, 1975.

Kolchin, Peter. *American Slavery: 1619–1877*. New York: Hill and Wang, 1994.

Labaree, Benjamin W. *America's Nation Time, 1607–1789*. New York: W. W. Norton, 1972.

Lang, A. S. *Financial History of the Public Lands of Texas*. Waco: Texian Press, 1932.

Laslett, Barbara. "The Family as a Public and Private Institution: A Historical Perspecitve." *Journal of Marriage and Family*, 35 (1973), 480–492.

Ledbetter, Billy D. "Politics and Society: The Popular Response to Political Rhetoric in Texas, 1857–1860." *East Texas Historical Journal*, 13 (Fall 1975), 11–20.

Lee, Charles R., Jr. *The Confederate Constitution*. Chapel Hill: University of North Carolina Press, 1963.

Lemmon, James T. *The Best Poor Man's Country*. New York: Oxford University Press, 1972.

Levinson, Daniel J. *The Seasons of a Man's Life*. New York: Ballantine Books, 1978.

―――. "Exploration in Biography: Evolution of the Individual Life Structure in Adulthood." In A. I. Rabin, et al., eds., *Further Explorations in Personality*. New York: John Wiley and Sons, 1981.

Litwack, Leon. *Been in the Storm So Long: The Aftermath of Slavery*. New York: Alfred Knopf, 1979.

Long, Clarence. *Wages and Earnings in the United States, 1860–1890*. Princeton: Princeton University Press, 1960.

McCardell, John. *The Idea of a Southern Nation: Southern Nationalists and Southern Nationalism, 1830–1860*. New York: W. W. Norton, 1979.

McComb, David. *Houston: The Bayou City*. Austin: University of Texas Press, 1969.

―――. *Galveston: A History*. Austin: University of Texas Press, 1986.

McKay, Seth Shepard. *Making the Texas Constitution of 1876*. Philadelphia: University of Pennsylvania Press, 1924.

―――. *Debates of the Texas Constitution of 1876*. Austin: University of Texas Press, 1930.

McKitrick, Eric. *Andrew Johnson and Reconstruction*. Chicago: University of Chicago Press, 1960.

McKitrick, Reuben. *The Public Land System of Texas, 1823–1910*. Madison: University of Wisconsin Press, 1918.

McPherson, James M. *Battle Cry of Freedom:The Civil War Era*. New York: Oxford University Press, 1988.

―――. *Ordeal by Fire: The Civil War and Reconstruction*. New York: Alfred Knopf, 1982.

Marten, James. *Texas Divided: Loyalty and Dissent in the Lone Star State*. Lexington: University Press of Kentucky, 1990.

―――. "Slaves and Rebels: The Peculiar Institution in Texas, 1861–1865." *East Texas Historical Journal*, 28 (Spring 1990), 29–36.

Meiners, Fredericka. "The Texas Border Cotton Trade, 1862–1863." *Civil War History*, 23 (Dec. 1977), 293–306.

Merk, Frederick. *Manifest Destiny and Mission in American History*. Recent edition. Westport, Conn.: Greenwood Press, 1983.

Mering, John V. "The Constitutional Union Campaign of 1860: An Example of the Paranoid Style." *Mid-America*, 60 (Apr.–July 1978), 95–106.

―――. "The Slave-State Constitutional Unionists and the Politics of Consensus." *Journal of Southern History*, 43 (Aug. 1977), 395–410.

―――. "Persistent Whiggery in the Confederate South: A Reconsideration." *South Atlantic Quarterly*, 69 (Winter 1970), 124–143.

Merriam, Charles Edward. "The Political Philosophy of John C. Calhoun." In *Studies in Southern History and Politics*. Inscribed to William Archibald Dunning. New York: Columbia University Press, 1914.

Miller, John C. *The Federalist Era, 1789–1801*. New York: Harper and Row, 1960.

Miller, Thomas L. *The Public Lands of Texas, 1519–1970*. Norman:

Selected Bibliography

University of Oklahoma Press, 1972.
Mintz, Steven and Susan Kellogg. *Domestic Revolutions: A Social History of the American Family*. New York: Free Press, 1988.
Moneyhon, Carl H. *Republicanism in Reconstruction Texas*. Austin: University of Texas Press, 1980.
Montejano, David. *Anglos and Mexicans in the Making of Texas, 1836-1986*. Austin: University of Texas Press, 1987.
Moore, Albert B. *Conscription and Conflict in the Confederacy*. New York: Macmillan, 1924.
Moore, Richard. "Radical Reconstruction: The Texas Choice." *East Texas Historical Journal*, 16 (Spring 1978), 15-21.
———. "Reconstruction." In Ben Procter and Archie P. McDonald, eds., *The Texas Heritage*. St Louis: Forum Press, 1980. Pp. 95-107
Moretta, John. "Jose Maria Jesus Carvajal, United States Foreign Policy and the Filibustering Spirit in Texas, 1846-1853." *East Texas Historical Journal*, 33 (Fall 1995), 3-20.
———. "The Censoring of Lorenzo Sherwood: The Politics of Railroads, Slavery, and Southernism in Antebellum Texas." *East Texas Historical Association Journal* (Fall 1997), 39-52.
———. "Pendleton Murrah and States Rights in Civil War Texas." *Civil War History*, 45 (June 1999), 126-146.
Muir, Andrew Forest. "The Destiny of Buffalo Bayou." *Southwestern Historical Quarterly*, 47 (Oct. 1943), 91-106.
———. "Railroads Come to Houston." *Southwestern Historical Quarterly*, 64 (July 1960), 42-63.
———. "The Free Negro in Harris County, Texas." *Southwestern Historical Quarterly*, 46 (Jan. 1943), 214-238.
Myers, S. D. "Mysticism, Realism, and the Texas Constitution of 1876." *Southwest Social Science Quarterly*, 9 (Sept. 1929), 166-184.
Nash, Gary B. *Quakers and Politics: Pennsylvania, 1681-1726*. New edition. Boston: Northeastern University Press, 1993.
Nackman, Mark W. *A Nation Within a Nation: The Rise of Texas Nationalism*. Port Washington, N.Y.: Kennikat Press, 1975.
Nieman, Donald G. *To Set the Law in Motion: The Freedmen's Bureau and the Legal Rights of Blacks, 1865-1868*. Millwood, N.Y.: KTO Press, 1979.
Norvell, James R. "The Reconstruction Courts of Texas, 1867-1873." *Southwestern Historical Quarterly*, 62 (Oct. 1968), 141-163.
Nunn, Wiliam Curtis. *Texas Under the Carpetbaggers*. Austin: University of Texas Press, 1962.
Oakes, James. *The Ruling Race: A History of American Slaveholders*. New York: Vintage Books, 1982.
Oates, Stephen B. *Visions of Glory: Texans on the Southwestern Frontier*. Norman: University of Oklahoma Press, 1970.
———. "Texas Under the Secessionists." *Southwestern Historical Quarterly*, 67 (Oct. 1963), 167-212.
Olsen, Otto. "Reconsidering the Scalawags." *Civil War History*, 12 (Dec. 1966), 304-320.
———, ed. *Reconstruction and Redemption in the South*. Baton Rouge: Louisiana State University Press, 1980.
Osterweis, Rollin G. *The Myth of the Lost Cause, 1865-1900*. Hamden, Conn.: Archon Books, 1973.
———. *Romanticism and Nationalism in the Old South*. New Haven, Conn.: Yale University Press, 1949.
Owsley, Frank L. "Defeatism in the Confederacy." *North Carolina Historical Review*, 3 (July 1926), 446-456.
———. "The Fundamental Cause of the

Civil War: Egocentric Sectionalism." *Journal of Southern History*, 7 (Feb. 1941), 3–18.

———. *State Rights in the Confederacy*. Chicago: University of Chicago Press, 1925; Glouchester, Mass.: Peter Smith, 1961.

Parks, Joseph H. *General Edmund Kirby Smith, CSA*. Baton Rouge: Louisiana State University Press, 1954.

Perman, Michael. *Reunion Without Compromise: The South and Reconstruction, 1865–1868*. Cambridge: Cambridge University Press, 1973.

———. *The Road to Redemption: Southern Politics, 1869–1879*. Chapel Hill: University of North Carolina Press, 1984.

Peskin, Allan. "Was There a Compromise of 1877?" *Journal of American History*, 60 (June 1973), 63–75.

Potter, David M. *The Impending Crisis, 1848–1861*. New York: Harper and Row, 1976.

———. *The South and the Sectional Conflict*. Baton Rouge: Louisiana State University Press, 1968.

Powell, Lawrence N., and Michael S. Wayne. "Self-Interest and the Decline of Confederate Nationalism." In Harry P. Owens and James J. Cooke, eds., *The Old South in the Crucible of War*, 29–45. Jackson: University Press of Mississippi, 1983.

Power, Edward J. *A History of Catholic Higher Education in the United States*. Milwaukee: Marquette University Press, 1958.

Procter, Ben H. *Not Without Honor: The Life of John H. Reagan*. Austin: University of Texas Press, 1962.

Prucha, Paul. *The Sword of the Republic: The United States Army on the Frontier, 1783–1846*. Reprint Edition. Lincoln: University of Nebraska Press, 1995.

Rable, George C. *But There was No Peace: The Role of Violence in the Politics of Reconstruction*. Athens: University of Georgia Press, 1984.

Rabinowitz, Howard N. "From Exclusion to Segregation: Southern Race Relations, 1865–1890." *Journal of American History*, 63 (Sept. 1976), 325–350.

Ramsdell, Charles W. *Behind the Lines in the Southern Confederacy*. Baton Rouge: Louisiana State University Press, 1944.

———. *Reconstruction in Texas*. New York: Columbia University Press, 1910.

———. "The Frontier and Secession." *Studies in Southern History and Politics*. New York: Columbia University Press, 1914.

———. "The Texas State Military Board, 1862–1865." *Southwestern Historical Quarterly*, 27 (Apr. 1924), 253–275.

Randolph, Nowlin. "Judge William Pinckney Hill Aids the Confederate War Effort." *Southwestern Historical Quarterly*, 68 (July 1964), 14–28.

Reynolds, Donald E. *Editors Make War: Southern Newspapers in the Secession Crisis*. Nashville, Tenn.: Vanderbilt University Press, 1970.

Rice, Lawrence D. *The Negro in Texas, 1874–1900*. Baton Rouge: Louisiana State University Press, 1971.

Richter, William L. "The Army and the Negro in Texas During Reconstruction, 1865–1870." *East Texas Historical Journal*, 10 (Spring 1970), 7–19.

———. *The Army in Texas During Reconstruction, 1865–1870*. College Station: Texas A&M University Press, 1987.

———. "'Devil Take Them All': Military Rule in Texas." *Southern Studies*, 26 (Spring 1986), 5–29.

———. "Spread-Eagle Eccentricities: Military-Civilian Relations in Reconstruction Texas." *Texana*, 8, no. 4 (1970), 311–327.

———. "'We Must Rub Out and Begin Anew':The Army and the Republican

Selected Bibliography

Party in Texas Reconstruction, 1867–1970." *Civil War History,* 19 (Dec. 1973), 334–352.
Reed, S. G. *A History of Texas Railroads.* Houston: St. Clair Press, 1941.
Ringold, May Spencer. *The Role of the State Legislatures in the Confederacy.* Athens: University of Georgia Press, 1966.
Rippy, J. Fred. "Border Troubles Along the Rio Grande." *Southwestern Historical Quarterly,* 23 (Oct 1919), 91–110.
Roark, James L. *Masters Without Slaves: Southern Planters in the Civil War and Reconstruction.* New York: W. W. Norton, 1978.
Roberts, Oran M. "The Political, Legislative, and Judicial History of Texas for Its Fifty Years of Statehood, 1845–1895." In Dudley G. Wooten, ed., *A Comprehensive History of Texas, 1865–1897.* 2 vols. Dallas: William G. Scarff, 1898.
Robinson, William M., Jr. *Justice in Grey: A History of the Judicial System of the Confederate States of America.* Cambridge: Harvard University Press, 1941.
Roland, Charles P. *Albert Sidney Johnston: Soldier of Three Republics.* Austin: University of Texas Press, 1964.
Rugoff, Milton. *America's Gilded Age: Intimate Portraits from an Era of Extravagance and Change, 1850–1890.* New York: Henry Holt, 1989.
Russ, William. "Radical Disfranchisement in Texas, 1867–1870." *Southwestern Historical Quarterly* (July 1934), 40–53.
Sandbo, Anna Irene. "Beginnings of the Secession Movement in Texas." *Southwestern Historical Quarterly,* 18 (Oct. 1914), 162–194.
———. "The First Session of the Secesssion Convention of Texas." *Southwestern Historical Quarterly,* 18 (Oct. 1914), 162–194.
Schooner, Thomas. "Confederate Diplomacy and the Texas-Mexican Border, 1861–1865." *East Texas Historical Journal,* 11 (Spring 1973), 33–39.
Sefton, James E. *The United States Army and Reconstructin, 1865–1877.* Baton Rouge: Louisiana State University Press, 1967.
Seip, Terry L. *The South Returns to Congress: Men, Economic Measures, and Intersectional Relationships, 1868–1879.* Baton Rouge: Louisiana State University Press, 1983.
Shafer, Boyd C. *Faces of Nationalism: New Realities and Old Myths.* New York: Harcourt Brace and Co., 1972.
———. *Nationalism, Myth and Reality.* New York: Harcourt Brace and Co., 1955.
Shearer, Ernest. "The Carvajal Disturbances." *Southwestern Historical Quarterly,* 55 (Oct. 1951), 208–235.
Shelley, George. "The Semicolon Court of Texas." *Southwestern Historical Quarterly,* 48 (Apr. 1945), 449–468.
Shepard, E. Lee. "Breaking into the Profession: Establishing a Law Practice in Antebellum Virginia." *Journal of Southern History,* 49 (Aug. 1982), 382–400.
Shook, Robert. "The Federal Military in Texas, 1865–1870." *Texas Military History,* 6 (Spring 1967), 3–45.
Silverthorne, Elizabeth. *Ashbel Smith of Texas: Pioneer, Patriot, Statesman, 1805–1886.* College Station: Texas A&M University Press, 1982.
Simmons, R. C. *The American Colonies from Settlement to Independence.* New York: W. W. Norton, 1981.
Singletary, Otis A. *The Mexican War.* Chicago: University of Chicago Press, 1960.
———. "The Texas Militia During Reconstruction." *Southwestern Historical Quarterly,* 60 (July 1956), 23–35.
Smallwood, James. *Time of Hope, Time of Despair: Black Texans During Reconstruction.* Port Washington, N.Y.: Kennikat Press, 1981.

———. "When the Klan Rode: White Terror in Reconstruction Texas." *Journal of the West*, 25 (Oct. 1986), 4–13.

———. "Perpetuation of Caste: Black Agricultural Workers in Reconstruction Texas." *Mid-America*, 61 (Jan. 1979), 2–24.

Smelser, Marshall. *The Democratic Republic, 1801–1815*. New York: Harper and Row, 1968.

Smith, David P. *Frontier Defense in the Civil War: Rangers and Rebels*. College Station: Texas A&M University Press, 1992.

———. "Conscription and Conflict on the Texas Frontier, 1863–1865." *Civil War History*, 36 (Sept. 1990), 250–261.

Smith, Justin H. *The War With Mexico*. 2 vols. New York: Macmillan Co., 1919.

Smith, Mitchell, "The 'Neutral' Matamoros Trade, 1861–1865." *Southwest Review*, 37 (Autumn 1952), 319–324.

Smyrl, Frank. "Unionism in Texas, 1856–1861." *Southwestern Historical Quarterly*, 68 (Oct. 1964), 172–195.

Snead, Edgar P. "A Historiography of Reconstruction in Texas: Some Myths and Realities." *Southwestern Historical Quarterly*, 72 (Apr. 1969), 435–448.

Somers, Dale A. "James P. Newcomb: The Making of a Radical." *Southwestern Historical Quarterly*, 72 (Apr. 1969), 449–469.

Stambaugh, J. Lee and Lillian J. Stambaugh. *The Lower Rio Grande Valley of Texas*. San Antonio: Naylor Co., 1954.

Stampp, Kenneth. *And the War Came: The North and the Secession Crisis, 1860–1861*. Baton Rouge: Louisiana State University Press, 1970.

———. *Imperiled Union: Essays on the Background of the Civil War*. New York: Oxford University Press, 1981.

———. *The Era of Reconstruction, 1865–1877*. New York: Alfred Knopf, 1965.

———. *The Peculiar Institution: Slavery in the Antebellum South*. New York: Vintage Books, 1956.

Steen Ralph W. "Texas Newspapers and Lincoln." *Southwestern Historical Quarterly*, 51 (Jan. 1948), 199–212.

Stover, John F. *The Railroads of the South, 1865–1900*. Chapel Hill: University of North Carolina Press, 1955.

Summers, Mark W. *Railroads, Reconstruction, and the Gospel of Prosperity: Aid Under the Radical Republicans, 1865–1877*. Princeton: Princeton University Press, 1984.

Sydnor, Charles S. *The Development of Southern Sectionalism, 1819–1848*. Baton Rouge: Louisiana State University Press, 1948.

Takaki, Ronald T. *A Proslavery Crusade: The Agitation to Reopen the African Slave Trade*. New York: Free Press, 1971.

Tatum, Georgia Lee. *Disloyalty in the Confederacy*. Chapel Hill: University of North Carolina Press, 1934.

Taylor, Paul S. *An American-Mexican Frontier—Nueces County, Texas*. Chapel Hill: University of North Carolina Press, 1934.

Thomas, Emory. *The Confederate Nation, 1861–1865*. New York: Harper and Row, 1979.

———. "Rebel Nationalism: E. H. Cushing and the Confederate Experience." *Southwestern Historical Quarterly*, 73 (Jan. 1970), 343–355.

Timmons, Joe T. "The Referendum in Texas on the Ordinance of Secession, February 23, 1861: The Vote." *East Texas Historical Journal*, 11 (Fall 1973), 12–28.

Toller, Frederick B. *Quakers and Atlantic Culture*. New York: W. W. Norton, 1960.

———. *Meeting House and Counting House: The Quaker Merchants of Philadelphia*.

Selected Bibliography

Chapel Hill: University of North Carolina Press, 1948.

Trefousse, Hans. *The Radical Republicans: Lincoln's Vanguard for Racial Justice.* New York: W. W. Norton, 1969.

Trelease, Allen W. *White Terror: The Ku Klux Klan Conspiracy and Southern Reconstruction.* New York: Harper and Row, 1971.

———. "Who Were the Scalawags?" *Journal of Southern History,* 29 (Nov. 1963), 445–468.

Trexler, H. A. "The *Harriet Lane* and the Blockade of Galveston." *Southwestern Historical Quarterly,* 35 (Oct. 1931), 109–123.

Tucker, Philip C., III. "The United States Gunboat *Harriet Lane.*" *Southwestern Historical Quarterly,* 22 (Apr. 1918), 360–380.

Tyler, Ron, et al., eds., *The New Handbook of Texas.* 6 vols. Austin: Texas State Historical Association, 1996.

———. "Cotton on the Border, 1861–1865." *Southwestern Historical Quarterly,* 73 (Apr. 1970), 456–477.

Ver Steeg, Clarence L. *The Formative Years, 1607–1763.* New York: Hill and Wang, 1964.

Wacker, Peter. *Land and People: A Cultural Geography of Preindustrial New Jersey.* Princeton: Princeton University Press, 1975.

Waller, John L. *Colossal Hamilton of Texas: A Biography of Andrew Jackson Hamilton, Militant Unionist and Reconstruction Governor.* El Paso: Texas Western Press, 1968.

Wallace, Ernest. *Texas in Turmoil: The Saga of Texas, 1849–1875.* Austin: Steck-Vaughn, 1965.

Walther, Eric H. *The Fire-eaters.* Baton Rouge: Louisiana State University Press, 1992.

Webb, Walter Prescott. *The Texas Rangers: A Century of Frontier Defense.* Boston: Houghton Mifflin, 1935.

Weisberger, Bernard A. "The Dark and Bloody Ground of Reconstruction Historiography." *Journal of Southern History,* 25 (Nov. 1959), 427–447.

Wesley, Charles H. *The Collapse of the Confederacy.* Washington, D.C.: Associated Publishers, 1937.

White, William W. "The Distintegration of an Army: Confederate Forces in Texas, April–June 1865." *East Texas Historical Journal,* 26 (Fall 1988), 4–47.

———. "The Texas Slave Insurrection in 1860." *Southwestern Historical Quarterly,* 52 (Jan. 1949), 259–285.

Wiebe, Robert H. *The Search for Order, 1877–1920.* New York: Hill and Wang, 1967.

Wiecek, William M. "The Reconstruction of Federal Judicial Power, 1863–1875." *American Journal of Legal History,* 13 (Oct. 1969), 333–359.

Wiley, Bell I. *Southern Negroes, 1861–1865.* New Haven, Conn.: Yale University Press, 1938.

———. *The Life of Johnny Reb: The Common Soldier of the Confederacy.* Baton Rouge: Louisiana State University Press, 1978.

Williams, T. Harry. "An Analysis of Some Reconstruction Attitudes." *Journal of Southern History,* 12 (Nov. 1946), 469–486.

Wilson, Major L. *Space, Time, and Freedom: The Quest for Nationality and the Irrepressible Conflict, 1815–1861.* Westport, Conn.: The Greenwood Press, 1974.

Wish, Harvey. "The Revival of the African Slave Trade in the United States, 1856–1860." *Mississippi Valley Historical Review,* 27 (1941), 569–588.

Winkler, Ernest W. "The Bryan-Hayes Correspondence." *Southwestern Historical Quarterly,* 25, 27 (Jan. 1923, Apr.–Oct. 1924), 100; 164–175; 243–245; 246–250.

Woodward, C. Vann. *Origins of the New South, 1877–1913.* Baton Rouge:

Louisiana State University Press, 1951.

———. *Reunion and Reaction: The Compromise of 1877 and the End of Reconstruction.* Revised edition. New York: Oxford University Press, 1991.

Wooster, Ralph A. *The Secession Conventions of the South.* Princeton: Princeton University Press, 1962.

———, ed. *Lone Star Blue and Gray: Essays on Texas in the Civil War.* Austin: Texas State Historical Association, 1995.

———. *Texas and Texans in the Civil War.* Austin: Eakin Press, 1995.

———. "An Analysis of Texas Know-Nothings." *Southwestern Historical Quarterly,* 70 (Jan. 1967), 414–423.

———. "An Analysis of the Membership of the Texas Secession Convention." *Southwestern Historical Quarterly,* 62 (Jan. 1959), 322–335.

———. "The Texas Gulf Coast in the Civil War." *Texas Gulf Historical and Biographical Record,* 1 (Nov. 1965), 7–16.

———. "Wealthy Texans, 1860." *Southwestern Historical Quarterly,* 71 (Oct. 1967), 163–180.

———. "Wealthy Texans, 1870." *Southwestern Historical Quarterly,* 74 (Oct. 1970), 24–35.

Wyatt-Brown, Bertram. *Southern Honor: Ethics and Behavior in the Old South.* New York: Oxford University Press, 1982.

Yearns, Wilfrid Buck. *The Confederate Congress.* Athens: University of Georgia Press, 1960.

———, ed. *The Confederate Governors.* Athens: University of Georgia Press, 1985.

Ziegler, Jesse A. *Wave of the Gulf.* San Antonio: Naylor Co., 1938.

VIII. Theses and Dissertations

Ashcraft, Allan C. "Texas: 1860–1866. The Lone Star State in the Civil War." Ph.D. diss., Columbia University, 1960.

Baggett, James A. "The Rise and Fall of the Texas Radicals, 1867–1883." Ph.D. diss., North Texas University, 1972.

Bowen, Nancy Head. "A Political Labyrinth: Texas in the Civil War—Questions in Continuity." Ph.D. diss., Rice University, 1974.

Carrier, John Presley. "A Political History of Texas During Reconstruction, 1865–1874." Ph.D. diss., Vanderbilt University, 1971.

Cowling, Annie "The Civil War Trade of the Lower Rio Grande Valley." M.A. thesis, University of Texas, 1926.

Dugas, Vera Lea. "A Social and Economic History of Texas in the Civil War and Reconstruction Period." Ph.D. diss., University of Texas, 1963.

Fanzetti, Robert Joseph. "Elisha Marshall Pease and Reconstruction." M.A. thesis, Southwest Texas State University, 1970.

Glover, Robert W. "The West Gulf Blockade, 1861–1865: An Evaluation." Ph.D. diss., North Texas State University, 1974.

Gray, Ronald N. "Edmund J. Davis: Radical Republican and Reconstruction Governor of Texas." Ph.D. diss., Texas Tech University, 1976.

Griffin, Roger Allen. "Connecticut Yankee in Texas: A Biography of Elisha Marshall Pease." Ph.D. diss., University of Texas, 1973.

Lack, Paul D. "Urban Slavery in the Southwest." Ph.D. diss., Texas Tech University, 1973.

Ledbetter, Billy Don. "Slavery, Fear and Disunion in the Lone Star State: Texans' Attitudes toward Secession and the Union, 1846–1861." Ph.D. diss., North Texas State University, 1972.

Maher, Edward R., Jr. "Secession in Texas." Ph.D. diss., Fordham University, 1960.

Selected Bibliography

Meiners, Fredericka Ann. "The Texas Governorship, 1861–1865: Biography of an Office." Ph.D. diss., Rice University, 1974.

Moretta, John Anthony. "William Pitt Ballinger: Public Servant, Private Pragmatist." Ph.D. diss., Rice University, 1985.

Sandlin, Betty J. "The Texas Reconstruction Constitutional Convention of 1868–1869." Ph.D. diss., Texas Tech University, 1970.

Scarborough, Jane Lynn. "George W. Paschal: Texas Unionist and Scalawag Jurisprudent." Ph.D. diss., Rice University, 1972.

Settles, Thomas M. "The Military Career of John Bankhead Magruder." Ph.D. diss., Texas Christian University, 1972.

Shook, Robert W. "Federal Occupation and Administration of Texas, 1865–1870." Ph.D. diss., North Texas State University, 1970.

Sinclair, Oran Lonnie. "Crossroads of Conviction: A Study of the Texas Political Mind, 1856–1861." Ph.D. diss., Rice University, 1975.

Smyrl, Frank H. "Unionism, Abolitionism, and Vigilantism in Texas, 1856–1865." M.A. thesis, University of Texas, 1961.

Notes

Abbreviations:
    Ballinger Papers: William Pitt Ballinger Papers
    CAH: Center for American History, University of Texas at Austin
    HMRC: Houston Metropolitan Research Center
    NAMS M-179: Microfilm Series M-179, National Archives
    PC: Private Collection, Galveston
    RL: Rosenberg Library, Galveston
    SHQ: Southwestern Historical Quarterly
    TSA: Archives Division, Texas State Library, Austin
    WPB, Diary: in Ballinger Papers (Rosenberg Library, Galveston)

Introduction

1. Marcus Mott, "Recollections," Ballinger and Associates (HMRC); cited hereafter as WPB & Assoc. (HMRC).
2. Jay Gould to Ballinger, Mar. 1, 1881, ibid.
3. Betty Ballinger to Ballinger Mills, Dec. 5, 1930, Ballinger Mills Papers (PC).
4. Thomas Jack Ballinger, undated entry in WBP, "Family Notes," Ballinger Papers (RL). Also see Galveston *News*, Mar. 8, 1881.
5. WPB, "Family Notes," Ballinger Papers (RL).
6. William Pitt Ballinger, Diary, Mar. 11, 1881, ibid.
7. Gould to WPB, Apr. 29, 1881, WPB & Assoc. (HMRC).
8. James Baker to Marcus Mott, Mar. 4, 1888, ibid.
9. Oran Roberts to Thomas Jack Ballinger, Sept. 5, 1890, ibid.
10. Marcus Mott to John S. Davenport, Feb. 18, 1888, ibid.
11. Walter Botts to Thomas Jack Ballinger, Mar. 1, 1888, ibid.
12. One of the many quotations found in Ballinger's "Sketchbook," which was a compilation of personal essays, observations, quotations, and simple musings about his life in general. The "Sketchbook" provides invaluable insights into Ballinger's personality and the way he viewed his world and the way he wanted to be perceived by others. The "Sketchbook" is in the Ballinger Papers, Miscellaneous Notes and Documents (RL).
13. Mott, "Recollections," WPB & Assoc. (HMRC).
14. Speech given before a gathering of Houston and Galveston attorneys, May 9, 1874, in Houston. Copy of speech in WPB & Assoc. (HMRC).

Chapter One

1. WPB, "Family Notes," Ballinger Papers (RL).
2. Ballinger, Diary, June 7, 1870.
3. Thomas Jack Ballinger, "Entry," in Betty Ballinger, "Our Family History," Betty Ballinger Papers (RL).
4. Bradley Chapin, *Early America* (rev. ed.; New York: Jerome S. Ozer, 1984), 126; Benjamin W. Labaree, *America's Nation Time, 1607-1789* (New York: W. W. Norton, 1972), 38-39; Clarence L. Ver Steeg, *The Formative Years, 1607-1763* (New York: Hill and Wang, 1964), 18, 117-118; "William Penn: The Aristocrat as Democrat," in Norman K. Risjord, *Representative Americans: The Colonists* (Lexington, Mass.: D. C. Heath, 1981), 88. For a general history of the Quakers see Frederick B. Tolles, *Quakers and Atlantic Culture* (New York: Macmillan, 1960) and *Meeting House and Counting House: The Quaker Merchants of Colonial Philadelphia, 1682-1763* (Chapel Hill: Univeristy of North Carolina Press, 1948); James T. Lemmon, *The Best Poor Man's Country* (New York: Oxford University Press, 1972); Gary B. Nash, *Quakers and Politics: Pennsylvania, 1681-1726* (new ed.; Boston: Northeastern University Press, 1993); Sally Schwartz, *"A Mixed Multitude:" The Struggle for Toleration in Colonial Pennsylvania* (New York: New York University Press, 1987); WPB, "Family Notes," Ballinger Papers (RL); On the history of colonial New Jersey, see Peter Wacker, *Land and People: A Cultural Geography of Preindustrial New Jersey* (New Brunswick, N.J.: Rutgers University Press, 1975); J. E. Pomfret, *The Province of West New Jersey, 1609-1702: A History of the Origins of an American Colony* (Princeton: Princeton University Press, 1956), and *The Province of East New Jersey, 1609-1702: The Rebelious Proprietary* (Princeton: Princeton University Press, 1962). Also see Chapin, *Early America*, 124-125; R. C. Simmons, *The American Colonies: From Settlement to Independence* (New York: Norton, 1976), 132-133; Ver Steeg, *The Formative years*, 116-117.
5. WPB, "Family Notes,"Ballinger Papers (RL).
6. Ibid.
7. Ibid.
8. Ibid; John C. Miller, *The Federalist Era, 1789-1801* (New York: Harper and Row, 1960), 146-147; Reginald Horsman, *Expansion and American Indian Policy, 1783-1812* (Norman: University of Oklahoma Press, 1992) 42-49; Gregory Dowd, *A Spirited Resistance: The North American Indian Struggle for Unity, 1745-1815* (Baltimore: Johns Hopkins University Press, 1992), 90-115; Paul Prucha, *The Sword of the Republic: The United States Army on the Frontier, 1783-1846* (New York: Macmillan, 1969), 22-27; Richard Kohn, *Eagle and Sword: the Federalists and the Creation of the Military Establishment in America, 1783-1802* (New York: Free Press, 1975), 91-128; Paul A. Hutton, "William Wells: Frontier Scout and Indian Agent," *Indian Magazine of History*, 74 (Sept. 1978), 187-189.
9. WPB, "Family Notes," Ballinger Papers (RL).
10. Ibid.; Marshall Smelser, *The Democratic Republic, 1801-1815* (New York: Harper and Row, 1968), 252-253; Prucha, *The Sword of the Republic*, 110-115; Dowd, *A Spirted Resistance*, 123-147.
11. WPB, "Family Notes," Ballinger Papers (RL); Betty Ballinger, "Our Family History," Betty Ballinger Papers (RL).
12. WPB, "Family Notes," Ballinger Papers (RL); Betty Ballinger, "Our Family History," Betty Ballinger Papers (RL).
13. WPB, "Family Notes," Ballinger Papers (RL); Betty Ballinger, "Our Family History," Betty Ballinger Papers (RL).

14. WPB to daughter, Dec. 1, 1886, Ballinger Mills Papers (PC).
15. WPB to daughter, Nov. 20, 1887, ibid.
16. WPB to daughter, Oct. 22, 1887, ibid.
17. WPB to daughter, Nov. 1, Dec. 4, 1887, ibid.
18. WPB, "Family Notes,"Ballinger Papers (RL); Charles Fairman, *Mr. Justice Miller and the Supreme Court, 1862-1890* (New York: Russell and Russell, 1939), 3-5.
19. Fairman, *Mr. Justice Miller*, 6-12.
20. WPB to daughter, Aug. 5, 1887, B. Mills Paper (PC).
21. For Ballinger's interpretation of Plutarch as well as his observations regarding other classical writers, see his comments in his "Sketchbook," in Ballinger Papers (RL).
22. Jay P. Dolan, *The American Catholic Experience: A History From Colonial Times to the Present* (Garden City, N.Y.: Image Books, 1985), 249-250; John B. Boles, *Religion in Antebellum Kentucky* (Lexington: University Press of Kentucky, 1976), 70; Edward J. Power, *A History of Catholic Higher Education in the United States* (Milwaukee: Marquette University Press, 1958), 333; Richard R. Duncan, "Catholics and the Church in the Antebellum Upper South," in Randall M. Miller and Jon L. Wakelyn (eds.), *Catholics in the Old South: Essays on Church and Culture* (Macon, Ga.: Mercer University Press, 1983), 80-81; Francis X. Curran, "The Jesuits in Kentucky, 1831-1846," *Mid America*, 35 (Jan. 1953), 231.
23. WPB to son, Sept. 15, 1885, Misc. Letters, 1854-1894, WPB & Assoc. (HMRC).
24. WPB to son, Oct. 22, 1885, ibid.
25. WPB to son, Dec. 1, 1885, ibid.
26. Thomas Jack Ballinger, "Entry," in Ballinger Mill's "The Ballinger Family History," B. Mills Papers (PC).
27. Curran, "The Jesuits in Kentucky," 240-242.
28. WPB to son, Jan. 5, 1886, B. Mills Papers (PC).
29. WPB to son Apr. 11, 1886, ibid.
30. WPB to daughter, July 7, 1886, ibid.
31. WPB to daughter, Jan. 3, 1887, ibid.
32. Ibid.
33. WPB to daughter, Aug. 17, 1887, ibid.
34. WPB to son, Oct. 22, 1884, ibid.
35. Ibid.
36. Lawrence M. Friedman, *A History of American Law* (New York: Simon and Schuster, 1973), 278-279; E. Lee Shepard, "Breaking into the Profession: Establishing a Law Practice in Antebellum Virginia," *Journal of Southern History*, 49 (Aug. 1982), 394; Charles Warren, *A History of the American Bar* (Boston: Little, Brown, and Co., 1911), 166.
37. WPB, "Family Notes," Ballinger Papers (RL); Ballinger Mills, "The Ballinger Family History," B. Mills Paper (PC); Galveston *News*, June 12, 1874; Ron Tyler, et al. (eds.), *The New Handbook of Texas* (6 vols.; Austin: Texas State Historical Association, 1996), IV, 305; Charles Waldo Hayes, *History of the Island and City of Galveston* (2 vols.; Austin: Jenkins Press, 1974), II, 839-841.

Chapter Two

1. WPB to daughter, June 17, 1887, B. Mills Papers (PC).
2. Ibid.
3. James Love to Tom Jack, Mar. 15, 1871, Misc. Papers, WPB & Assoc. (HMRC).
4. Ballinger's "Study Guide" can be found in Misc. Papers, WPB & Assoc. (HMRC).

WPB to daughter, June 17, 1887, B. Mills Paper (PC).

5. Henry W. Barton, *Texas Volunteers in the Mexican War* (Wichita Falls: Texian Press, 1970), 22-25.

6. WPB to father, May 1, 1846, B. Mills Papers (PC).

7. Barton, *Texas Volunteers*, 22-25; Alexander Lander, *A Trip to the Wars: Comprising the History of the Galveston Riflemen Formed Apr. 28, 1846, at Galveston, Texas: Together With the History of the Battle of Monterey: Also Description of Mexico and Its People* (Monmouth, Ill.: Printed at the "Atlas Office," 1847).

8. WPB to James Love, May 30, 1846, Ballinger Papers (CAH).

9. Barton, *Texas Volunteers*, 52-55.

10. Ibid.

11. For Ballinger's duties and activities as adjutant see his letters to his uncle, June 22, July 7, 29, Aug. 5, 1846, Ballinger Papers (CAH). Also see Albert Sidney Johnston to James Love, July 17, 1846, B. Mills Papers (PC).

12. Barton, *Texas Volunteers*, 60-63.

13. WPB to uncle, July 30, 1846, Ballinger Papers (CAH).

14. On the concept of Manifest Destiny as one of the driving forces in the Mexican War see Frederick Merk, *Manifest Destiny and Mission in American History* (Westpoint, Conn.: Greenwood Press, 1983); Norman Graebner, *The Foundation of American Foreign Policy* (New York: Harlan Davidson, 1985); Thomas R. Hietala, *Manifest Design: Anxious Aggrandizement in Late Jacksonian America* (New York: Cornell University Press, 1985); Reginald Horsman, *Race and Manifest Destiny: The Origins of American Racial Anglo-Saxonism* (East Lansing: Michigan State University Press, 1981).

15. WPB to Guy Bryan, Nov. 1, 1864, Guy Bryan Papers (CAH); John D. Eisenhower, *So Far From God: The United States War with Mexico* (New York: Random House, 1989), 107-110; Lander, *A Trip to the Wars*, 28.

16. WPB to uncle, Aug. 25, 1846, Ballinger Papers (CAH); Barton, *Texas Volunteers*, 75.

17. Justin H. Smith, *The War With Mexico* (2 vols.; New York: Macmillan Co., 1919), I, 232-234, 249-250; Otis A. Singletary, *The Mexican War* (Chicago: University of Chicago Press, 1960), 33-36; Eisenhower, *So Far From God*, 120-121.

18. Smith, *The War With Mexico*, 250-252; Eisenhower, *So Far From God*, 127-132.

19. Ephraim MacLean to James Love, Oct. 1, 1846, James Love Papers (RL); Ephraim Mclean, "My Connexion With the Mexican War," in Ballinger Papers (RL).

20. Singletary, *The Mexican War*, 39; Eisenhower, *So Far From God*, 138.

21. McLean, "My Connexion with the Mexican War."

22. Ibid.

23. Albert Sidney Johnston to James Love, Oct. 22, 1846, Ballinger Papers (CAH).

24. Eisenhower, *So Far From God*, 138-147; Singletary, *The Mexican War*, 41-42; T. Harry Williams, *The History of American Wars from 1745 to 1918* (New York: Knopf, 1981), 172.

25. The recommendations of Ballinger's committee, his oath, and a copy of his license can be found in the Ballinger Papers (RL).

26. J. Jones to Samuel May Williams, May 9, 1849, Ballinger Papers (CAH); J. Butler to Williams, Apr. 4, 1850, ibid.; WPB to Williams, Sept. 4, 14, Oct. 1, 30, Nov. 23, Dec. 1, 1849, Feb. 18, Apr. 24, May 24, 27, 1850, ibid. Also see Samuel May Williams to Jones, Butler and Ballinger, Sept. 1849-June 1850, Samuel May Williams Papers (RL).

27. Rueben McKitrick, *The Public Land System of Texas, 1823-1910* (Madison:

University of Wisconsin Press, 1918), 20–23. A contemporary decription of the various types of grants can be found in Jacob de Cordova, *Texas: Her Resources and Her Public Men* (Philadelphia: E. Crozet, 1858), 6–10. The theory was that the oldest grant took precedence but since many of these grants were later declared invalid, no title to land acquired through a grant was completely safe until a court ruled on it. Galen D. Greaser and Jesus de la Teja, "Quieting Titles to Spanish and Mexican Land Grants in the Trans–Nueces: The Bourland and Miller Commission, 1850–1852," *SHQ*, 95 (Apr. 1992), 445–447.

28. Mexican law required that grants be made to Mexican citizens only. However, by the time of the Texas rebellion much of this land was in the hands of Anglo speculators. The opinion in *League v. Egery, et al.*, 65 U.S. 264, describes the background of the Littoral and Border grants. Also see McKitrick, *The Public Land System of Texas*, 39; Greaser and de la Teja, "Quieting Titles to Spanish and Mexican Land Grants in the Trans–Nueces."

29. McKitrick, *The Public Land System of Texas*, 39. For discussion of the issue of land transfers from Tejanos to Anglos see Paul Schuster Taylor, *An American–Mexican Frontier—Nueces County, Texas* (Chapel Hill: University of North Carolina Press, 1934).

30. On Anglo determination to strip Tejanos of their land and status, see Arnoldo De Leon, *The Tejano Community, 1836–1900* (Albuquerque: University of New Mexico Press, 1892) and *They Called Them Greasers: Anglo Attitudes toward Mexicans in Texas, 1821–1900* (Austin: University of Texas Press, 1983). Also see David Montejano, *Anglos and Mexicans in the Making of Texas, 1836–1986* (Austin: University of Texas Press, 1987).

31. Leonardo Manso to WPB, May–July 1847, Ballinger Papers (CAH); Joaquin Arguelles to WPB, June–Oct. 1847, ibid.; WPB to Manso, Nov. 3, 28, 1847, ibid.

32. Peter Powell to Jones, Butler and Ballinger, Nov. 22, 1848, ibid.

33. WPB to uncle, Dec. 2, 1847, B. Mills Papers (PC).

34. Love to WPB, Dec. 15, 1847, ibid.

35. WPB to Love, Dec. 30, 1847, ibid.

36. City of Galveston to Ballinger, Jan.–June 1850, Ballinger Papers (CAH).

37. WPB to M. Buechner and J. A. Sauter, Sept. 15, 1850, ibid.

38. Robert Walker to WPB Mar. 30, 1847, ibid.; James Merrill to WPB, Apr. 1, 1847, ibid.

39. WPB, undated notes on case, ibid.

40. Merrill to WPB, May 2, 1847, ibid.

41. Earl Wesley Fornell, *The Galveston Era: The Texas Crescent on the Eve of Secession* (Austin: University of Texas Press, 1961) 241–242; Fred H. Robbins, "The Origins and Development of the African Slave Trade into Texas, 1816–1860" (M.A. thesis, University of Houston, 1972), 111, 119–120, 139–140; Randolph B. Campbell, *An Empire for Slavery: The Peculiar Institution in Texas, 1821–1865* (Baton Rouge: Louisiana State University Press, 1989), 53–54, 72–73.

42. WPB, undated notes in case, Ballinger Papers (CAH); Robert Walker to WPB, May 25, 1847, ibid.

43. Harvey Wish, "The Revival of the African Slave Trade in the United States, 1856–1860," *Mississippi Valley Historical Review*, 27 (1941), 569–588; Fornell, *The Galveston Era*, 248–250, 262–264; Kenneth Stampp, *The Peculiar Institution: Slavery in the Antebellum South* (New York: Knopf, 1956), 270–272.

44. James Love to WPB, May 1, 1849, Ballinger Papers (CAH).

45. Some of Love's more notable Whig associates personally endorsing Ballinger were Texas Supreme Court justice R. T. Wheeler, Col. Albert Sidney Johnston, and eminent Galvestonians John B. Ash, Levi Jones, and Thomas F. McKinney. R. T. Wheeler to

Thomas Ewing, June 1, 1849, M873, R659, frame 614 (National Archives); Albert Sidney Johnston to Ewing, June 2, 1849, frame 626, ibid.; John B. Ash to Ewing, May 1, 1849, frame 620, ibid.; J. L. Bates to Ewing, May 1, June 1, 1849, frames 614 and 620, ibid.

46. Galveston *News*, Sept. 4, 1897; Galveston *Tribune*, Aug. 29, 1924. Also see "William Houston Jack" in Tyler, et al. (eds)., *The New Handbook of Texas*, III, 888–889. By 1840 Jack owned 2,574 acres in Brazoria County as well as 17 town lots in Velasco, and 31 slaves.

47. WPB to daughter, Mar. 16, 1886, B. Mills Papers (PC).

48. The assessment of Hally Ballinger's personality and relationship with Ballinger is based on extrapolation of the numerous letters between the two, as well as diary entries and other personal notes found in Ballinger's various papers in all the collections.

49. James Love to Laura Jack, Apr. 21, 1849.

50. "Family Register," in Ballinger Mills, "The Ballinger Family History," B. Mills Papers (PC); Also Thomas Harrison to Robert Mills, May 2, 1850, ibid.

51. Before actively keeping a diary, Ballinger wrote sporadically about the events in his life in undated notebooks. His description of his first house as well as his mother-in-law's insistence that he accept her generosity, was found in one of his notebooks in the Ballinger Papers (RL).

Chapter Three

1. WPB to wife, Feb. 11, 1851, B. Mills Papers (PC).
2. WPB to wife, Mar. 12, 1851, May 3, 1852, ibid.
3. WPB to wife, Jan. 6, 1852, ibid.
4. Charles H. Brown, *Agents of Manifest Destiny: The Lives and Times of the Filibusters* (Chapel Hill: University of North Carolina Press, 1980), 147–148; J. Fred Rippy, "Border Troubles Along the Rio Grande," *SHQ*, 23 (Oct. 1919), 91–93; John Moretta, "Jose Maria Carvajal, United States Foreign Policy and the Filibustering Spirit in Texas, 1846–1853," *East Texas Historical Journal*, 33 (Fall 1995), 3.
5. Ovid F. Johnson to Robert Hughes, Nov. 5, 1849, in William R. Manning (ed.), *Diplomatic Correspondence of the United States, Inter-American Affairs, 1831–1860* (12 vols.; Washington D.C.: Carnegie Endowment for International Peace, 1932–1939), IX, 45–47. Moretta, "Carvajal," 8–9; July 18, 1852, Sen. Exec. Doc. 1, 32nd Cong., 2nd Sess.; Ernest Shearer, "The Carvajal Disturbances," *SHQ*, 55 (Oct. 1951), 208–210; Charles L. Dufour, *Gentle Tiger: The Gallant Life of Roberdeau Wheat* (Baton Rouge: Louisiana State University Press, 1957), 62–63; New Orleans *Daily Picayune*, Dec. 6, 1851; John Salmon Ford, *Rip Ford's Texas*, ed. Stephen B. Oates (Austin: University of Texas Press, 1963); T. R. Fehrenbach, *Lone Star: A History of Texas and Texans* (New York: Macmillan, 1968), 374–392, 500–502; Ben Proctor, "The Texas Rangers: An Overview," in Ben Procter and Archie P. McDonald (eds.), *The Texas Heritage* (St. Louis: Forum Press, 1980), 119–130; Thomas W. Cutrer, *Ben McCulloch and the Frontier Military Tradition* (Chapel Hill: University of North Carolina Press, 1993). Considered the definitive work on the Rangers is Walter Prescott Webb's *The Texas Rangers: A Century of Frontier Defense* (2nd ed.; Austin: University of Texas Press, 1965). Webb's work, though factually accurate and rich in adventure, dismisses—as does Cutrer's monograph on McCulloch—much of the Rangers' cruelty, law-breaking, and bigotry, especially toward Hispanics.
6. Daniel Webster to WPB, Aug. 25, 1851, Ballinger Papers (CAH).
7. WPB to Webster, Oct. 3, 1851, Microfilm Series M-179, roll 127, frame 453 (National Archives).

8. WPB to Webster, Oct. 24, 1851, ibid.
9. Moretta, "Carvajal," 20; Dufour, *Gentle Tiger*, 64; Brown, *Agents of Manifest Destiny*, 152; Shearer, "Carvajal Disturbances," 209.
10. WPB to Webster, Mar. 3, 1852, NAMS M-179, R130, frame 20.
11. Ibid., frame 21; Moretta, "Carvajal," 15; Sheater, "Carvajal Disturbances," 222-223; Oates, *Rip Ford's Texas*, 203-204; Dufour, *Gentle Tiger*, 68.
12. WPB to Webster, Mar. 3, 1852, NAMS M-179, R130, frame 21; WPB to wife, Mar. 5, 1852, B. Mills Papers (PC).
13. WPB to Webster, Mar. 3, 6, 1852, NAMS M-179, R130, frame 21; Moretta, "Carvajal," 15-16.
14. Manuel Larrainzar to William Marcy, Apr. 21, 1853, in Manning (ed.), *Diplomatic Correspondence*, IX, 558; Austin *Texas States Gazette*, Apr. 17, 1852.
15. Moretta, "Carvajal," 17; Brownsville *American Flag*, Apr. 30, 1853; Shearer, "Carvajal Disturbances," 226-227; New Orleans *Daily Picayune*, Apr. 20, 1853; WPB to Wm. Marcy, Apr. 1, 1853, NAMS M-179, R132, frame 45.
16. WPB to Marcy, Apr. 1, 1853, NAMS M-179, R132, frame 45; WPB to wife, Apr. 3, 1853, B. Mills Papers (PC).
17. WPB, Diary, Nov. 30, 1958.
18. Brownsville *American Flag*, Apr. 10, 1853.
19. WPB to Caleb Cushing, Apr. 6, 1853, NAMS M-179, R132, frame 52.
20. WPB to Cushing, Apr. 9, 1853, Letters Received, Dept. of Justice, RG 60 (National Archives).
21. WPB to wife, Apr. 15, 1853, B. Mills Papers (PC).
22. Ballinger to James Love, July 9, 1853, WPB & Assoc. (HMRC).
23. Hay to Cushing, Aug. 6, 1853, Letters Received, Dept. of Justice, RG 60 (National Archives).
24. Hay to Cushing, Jan. 17, 1854, ibid.
25. WPB to Hay, Jan. 25, 1854, Ballinger Papers (CAH).
26. Hay to Cushing, Jan. 3, 1854, Letters Received, Dept. of Justice, RG 60 (NA); Hay to Ballinger, Jan. 16, 1854, Ballinger Papers (CAH).
27. Ballinger, Diary, Jan. 29, 1854.
28. Moretta, "Carvajal," 25.
29. WPB, Family Papers, B. Mills Papers (PC).
30. Ballinger, Diary, Aug. 8, 1853.
31. See Ballinger Diary entries, years 1852-1884.
32. Ibid. Also see WPB, Family Papers, B. Mills Papers (PC).
33. WPB, Family Papers, ibid.
34. WPB, "Sketchbook," Ballinger Papers (RL).
35. WPB, Family Papers, B. Mills Papers (PC). On Ballinger's notoriety as an amateur botanist, see Galveston *News*, June 12, 1860, and Galveston *Civilian*, Apr. 3, 1860.
36. WPB, Family Papers, B. Mills Papers (PC).
37. WPB to daughter, Feb. 18, 1884, B. Mills Papers (PC).
38. WPB, Family Papers, B. Mills Papers (PC).
39. WPB, Diary, Oct. 10, 1853.

Chapter Four

1. L. A. Thompson to WPB, Oct., 25, 27, Nov. 1, 4, 7, 10, 14, 1853, Ballinger Papers (CAH). James Love to Ballinger, Dec. 10, 1853, WPB & Assoc. (HMRC).

2. Love to WPB, Dec. 10, 1853, WPB & Assoc. (HMRC).
3. Love to WPB, Jan. 21, 1854, ibid.
4. WPB to James Love, Feb. 18, 1854, ibid.
5. Assessments of Jack's character, temperament, and personality, can be found in WPB, Family Papers, B. Mills Papers (PC) as well as in Marcus Mott, "Recollections," Ballinger Papers (HMRC) and "Our Family History," Betty Ballinger Papers (RL).
6. George Armstrong Jones to WPB, Aug., 6, 22, Sept. 1, 1863, Balllinger Papers (CAH). Also see WPB, Diary, Aug. 9, 29, Sept. 6, 20, 1863, Ballinger Papers (RL).
7. WPB to James Love, Aug. 13, 1857, B. Mills Papers (PC).
8. Thomas Jack to his mother, July 1, 1856, Jack Family Papers (RL).
9. WPB, Diary, Nov., 12, Dec. 22, 1857, Feb. 18, 1858, Aug. 5, 1859.
10. WPB to son, May 2, 1886, B. Mills Papers (PC).
11. Royall T. Wheeler to Oran M. Roberts, May 29, 1857, Oran M. Roberts Papers (CAH).
12. For a general discussion of this issue, see McKitrick, *The Public Land System of Texas, 1823-1910*; A. S. Lang, *Financial History of the Public Lands of Texas* (Waco: Texian Press, 1932); Thomas L. Miller, *The Public Lands of Texas, 1519-1970* (Norman: University of Oklahoma Press, 1972); and James Day, *Jacob de Cordova: Land Merchant of Texas* (Waco: Texian Press, 1962).
13. Before his death. Ballinger recapped for his son the entire Grayson episode in a twenty-page brief dated Sept. 21, 1887, which can be found in the Ballinger Papers, Misc. Letters, Notes, and Documents (RL). Also Muldoon's original grant from the governor of Coahuila-Texas as well as the original transfer documents to Grayson can be found in the Peter W. Grayson Papers (RL).
14. Brief dated Sept. 21, 1887, Ballinger Papers, Misc. Letters, Notes, and Documents (RL), 6.
15. Ibid., 7-B.
16. Ibid., 9.
17. WPB to F. Grayson, Nov. 22, 1859, Grayson Papers (RL).
18. Cornelius Peterson to WPB, Feb. 15, 1860, Ballinger Papers (HMRC); WPB to Peterson, Mar. 3, 1860, WPB & Assoc., Misc. Letters and Notes, 1854-1874 (HMRC).
19. Peterson to WPB, May 1, 1860, WPB & Assoc., Misc. Letters and Notes, 1854-1874 (HMRC).
20. Ballinger, Diary, Dec. 16, 1859.
21. William B. Strong to John Wharton Terry, Feb. 9, 1897, WPB & Assoc. (HMRC).
22. Ballinger, Diary, for the year 1858. Beginning in 1858 and for the next ten years, Ballinger kept a complete record of all his expenses, income, and his fee schedule in the back of his diaries. Not until the 1870s did he hire a "professional bookkeeper" to handle the firm's financial affairs.
23. WPB, Diary, Jan. 17, 1855; William Morris to WPB, Oct. 13, 1859, Ballinger Papers (CAH).
24. See "Record Books," years 1874-1890, WPB & Assoc. (HMRC).
25. WPB, "Professional Notes & Speeches," Apr. 24, 1878, WPB & Assoc. (HMRC).
26. Michel Menard to James Love, Jan. 5, Mar. 3, 1855, B. Mills Papers (PC).
27. WPB, Diary, Mar. 22, 1855.
28. Fornell, *The Galveston Era*, 15-16; David G. McComb, *Galveston: A History*

Notes to Pages 74–84

(Austin: University of Texas Press, 1986), 56; Willard Richardson (ed.), *Galveston Directory, 1859–60, with a Brief History of the Island* (Galveston: Galveston News, 1860); E. L. Wall (ed.), *Charter and Bylaws of the Galveston Wharf Company* (Galveston: Civilian Book and Job Printing Office, 1861), "The Port Situation," pp. 1–3. This study first appeared as a series of articles in the Galveston *News* in 1928.

29. *The Mayor Alderman, and Inhabitants of the City of Galveston v. Michel B. Menard*, 23 Texas 352 (1859).
30. Ibid., 353.
31. Ibid., 358–360.
32. Ibid., 366–367.
33. Ibid., 368.
34. Ibid., 379–380.
35. Ibid., 371–372, 383–385.
36. WPB, Diary, Oct. 10, 1859.
37. Ibid., Oct. 17, 19, 1859.
38. *City of Galveston v. Michel B. Menard*, 23 Texas 391.
39. L. A. Thompson to Ballinger, Nov. 5, 1859, Ballinger Papers (CAH).
40. WPB to Tom Jack, Oct. 22, 1859, WPB & Assoc., Misc. Letters, 1854–1874 (HMRC).
41. WPB to son, Nov. 2, 1886, B. Mills Papers (PC). For number of cases heard before the Texas State Supreme Court, see WPB & Assoc. (HMRC), files for the years 1860–1890.
42. WPB, Diary, Mar. 12, 1859, Aug. 5, 1858; WPB to W. B. Sorley, Aug. 24, 1858, WPB & Assoc. (HMRC).
43. WPB, Diary, Feb. 18, 1860.
44. WPB, Diary, Sept. 26, 1859, ibid.
45. WPB, "Professional Notes," Mar. 16, 1882, WPB & Assoc. (HMRC).
46. WPB to Tom Jack, July 17, 1856, ibid.
47. See WPB & Assoc. papers (HMRC) for the years 1854–1884, for examples of Ballinger's intense preparation for cases as well as his interpretation on points of law.
48. Marcus Mott, "Recollections," in WPB & Assoc. (HMRC).
49. See Ballinger Papers for the years 1855–1860 (CAH); Robert Mills to WPB, June 10, 16, 25, 1860; Victor Girandeau to WPB, June 12, 28, 1860, Ballinger Papers (CAH).
50. WPB & Assoc. (HMRC), Aug. 1855–1884.
51. WPB, Diary, July 30, 1854.
52. WPB to Tom Jack, Aug. 2, 1854, WPB & Assoc. (HMRC).
53. WPB, Diary, Aug. 4, 1854.
54. WPB, Diary, Aug. 6, 1854; Binford Tate to WPB, Sept. 22, Oct. 1, 10, 1854, Ballinger and Assoc. (HMRC).
55. Johnston Brothers to WPB, Oct., 22, 30, Nov. 8, 18, 27, Dec. 5, 14, 20, 1860, Jan. 7, 16, 27, Apr. 14, 1861, WPB & Assoc. (HMRC).
56. WPB, Diary, July 23, 1862; WPB to James Sorley, July 25, 1862, WPB & Assoc. (HMRC); Sorley to WPB, Aug. 5, 1862, ibid.
57. The best account of Southerners' Northern sojourns during the antebellum period is John Hope Franklin's *A Southern Odyssey: Travelers in the Antebellum North* (Baton Rouge: Louisiana State University Press, 1975).
58. WPB to Tom Jack, July 29, 1854, WPB & Assoc. (HMRC).
59. WPB to wife, Aug. 8, 1854, B. Mills Papers (PC); WPB, Diary, Aug. 7, 1854.

60. WPB to wife, Aug. 20, 1854, ibid.
61. WPB, Diary, Aug. 8, 1854, ibid.
62. WPB to Tom Jack, Aug. 23, 1854, WPB & Assoc. (HMRC).
63. WPB to Tom Jack, Aug. 19, 1854, ibid.
64. WPB to wife, Sept. 5, 1854, B. Mills Papers (PC).
65. Ibid.
66. WPB, Diary, Sept. 26, 1854.

Chapter Five

1. Fornell, *The Galveston Era*, 18–20; McComb, *Galveston: A History*, 47, 50, 68–69.
2. For an example of Ballinger's influence within the elite's inner circle as well as his ascendancy within Texas, see John Moretta, "The Censoring of Lorenzo Sherwood: The Politics of Railroads, Slavery, and Southernism in Antebellum Texas," *East Texas Historical Journal*, 35 (Fall 1997), 39–52.
3. WPB to Guy Bryan, Oct. 24, 1860, Bryan Papers (CAH).
4. Galveston *News*, July 31, 1856, Nov. 23, 1858, Mar. 28, 1858, Nov. 13, 1859.
5. Copy of Ballinger's speech can be found in his "Notebook," for the year 1856 in Ballinger Papers (RL).
6. Ibid.
7. Ibid.
8. Galveston *News*, Apr. 15, 1859, Galveston *Civilian*, May, 2, June 30, 1859; Houston *Telegraph*, Sept. 27, Nov. 10, 1860; WPB to son, Sept. 18, 1885, B. Mills Papers (PC).
9. WPB to daughter, Oct. 22, 1886, B. Mills Papers (PC).
10. WPB, Diary, Feb. 7, June 23, 1858.
11. WPB to James Love, Aug. 9, 1858, WPB & Assoc. (HMRC).
12. WPB to son, Oct. 1, 1885, B. Mills Papers (PC).
13. WPB, Diary, 1853–1859.
14. WPB, "Professional Notes," June 1880, WPB & Assoc. (HMRC).
15. Tom Jack to Marcus Mott, Oct. 10, 1878, ibid.
16. Galveston *Civilian*, July, 7, 14, Nov. 24, Dec. 5, 17, 19, 1857, Mar. 30, 1858; Houston, *Telegraph*, July 20, 1857.
17. WPB, Diary, Aug. 9, 1854, Feb. 3, Apr. 11, 1857, Oct. 20, Dec. 5, 1859, Mar. 16, 1863, Aug. 19, 1864.
18. Ibid., May 13, 1860.
19. Ibid., July 31, Aug. 8, Nov. 2, 1860.
20. Ibid., Apr. 26, 1858.
21. Ibid., Mar. 23, 1863.
22. Ibid., Oct. 22, 1872.
23. Undated copies of the *News* description of Ballinger's home found in the Betty Ballinger Papers (RL) and B. Mills Papers (PC).
24. WPB to Thomas Harrison, Mar. 3, 1854. Also see Ballinger Papers (CAH) for year 1860 for description, location, and amount of land Ballinger owned in Texas by the eve of the Civil War.
25. WPB, Diary, Feb. 27, Mar. 6, Apr. 18, 1857.
26. Ibid., Mar. 27, 1857.
27. Galveston *News*, Apr. 28, 1856; Galveston *Civilian*, Apr. 30,1856.
28. Steven Mintz and Susan Kellogg, *Domestic Revolutions: A Social History of American Family Life* (New York: Free Press, 1988), 43–45; David Brion Davis, "The American

Family and Boundaries in Historical Perspective," in *From Homicide to Slavery: Studies in American Culture* (New York: Oxford University Press, 1886), 166–183; Carl Degler, *At Odds: Women and the Family in America from the Revolution to the Present* (New York: Oxford University Press, 1980), 10–30, defines the characteristics of the new middle class democratic family that emerged between 1800 and 1860. On the changing image of the American family see John Demos, "The American Family in Past Times," *American Scholar*, 43 (Oct., 1974), 432–439.

29. Kirk Jeffrey, "The Family as Utopian Retreat From the City," *Soundings*, 55 (1972), 21–41; Barbara Laslett, "The Family as a Public and Private Institution: An Historical Perspective," *Journal of Marriage and the Family*, 35 (1973), 480–492; Mintz and Kellogg, *Domestic Revolutions*, 45–46.

30. WPB to Thomas Harrison, Mar. 1, 1860, Jack Family Papers (RL).

31. Fornell, *The Galveston Era*, 7–9.

32. WPB to daughter, Feb. 18, 1885, B. Mills Papers (PC).

33. Tom Jack to Thomas Harrison, May 15, 1859, Jack Family Papers (RL).

34. Ballinger, Diary, 1853–1860.

35. Beaver Williams to Marcus Mott, June 9, 1882, WPB & Assoc. (HMRC); WPB, Diary, Aug. 5, 1860.

36. WPB, Diary, Jan. 6, 1859.

37. WPB, undated entry in "Personal Notes," WPB & Assoc. (HMRC).

38. Ibid.; WPB, Diary, May 26, 1860.

39. WPB, Diary, Jan. 6, 1859.

40. ibid., Apr. 26, 1860.

41. The prices for staples and other goods for 1860 can be found in *Historical Statistics of the United States: Colonial Times to the Present, 1970* (New York: Basic Books, 1976), 205, 209, 213. For Ballinger's household expenditures, see Ballinger Papers for years 1858–1860 (CAH) and WPB, Diary, 1858–1860.

42. *Historical Statistics*, 163, 165; Clarence Long, *Wages and Earning in the United States, 1860–1890* (Princeton: Princeton University Press, 1960), 94–104. The conversion of Ballinger's 1860 income into 1998 dollars was done by economists Steven Pitts and Richard Gosselin of Houston Community College, Central College.

43. James Willard Hurst, *The Growth of American Law: The Law Makers* (Boston: Little, Brown and Co., 1950), 311.

44. Edward Albert Palmer, "Diary," in Edward C. Hutcheson (ed.), *The Houston Lawyer* (Houston: 1977), 9.

45. E. Lee Shepard, "Breaking into the Profession: Establishing a Law Practice in Antebellum Virginia," *Journal of Southern History*, 48 (1982), 408.

46. Ibid., 409.

47. Tom Jack to mother, May 10, 1858, Jack Family Papers (RL).

Chapter Six

1. WPB, Diary, Mar. 10, 1854.

2. There are numerous studies on the relationship between racism and slavery. This author found particularly insightful: George M. Fredrickson, *The Black Image in the White Mind: The Debate on Afro-American Character and Destiny, 1817–1914* (reprint; New York: Wesleyan University Press, 1987); Winthrop D. Jordan, *White Over Black: American Attitudes Toward the Negro, 1950–1812* (Chapel Hill: University of North Carolina Press, 1968); Leslie Howard Owens, *This Species of Property: Slave Life and Culture in the Old South*

Notes to Pages 112–117

(New York: Oxford University Press, 1976); Kenneth Stampp, *The Peculiar Institution: Slavery in the Antebellum South* (New York: Vintage Books, 1956); James Oakes, *The Ruling Race: A History of America Slaveholders* (New York: Vintage Books, 1982); Eugene D. Genovese, *Roll, Jordan, Roll: The World the Slaves Made* (New York: Pantheon Books, 1974).

3. WPB, "On the Importance & Necessity of Educating Our Negroes, Lyceum Address," "Personal Notes," Apr. 6, 1859, WPB & Assoc. (HMRC).

4. WPB, Diary, Apr.–June 1857, Dec. 11, 1858. Also see *State of Texas v. Theophilus Freeman*, District Court of Galveston, Jan. 6, 1857.

5. Campbell, *An Empire for Slavery*; United States Bureau of the Census, *Statistics of the United States (Including Mortality, Property, etc.) in 1860*, 337, shows that Texan slaveholders manumitted only five slaves in the census year 1850 and thirty-seven in 1860. For public condemnation of slaveholders who freed their slaves, see editorial of the Austin *Southern Intelligencer*, Jan. 5, 1859. For further legislative acts prohibiting manumission see *Journal of the Senate of Texas* (Austin: State Printers, 1859), 269, 284, 320, 337, 339; H. P. N. Gammel (comp.), *The Laws of Texas, 1822–1897* (10 vols.; Austin: Gammel Book Co., 1898–1902), V, 22–23.

6. *Betsy Webster v. T. J. Heard*, 32 Texas 656.

7. Ibid., 658; WPB, Diary, June 16, 1857.

8. Ira Berlin, *Slaves Without Masters: The Free Negro in the Antebellum South* (New York: Random House, 1974), 138–156; Helen Tunnicliff Catterall (ed.), *Judicial Cases Concerning Slavery* (5 vols.; New York: Negro Universities Press, 1926–1937), I, 243–244, II, 398, III, 23, 76–77, 166, IV, 68–69, V, 213–214; A. E. Keir Nash, "Fairness and Formalism in the Trials of Blacks in the State Supreme Courts of the Old South," *Virginia Law Review*, 56 (1970), 90–93 and "The Texas Supreme Court and the Trial Rights of Blacks, 1845–1860," *Journal of American History*, 58 (1971), 622–642; Campbell, *An Empire for Slavery*, 111–113, 206–207.

9. Berlin, *Slaves Without Masters*, 370–379. Berlin asserts that by the late 1850s the desire to enslave free blacks greatly intensified and, as a result, free blacks either had to leave the state or return to bondage. Also see Stampp, *The Peculiar Institution*, 216–217; Benjamin Quarles, *The Negro in the Making of America* (New York: Collier Books, 1969), 86–88; Clement Eaton, *The Growth of Southern Civilization, 1790–1860* (New York: Harper and Row, 1961), 92–94; Campbell, *An Empire for Slavery*, 111–113; McComb, *Galveston: A History*, 85; Gammel, *The Laws of Texas*, III, 1042; Andrew Forest Muir, "The Free Negro in Jefferson and Orange Counties, Texas," *Journal of Negro History*, 35 (1950), 183–206; and Muir, "The Free Negro in Harris County, Texas," *Southwestern Historical Quarterly*, 46 (Jan. 1943), 214–238. For other cases similar to Ballinger's see *Purvis v. Sherod*, 12 Texas 140; *Armstrong v. Jowell*, 24 Texas 58 (1859); *Philleo v. Holliday*, 24 Texas 38 (1859). Occasionally the state legislature allowed free blacks to remain in Texas. See Gammel, *The Laws of Texas*, III, 1042, 1045.

10. WPB to James Love, Sept. 16, 1857, B. Mills Papers (PC).

11. Love to WPB, June 5, 1858, WPB & Assoc. (HMRC).

12. Ballinger Papers for the year 1858, Ballinger Papers (CAH); WPB, Diary, June 23, 1858.

13. *Webster v. Heard*, 32 Texas 670.

14. Ibid., 677.

15. Ibid., 676.

16. Ibid., 680.

17. Ibid., 681.

18. WPB to Guy Bryan, Dec. 27, 1858, Bryan Papers (CAH).
19. WPB to James Love, Dec. 16, 1858, B. Mills Papers (PC).
20. In general Texas slave laws were similar to those of the rest of the slaveholding states. For a general discussion of those codes, see Mark Tushnet, *The American Law of Slavery, 1810–1860: Considerations of Humanity and Interest* (Princeton: Princeton University Press, 1981). Although Tushnet does not specifically deal with Texas or make state-by-state comparisons, Texans generally adopted the legislative acts of the older slave states.
21. Ballinger's papers for the years 1855–1861 contain numerous correspondence from slaveowners requesting the attorney's assistance in helping to retain or reclaim their slave property.
22. Galveston *Herald*, May 5, 1857; Galveston *Civilian*, Aug. 5, 1859; Houston *Telegraph*, May 13, 1857; Fornell, *The Galveston Era*, 116–117.
23. WPB, Diary, June 20, 1859.
24. Walter L. Buenger, "Texas and the Riddle of Secession," in Ralph A. Wooster (ed.), *Lone Star Blue and Gray: Essays on Texas in the Civil War* (Austin: Texas State Historical Association, 1995), 5, 9–12; Also see Buenger, *Secession and the Union in Texas* (Austin: University of Texas Press, 1984), 63–64, 120–126; John Moretta, "William Pitt Ballinger and the Travail of Texas Secession," *Houston Review*, 11, no. 1 (1989), 5–7; Fornell, *The Galveston Era*, 288–289; Claude Elliot, *Leathercoat: The Life History of a Texas Patriot* (San Antonio: Standard Printing Co., 1938), 46–49, 56–59; Jane L. Scarborough, "George W. Paschal, Texas Unionist and Scalawag Jurisprudent" (Ph.D. diss., Rice University, 1972), 58–60; Oran Lonnie Sinclair, "Crossroads of Conviction: The Texas Political Mind, 1856–1861" (Ph.D. diss., Rice University, 1975), 181–204; John L. Waller, *Colossal Hamilton of Texas: A Biography of Andrew Jackson Hamilton, Militant Unionist and Reconstruction Governor* (El Paso: Texas Western Press, 1968), 26–29; Alma Dexta King, "The Political Career of William Simpson Oldham," *Southwestern Historical Quarterly*, 33 (Oct. 1929), 112–131; Ben Procter, *Not Without Honor: The Life of John Reagan* (Austin: University of Texas Press, 1962), 315–318; Philip J. Avillo Jr., "John H. Reagan: Unionist or Secessionist?" *East Texas Historical Journal*, 13 (Spring 1975), 23–33. For examples of moderate-Unionist rhetoric, see George W. Paschal to Ashbel Smith, May 27, 1859, Ashbel Smith Papers (CAH); Smith to WPB, June 16, 1859, Ballinger Papers (CAH); Paschal to WPB, Aug. 2, 1860, WPB & Assoc. (HMRC); WPB to Guy Bryan, June 30, 1859, Bryan Papers (CAH).
25. On other Texas businessmen or professionals with national commercial interests similar to Ballinger's, see Thomas F. McKinney to Thomas Jack, WPB, and Guy M. Bryan, Nov. 22, 1860, Bryan Papers (CAH); Thomas F. McKinney to WPB, Sept. 13, 1860, WPB & Assoc. (HMRC); WPB to Guy Bryan, Aug. 15, 1860, Bryan Papers (CAH); Fornell, *The Galveston Era*, 278–293; Ralph A. Wooster, "Ben H. Epperson: East Texas Lawyer, Legislator, and Civil Leader," *East Texas Historical Journal*, 5 (Mar. 1967), 29–42; Sinclair, "Crossroads of Conviction," 129–181; Ernest Wallace, *Charles DeMorse: Pioneer Editor and Statesman* (Lubbock: Texas Tech Press, 1943), 1–142; Austin *Southern Intelligencer*, Sept. 5, Oct. 10, 1860, Jan., 20, 23, Feb. 6, 13, 1861; San Antonio *Weekly Alamo Express*, Feb. 9, 16, 23, 1661.
26. WPB to Guy Bryan, June 4, 1860, Bryan Papers (CAH).
27. WPB to Guy Bryan, Feb. 21, 1859. On Whig nationalism see Charles Grier Sellers Jr., "Who Were the Southern Whigs?" *American Historical Review*, 59 (Jan. 1954), 335–346; Arthur Charles Cole, *The Whig Party in the South* (Washington, D.C.: American

Historical Assoc., 1914; Gloucester, Mass.: P. Smith, 1962), 277–308, 309–343; Carl N. Degler, *The Other South: Southern Dissenters in the Nineteenth Century* (New York: Harper and Row, 1974), 105–116, 160–163, demonstrates the continuity of Whiggery and Unionism. For an excellent analysis of the various strands of Whig ideology and interest, see Daniel Walker Howe, *The Political Culture of the American Whigs* (Chicago: University of Chicago Press, 1979), 238–262.

28. WPB to Guy Bryan Feb. 7, 1859, Guy Bryan Papers (CAH).
29. WPB to Thomas Harrison, May 6, 1860, B. Mills Papers (PC).
30. WPB to Thomas Harrison, Aug. 18, 1860, ibid.
31. WPB to Guy Bryan, July 30, 1860, Bryan Papers (CAH).
32. Richard Sewell, *A House Divided: Sectionalism and Civil War, 1848–1865* (Baltimore: Johns Hopkins Press, 1988), 73–76; Eric Walthers, *The Fire-eaters* (Baton Rouge: Louisiana State University Press, 1992), 71, 73–75; Steven A. Channing, *Crisis of Fear: Secession in South Carolina* (New York: Simon and Schuster, 1970), 195–208.
33. James McPherson, *Battle Cry of Freedom: The Civil War Era* (New York: Oxford University Press, 1988), 221–222; Arthur M. Schlesinger Jr. (ed.), *History of American Presidential Elections* (4 vols.; New York: Chelsea House, 1971), II, 1124–1127; David M. Potter, *The Impending Crisis, 1848–1861* (New York: Harper and Row, 1976), 416–417. The fullest and best accounts of the Constitutional Union Party are in Dwight L. Dumond, *The Secession Movement, 1860–1861* (New York: Macmillan, 1931), 92–112, and in the various biographies of its organizers: Joseph H. Parks, *John Bell of Tennessee* (Baton Rouge: Louisiana State University Press, 1950), 339–360; Albert D. Kirwan, *John J. Crittenden: The Struggle for the Union* (Lexington: University of Kentucky Press, 1962), 336–365. Also see Arthur Cole, *The Whig Party in the South* (Washington, D.C., American Historical Association, 1913), 328–338; John V. Mering, "The Constitutional Union Campaign of 1860: An Example of the Paranoid Style," *Mid-America*, 60 (1978), 95–106, and "The Slave State Constitutional Unionists and the Politics of Consensus," *Journal of Southern History*, 43 (1977), 396–410; Thomas B. Alexander, "Persistent Whiggery in the Old South," *Journal of Southern History*, 27 (Aug. 1961), 305–329; Frank H. Smyrl, "Unionism in Texas, 1856–1861," *Southwestern Historical Quarterly*, 68 (Oct. 1964), 172–195; the best treatment of the party in Texas is James Alex Baggett's "The Constitutional Union Party in Texas," *Southwestern Historical Quarterly*, 82 (Jan. 1979), 233–264.
34. Oakes, *The Ruling Race*, 220–223. Further elaboration of Oakes's assertion can be found in Herbert J. Doherty Jr., "Union Nationalism in Georgia," *Georgia Historical Quarterly*, 37 (Mar. 1953), 18–38; for Whig Unionists' thoughts on the economics of slavery as well as on other economic issues, see Robert R. Russell, *Economic Aspects of Southern Sectionalism, 1840–1861* (Urbana: University of Illinois, 1924), 58, 85, 87, 179; James Marten, *Texas Divided: Loyalty and Dissent in the Lone Star State, 1856–1874* (Lexington: University Press of Kentucky, 1990), 31–32; John McCardell, *The Idea of a Southern Nation: Southern Nationalists and Southern Nationalism, 1830–1860* (New York: W. W. Norton, 1979), 91–140; For other Texas conservatives who shared Ballinger's views, see John P. Osterhout to Brother Orlando, Feb. 1, 1860, and Osterhout to Mother, Mar. 12, 1856, John Patterson Osterhout Papers (Fondren Library, Rice University); C. Alwyn Barr, "The Making of a Secessionist: The Antebellum Career of Roger Q. Mills," *Southwestern Historical Quarterly*, 79 (Oct. 1975), 129–144.
35. WPB, Diary, May, 13–24, Aug. 1, 1860.
36. Ibid., Aug. 17–21, 1860; Galveston *News*, Aug. 21, 1860; Galveston *Civilian*, Aug.

22, 1860; Houston *Telegraph*, Aug. 27, 1860.

37. Copy of Ballinger's speech delivered to the Montgomery County Bell–Everett Club, Sept. 10, 1860, found in WPB & Assoc. (HMRC).

38. "Secession," (draft of speech delivered by Ballinger on Aug. 23, 1860), Ballinger Papers (RL).

39. Ibid.

40. Ibid.

41. WPB, Diary, Aug. 23, 1860.

42. Ibid., Oct. 16, 1860.

43. Ibid., Nov. 1, 8, 1860.

44. James Bell to WPB, Dec. 1, 1860; Walter Botts to WPB, Nov. 17, 1860, WPB & Assoc. (HMRC).

45. WPB, Diary, Nov. 14, 15, 1860.

46. Houston *Telegraph*, Nov. 19, 21, 1860; Galveston *News*, Nov. 22, 1860.

47. Jimmie Hicks, "Texas and Separate Independence, 1860–61," *East Texas Historical Journal*, 4 (1966), 85–106; C. A. Bridges, "The Knights of the Golden Circle: A Filibustering Fantasy," *Southwestern Historical Quarterly*, 44 (Jan. 1941), 287–302; Llerena B. Friend, *Sam Houston: The Great Designer* (Austin: University of Texas Press, 1954), 330–335; Galveston *News*, Dec. 18, 22, 1860.

48. WPB, Diary, Dec. 21, 1860.

49. Ibid., Dec. 30, 1860.

50. Ibid., Dec. 31, 1860.

51. WPB to George Paschal, May 8, 1863, Ballinger Papers (CAH); Marshall *Texas Republican* Jan. 5, 12, 19, 26, 1861; Austin *State Gazette*, Dec. 29, 1860, Jan., 5, 12, 19, Feb. 16, 23, 1861; "A Declaration of Causes Which Impel the State of Texas to Secede from the Federal Union," in Ernest Winkler (ed.), *Journal of the Secession Convention of Texas, 1861* (Austin: Austin Printing Co., 1912), 65. One Texan steadfast in his commitment to the Union and who regarded secession as illegal, was lawyer-editor George Paschal of Austin. On his fight against secession, see Paschal to WPB, Nov. 20, Dec. 12, 30, 1860, Jan. 18, 1861; Scarborough, "George W. Paschal," 39–136. For other Texans who remained devoted Unionists see Marten, *Texas Divided*, 20–24. Most other Unionists followed in Ballinger's path. For example, James Throckmorton. See Elliot, *Leathercoat*, 50–51; Marten, *Texas Divided*, 25–26. For a brief description of conditional unionism in the South, see Degler, *The Other South*, 124–125. Secessionists and unconditional Unionists characterize what Morton Brodzins calls traitriots, individuals who renounce their country because it has somehow foresaken those values they held dear, or who are more devoted to personal principles or values than to national loyalty. Unionists like Ballinger withdrew their loyalty to the Union because in the end he believed the Republican Party had perverted the principles set forth by the founding fathers in the Constitution so that it no longer protected Southern property and rights. Unconditional Unionists such as George Paschal ignored the Confederate government's demands for their loyalty, remaining true to the principles they believed the United States still represented. Morton Grodzins, *The Loyal and the Disloyal: Social Boundaries of Patriotism and Treason* (Chicago: University of Chicago Press, 1956), 208–216.

52. WPB to George Paschal, May 8, 1863, Ballinger Papers (CAH).

53. WPB to James Love, Apr. 1, 1861, B. Mills Papers (PC).

54. WPB to Guy Bryan, Mar. 24, 1861, Bryan Papers (CAH). For examples of emerging Confederate nationalism and its similarity to unionism, see Winkler (ed.), *Journal of the*

Secession Convention, 64-65; Francis Lubbock, *Six Decades in Texas; or, Memoirs of Francis Richard Lubbock, Governor of Texas in War Time, 1861-1863: A Personal Experience in Business, War, and Politics*, ed. C. W. Raines (Austin: Ben C. Jones & Co., 1866), 304-313; Steven B. Oates, "Texas Under the Secessionists," *Southwestern Historical Quarterly*, 67 (Oct. 1963), 167-212; Buenger, "Texas and the Riddle of Secession," 24-26; McCardell, *The Idea of a Southern Nation*, 251, 271, 336-338. McCardell uses John H. Reagan, who, like Ballinger, did not become a Southern nationalist until after Texas seceded. He also uses Reagan to establish that moderates, even conservatives like Ballinger, with a strong nationalist tradition, led the Confederacy. As will be seen in Chapter 7, this was true for both Ballinger and Reagan. Many Texas newspapers were fond of equating emerging Confederate nationalism with the symbols and heritage of unionism. See for example Marshall *Texas Republican*, Dec. 1, 1860; Jan. 5, 12, 19, 26, Mar. 16, 1861; Austin *Texas State Gazette*, Sept. 1, Nov. 17, 1860.

55. James Harrison to WPB, Mar. 5, 1861, WPB & Assoc. (HMRC).

56. WPB, Diary, Feb. 23, 1862.

Chapter Seven

1. WPB to Jefferson Davis, Apr. 20, 1861, WPB & Assoc. (HMRC).

2. Ballinger's letter to Wigfall dated May 16, 1861, was found in the Jefferson Davis Papers (Rice University). Also see WPB to Earl Van Dorn, July 16, 1861, Ballinger Papers (CAH). Ballinger was not the only Texan worried about protecting the state's coastline and ports from Union assaults. See Alwyn Barr, "Texas Coastal Defense, 1861-1865," in Wooster (ed.), *Lone Star Blue and Gray*, 152-155; Lester N. Fitzhugh, "Saluria, Fort Esperanza, and Military Operations on the Texas Coast, 1861-1864," *Southwestern Historical Quarterly*, 61 (July 1957), 66-100; Ralph Wooster, "The Texas Gulf Coast in the Civil War," *Texas Gulf Historical and Biographical Record*, 1 (Nov. 1965), 7-16; and Wooster, *Texas and Texans in the Civil War* (Austin: Eakin Press, 1995), 45-47; Edward T. Cotham Jr., *Battle on the Bay: The Civil War Struggle for Galveston* (Austin: University of Texas Press, 1998), 13-28; Lubbock, *Six Decades in Texas*, 348-350.

3. Francis Lubbock to WPB, July 27, 1861, Ballinger Papers (CAH); Van Dorn to Ballinger, July 28, 1861, ibid.; WPB, Diary, July 27, 1861.

4. WPB, Diary, Aug. 8, 1861.

5. Ibid., Aug. 10, 12, 1861.

6. Ibid., Aug. 13, 1861.

7. Ibid; Wooster, *Texas and Texans in the Civil War*, 43-44; Oates, "Texas Under the Secessionists," 194-195; Robert G. Hartje, *Van Dorn: The Life and Times of a Confederate General* (Nashville: Vanderbilt University Press, 1967), 88-90.

8. WPB, Diary, Aug. 15, Sept. 1, 1861.

9. Ibid., Sept. 29 to Oct. 3, 1861.

10. Ibid., Oct. 10, 1861.

11. Ibid., Oct. 13-17, 1861.

12. Ibid., Oct. 22-27, 1861.

13. WPB to Guy Bryan, Nov. 10, 1861, Bryan Papers (CAH).

14. WPB to Tom Jack, Nov. 17, 1861, Ballinger Papers (CAH).

15. WPB, Diary, Oct. 4, 1862.

16. WPB, Diary, June 4, 28, July 10, 23, 1862; WPB to Paul Hebert, June 12, July 2, 1862, Ballinger Papers (CAH); William Oakes to WPB, Aug. 22, 1862, WPB & Assoc. (HMRC). Also see John Henry Brown, *History of Texas: 1865-1892* (2 vols.; St. Louis: L. E.

Daniell, 1892–1893), II, 408; Frank L. Owsley, *State Rights in the Confederacy* (Gloucester, Mass.: Peter Smith, 1961), 157–158; Stephen B. Oates, *Visions of Glory: Texans on the Southwestern Frontier* (Norman: University of Oklahoma Press, 1970), 117–118; McComb, *Galveston: A History*, 74; Cotham, *Battle on the Bay*, 37–41; Paeder Joel Hoovestol, "Galveston in the Civil War" (Master's thesis, University of Houston, 1950), 20. Galveston *News*, May 6, 21, July 2, 9, 25, Aug. 5, 19, 1862; Houston *Telegraph*, July 20, Aug. 14, 22, Sept. 3, 15, 19, 1862; Lubbock, *Six Decades in Texas*, 347–348, 350, 386–387, 606–607; WPB to Hebert, July 2, 1862, Ballinger Papers (CAH); John Franklin Smith to Justina Rowzee, June 28, 1862, John Franklin Smith Papers (CAH).

17. WPB to Hally, Jan. 13, 1862, Ballinger Papers (RL); Cotham, *Battle on the Bay*, 50–51.

18. WPB, Diary, Oct. 4, 5, 1862; Col. Joseph J. Cook to Paul O. Hebert, Oct. 9, 1862, in *Confederate Military History* (5 vols.; Atlanta: Confederate Publishing Co., 1899), II, 73–75. Also see Galveston *News*, Oct. 8, 1862; Charles C. Cumberland, "The Confederate Loss and Recapture of Galveston, 1862–1863," *Southwestern Historical Quarterly*, 51 (Oct. 1947), 110–114; McComb, *Galveston: A History*, 75; Cotham, *Battle on the Bay*, 51–64; Barr, "Texas Coastal Defense," 161–162; Wooster, *Texas and Texans in the Civil War*, 63.

19. WPB, Diary, Jan. 1–3, 1863; Cotham, *Battle on the Bay*, 105–134; Wooster, *Texas and Texans in the Civil War*, 65–68; McComb, *Galveston: A History*, 76–77; Cumberland, "The Confederate Loss and Recapture of Galveston, 1862–1863," 124–126; Barr, "Texas Coastal Defense," 162–165; Houston *Tri-Weekly Telegraph*, Jan. 5, 7, 12, 19, 1863; Hayes, *History of the Island and City of Galveston*, 549–579; Donald Frazier, "Sibley's Texans and the Battle of Galveston," *Southwestern Historical Quarterly*, 99 (Oct. 1995), 175–200.

20. Copy of Ballinger's "Circular" found in Ballinger Papers (RL). For more information on the sequestration law's purpose as well as on Confederate expectations, see William M. Robinson, *Justice in Grey: A History of the Judicial System of the Confederate States of America* (Cambridge: Harvard University Press, 1941), 493–496; Wilfred Buck Yearns, *The Confederate Congress* (Athens, Ga.: University of Georgia Press, 1960), 132–135, 191, 196.

21. Ballinger, "Circular," Ballinger Papers (RL); Robinson, *Justice in Grey*.

22. WPB, Diary, Feb. 12, 1862, Ballinger Papers (RL); Confederate Constitution, Article III, Section 2; Statutes at Large, Provisional Government of the Confederate States of America, 1st Sess., Sect. 44; Robinson, *Justice in Grey*, 1–51; T. R. Havins, "Administration of the Sequestration Act in the Confederate District Court for the Western District of Texas, 1862–1865," *Southwestern Historical Quarterly*, 43 (Jan. 1940), 281–322; Nowlin Randolph, "Judge William Pickney Hill Aids the Confederate War Effort," *Southwestern Historical Quarterly*, 68 (July 1964), 14–28.

23. Ballinger Papers, Oct.–Dec., 1861, Jan. 20, 1662 (CAH); Havins, "Administration of the Sequestration Act," 306, 311; Randoloph, "Judge William Pickney Hill," 17–18.

24. Ballinger Papers, Nov. 3, 1861 to Jan. 10, 1862 (CAH).

25. Ballinger Papers, Oct.–Dec. 1861, ibid.

26. Anonymous letter to WPB, dated Nov. 11, 1861. Also see WPB to William Pinckney Hill, Nov. 27, 1861, and Ballinger Papers, Oct.–Nov. 1861, all in (CAH).

27. WPB, Diary, Mar. 8, Apr. 16, 1863; WPB to James Love, Mar. 22, 1863, WPB & Assoc. (HMRC).

28. WPB, Diary, Jan. 13, 1862.

29. Robinson, *Justice in Grey*, 493–496

30. Houston *Telegraph*, July 20, 1863.

31. WPB, Diary, Sept. 17, Nov. 26, 1863.
32. Peter W. Gray to WPB, Oct. 14, 1863, Ballinger Papers (CAH); WPB, Diary, Oct. 26, Nov. 17, 1863.
33. Robinson, *Justice in Grey*, 263–264; Ballinger Papers, Jan. 2 to May 3, 1865 (CAH).
34. Murray to WPB, Nov. 2, 21, 1863, Ballinger Papers (CAH); WPB to Tom Jack, Dec. 12, 1863, WPB & Assoc. (HMRC).
35. WPB to Tom Jack, Mar. 12, Apr. 9, 1864, Ballinger Papers (CAH).
36. WPB to Tom Jack, Oct. 12, 1864, ibid.
37. WPB to Tom Jack, Nov. 3, 1864, ibid.
38. WPB to Guy Bryan, Sept. 26, 1864, Bryan Papers (CAH). Anonymous undated note to Ballinger found in Ballinger Papers for the year 1864 (CAH).
39. WPB to Col. William Bates, Oct. 8, 1864, Ballinger Papers (CAH).
40. Love to WPB, Oct. 10, 1864, ibid.
41. WPB to James Love, Nov. 5, 1864, B. Mills Papers (PC).
42. Albert B. Moore, *Conscription and Conflict in the Confederacy* (New York: Macmillan, 1924), 52–53; Emory M. Thomas, *The Confederate Nation: 1861–1865* (New York: Harper and Row, 1979), 152–153; Wooster, *Texas and Texans in the Civil War*, 32; McPherson, *Battle Cry of Freedom*, 428–432; McPherson, *Ordeal By Fire: The Civil War and Reconstruction* (New York: Alfred Knopf, 1982), 182–183; Frank Owsley, *State Rights in the Confederacy* (Chicago: University of Chicago Press, 1931), 176–202; Paul D. Escott, *After Secession: Jefferson Davis and the Failure of Confederate Nationalism* (Baton Rouge: Louisiana State University Press, 1978), 73–88, 138–149, 151, 152–153; Richard Beringer, Herman Hattaway, Archer Jones, and William N. Still Jr., *Why the South Lost the Civil War* (Athens, Ga.: University of Georgia Press, 1986), 220–227; John Brawner Robbins, "Confederate Nationalism: Politics and Government in the Confederate South, 1861–1865" (Ph.D diss., Rice University, 1964), 108–109; Rupert N. Richardson, Ernest Wallace, and Adrian Anderson, *Texas The Lone Star State* (Englewood Cliffs, N.J.: Prentice Hall, 1988), 218.
43. WPB, editorial for the Houston *Telegraph*, Dec. 12, 1863; WPB to Peter W. Gray, July 26, 1862, WPB & Assoc. (HMRC); Ernest Wallace, *Texas in Turmoil: The Saga of Texas, 1849–1875* (Austin: Steck-Vaughn, 1965), 78–79; Thomas, *The Confederate Nation*, 152–154; Moore, *Conscription and Conflict in the Confederacy*, 27–82, 230–231, 255–296; Alwyn Barr (ed.), "Records of the Confederate Military Commission in San Antonio, July 2–Oct. 10, 1862," *Southwestern Historical Quarterly*, 70 (July 1966), 94–95.
44. WPB, editorial, Houston *Telegraph*, June 15, 1862; Galveston *News*, June 19, 1862.
45. Marten, *Texas Divided*, 49–50; McPherson, *Battle Cry of Freedom*, 433–435; John B. Robbins, "The Confederacy and the Writ of Habeas Corpus," *Georgia Historical Quarterly*, 55 (1971), 83–101; Owsley, *State Rights in the Confederacy*, 162–164, 184–191; Beringer, Hattaway, et al., *Why the South Lost the Civil War*, 22–224; Robbins, "Confederate Nationalism," 64–86; Robert P. Felgar, "Texas in the War for Southern Independence, 1861–1865" (Ph.D. diss., University of Texas, 1935), 204–225; Claude Elliot, "Union Sentiment in Texas, 1861–1865," in Wooster (ed.), *Lone Star Blue and Gray*, 95.
46. WPB, editorial, Houston *Telegraph*, Mar. 23, 1864
47. WPB, Diary, Sept. 29, Oct. 2, 1864.
48. Houston *Telegraph*, Nov. 21, 1864.
49. Ibid., Feb., 8, 1865.

Notes to Pages 152–157

50. Ibid., Feb., 15, 1865.
51. Ibid., June 5, 1863.
52. Thomas Harrison to WPB, Nov. 11, 1862, Ballinger Papers (CAH).
53. Frank L. Owsley, *King Cotton Diplomacy: Foreign Relations of the Confederate States of America* (Chicago: University of Chicago Press, 1931), 16–25, 43–50, 465; McPherson, *Ordeal by Fire*, 217–218, 301–302, 342; Henry Bluementhal, "Confederate Diplomacy: Popular Notions and International Realities," *Journal of Southern History*, 32 (May 1966), 151–171; Stuart Bruchey (ed.), *Cotton and the Growth of the American Economy: 1790–1860* (New York: W. W. Norton, 1967), 73–75; J. M. Callahan, *The Diplomatic History of the Southern Confederation* (Baltimore: Johns Hopkins University Press, 1901), 102–159.
54. Houston *Telegraph*, June 11, 1863.
55. Ibid., June 28, 1863.
56. McPherson, *Ordeal by Fire*, 218; Houston *Telegraph*, Dec. 13, 1862.
57. WPB to Francis Lubbock, Aug. 26, 1863, Ballinger Papers (CAH).
58. WPB, Diary, July 27, 1863.
59. James Love to WPB, Aug. 4, 1863, Ballinger Papers (CAH); WPB to Guy Bryan, Oct. 10, 1863, Bryan Papers (CAH); WPB, Diary, Aug. 1, 1863.
60. Houston *Telegraph*, July 17, 1863.
61. Ezra J. Warner and W. Buck Yearns, *Biographical Register of the Confederate Congress* (Baton Rouge: Louisiana State University Press, 1975), 187–168, 256–257; Thomas B. Alexander and Richard E. Beringer, *The Anatomy of the Confederate Congress: A Study of the Influences of Member Characteristics on Legislative Voting Behavior, 1861–1865* (Nashville: Vanderbilt University Press, 1972), 14–15, 57–58, 106; Yearns, *Biographical Register of the Confederate Congress*, 234–235; Alvy L. King, *Louis T. Wigfall, Southern Fire-eater* (Baton Rouge: Louisiana State University Press, 1970); 135–153; Walther, *The Fire-eaters*, 189–190; Benny E. Deuson, "Pendleton Murrah," in W. C. Nunn (ed.), *Ten Texans in Gray* (Hillsboro, Tex.: Hill Junior College Press, 1968), 122–123; James T. DeShields, *They Sat in High Places* (San Antonio: Naylor Press, 1940), 247–248; Fredericka Meiners, "The Texas Governorship, 1861–1865: Biogrpahy of an Office" (Ph.D diss., Rice University, 1974), 258–262; Nancy Head Bowen, "A Political Labyrinth: Texas in the Civil War—Questions in Continuity" (Ph.D. diss., Rice University, 1974), 137–139; Wooster, *Texas and Texans in the Civil War*, 105.
62. Meiners, "The Texas Governorship, 1861–1865," 293–294; David P. Smith, "Conscription and Conflict on the Texas Frontier, 1863–1865," *Civil War History*, 36 (Sept. 1990), 252–254; David P. Smith, *Frontier Defense in the Civil War: Texas Rangers and Rebels* (College Station: Texas A&M University Press, 1992), 88–98; Robert L. Kerby, *Kirby Smith's Confederacy: The Trans-Mississippi South, 1863–1865* (New York: Columbia University Press, 1972), 217–219; Moore, *Conscription and Conflict in the Confederacy*, 247–248; Felgar, "Texas in the War," 200–225; Escott, *After Secession*, 80–88; Mary Spencer Ringold, *The Role of the State Legislatures in the Confederacy* (Athens, Ga.: Univeristy of Georgia Press, 1966), 14–18.
63. WPB, Diary, Apr. 10, 11, 1864; Houston *Telegraph*, May 5, 1864.
64. Houston *Telegraph*, May 12, 1864; WPB to Fletcher Stockdale, May 31, 1864, Ballinger Papers (CAH).
65. WPB to Pendleton Murrah, Apr. 20, 1864, Pendleton Murrah Papers (TSA).
66. Houston *Telegraph*, May 4, 1864; WPB, Diary, Apr. 15–May 22, 1864.
67. *The War of the Rebellion: A Compilation of the Official Records of the Union and Confederate Armies* (70 vols., in 128; Washington, D.C.: Government Printing Office,

1880–1901), Ser. I, Vol. XLI, Pt. IV, 1006; LIII, 926; XXXIV, Pt. III, 726, 735, 739, 747, 786–788; Smith, "Conscription and Conflict," 281; Kerby, *Kirby Smith's Confederacy*, 279; Gammel, *The Laws of Texas*, V, 773–775.

68. Kerby, *Kirby Smith's Confederacy*, 138–139, 159–160; Meiners, " The Texas Governorship, 1861–1865," 326–327; James L. Nichols, *The Confederate Quartermaster in the Trans-Mississippi* (Austin: University of Texas Press, 1964), 58–75; Allan C. Ashcraft, "Texas: 1860–1866: The Lone Star State in the Civil War" (Ph.D. diss., Columbia University, 1960), 179–180, 218–221.

69. W. Buck Yearns (ed.), *The Confederate Governors* (Athens, Ga.: University of Georgia Press, 1985), 200; Meiners, "The Texas Governorship, 1861–1865," 99–101, 329–330; Charles W. Ramsdell, "The Texas State Military Board, 1862–1865," *Southwestern Historical Quarterly*, 27 (Apr. 1924), 257–272; Michael Robert Green, "'. . . so Illy Provided . . .' Events Leading to the Creation of the Texas Military Board," *Military History of Texas and the Southwest*, 10 (1972), 115–125; Lubbock, *Six Decades in Texas*, 365–371; Ronnie C. Tyler, "Cotton on the Border," *Southwestern Historical Quarterly*, 73 (Apr. 1970), 456–477; Fredericka Meiners, "The Texas Border Cotton Trade, 1862–1865," *Civil War History*, 23 (Dec. 1977), 293–306.

70. Houston *Telegraph*, Jan. 9, Mar. 14, 1864. On Confederate impressment of supplies, see Owsley, *State Rights in the Confederacy*, 229; Escott, *After Secession*, 100–121; Stephen E. Ambrose, "Yeoman Discontent in the Confederacy," *Civil War History*, 8 (1962), 259–268; McPherson, *Ordeal By Fire*, 378.

71. Murrah to WPB, Apr. 3, 1864, Ballinger Papers (CAH); WPB, Diary, Apr. 11, 1864.

72. WPB to Guy Bryan, June 30, 1864, Bryan Papers (CAH).

73. Kirby Smith to WPB, July 1, 1864, Ballinger Papers (CAH). For Smith's missives to Murrah and Murrah's responses, see *Official Records*, 53: 979–980, 1008–1015; Smith to Murrah, Mar. 1, 1864, Murrah to Smith, June 17, 21, 24, 25, 28, 1864, Governor's Letters (TSA); Kerby, *Kirby Smith's Confederacy*, 201–202.

74. WPB to Kirby Smith, July 7, 1864, ibid.

75. Ibid.

76. Kirby Smith to Murrah, July 13, 1864, Governor's Letters (TSA); Murrah to the People of Texas, July 19, 1864, Governor's Proclamations (TSA); Joseph H. Parks, *General Edmund Kirby Smith, CSA* (Baton Rouge: Louisiana State University Press, 1954), 364–365.

77. Houston *Telegraph*, Sept. 10, 12, 19, 1864; Galveston *News*, Sept. 19, 30, 1864.

78. WPB, Diary, Oct. 1, 1864.

79. Houston *Telegraph*, Dec. 2, 1964, Jan. 6, 1865.

80. WPB to James Love, Aug. 5, 1860, B. Mills Papers (PC).

81. For examples of the impact of the war on Ballinger's family as well as his feelings of having neglected them because of his devotion to the Confederacy, see his Diary, Feb. 3, June 12, Oct. 22, 1862, and Jan. 13, Nov. 25, 1864.

82. WPB to Guy Bryan, Nov. 11, 1864, Jan. 8, 1865, Bryan Papers (CAH). On the peace movement, see Moore, *Conscription and Conflict in the Confederacy*, 272–273; John R. Brumgardt, "The Confederate Career of Alexander H. Stephens: The Case Reopened," *Civil War History*, 27 (1981), 64–81; Horace W. Raper, "William W. Holden and the Peace Movement in North Carolina," *North Carolina Historical Review*, 31 (1954), 493–516.

83. Peter W. Gray to WPB, Jan. 5, 1865, WPB & Assoc. (HMRC); WPB, Diary, Jan. 7, 1865.

84. Pendleton Murrah to WPB, Jan. 7, 1865, Ballinger Papers (CAH).

Notes to Pages 163–170

85. WPB to Murrah, Jan. 26, 1865, ibid. Also see WPB to Murrah, Jan. 30, 1865, Governor's Letters (TSA).

86. Owsley, *King Cotton Diplomacy*, 86–145, 438–442, 447–449, 527–549; Lynn M. Case and Warren F. Spencer, *The United States and France: Civil War Diplomacy* (Philadelphia: University of Pennsylvania Press, 1970), 427–480; McPherson, *Ordeal by Fire*, 344.

87. WPB to Francis Lubbock, Sept. 25, 1862, Governor's Letters (TSA). Also see Lubbock to WPB, Oct. 5, 1862 and WPB to Lubbock, Oct. 20, 1862, Ballinger Papers (CAH). For discussion of this most controversial issue in the short history of the CSA, see Berringer, Hattaway, et al., *Why the South Lost the Civil War*, 368–397; Robert F. Durden, *The Gray and the Black: The Confederate Debate on Emancipation* (Baton Rouge: Louisiana State University Press, 1972).

88. Houston *Telegraph*, Feb. 12, 1665.

89. WPB to Fletcher Stockdale, Mar. 7, 1865, Ballinger Papers (CAH).

90. WPB to James Love, Mar. 8, 1865, WPB & Assoc. (HMRC).

91. Berringer, Hattaway, et al., *Why the South Lost the Civil War*, 373; McPherson, *Ordeal by Fire*, 478 and *Battle Cry of Freedom*, 832–837; Durden, *The Gray and the Black*, 181–267; Thomas, *The Confederate Nation*, 292–293; Frank Vandiver, *Their Tattered Flags: The Epic of the Confederacy* (New York: Harper's Magazine Press, 1970), 260–262. On how the Texas Congressional delegation responded to the proposal and how they voted, see *Proceedings of the Second Confederate Congress, Second Session. Dec. 15, 1864 to Mar. 18, 1865*, in Frank Vandiver (ed.), *Southern Historical Society Papers*, Vol. 52 (38 vols.; Richmond, Va.: Southern Historical Society, 1959), 176, 181–183, 257–258, 325, 329–330, 337–338, 362–363, 365, 377, 383, 387, 452–457, 464–465; King, *Louis T. Wigfall*, 205–208; King, "Political Career of William Simpson Oldham," 130–131; Wooster, *Texas and Texans in the Civil War*, 174–175; WPB, editorials, Houston *Telegraph*, Mar. 24, 29, 1865.

92. McPherson, *Ordeal by Fire*, 478–482 and *Battle Cry of Freedom*, 844–850.

93. Yearns (ed.), *The Confederate Governors*, 214; William W. White, "The Distintegration of an Army: Confederate Forces in Texas, Apr.–June 1865," *East Texas Historical Journal*, 26 (Fall 1988), 41–42; Emory Thomas, "Rebel Nationalism: E. H. Cushing and the Confederate Experience," *Southwestern Historical Quarterly*, 73 (Jan. 1970), 348–349; Wooster, *Texas and Texans in the Civil War*, 179.

94. WPB, Diary, Apr. 14, 1865.

95. Ibid.; Houston *Telegraph*, Apr. 25, 1865.

Chapter Eight

1. Houston *Telegraph*, May 11, 1865; WPB, Diary, May 13, 1865. Also see William White, "The Disintegration of an Army: Confederate Forces in Texas, Apr.–June, 1865," *East Texas Historical Journal*, 26 (1988), 40–46; Charles W. Ramsdell, "Texas From the Fall of the Confederacy to the Beginning of Reconstruction," *Quarterly of the Texas State Historical Association*, 11 (Jan. 1908), 205–207, and *Reconstruction in Texas* (New York: Columbia University Press, 1910), 30–31; William L. Richter, *The Army in Texas During Reconstruction, 1865–1870* (College Station: Texas A&M University Press, 1987), 6.

2. Houston *Telegraph*, Apr. 29, 1865; WPB, Diary, May 17, 1865. On the breakdown of law and order soon after Texas heard of Smith's surrender, see Houston *Telegraph*, May 24, 31, June 6, 9, 16, 1865.

3. WPB, Diary, May 17, 1865; Ramsdell, *Reconstruction in Texas*, 36–39; Ashcraft, "Texas: 1860–66"; Wooster, *Texas and Texans in the Civil War*, 182.

4. WPB, Diary, May 17, 1865.
5. Ibid., May 18–27, 1865.
6. Ibid., May 28, 1865.
7. Ibid., May 29, 1865.
8. Ibid., May 30, 1865; WPB to Pendleton Murrah, June 1, 1865, Ashbel Smith Papers (CAH).
9. WPB, Diary, June 2, 1865.
10. Ibid., June 11, 1865; Kenneth Stampp, *The Era of Reconstruction, 1865–1877* (New York: Alfred Knopf, 1965), 62–63; Jonathan T. Dorris, *Pardon and Amnesty Under Lincoln and Johnson: The Restoration of Confederates to Their Rights and Privileges, 1861–1898* (Chapel Hill: University of North Carolina Press, 1953), 135–136; Dan T. Carter, *When the War Was Over: The Failure of Self-Reconstruction in the South, 1865–1867* (Baton Rouge: Louisiana State University Press, 1985), 25; James McPherson, *Ordeal by Fire*, 498–499; John Hope Franklin, *Reconstruction After the Civil War* (Chicago: University of Chicago Press, 1961), 33–34; Eric Foner, *Reconstruction: America's Unfinished* Revolution, 1863–1877 (New York: Harper and Row, 1988), 183; James D. Richardson (ed.), *A Compilation of the Messages and Papers of the Presidents, 1789–1897* (10 vols.; Washington, D.C.: Bureau of National Literature and Art, 1896–1899), VI, 310–314.
11. Ballinger's undated June letter to Andrew Johnson found in Ballinger Papers (RL).
12. Richter, *The Army in Texas During Reconstruction*, 11–16; Robert W. Shook, "Federal Occupation and Administration of Texas, 1865–1870" (Ph.D. diss., North Texas State University, 1970), 76–78; Ramsdell, *Reconstruction in Texas*, 48–49; Stephen F. Shannon, "Galvestonians and Military Reconstruction, 1865–1867" (Master's thesis, Rice University, 1975), 102–108; Campbell, *Empire for Slavery*, 249–251; WPB to Aaron Coffee, July 1, 1865, WPB & Assoc. (HMRC).
13. WPB, Diary, July 16, 1865.
14. Shannon, "Galvestonians and Military Reconstruction, 1865–1867," 106–108, 119; Ramsdell, *Reconstruction in Texas*, 48–49; Ira Christian Colby, "The Freedmen's Bureau of Texas and its Impact on the Emerging Social Welfare System and Black–White Relations, 1865–1885" (Ph.D. diss., University of Pennsylvania, 1984), 60–62; Claude Elliot, "The Freedmen's Bureau in Texas," *Southwestern Historical Quarterly*, 56 (July 1952), 3; Nancy Cohen-Lack, "A Struggle for Sovereignty: National Consolidation, Emancipation, and Free Labor in Texas, 1865," *Journal of Southern History*, 58 (1992), 63–66; Richter, *The Army in Texas During Reconstruction*, 33.
15. WPB to John Hancock, Mar. 4, 1866, Ballinger Papers (CAH).
16. Ibid. On the Black Codes and for other white Southerners who shared Ballinger's "solicitude" toward freedmen as well as his antipathy toward the Freedmen's Bureau, see Carter, *When the War Was Over*, 176–321; William L. Richter, *Overreached on All Sides: The Freedmen's Bureau Administrators in Texas, 1865–1868* (College Station: Texas A&M University Press, 1991), 20–22, and *The Army in Texas During Reconstruction*, 49–61; Ramsdell, *Reconstruction in Texas*, 120–127; Foner, *Reconstruction: America's Unfinished Revolution*, 199–202; McPherson, *Ordeal by Fire*, 511–512; Barry A. Crouch, "All the Vile Passions: The Texas Black Code of 1866," *Southwestern Historical Quarterly*, 97 (July 1993), 13–34; Gammel, *The Laws of Texas*, V, 979–981, 994–999, 1020–1022.
17. WPB to John Hancock, Mar. 4, 1866, Ballinger Papers (CAH); also see WPB to William Pinckney Hill, unsent letter, Dec. 21, 1866 (CAH); Carter, *When the War Was Over*, 183–187.

18. See WPB & Assoc. (HMRC), especially the years 1865–1868 for examples of his solicitude/paternalism toward freedmen.

19. WPB to Guy Bryan, Oct. 22, 1887, Bryan Papers (CAH).

20. WPB, Diary, July 22, 1865.

21. Foner, *Reconstruction: America's Unfinished Revolution*, 183–184; Carter, *When the War Was Over*, 25; Richardson (ed.), *Compilation of the Messages and Papers of the Presidents*, VI, 213–218; Dorris, "Pardon Seekers and Brokers: A Sequel to Appomattox," *Journal of Southern History*, 1 (1935), 291.

22. WPB, Diary, July 28, Aug. 8, 1865; WPB to Guy Bryan, June 17, 1865, Bryan Papers (CAH). Hamilton's biographer has concluded that the governor liberally recommended pardoning for many Texans, rejecting only those who had gone to West Point or Annapolis. Motivating Hamilton was his hope that his generosity would attract loyal allies from among those pardoned. See Waller, *Colossal Hamilton of Texas*, 82–83.

23. For background on Samuel Miller see Fairman, *Mr. Justice Miller*. Also contained in Fairman's work is the substantial correspondence between Miller and Ballinger, to be cited henceforth as Miller to WPB, date, page number, *Mr. Justice Miller*. For example, quotes in this particular notation are found in a letter from Miller dated Aug. 31, 1865, p. 124.

24. Miller to WPB, Jan. 11, 1866, ibid.

25. Miller to WPB, Aug. 31, 1865, ibid., 126–127.

26. Ibid.

27. WPB to wife, Aug. 23, 1865, B. Mills Papers (PC); Miller to Johnson, Aug. 13, 1865, Ballinger Papers (CAH); Miller to WPB, Sept. 3, 1865, Ballinger Papers (CAH); WPB, Diary, Aug. 25, undated entry, Oct. 1865.

28. Houston *Telegraph*, Apr. 28, 1865.

29. WPB, Diary, Aug. 25, 1865.

30. Stampp, *Era of Reconstruction*, 67–69; Franklin, *Reconstruction After the Civil War*, 34; Foner, *Reconstruction: America's Unfinished Revolution*, 190–191; Ray F. Nichols, "United States vs. Jefferson Davis," *American Historical Review*, 31 (1926), 266–284; Dorris, *Pardon and Amnesty*, 135–146; Eric L. McKitrick, Andrew Johnson and Reconstruction (Chicago: University of Chicago Press, 1960), 142–148; Harold M. Hyman and Benjamin P. Thomas, *Stanton: The Life and Times of Lincoln's Secretary of War* (New York: Knopf, 1962), 447–452; McPherson, *Ordeal by Fire*, 504–505.

31. WPB, Diary, Aug. 27, 1865.

32. Ibid.

33. Fairman, *Mr. Justice Miller*, 125; Miller to WPB, Aug. 21, 1865; Miller to Andrew Johnson, Aug. 31, 1865, Ballinger Papers (CAH); WPB, Diary, Oct. 19, 21, 1865. On the use of pardon agents or "brokers" see Franklin, *Reconstruction*, 34; McKitrick, *Andrew Johnson*, 173; McPherson, *Ordeal by Fire*, 504; Dorris, "Pardon Seekers and Brokers," 295–298.

34. WPB, Diary, Sept. 1, 1865.

35. Ibid., Nov. 10, 11, 23, 1865. Ballinger also received a gift of land from one grateful relative, Moses Bryan. See WPB to Moses Bryan, Jan. 1, 1866, Moses Austin Bryan Papers (CAH). As late as Feb. 1867, Adams was forwarding pardons to Ballinger. See Green Adams to WPB, Feb. 14, 1867, WPB & Assoc. (HMRC).

36. WPB, Diary, Nov. 13, 1865.

37. Ibid., Nov. 15, 1865.

38. Ibid., Nov. 20, 1865.

Notes to Pages 182-190

39. Ibid., Nov. 25, 1865.
40. Ibid., Jan. 24, 1866.
41. Hurst, *The Growth of American Law: The Law Makers*, 305-308.
42. On the division of labor within the partnership, as well as insights into their personal and working relationship, see WPB & Assoc. (HMRC), years 1865-1880.
43. D. Appleton & Co. to WPB, Nov. 11, 1865, WPB & Assoc. (HMRC). Also see Galveston District Court Dockets, Jan. 1866, June 1866, Jan. 1867, June 1867 terms, Galveston County Court House.
44. J. B. Bees to WPB, Octobeer 17, Dec. 9, 1865; Cook & Collier to WPB, Aug. 31, 1866; Leon Blum to WPB, July 20, 1866; Fairthorne & Rand to WPB, June 5, July 20, Aug. 16, Sept. 4, 1866, WPB & Assoc. (HMRC); W. Killop, Sprague & Co. of the Commercial Agency of New York to WPB, Sept. 10, 21, 1866, Ballinger Papers (CAH).
45. "Statement of claims unaccounted for to R. A. Stephens by W. P. Ballinger, late C.S. Receiver, Feb. 14, 1866, Ballinger Papers (CAH); WPB, Diary, Aug. 22, 1667, Ballinger Papers (RL); Charles Fairman, *A History of the Supreme Court of the United States: Reconstruction and Reunion, 1864-1888* (9 vols.; New York: Macmillan, 1971), VI, 861-863.
46. D. E. Braman to WPB, Aug. 24, 1866, WPB & Assoc. (HMRC); P. Briscoe to WPB, June 12, July 8, Aug. 13, Dec. 29, 1866, ibid.; F. P. Hood to WPB, Feb. 4, 1867, ibid. Also see extensive correspondence and documents relating to Arthur James estate involving settling claims and selling land. James Family to WPB, Mar. 20, 31, May 7, July 7, Sept. 11, Nov. 24, Dec. 15, 1866, Ballinger Papers (CAH).
47. WPB, Diary, July 15, 1866, Nov. 20, 1867; WPB to Guy Bryan, Mar. 19, 1866, Bryan Papers (CAH).
48. WPB to Baker & Voorhis, May 4, July 12, 1866, WPB and Assoc. (HMRC); WPB, Diary, Oct. 19, 1866; WPB to Oran Roberts, Feb. 19, 1874, Oran M. Roberts Papers (CAH); Fairman, *Mr. Justice Miller*, 353.
49. Jane Lane Scarborough, "George W. Paschal: Texas Unionist and Scalawag Jurisprudent" (Ph.D. diss., Rice University, 1972), 1-38; James P. Hart, "George W. Paschal," *Texas Law Review*, 28 (1949), 23-42; WPB, Diary, Dec. 12, 1863.
50. Scarborough, "George W. Paschal: Texas Unionist and Scalawag Jurisprudent," 30-35.
51. WPB to George Paschal, Oct. 1, 1862, Ballinger Papers (CAH); Scarborough, "George W. Paschal: Texas Unionist and Scalawag Jurisprudent," 72-97; Marshall *Texas Republican*, Sept. 13, 1862; *War of the Rebellion*, Series II, Vol. IV, 872.
52. WPB to Fletcher Stockdale, Nov. 21, 1862, Ballinger Papers (CAH); WPB, to Francis Lubbock, Oct. 15, 1862, Governor's Records (TSA); *War of the Rebellion*, Series II, Vol. IV, 890; WPB, editorial, Houston *Telegraph*, Jan. 2, 1863; Marten, *Texas Divided*, 74.
53. Paschal to WPB, May 4, 1863, Ballinger Papers (CAH).
54. WPB to Paschal, Aug. 2, 1865, Ballinger Papers (HMRC); Paschal to WPB, Feb. 4 12, 23, Mar. 15, Apr. 22, May 12, June 6, 1866, WPB & Assoc. (HMRC).
55. Paschal to WPB, June 3, July 17, 1866, WPB & Assoc. (HMRC).
56. WPB, "Letters to Editors," ibid; WPB to Paschal, Sept. 10, 1866, ibid.
57. Galveston *News*, Oct. 15, 1866; Austin *Weekly Southern Intelligencer*, July 5, 1865; Paschal to WPB, June 3, 1866, WPB & Assoc. (HMRC); Baker & Voorhis & Co. advertisement found in Ballinger Papers (CAH); Scarborough, "George W. Paschal," 83-84.
58. WPB to Fletcher Stockdale, Oct. 24, 1866, Ballinger Papers (CAH).
59. WPB to Paschal, Dec. 1, 1866, WPB & Assoc. (HMRC).
60. "American Legal Periodicals," *Albany Law Journal*, 2 (Dec. 1870), 449; "Book

Notices," *American Law Review*, 1 (Jan. 1867), 378; "List of Law Books," published by W. H. & O. H. Morrison, Washington D.C., attached to Paschal's 29th volume of the Texas Report; *Journal of the Constitutional Convention of the State of Texas* (Austin, News Printing Office, 1875), 26; Hart, "George W. Paschal," 32; Scarborough, "George W. Paschal," 86–87.

Chapter Nine

1. WPB, Diary, May 27–30, 1866. After modifying Lincoln's ten percent proposal, Johnson, like his predecessor, expected Southern whites to take the lead in establishing new state governments loyal to the Union. To initiate this process, which he announced in May 1864, Johnson appointed a provisional governor for each former Confederate state, directing him to convene constitutional conventions as soon as the state had been stabilized. The governors were responsible for ensuring that only loyal whites voted for delegates. However, ex-Confederates like Ballinger, personally pardoned by the president, could engage in state affairs. Because of the state's vastness and the tensions between loyalists and secessionists, and between blacks and whites, in provisional governor Andrew Jackson Hamilton's opinion Texans would not be ready to elect a constitutional convention until January 1866. The delegates were to convene in Austin the next month. A. J. Hamilton to Andrew Johnson, Aug. 30, Sept. 28, Nov. 27, 1865, Feb. 26, 1866, Johnson Papers (UTAL); Richter, *The Army in Texas During Reconstruction*, 48–49; Marten, *Texas Divided*, 130–131; Ramsdell, *Reconstruction in Texas*, 59–62; Carl H. Moneyhon, *Republicanism in Reconstruction Texas* (Austin: University of Texas Press, 1980)), 20–24; Foner, *Reconstruction: America's Unfinished Revolution*, 187–190; Carter, *When the War Was Over*, 25–30. The convention was to abolish slavery, provide for the status of the freedmen, repudiate secession, and renounce the Confederate debt. Though reluctantly accepting the federal government's demands, the delegates made it clear that these concessions resulted from a force of arms. The conservatives dodged the secession question by proclaiming that the Confederacy's defeat served as de facto evidence of the movement's failure but denied that it had been illegal. The delegates also refused to ratify the Thirteenth Amendment outlawing slavery, declaring the amendment already was in effect. The convention did amend the new state constitution to exclude slavery. As did all other Southern conventions, the Texas assemblage refused to grant freedmen equal rights with whites. It extended more privileges than most Southern states did, such as the right to testify in court and sit on juries when blacks were on trial. The convention repudiated the war and cancelled all state debts incurred during the war, whether they had to do with the conflict or not. These measures and other changes to the 1845 constitution were adopted and submitted to the people for ratification on June 15, 1866. Ramsdell, *Reconstruction in Texas*, 85, 89–112; Crouch, "All the Vile Passions," 21; Waller, *Colossal Hamilton*, 78–94; Moneyhon, *Republicanism in Reconstruction Texas*, 42–47; James A. Baggett, "Birth of the Texas Republican Party," *Southwestern Historical Quarterly*, 78 (July 1974), 9; John P. Carrier, "A Political History of Texas During Reconstruction, 1865–1874" (Ph.D. diss., Vanderbilt University, 1971), 40–43; One of the best analyses of the proceedings is John Conger McGraw, "The Texas Constitution of 1866" (Ph.D. diss., Texas Tech University, 1959); Ronald N. Gray, "Edmund J. Davis: Radical Republican and Reconstruction Governor of Texas" (Ph.D. diss., Texas Tech University, 1976), 72–95.

2. WPB to Oran Roberts, Mar. 9, 1866, Roberts Papers (CAH).
3. Paschal to WPB, Apr. 26, 1866, WPB & Assoc. (HMRC).
4. WPB to John Hancock, Mar. 4, 1866, Ballinger Papers (CAH); WPB to Elisha M.

Pease, Feb. 24, 1866, Pease Family Papers (Austin Public Library, Austin, Tex.).

5. Texas Constitution of 1866, Article IV, Section 2 (TSA); Paschal to WPB, Oct. 4, 1866, WPB & Assoc. (HMRC).

6. WPB, Diary, May 22, 1865; Carter, *When the War Was Over*, 28-31; Foner, *Reconstruction: America's Unfinished Revolution*, 189-192; Michael Perman, *Reunion Without Compromise: The South and Reconstruction, 1865-1868* (Cambridge: Cambridge University Press, 1973), 152-171; McKitrick, *Andrew Johnson and Reconstruction*, 173-183; McPherson, *Ordeal by Fire*, 503-504.

7. WPB to Guy Bryan, Aug. 5, 1866, Bryan Papers (CAH); Galveston *News*, July 3, 1866; Houston *Telegraph*, July 10, 1866; Marshall *Texas Republican*, July 7, 1866.

8. WPB to Guy Bryan, July 24, 1866, Bryan Papers (CAH).

9. WPB, Diary, July 27-29, 1866.

10. Ibid., July 30, 1866; Smith to WPB, Aug. 5, 1866, WPB & Assoc. (HMRC); WPB to Smith, Aug. 8, 1866, Ashbel Smith Papers (CAH). Smith was not alone in his concerns that state National Union gatherings were not electing delegates "of character, ability, and intelligence." Most important, they had to be individuals who had not been "very prominent or active either for or against secession." Sellers, apparently in Smith's view, failed on both accounts. See Carter, *When the War Was Over*, 237-238, 246-247; Perman, *Reunion Without Compromise*, 214-222; Thomas Wagstaff, "Andrew Johnson and the National Union Movement, 1865-1866" (Ph.D. diss., University of Wisconsin, 1967), 283-284.

11. Thomas Wagstaff, "The Arm-in-Arm Convention," *Civil War History*, 14 (June 1968), 101-119; Perman, *Reunion Without Compromise*, 220-221; Foner, *Reconstruction: America's Unfinished Revolution*, 64; McPherson, *Ordeal by Fire*, 518-520; McKitrick, *Andrew Johnson and Reconstruction*, 318-320.

12. WPB, Diary, Dec. 1, 1866.

13. Ramsdell, *Reconstruction in Texas*, 112-117; Moneyhon, *Republicanism in Reconstruction Texas*, 44-52; Alwyn Barr, *Black Texans*, 56-57; Elliot, *Leathercoat*, 110-112, 161-178; Randolph B. Campbell, "The District Judges of Texas in 1866-1867: An Episode in the Failure of Presidential Reconstruction," *Southwestern Historical Quarterly*, 93 (Jan. 1990), 360-364; Richter, *The Army in Texas During Reconstruction*, 51-91; Moore, "Radical Reconstruction," 15-17; Perman, *Reunion Without Compromise*, 13-21; Barry Crouch, "A Spirit of Lawlessness: White Violence; Texas Blacks, 1865-1868," *Journal of Social History*, 18 (1984), 217-232; Leon F. Litwactk, *Been in the Storm So Long: The Aftermath of Slavery* (New York: Alfred Knopf, 1979), 274-282; Robert Shook, "Federal Occupation and Administration of Texas, 1865-1870" (Ph.D. diss., North Texas State University, 1970), 193-207; James M. Smallwood, *Time of Hope, Time of Despair: Black Texans During Reconstruction* (Port Washington, N.Y.: Kennikat Press, 1981), 128-158; Allen W. Trelease, *White Terror: The Ku Klux Klan Conspiracy and Southern Reconstruction* (New York: Harper and Row, 1971), 137-148; Gregg Cantrell, "Racial Violence and Reconstruction Politics in Texas, 1867-1968," *Southwestern Historical Quarterly*, 93 (Jan. 1990), 333-356.

14. Paschal to WPB, July 16, 1866, WPB & Assoc. (HMRC).

15. WPB to Guy Bryan, Sept. 26, 1866, Bryan Papers (CAH).

16. The best overview of the congressional, radical takeover of Reconstruction is found in Foner, *Reconstruction: America's Unfinished Revolution*, 221-280. Also see Carter, *When the War Was Over*, 237-275; Richter, *The Army in Texas During Reconstructon*, 92-125; Ramsdell, *Reconstruction in Texas*, 94-96, 145-175; Moneyhon, *Republicanism in Reconstruction Texas*, 68-69; Carrier, "Texas During Reconstruction," 202.

17. WPB to John Hancock, Dec. 4, 1867; WPB to Joseph J. Reynolds, Nov. 27, 1867,

Ballinger Papers (CAH); WPB to Philip Sheridan, Dec. 27, 1867, ibid.; WPB to Elisha M. Pease, Nov. 29, 1867, WPB & Assoc. (HMRC); Galveston *News*, Nov. 22, 26, 1867; Houston *Telegraph*, Nov. 29, Dec. 5, 7, 12, 14, 20, 1867; Ramsdell, *Reconstruction in Texas*, 168-170; Richter, *The Army in Texas During Reconstruction*, 124. Ballinger's letters to Union officials, both military and civilian can also be found in Letters Received by the Office of the Adjutant General (Main Series), 1861-1870, United States Department of War, Records of the Adjutant General's Office, RG 94 and RG 407 (National Archives). For more on Elisha M. Pease, see Roger Allen Griffin, "Conneticut Yankee in Texas: A Biography of Elisha Marshall Pease" (Ph.D. diss., University of Texas at Austin, 1973), esp. pages 225-271 for his role during Reconstruction.

18. Elisha M. Pease, Oct. 15, 1869, Ballinger Papers (CAH)

19. WPB, Diary Dec. 1, 1869.

20. Ramsdell, *Reconstruction in Texas*, 261-267, 274-278; Moneyhon, *Republicanism in Reconstruction Texas*, 103-117,127-128, 134; Wallace, *Texas in Turmoil*, 206-210; Carrier, "Texas During Reconstruction," 389-426; Richter, *The Army in Texas During Reconstruction*, 182-186; Winkler (ed.), *Platforms of the Political Parties in Texas*, 117, 119-121; Baggett, "Birth of the Texas Republican Party," 11; WPB, Diary, June 8, 1869.

21. WPB to Fletcher Stockdale, Dec. 20, 1869, Ballinger Papers (CAH); For conservative reaction to the 1869 election, see Ramsdell, *Reconstruction in Texas*, 285-292; Moneyhon, *Republicanism in Reconstruction Texas*, 122-126; Richter, *The Army in Texas During Reconstruction*, 172-186.

22. WPB, Diary, Mar. 6, 11, 18, 21, 1871.

23. Ibid., Mar. 23, 1871.

24. Ibid., Mar. 31, Apr. 10, 11, 1871.

25. Ibid., May 25, 1871.

26. WPB, "Family Notes," Ballinger Papers (RL); WPB, Diary for the years 1868-1871; Betty Ballinger's entry in "Our Family History: Personal Notes," B. Mills Papers (PC); WPB to Guy Bryan, Oct. 2, 8, Nov. 1869, Bryan Papers (CAH).

27. WPB, "Family Notes," Ballinger Papers (RL); WPB, Diary for the years 1868-1871; Betty Ballinger's entry in "Our Family History: Personal Notes," B. Mills Papers (PC); WPB to Guy Bryan, Sept. 12, Dec. 1, 1869.

28. WPB, Diary, June 15-18, 1871; Betty Ballinger to Ballinger Mills, Aug. 5, 1932, B. Mills Papers (PC).

29. WPB, Diary, June 23, 1871.

30. Ibid., June 29, July 16, 21, 1871.

31. Ibid., Aug. 18, 21, 1871.

32. Ibid., Aug. 24, 1871.

33. Ibid., Aug. 28, 1871.

34. Ibid., Sept. 25, Oct. 6, 22, 1871.

35. Ibid., Nov. 12, 1871; WPB to Fletcher Stockdale, Nov. 24, 1871, Ballinger Papers (CAH). Most of the state's papers supported Ballinger's view of Davis. See, for example Houston *Telegraph*, Oct. 1, Nov. 8, 1870; San Antonio *Herald*, Sept. 27, Oct. 4, 20, Nov. 24, 1870; Galveston *News*, Feb. 12, Aug. 13, Oct. 19, 20, 1871; Austin *Democratic Statesman*, Oct. 3, 5, 1871.

36. Foner, *Reconstruction: America's Unfinished Revolution*, 412-421; Moneyhon, *Republicanism in Reconstruction Texas*, 104-124; Carrier, "Political History of Texas During Reconstruction," 355; Thomas B. Alexander, "Persistent Whiggery in the Confederate South, 1860-1877," in Kenneth Stampp and Leon F. Litwack (eds)., *Reconstruction: An*

Anthology of Revisionist Writings (Baton Rouge: Louisiana State University Press, 1976), 289–292; Michael Perman, *The Road to Redemption: Southern Politics, 1869–1879* (Chapel Hill: University of North Carolina Press, 1984), 16–21.

37. For other ex–Whig conservative white Southerners who shared Ballinger's view, see Joel Williamson, *After Slavery: The Negro in South Carolina During Reconstruction, 1861–1877* (Chapel Hill: University of North Carolina Press, 1965), 274–300; C. Vann Woodward, *The Strange Career of Jim Crow* (4th ed.; New York: Oxford University Press, 1985), 31–66; C. Vann Woodward, "The Strange Career of a Historical Controversy," in C. Vann Woodward, *American Counterpoint: Slavery and Racism in the North-South Dialogue* (Boston: Little, Brown, and Co., 1971), 234–260.

38. WPB to Guy Bryan, Aug. 5, 1871, Bryan Papers (CAH).

39. Galveston *News*, July 15, 1871; Houston *Telegraph*, Oct. 22, 1871; WPB to Guy Bryan, Aug. 5, 1871, Bryan Papers (CAH).

40. Quoted in Foner, *Reconstruction: America's Unfinished Revolution*, 417.

41. Austin *Democratic Statesman*, July 26, Aug. 20, 1871. Also see Moneyhon, *Republicanism in Reconstruction Texas*, 164–167.

42. WPB to Fletcher Stockdale, Sept. 5, 1871, Ballinger Papers (CAH).

43. Foner, *Reconstruction: America's Unfinished Revolution*, 547–549; Perman, *Road to Redemption*, 127–128, 150–155, 173–177; Alexander, "Persistent Whiggery," 292–293.

44. Moneyhon, *Republicanism in Reconstruction Texas*, 162–167; Wallace, *Texas in Turmoil*, 213–215; Ramsdell, *Reconstruction in Texas*, 300–314; Moore, "Radical Reconstruction," 102; William A. Russ Jr., "Radical Disfranchisement in Texas, 1867–1870," *Southwestern Historical Quarterly*, 38 (July 1934), 40–52.

45. WPB, Diary, Dec. 12, 1872; WPB to Guy Bryan, Jan. 5, 1873, Bryan Papers (CAH).

46. Davis sensed his increasing isolation. He sent the Thirteenth Legislature a conciliatory message, suggesting a willingness to change some laws. The governor's overture fell on deaf ears as the Conservative–Democratic coalition repealed everything that was left of the so-called "Obnoxious Acts" passed soon after Davis took office in 1870. For example, the state police force was abolished, the governor's appointive powers were reduced, and the governor's authority to declare martial law was restricted. Perhaps most important, the legislature simplified voter registration procedures as well as limiting the election to a single day instead of four. The next election was set for the first Tuesday of December 1873. Moneyhon, *Republicanism in Reconstruction Texas*, 183–185, 192; Richardson, Wallace, and Anderson, *Texas*, 244; Wallace, *Texas in Turmoil*, 216; Ramsdell, *Reconstruction in Texas*, 313–315; Gammel, *The Laws of Texas*, VIII, 456, 468, 493; Fehrenbach, *Lone Star*, 428–429; Austin *Democratic Statesman*, Jan. 14, 1873. In 1871 the Conservative/ex-Whig Democratic coalition began their assault on the radical governments throughout the South, not by attacking radical racial policies but by criticizing Republican rule for its alleged financial corruption and extravagance, demanding a reduction in taxes and state expenditures. In several states, including Texas, this coalition organized Taxpayer's Conventions through which they hoped to start their "redemption." On the convention held in Austin in the fall of 1871, see Moneyhon, *Republicanism in Reconstruction Texas*, 152–162; Ramsdell, *Reconstruction in Texas*, 301–309; Richardson, Wallace, and Anderson, *Texas*, 242; Winkler (ed.), *Platforms of the Political Parties in Texas*, 128–140; Austin *Democratic Statesman*, Sept. 21, 23, 25, 27, 30, Oct. 2, 5, 9, 1871; Houston *Telegraph*, Sept. 24, 28, Oct. 3, 5, 10, 1871; *Colorado Citizen*, Oct. 5, 1871. On similar convocations held in other Southern states, see Foner, *Reconstruction: America's Unfinished Revolution*, 415–416; J. Mills Thornton III,

"Fiscal Policy and the Failure of Radical Reconstruction in the Lower South," in J. Morgan Kousser and James M. McPherson (eds.), *Region, Race and Reconstruction: Essays in Honor of C. Vann Woodward* (New York: Oxford University Press, 1982), 367–371. A more objective analysis of the Davis administration leads to a very different assessment. Though the cost of state government increased under the radicals, there were several reasons for the escalation. Texas had grown appreciably both in population and territory inhabited since 1860. The still unsettled frontier conditions, where lawlessness was rampant, warranted the existence of both a militia and state law enforcement agency. In a little over two years the State Police made more than 1300 arrests for murder or attempted murder. The increased taxation lambasted by the opposition was used to finance a desperately needed free public school system, which can by no means be a waste of money. Davis's use of taxes for educational purposes is to be lauded rather than condemned. Indeed, Davis vetoed several bills giving large land grants of school lands to railroads—bills for which convention leaders like James Throckmorton had served as lobbyists for the Southern Pacific Railroad. Still, it was the governor who was chastised for his association with the robber barons. See Moneyhon, *Republicanism in Texas*, 137–150; Mark W. Summers, *Railroads, Reconstruction, and the Gospel to Prosperity: Aid Under the Radical Republicans, 1865–1877* (Princeton: Princeton University Press, 1984), 84–51; Homer L. Kerr, "Migration into Texas, 1860–1880," *Southwestern Historical Quarterly*, 70 (Oct. 1966), 189–192; Moore, "Radical Reconstruction," 101–102; James A. Baggett, "Beginnings of Radical Rule in Texas: The Special Legislative Session of 1870," *Southwestern Journal of Social Education*, 2 (Spring-Summer, 1972), 27–35; Carl H. Moneyhon, "Public Education and Texas Reconstruction Politics, 1871–1874," *Southwestern Historical Quarterly*, 92 (Jan. 1989), 392–416; Anne P. Baenziger, "The Texas State Police Force During Reconstruction: A Reexamination," *Southwestern Historical Quarterly*, 72 (Apr. 1969), 470–491; Randolph B. Campbell, "Carpetbagger Rule in Reconstruction Texas: An Enduring Myth," *Southwestern Historical Quarterly*, 97 (Apr. 1994), 587–598; and "Scalawag District Judges: The E. J. Davis Appointees," *Houston Review*, 14 (1992), 75–88; Ralph A. Wooster, "Statehood, War, and Reconstruction," in Donald W. Whisehunt (ed.), *Texas: A Sesquicentennial Celebration* (Austin: Eakin Press, 1984), 114–120; Richter, *The Army in Texas During Reconstruction*, 191–193; Ronald N. Gray, "Edmund J. Davis;" William T. Hooper Jr., "Governor Edmund J. Davis, Ezra Cornell, and the A&M College of Texas," *Southwestern Historical Quarterly*, 78 (Jan. 1975), 307–312; Ramsdell, *Reconstruction in Texas*, 313–315; Moneyhon, *Republicanism in Reconstruction Texas*, 163–196; Fehrenbach, *Lone Star*, 428–429; Richardson, Wallace, Anderson, *Texas: The Lone Star State*, 244; Gammel, *The Laws of Texas*, VII, 456, 468, 493; Austin *Democratic Statesman*, Jan. 14, 1873.

47. WPB. Diary, Nov. 12, 1673.

48. Moneyhon, *Republicanism in Reconstruction Texas*, 185–191; Also see Moneyhon, "Edmund J. Davis in the Coke-Davis Election Dispute of 1874: A Reassessment of Character," *Southwestern Historical Quarterly*, 100 (Oct. 1996), 131–145; Moore, "Radical Reconstruction," 102; Wallace, *Texas in Turmoil*, 217–220; Ramsdell, *Reconstruction in Texas*, 314–317; Fehrenbach, *Lone Star*, 429–432; Richardson, Wallace, Anderson, *Texas*, 244; George Shelley, "The Semicolon Court of Texas," *Southwestern Historical Quarterly*, 48 (Apr. 1945), 449–468; *Ex Parte Rodriquiz*, 39 Texas Reports, 709.

49. WPB, Diary, Jan. 29, 1874; Moneyhon, *Republicanism in Texas*, 191–194; Moneyhon, "Edmund J. Davis in the Coke, Davis Election Dispute of 1874," 149–152; Dallas *Herald*, Jan. 24, 1874.

50. WPB, Diary, Jan. 23, 1874; Coke to WPB, Jan. 24, 1874, WPB & Assoc. (HMRC).

51. Coke to WPB, Jan. 30, 1874, Ballinger Papers (CAH). A copy of Coke's letter also appeared in the Austin *Democratic Statesman*, Jan. 30, 1874. For Bryan's activities on Ballinger's behalf, see Bryan to Coke, Jan. 20, 27, 1874, Bryan Papers (CAH) and Governor's Papers (TSA).
52. WPB, Diary, Jan. 23, 1874.
53. Ibid., Jan. 27, 28, 1874.
54. WPB to Guy Bryan, Mar. 13, 1878, Bryan Papers (CAH).
55. WPB to Coke, Feb. 3, 1874, Governor's Papers (TSA). Ballinger's letter was also printed in the Austin *Democratic Statesman*, Feb. 4, 1874.
56. Austin *Democratic Statesman*, Feb. 5, 1874; Dallas *Herald*, Feb. 6, 1874.
57. Foner, *Reconstruction: America's Unfinished Revolution*, 512–513; Rendigs Fels, *American Business Cycles*, 1865–1897 (Chapel Hill: Univeristy of North Carolina Press, 1959), 83–111; Eric Hobsbawm, *The Age of Capital, 1848–1875* (London: Weidenfeld and Nicolson, 1975), 4–5, 46; Allan Nevins, *The Emergence of Modern America, 1865-1878* (New York: Macmillan, 1927), 293–303; Irwin Unger, *The Greenback Era: A Social and Political History of American Finance, 1865–1879* (Princeton: Princeton University Press, 1964), 213–224.
58. WPB to Fletcher Stockdale, Dec. 28, 1872, Ballinger Papers (CAH); WPB to Guy Bryan, July 26, 1874, Bryan Papers (CAH). Also see WPB & Assoc. Papers (HMRC) for the years 1870–1875.
59. WPB, Diary, Dec. 30, 1879.
60. WPB to Guy Bryan, Aug. 9, 1875, Bryan Papers (CAH); WPB, Diary, Aug. 15, 25, 1875.
61. Wallace, *Texas in Turmoil*, 224; Seth Shepard McKay, *Making the Texas Constitution of 1876* (Philadelphia: University of Pennslyvania, 1924), 76–77; Austin *State Gazette*, Sept. 15, 17, 1875; Dallas *Herald*, Sept. 23, 1875; *Journal of the Constitutional Convention of 1875* (Galveston: Galveston *News*, 1905), 101, 128; WPB to wife, Sept. 7, 1875, B. Mills Papers (PC),
62. WPB, Diary, Sept. 6, 7, 1875.
63. WPB to wife, Sept. 21, 1875, B. Mills Papers (PC); Seth Shepard McKay, *Debates in the Texas Constitutional Convention of 1875* (Austin: University of Texas, 1930), 69.
64. Austin *State Gazette*, Sept. 22–25 , 1875; McKay, *Debates*, 49–54.
65. Austin *State Gazette*, Sept. 22–25; Austin *Democratic Statesman*, Sept. 24, 1875; *Journal of the Constitutional Convention of 1875*, 176, 182.
66. Austin *Democratic Statesman*, Sept. 24, 1875; McKay, *Debates*, 69.
67. WPB. Diary, Sept. 17, 21–23, 1875. Also see Oscar Walter Roberts, "Richard Coke on Constitution-Making, *Southwestern Historical Quarterly*, 78 (July 1974), 69–75.
68. Austin *Democratic Statesman*, Sept. 25, 1875. Most of the state's leading newspapers endorsed the majority report. The Houston *Telegraph*, however, dissented, praising the minority report for its "apprehension of the legal side of the argument." See *Telegraph*, Sept. 22, 1875. Other dissenting editorials can be found in the Galveston *News*, Sept. 25, 1875; Austin *State Gazette*, Sept. 23, 1875; and the San Antonio *Herald*, Sept. 25, 1855. The *Herald* agreed that the majority report was without legal ground but should nonetheless be accepted for its "economy."
69. McKay, *Making the Texas Constitution*, 81; McKay, *Debates*, 138; Austin *State Gazette*, Oct. 23, 1875.
70. Austin *State Gazette*, Oct. 3, 1675; McKay, *Debates*, 139–140; McKay, *Making the Texas Constitution*, 82; WPB, Diary, Oct. 7, 1875.
71. Richardson, Wallace, Anderson, *Texas*, 252; Texas, Constitution of 1876, Article

Notes to Pages 215–223

IV; *Journal of the Constitutional Convention*, 228–234; McKay, *Debates*, 147–154; McKay, *Making the Texas Constitution*, 87.

72. McKay, *Debates*, 155; Austin *State Gazette*, Oct. 5, 1875; WPB, Diary, Sept. 21, 1875. Most of the state's leading papers condemned the "bounteous provision" for the governor and other executive officers. See Austin *Democratic Statesman*, Oct. 20, 1875 and Galveston *News*, Oct. 13, 1875. The Houston *Telegraph*, Oct. 8, 1875, suggested the convention should have stipulated that only single men be elected to state offices, for it would be impossible for married men with families to live on the salaries specified.

73. Richardson, Wallace, Anderson, *Texas*, 253; Seth Shepard McKay, "Some Attitudes of West Texas Delegates in the Constitutional Convention of 1875," *West Texas Historical Association Yearbook*, V, 100–106; Ralph Smith, "The Grange Movement in Texas, 1873–1900," *Southwestern Historical Quarterly*, 42 (Apr. 1939), 297–315; WPB, Diary, Oct. 10, 1875.

74. McKay, *Debates*, 175–180; McKay, *Making the Texas Constitution*, 96–97; Austin *State Gazette*, Oct. 7, 8, 13, 1875; Austin *Democratic Statesman*, Oct. 8, 1675.

75. McKay, *Debates*, 180–181.

76. Ibid.; Austin *State Gazette*, Oct. 6, 1875.

77. S. D. Myers Jr., "Mysticism, Realism, and the Texas Constitution of 1876," *Southwestern Political and Social Science Quarterly*, 9 (Sept. 1929), 172–176; Richardson, Wallace, and Anderson, *Texas*, 253.

78. Austin *State Gazette*, Oct. 12, 1875; McKay, *Debates*, 232–233.

79. Austin *State Gazette*, Oct. 12, 1875; McKay, *Debates*, 233, Texas, Constitution of 1876, Article VII.

80. WPB, Diary, Oct. 20, 1875; Austin *State Gazette*, Oct. 23, 1875; Houston *Telegraph*, Oct. 23, 1875; Galveston *News*, Oct. 13, 1875.

81. Wallace, *Texas in Turmoil*, 225; Richardson, Wallace, and Anderson, *Texas*, 252; McKay, *Making the Texas Constitution*, 88–94; McKay, *Debates*, 381–383, 430; *Journal of the Constitutional Convention*, 406, 413, 457; WPB, Diary, Nov. 16, 1875; Austin *State Gazette*, Nov. 5, 12, 14, 1875.

82. Friedman, *A History of American Law*, 336–338, 347–348. Also see *Harwell v. State*, 22 Tex. App. 251, 2 S.W. 606 (1886); *Taylor v. State*, 5 Tex. App. 569 (1877); *Wilson v. State*, 12 Tex. App. 481 (1882); *Shaw v. State*, 2 Tex. App 487 (1877); *Curry v. State*, 7 Tex. App. 91 (1879).

83. *Journal of the Constitutional Convention*, 772; Austin *State Gazette*, Nov. 23, 1875; McKay, *Making the Texas Constitution*, 145–147.

84. WPB to Tom Jack, Oct. 22, 1875, WPB & Assoc. (HMRC); WPB, Diary, Nov. 10, 1875.

85. Galveston *News*, Jan. 2, 1876; Houston *Telegraph*, Jan. 5, 1876; WPB to Willard Richardson, Feb. 15, 1876, WPB & Assoc. (HMRC).

86. Galveston *News*, Jan. 30, 1876; Richardson to WPB, Jan. 13, 1876, WPB & Assoc. (HMRC).

87. See Ballinger's editorials in Houston *Telegraph*, Dec. 12, 14, 21, 23, 1875, Jan. 12, 15, 1876.

88. Ibid., Jan. 15, 1876.

89. WPB, Diary, Feb. 11, 1876.

Chapter Ten

1. WPB, Diary, Apr. 1, 1876.

2. Foner, *Reconstruction: America's Unfinished Revolution*, 565–575; McPherson, *Ordeal by Fire*, 596–600.

3. Foner, *Reconstruction: America's Unfinished Revolution*, 575–586.

4. WPB, Diary, Mar. 1, 6, 1876.

5. Copies of the letters sent to Hayes were also forwarded to Ballinger and Guy Bryan. See Richard Coke to Byran, Mar. 9, 1877, Bryan Papers (CAH); Coke to Ballinger, Mar. 9, 1877, WPB & Assoc. (HMRC); E. J. Davis to WPB, Mar. 11, 1877, ibid.; A. J. Hamilton to WPB, Mar. 10, 1877, ibid.; Elisha M. Pease to Guy Bryan, Mar. 15, 1877, Bryan Papers (CAH); Pease to WPB, 15 Mar. 15, 1877, ibid.

6. Miller to WPB, Mar. 21, 1874, in Fairman, *Mr. Justice Miller*, 347–348.

7. George P. Garrison, "Guy Bryan," *Quarterly of the Texas State Historical Association*, V (Oct. 1901), 121–136; Fairman, *Mr. Justice Miller*, 349; E. W. Winkler, "The Bryan–Hayes Correspondence," *Southwestern Historical Quarterly*, 25 (Jan. 1922), 98–100.

8. Garrison, "Guy Bryan." Also see WPB, "Family Notes," Ballinger Papers (RL); Betty Ballinger, "Our Family History," Betty Ballinger Papers (RL); and Ballinger Mills, "The Ballinger Family History," B. Mills Papers (PC).

9. Hayes to Bryan, May 5, 1859, Bryan Papers (CAH).

10. Winkler, "Bryan–Hayes Correspondence," *Southwestern Historical Quarterly*, 27 (July 1932), 72–73, 164–165.

11. Elisha M. Pease to Rutherford B. Hayes, June 13, 1877, Ballinger Papers (CAH); Winkler, "Bryan–Hayes Correspondence," 27 (Jan. 1924), 242–243; WPB to Bryan, Mar. 20, 1877, Bryan Papers (CAH).

12. WPB to Miller, Mar. 15, 1877, WPB & Assoc. (HMRC); WPB, Diary, Mar. 12, 1877.

13. Miller to WPB, Mar. 18, 1877, Ballinger Papers (CAH). Also see Fairman, *Mr. Justice Miller*, 351–353.

14. Miller to WPB, Apr. 23, May 6, 1877, Ballinger Papers (CAH).

15. Fairman, *Mr. Justice Miller*, 357–358; WPB, Diary, May 28, 1877.

16. WPB, Diary, July 15, 1877; WPB to Guy Bryan, Sept. 12, 1877, Feb. 23, 1879, Bryan Papers (CAH); WPB to Samuel Miller, Sept. 5, 1877, WPB & Assoc. (HMRC).

17. Winkler, "Bryan–Hayes Correspondence," 27 (Apr. 1924), 246–249.

18. Galveston *News*, Oct. 21, 26, 1877

19. WPB to Miller, Nov. 1, 1877, Ballinger Papers (CAH); Galveston *News*, Nov. 2, 1877.

20. Miller to WPB, Jan. 20, Feb. 3, 1878, Ballinger Papers (CAH); WPB, Diary, Jan. 23, 1878; Miller to WPB, Dec. 25, 1880, Jan. 2, 1881, Ballinger Papers (CAH); Miller to WPB, Jan. 6, Apr. 17, 1883, ibid.; Miller to WPB, May 2, June 1, 1883, ibid.; WPB to Miller, May 21, 1883, ibid.

21. Richardson, Wallace, and Anderson, *Texas*, 265–271; Fehrenbach, *Lone Star*, 604–605; John Spratt, *The Road to Spindletop: Economic Change in Texas, 1875–1901* (Austin: University of Texas Press, 1970, 1983), 190–220. The two standard studies on Texas railroads are S. G. Reed, *A history of the Texas Railroads and of Transportation Conditions under Spain and Mexico and the Republic and the State* (Houston: St. Clair Publishing Co., 1941); and C. S. Potts, *Railroad Transportation in Texas* (Austin: University of Texas, 1909). Also see Ira B. Clark, *Then came the Railroads: The Century from Steam to Diesel in the Southwest* (Norman, Okla.: University of Oklahoma Press, 1958). For background on Southern railroads in general, including Texas, see John Stover, *The Railroads of the South, 1865–1900: A Study of Finance and Control* (Chapel Hill: University of North Carolina Press, 1955).

22. Friedman, *A History of American Law*, 389–395. Also see Gabriel Kolko, *Railroads and Regulation, 1877–1916* (Princeton: Princeton University Press, 1965), esp. pages 10–105; Robert Wiebe, *The Search for Order, 1877–1920* (New York: Hill and Wang, 1967), 52–54.

23. Harry N. Schreiber,"Federalism, the Southern Regional Economy, and Public Policy Since 1865," in David J. Bodenhammer and James W. Ely Jr. (eds.), *Ambivalent Legacy: A Legal History of the South* (Jackson: University of Mississippi Press, 1964), 69–105; Spratt, *The Road to Spindletop*, 13–25.

24. WPB, Diary, June 23, 1860.

25. WPB to Guy Bryan, Aug. 17, 1882, Bryan Papers (CAH).

26. WPB to J. E. Poole, Oct. 22, 1881, WPB & Assoc. (HMRC).

27. WPB to Marcus Mott, Mar. 4, 1685, ibid.

28. WPB, Diary, Nov. 17, 1867; Thomas Harrison to WPB, Aug. 5, Oct. 12, 1866, Apr. 2, 1867; Galveston *News*, Nov. 19, 1906.

29. See WPB & Assoc. (HMRC), Files and Papers, for the years 1873–1878.

30. Charles O. Gregory, "Trespass to Negligence to Absolute Liability," *Virginia Law Review*, 37 (1951), 359–379.

31. See WPB & Assoc. (HMRC), Files and Papers, for the years 1871–1886.

32. Oscar G. Murray to WPB, Apr. 16, 19, 1878, WPB & Assoc. (HMRC); WPB to Murray, May 12, June 7, July 21, 26, 1879, ibid.

33. See WPB & Assoc. (HMRC), Files and Papers, July–Sept. 1878, ibid.

34. Ibid., 1877–1878. Newspaper article explaining the Georgia court's ruling was found in WPB & Assoc. Papers for the year 1878.

35. J. H. Crowley to WPB, Jan. 8, 1879, WPB & Assoc. (HMRC).

36. WPB & Assoc. (HMRC), Files and Papers, Feb.–Aug. 1879.

37. Friedman, *A History of American Law*, 412.

38. Ibid., 413.

39. Ibid.

40. Between 1870 and 1900, some state supreme courts behaved as if their primary function was to reverse decisions of their lower courts for supposed "technical errors." This seemed particularly true in Texas. An 1887 article in the *American Law Review* noted that the Texas Court of Appeals (a sort of auxiliary court of the state supreme court) "seems to have been organized to overrule and reverse. At least, since its organization that has been its chief employment." To support its contention, the *Review* cited a rather revealing fact: during the twelve years of the court's existence, it had reversed 1,604 cases, and affirmed only 802—a margin of almost two to one. In one volume of reports, there were five reversals to every single affirmance. Further investigation uncovered a more relevant statistic: Over 60 percent of the cases reversed involved railroad accidents or other suits against the lines for negligence. "Overruled by Their Judicial Superiors," *American Law Review*, 21 (1887), 610; Roscoe Pound, *Appellate Procedure in Civil Cases* (Boston: Little, Brown, and Co., 1941), 260–261. For Texas cases, see note 82, Chapter 9.

41. WPB & Assoc. (HMRC), Files and Papers for the years 1880–1886.

42. WPB to J. H. Crowley, Oct. 8, 1882, June 21, Sept. 13, Oct. 1, 10, 22, Nov. 4, 12, 1883, ibid.

43. WPB to J. H. Crowley, Apr. 4, 10, 14, 1884, ibid.

44. J. H. Crowley to WPB, Apr. 18, 22, 1884, ibid.; WPB to Crowley, Apr. 27, May 5, 10, 1884, ibid. Also see *Malcolm G. Douglas v. Galveston, Houston & Henderson Railway Company*, 55 Texas Reports, 564–567.

45. WPB, Diary, Mar. 13, 1883; WPB to son, Oct. 14, 1886, B. Mills Papers (PC).

46. WPB to Marcus Mott, May 1, 1883, WPB & Assoc. (HMRC); WPB, Diary, Aug. 5, 18, 1883.

47. On Jay Gould see Maury Klein's biography, *The Life and Legend of Jay Gould* (Baltimore: Johns Hopkings Press, 1986). Also see Milton Rugoff, *America's Gilded Age: Intimate Portraits from an Era of Extravagance and Change, 1850–1890* (New York: Holt, 1989), 52–54, 58–67.

48. Donovan Hofsommer, "Texas Railroads" in *Texas: A Sesquicentennial Celebration*, 244; Reed, *A History of the Texas Railroads*, 569–574; Spratt, *The Road to Spindletop*, 13–15.

49. *International & Great Northern Railroad Co., Moses Taylor et al. v. Paul Bremond*, 47 Texas Reports, 97.

50. Shearman & Sterling to WPB, Feb. 4, 5, 1880; Baker & Botts to WPB, Feb. 14, 1880, WPB & Assoc. (HMRC).

51. *International & Great Northern v. Paul Bremond*, 47 Texas Reports, 98–101.

52. WPB to Shearman & Sterling, Feb. 20, 1880, WPB & Assoc. (HMRC).

53. Shearman & Sterling to WPB, Feb. 27, 1880, ibid; *International & Great Northern v. Paul Bremond*, 47 Texas Reports,, 110–117. For an interpretation of ultra vires, see Friedman, *A History of American Law*, 453–454.

54. *International & Great Northern v. Paul Bremond*, 47 Texas 117–121.

55. WPB to Marcus Mott, Apr. 10, 1881, WPB & Assoc. (HMRC); WPB to Jay Gould, May 1, 1881, ibid.; Jay Gould to WPB, May 12, 1881, ibid.

56. Shearman & Sterling to WPB, Feb. 25, Mar. 4, Apr. 9, 1880, ibid.; WPB to Marcus Mott, Mar. 15, 1880, ibid.

57. J. E. Poole to WPB, July 29, 1878, ibid.

58. WPB, Diary, Aug. 3, 1880.

59. Ibid., June 15, 1883.

60. WPB to wife, June 21, 1880, B. Mills Papers (PC).

61. Gustav Ranger to WPB, Jan. 30, 1881, WPB & Assoc. (HMRC).

62. Edward Thompson to WPB, Dec. 16, 1886, ibid.

63. WPB, Diary, Oct. 29, 1883; Southwestern Telegraph & Telephone Company to Ballinger & Jack, May 30, 1883; WPB to brother, Aug. 5, 1863, ibid.

64. See Ballinger Papers, WPB & Assoc. (HMRC), for the years 1883–1887.

65. Ibid.

66. Ibid.

67. Ibid.

68. Deberry & Smith to WPB, Jan. 2, 1884, ibid.; Hefley & Wallace to WPB, Jan. 4, 1884, ibid.; WPB to George Sealy, Jan. 12, July 15, 1885, ibid.

69. WPB to George Sealy, Jan. 17, 30, 1885, ibid.

70. See copy of Ballinger's instructions to all division attorneys, dated Feb. 2, 1885, in ibid. for year 1885.

71. George Peck to WPB, May 16, 1886, ibid.

72. George Peck to WPB, May 31, June 26, 1886, ibid.

73. WPB to Marcus Mott, Oct. 4, 1886, ibid.

74. WPB, "Circular," Mar. 1, 1887, ibid.

75. George Peck to WPB, Oct. 15, 21, 1887, ibid.

76. Davis Garrett to WPB, Aug. 12, 1887; Deberry & Smith to WPB, Sept. 2, 1887; WPB to Deberry & Smith, Sept. 23, 1887, ibid.

Chapter Eleven

1. WPB, Diary, June 17, 28, 1885.
2. WPB, Diary, Apr. 9, 1866; WPB to wife, Aug. 17, 1886, B. Mills Papers (PC).
3. WPB, Diary, Oct. 1, 1887.
4. Houston *Telegraph*, Jan. 27, 1888; Galveston *News*, Jan. 21, 26, 1888.
5. John S. Davenport to Hally Ballinger, Jan. 30, 1888; George Sullivan to Marcus Mott, Feb. 14, 1888, WPB & Assoc. (HMRC).
6. Copy of Roberts address, dated Feb. 9, 1888, in Betty Ballinger Papers (RL). Also see Galveston *News*, Feb. 8, 9, 1888. For other statewide tributes to Ballinger, see Austin *State Gazette* and Dallas *Herald*, Jan. 23, 1888; also see speech given by State Supreme Court Justice Thomas N. Waul, printed in both Austin *State Gazette* and *Democratic Statesman*, Feb. 8, 9, 1888.
7. "Remarks of Judge James A. Baker on Presenting the Resolutions of the Bar of Galveston to the United States District Court," Mar. 5, 1888, p. 3, Ballinger Papers (RL).
8. Ibid., 4
9. Ibid., 5
10. Thomas Jack Ballinger, "Recollections," in B. Mills Papers (PC); James Baker to Thomas Jack Ballinger, Feb. 18, 1888, WPB & Assoc. (HMRC); Galveston *News*, Mar. 5, 1888.

INDEX

A

A. Blum and Company: 185
abolitionism: 82, 85, 93, 165
Adams, America: 16
Adams, Green: 177, 180
Adams, John: 16
Adams, Olivia: 15–17
Adams, Sarah Herndon: 16
Adams, Thomas Randolph: 16
advertising: 81–82
African Americans. *See* freedmen; slavery
afternoon tea: 100
amnesty: 173, 179–180
Ampudia, Pedro: 31
Antona: 171
Arguelles, Joaquin: 35
Arthur, Chester Alan: 229
Articles of Annexation: 189
asthma: and travel, 11; and physical appearance, 12; in childhood, 17–18; father's attitude toward, 17–18, 22; severe attacks of, 17, 57–58, 255, 256; control over, 22; impact of, on Ballinger's life choices, 23, 98, 140; and Mexican War, 29; and Civil War, 140; subsiding of, 197
Atchison, Topeka & Santa Fe: 250, 251–253
Atlanta: 159–160
Austin *Democratic Statesman*: 204, 209
Austin *State Gazette*: 189

B

Baker, James A.: 258–259
Baker & Botts: 4, 241, 245, 248, 258
Baker & Voorhis: 186

Ballinger, Betty: 1–2, 15–16, 98, 198–199
Ballinger, Elizabeth: 14
Ballinger, Elizabeth Jenkins: 22–23, 59
Ballinger, Harriet (daughter): 98
Ballinger, Harriet "Hally" Patrick Jack: relationship with W. Ballinger, 42–43, 45–46, 100–103, 197–198, 208, 255, 260; family history of, 43; photograph of, 44; marriage to W. Ballinger, 45–46; homes of, 46, 96, 98–101; children of, 50, 98, 102, 255; correspondence with W. Ballinger, 50, 53, 54, 55–56; and asthma of W. Ballinger, 57–58; breakdown of, 58; and family vacations, 59, 199–202; and father-in-law, 59; and entertaining, 100–101; emancipated slaves of, 174; and death and funeral of W. Ballinger, 256, 258, 260
Ballinger, Henry: 13, 86
Ballinger, James Franklin: marriages of, 15, 22–23; military experiences, 15; attitude toward asthma, 17–18, 22; relationship with W. Ballinger, 17–19, 23–24, 26–27, 59–61, 181; and H. Ballinger, 59; emigration to Texas, 181–182; illness of, 181
Ballinger, Joseph: 13–14
Ballinger, Laura Jack: 50
Ballinger, Lucy: 98, 198, 199
Ballinger, Olivia Adams: 15–17
Ballinger, Richard: 14–15
Ballinger, Thomas Jack: on J. Gould meeting, 2; and Grayson Case, 70; birth of, 198, 255; legal career of, 255; relationship with W. Ballinger, 255–256; photograph of, 257; and father's death, 259–260

Ballinger, William Pitt: O. Roberts's relationship with, 4–5; oratory of, 7, 79, 91–92, 124–125; photograph of, 10; emigration to Texas, 11, 25; fame of, 11–12; physical appearance and clothing of, 12, 64, 109; family history of, 13–17; Quaker heritage of, 13–17, 86; "Family Notes" of, 15; writings of, 15, 25–26, 59–60, 144–145, 150–151, 154, 156, 158, 160, 166–167, 203, 220; childhood of, 16–23; mother's death, 16–17; father's relationship with, 17–19, 23–24, 26–27, 59–61, 98, 181–182; as Kentucky resident, 18–24; education of, 19–21; Mexican War service of, 26–32; relationship with wife, 42–43, 45–46, 100–103, 197–198, 208; marriage of, 45–46; homes of, 46, 96, 98–101; and birth of L. Ballinger, 50; and family vacations, 58–61, 199–202; travel of, 58–61, 83–87, 134–138, 255–256; "Sketchbook" of, 59–60; friendships of, 93, 110; as entertainment reviewer, 94–95; income of, 99–100, 106–107, 210–211, 251; entertaining at home, 100–101; relationship with children, 102, 160–161, 255–256; daily routine of, 104–105; newspaper reading by, 104; children's deaths, 160–161; "Family Notebook" of, 199; birthday celebrations of, 201–202; land holdings of, 248–249; death and funeral of, 256, 258, 260; homages for, 258–260

———, Civil War: Unionist feelings, 120–121, 123–126, 128, 129–130; attempts at preventing, 123–132; "Secession Speech" of, 124–125; and secession, 131, 132, 226; Confederate loyalty, 133, 261; and J. Davis, 133–134; armaments purchases, 134–138; Galveston's surrender, 139–140; civilian status during, 140; receiver of enemy property, 141–145, 185; defense of Sequestration Act, 144–145; legal cases, 145–148; habeas corpus restrictions support, 149–150; martial law support, 149; journalism during, 150–151, 154, 156, 158, 160, 166–167; and conscription, 155–157, 164–165; and state sovereignty, 156; and cotton impressment, 157–159; personal conflict about, 161–162; and Texas as French protectorate, 162–164; and slave conscription, 164–165; peace negotiations for Texas, 169–182; prosecution for treason after, 169

———, correspondence with: T. Ballinger, 20; G. Bryan, 29; J. Love, 29–30, 36–37, 147–148; H. Ballinger, 50, 53, 54, 55–56, 178–179; J. Davis, 133–134; T. Jack, 137–138; P. Murrah, 158; K. Smith, 158–159

———, health: asthma, 11–12, 17–18, 22–23, 29, 57–58, 98, 140, 197, 255, 256; insomnia, 104–105; diarrhea, 197–198; collapsed lung ailment, 198; depression, 255

———, legal career: and J. Gould, 1–3, 240–245; and railroad law, 1–4, 11, 211, 232–245, 248–253; reputation of, 4, 37–38, 77, 93–94, 247; choice of, 6–7; as jury pleader, 6; appointment to Texas Supreme Court, 8, 206–209; as freedmen's advocate, 8, 175–176, 195, 202–204; and Texas Supreme Court, 8, 11, 42, 77–78, 191–192, 206–209, 243; training for, 23–26; practice manual composition, 25–26; bar examination, 32; and Jones and Butler partnership, 32–42, 63–64; and real estate law, 33–36, 63; conscience conflicts in, 36–38, 63–64, 231; lost cases, 39–41, 94; illegal activities of partners, 40–41; as U.S. district attorney for East Texas, 42, 47, 49–56; J. Carvajal prosecution, 50–57; resignation as U.S. district attorney, 55–58; recruitment offers, 63; beginning of Ballinger & Jack law firm, 65–66; Grayson Case, 67–71; fees charged, 71–73, 254; reduced fees for poor, 71, 254; and Flats Case, 72–77; anxiety over cases, 76; humor used in, 79–80; and oration, 79, 91–92; as land agent, 80–81; travel to Northeast, 83–87; legal document preparation by, 94; reaction to winning cases, 94; arbitrary style in, 105–106; emancipation cases, 112–118; and hate mail, 115; slaveholders as clients, 118; and Democratic

Index

Party, 122–123, 193–194, 220; Civil War-related cases, 145–148; and A. Johnson, 170, 177–181, 180–181, 192; pardon-seeking for Confederate clients, 176–177, 179–181; and S. Miller, 177–180, 224–226; as estate administrator, 185–186; support for codifying Texas laws, 186–190; and judiciary reform, 191–192, 218; and cattle industry, 210–211; and Texas Constitution of 1876, 211–220; and poll tax, 215–217, 220–222; U.S. Supreme Court nomination of, 223–228; and R. Hayes, 224–225; and tort law, 233–239; correspondent ties with other law firms, 247; as editor of encyclopedia of legal cases, 247; as supervisor, 251–253; and corporate image, 253–254; and Texas Bar Association, 258. *See also* Ballinger law firm

———, opinions on: secession, 7–8, 124–132, 162, 226; education, 21–22, 122, 221–222; race relations, 29–30, 164–165, 201; war, 29; slavery, 82, 85, 93, 111–112, 117–119, 129, 152, 164–165, 174; New York, 84–85; respect for law, 91–92, 122, 125; creating enemies, 93; being challenged, 117; A. Lincoln's assassination, 166–167; interracial marriage, 201

———, personality, interests, skills: character traits, 6–7, 37–38, 116–117, 175–176, 184–185, 239–240, 259–261; debating skill, 20; photographic memory, 21; Spanish fluency, 38; achievement obsession, 54–55; butterfly collector, 60; elitism, 90; artistic appreciation, 94–98; bibliophile, 95–98; hypocrisy, 175–176, 204; fatalism, 261

———, politics: Unionist sentiments, 120–121, 123–126, 128, 129–130; Whig Party, 121, 124; Democratic Party, 122–123, 192–194, 220; National Union Convention, 193–195

———, Reconstruction: prosecution for treason, 169, 173; negotiated peace for Texas, 170–173; pardon for treason, 176–182, 192

Ballinger, William Pitt, Jr.: 98, 160–161, 255

Ballinger, Jack, Mott, Terry & Ballinger: 256

Ballinger law firm: beginnings of Ballinger & Jack, 65–66; and real estate law, 67–71, 182; accounts receivable of, 71–72; income of, 71–72, 109, 210–211, 248, 251; clients of, 72–77, 81–84, 105–106; and *Mayor Aldermen and Inhabitants of Galveston v. Michel B. Menard*, 73–77; reputation of, 77; as land agents, 80–81; as debt collecting agents, 81–83, 185, 245; success of, 81–82, 89–90, 92–93, 105–106, 229; and W. Ballinger's trip to Northeast, 83–87; law library of, 96–98, 186–190; clerks hired by, 182; rebuilding practice after Civil War, 182, 184; division of duties at, 184–185, 231–232, 245; land investments of, 186; and Panic of 1873, 209–211; and cattle industry, 210–211; and railroad law, 211, 229, 232–245, 248–249, 251–253; clerks at, 245; working relationships at, 245–247; correspondent ties with other law firms, 247; secretaries at, 247–248; salaries at, 248; telephone service at, 248; typewriters at, 248; and "free use of the wires," 249, 250; insurance policies for, 249; and corporate image, 253–254. *See also* Ballinger, William Pitt: legal career

Bates, J. L.: 42
Bates, William: 147
Bell, James: 127
Bell, John: 123, 126–127
Bell and Everett Club: 124
Belle Sulphur (gunboat): 137
Benjamin, Judah P.: 108
Bennett, William: 247–248
Berkeley, John: 13
Binford Tate Plow Company: 83
"Black Belt": 223
Black Codes: 175, 195
Blacks. *See* freedmen; slavery
Booth, J. W.: 166
Boston: 85–86
Botts, Walter: 5, 127
Bowen McNamee & Company of Boston: 82
Breckenridge, Samuel Miller: 227

Breckinridge, John C.: 123
Bremond, Paul: 241, 243–244
Bristow, Benjamin H.: 227
Brownsville *American Flag*: 55
Bryan, Guy: correspondence of, 29; income of, 100; and conservatism, 121; and cotton impressment, 158; and racism, 176; pardon for treason, 180; and national elections of 1866, 194; and Black Codes, 195; and freedmen, 203; and W. Ballinger's appointment to Texas Supreme Court, 207–208; photograph of, 207; and Panic of 1873, 210; and W. Ballinger's nomination to U.S. Supreme Court, 224, 226–228; career of, 224–225; friendship with R. Hayes, 224–225
bureaucracy: 249–250, 252
Burke, Edmond: 211
Butler, General: 30
Butler, Jonas: 32–35, 65; photograph of, 33

C

Campbell, John A.: 226, 228
Canada: 200–201
Canby, Edward R. S.: 171–172
Carteret, George: 13
Carvajal, José María Jesús: 50–57
Catholic Church: 9, 19–21, 68–70. *See also* Jesuits
cattle industry: 210–211, 233, 234–235
Cavalry. *See* Texas Cavalry Regiment
Civil War: and secessionists, 7–8, 122–132, 162, 171, 193, 226; and Texas, 7–8, 134–167, 169–172; and Confederate Sequestration Law, 83; conditions leading to, 120–132; and sectionalism, 120–121, 123, 130; W. Ballinger's attempts at prevention of, 123–132; Galveston's surrender, 138–140; and confiscation of Northern property, 141–144; and Sequestration Act, 141–145; and General Sequestration Act, 143–144; conscription during, 149, 155–157; and habeas corpus restrictions, 149–150; British intervention in, 151–152; French intevention in, 151–152; King Cotton diplomacy, 151, 153, 159; battle of Gettysburg, 152; cotton embargo, 152–153; propaganda during, 154; Texas troops stationed only in Texas during, 155–157; cotton impressment, 157–159; ending of, 159–160, 165–166; R. Lee's surrender, 165–166. *See also* Confederacy; Reconstruction
Clarksville *Standard*: 189
Clay, Henry: 121
Clayton, John: 51
Coahuila-Texas: 34
Cochran, S.: 82
Cocke, James: 39
Coke, Lord: 5
Coke, Richard: and W. Ballinger's appointment to Texas Supreme Court, 8, 206–209; election as Texas governor, 205; and postponement of 1876 elections, 213–214
Colgate, Samuel: 82–83
collection agents: 81–83, 185, 245
common law: 75
"Compromise of 1877": 223
concomitant assumption of risk: 236. *See also* tort law
Confederacy: Sequestration Act, 83, 141–145; and Texas, 132, 134–167, 231; and Unionists, 133; Congress of, 149, 150; conscription laws, 149, 155–157; habeas corpus restrictions of, 149–150; cotton embargo, 152–153; Constitution of, 155–156; induction of state militias into, 155; Trans-Mississippi Military Department of, 155, 157; cotton impressment, 157–159; collapse of, 159–160; and conscription of slaves, 164–165; and Reconstruction, 169–186; general amnesty grant for Confederates, 173; pardons for Confederate officials, 176–182. *See also* Civil War; Secessionists
conscription: 149, 155–157
conservatives: 121
Constitutional Union Party: 123–126
Constitution of the Confederacy: 155–156
Constitution of the Republic of Texas: 189
Constitution of the United States: 155, 189
Constitutions of Texas: 189, 211–220
contributory negligence: 235, 236–238
Cook, Joseph J.: 139

Index

cotton: and slavery, 113; King Cotton diplomacy, 151, 153, 159; Civil War cotton embargo, 152–153; impressment by Confederacy, 157–159; Texas production of, 171
Crouch, Darius N.: 194
Crowley, J. H.: 235, 238
Cuba: 39
Cummings, Frederick: 54
Curtis, Benjamin R.: 108
Cushing, Caleb: 55, 56
Cushing, E. H.: 151
Custom House photograph: 125

D

Dallas *Herald*: 189, 209
Daughters of the Texas Republic: 199
Davenport, John S.: 256, 258
Davis, David: 223, 225
Davis, Edmund J.: 196–197, 202, 204, 205, 219, 224
Davis, Jefferson: W. Ballinger's support of, 133–134; and suspension of habeas corpus, 150; criticism of, 154–155; and cotton impressment, 157; and conscription of slaves, 164
Davis & Beall: 250
Deberry & Smith: 250
Democratic Party: and slavery, 122–123; W. Ballinger's antipathy toward, 192–193, 220; and National Union Convention, 193–194; and freedmen's suffrage, 195; racist policies of, 202, 205
desertion cases: 145–148
Devine, Thomas J.: 141
diarrhea: 197–198
Dickson case: 237–238
Digest of the Laws of Texas (Paschal): 187–190
Dillaway, Davenport & Leeds: 247
diseases. *See* specific diseases
Douglas, Malcolm: 238–239
Douglas, Steven: 122–123
Dudley, William: 15

E

Eaton, Benjamin: 110
education: 19–26, 215–218, 221–222
elections: A. Lincoln's election, 127–128; national elections, 127–128, 194, 223; post–Civil War election of Confederates, 195–196; corruption of, 206; postponement of Texas elections of 1876, 213–214, 221
emancipation cases: 112–118
Emancipation Proclamation: 173
England: 75, 151–152
estate administration: 185–186
Evarts, William M.: 108
Executive Bureau: 180

F

Farish, Oscar: 124, 128
fatalism: 261
fellow-servant rule: 236, 238–239. *See also* tort law
Fifteenth Amendment: 197
Fillmore, Millard: 54
Fitzhugh, George: 112
Flaget, Benedict: 19
Flanagan, James W.: 205
Flats Case: 72–77, 90, 94
flogging: 112
Fort Jackson (flagship): 170
Fourteenth Amendment: 195–196, 197, 216
Fox, George: 13
France: 151–152
freedmen: mobility of, 171–172; response to Emancipation Proclamation, 173–174; Federal treatment of, 174; and Freedmen's Bureau, 174–176; W. Ballinger as advocate of, 175–176, 202–204; and Black Codes, 175, 195; and voting, 195, 203–204, 206, 221–222; and interracial marriage, 201; and poll tax, 215–217; and Fourteenth Amendment, 216; and "Black Belt," 221. *See also* Slavery
Freedmen's Bureau: 174–176
frontier defense act: 155

G

Galveston: W. Ballinger's arrival in, 11; affluence in, 39–40; slave smuggling in, 39–41; photographs and drawing of, 68, 103, 125, 139; and *Mayor Aldermen and Inhabitants of Galveston v. Michel B.*

Menard, 73–77; antebellum society of, 89–90; description of antebellum Galveston, 103; and Civil War, 134, 138–140; as Queen City, 134, 138; under martial law, 138
Galveston *Civilian*: 94–95, 101, 189
Galveston German Association: 38
Galveston, Harrisburg & San Antonio Railroad: 232, 248
Galveston, Houston and Henderson Railroad Company (GH&H): J. Gould acquisition of, 2–3, 240; land sales to, 80–81; legal problems of, 232–240
Galveston, Houston & Henderson Railway Co. v. Anne Dickson: 237–238
Galveston *News*: 101, 128, 189, 220, 256
Galveston Wharf and Cotton Press Company: 72, 73, 90
Garrison, William Lloyd: 85
General Sequestration Act: 143–144. *See also* Sequestration Act
Georgia Railroad and Banking Company case: 235
Gettysburg: 152
———, Battle of: 152
GH&H. *See* Galveston, Houston and Henderson Railroad Company (GH&H)
Gibson, Paul: 235
Gorgas, Josiah: 135
Gould, Associate Justice: 243
Gould, Jay: 1–4, 240–245
Granger, Gordon: 173
Grant, U. S.: 165, 205
Gray, Peter W.: 162
Grayson, Frederick William: 67–68
Grayson, Peter W.: 67
Grayson Case: 67–71
Green, Tom: 146
Greenwood, Martha: 114
Groff, Samuel: 14
Gulf Colorado and Santa Fe Railroad: 234, 237, 248, 250

H

habeas corpus: 149–150
Hamer, Thomas L.: 30
Hamilton, Andrew Jackson: 176, 181, 197, 224

Hamilton, Morgan C.: 205
Hanagar, Walter: 238–239
Hancock, John: 191
Hancock, Winfield S.: 196
Hardin, E. J.: 113, 116
Harlan, John Marshall: 227, 228
Harrison, Laura: 43
Harrison, Thomas: 99–100, 129, 132, 152, 174
Harrison, William Henry: 15
Hartley, Oliver C.: 27
Hay, Samuel: 56–57
Hayes, Rutherford B.: 223, 224–227
health problems. *See* specific illnesses
Hebert, Paul O.: 135, 136, 138, 149, 150
Hefley & Wallace: 250
Henderson, J. Pinckney: 27
Herndon, Sarah: 16
Hill, William Pinckney: 141, 143
Hitchcock, Henry: 227
House, T. W.: 177
Houston & Texas Central R.R. Co. v. J. A. Nixon and Wife: 237
Houston Tap & Brazoria Railroad (HT&B): 241–244
Houston *Telegraph*: 150, 151, 179, 189, 218, 220, 221
HT&B. *See* Houston Tap & Brazoria Railroad (HT&B)
Hughes, Robert: 51
humor: 79–80
Hunt, William H.: 227
Hutcheson & Carrington: 241
Hutchings, R. J.: 177

I

I&GN. *See* International & Great Northern Railroad Company (I&GN)
Illinois Regiment: 176
illnesses. *See* specific illnesses
industrial revolution: 233
insomnia: 104–105
International & Great Northern Railroad Company (I&GN): 240–243
interracial marriage: 201

J

Jack, Harriet Patrick: 42–43. *See also* Ballinger, Harriet "Hally" Patrick Jack

Index

Jack, Laura Harrison: 43, 45, 225
Jack, Thomas: apprenticeship with W. Ballinger, 64; description of, 64–65; law firm partnership with W. Ballinger, 65–66; on W. Ballinger, 66, 104–105, 109; and oration, 79; income of, 100; as Confederate soldier, 137; photograph of, 183; duties at Ballinger law firm, 184–185, 231–232; as legal researcher, 184
Jack, William: 43, 224
Jackson, Andrew: 58
Jackson v. Lamphire: 50
Jay Cooke and Company: 210
Jeff Davis (gunboat): 137
Jenkins, Elizabeth: 22–23, 59
Jesuits: 9, 19–21, 95. See also Catholic Church
Johnson, Andrew: W. Ballinger's feelings toward, 170, 179, 192; and negotiated peace for Texas, 172; general amnesty grant for Confederates, 173; and pardons for Confederate officials, 177, 178–181; meeting with A. Ballinger, 180–181; and freedmen's suffrage, 195
Johnson, Herschel V.: 227
Johnson-Union club: 193
Johnston, Albert Sidney: 27, 30, 31
Johnston Brothers: 83
Jones, Gustavus (George) Armstrong: 65
Jones, John: 65
Jones, John B.: 32, 34, 35
Jones & Butler: 32–42, 63–64, 73
Jones & Garrett: 250
Juarez, Benito: 163
judiciary reform: 218
"Juneteenth": 173

K
Kentucky: 14, 181
Kenyon College: 224
King Cotton: 151, 153, 159
Kirby Smith, Edmund: 155, 157–159, 166, 167, 169
Know-Nothing Party: 123

L
Lamphire case: 50
land grants: in Texas, 33–36, 74–76, 232; nullification of Mexican land grants, 34–36; and English common law, 75; and Spanish civil law, 75. See also real estate law
Larrainzar, Manuel: 53–54
law and lawyers: railroad law, 1–4, 11, 211, 232–245; training of lawyers, 23–24, 182, 245; real estate law, 34–36, 67–71, 229, 251–253; reputation of lawyers, 37, 93; English common law, 75; Spanish civil law, 75; entertainment nature of law, 78–79; W. Ballinger's speech on respect for, 91–92; income of lawyers, 106–108; competition among lawyers, 108; codifying of Texas laws, 186–190; tort law, 233–239
law library: 96–98, 186–190
League v. Nichols: 70
Lee, Robert E.: 154, 165
Lewis, Allen: 176–177
Lincoln, Abraham: as presidential candidate, 123, 126; election of, 127–128; W. Ballinger's opinion of, 131; and secession, 132; and French governance of Mexico, 152; and Civil War, 162; and Mexican liberation from France, 163; assassination of, 166; Emancipation Proclamation of, 173–174; Supreme Court appointees of, 177; "ten percent" proposal of, 192
"littoral and border leagues": 34
livestock, tort law on: 234–235
Livingston, John: 81
Lone Star Association: 128
"Lone Star" movement: 128
Louis Napoleon (emperor of France): 152, 163
Love, James: influence on W. Ballinger residing in Texas, 11, 24, 41–42; description of, 25; correspondence of, 29–30, 31, 36–37; and career of W. Ballinger, 32, 42–43, 64, 73; knowledge of illegal slave trade, 40; and marriage arrangements for W. Ballinger, 45; disapproval of W. Ballinger's choice of cases, 115, 147–148; and legal challenges, 117; and Whig Party, 124; and J. Davis, 154; pardon for treason, 176; removal from office, 196
Lovett, Joseph A.: 32

Lubbock, Francis: 134, 149, 153

M

McKay, Seth Shepard: 212–214
McLean, Ephraim W.: 27, 30–31
McMahan, T. R.: 176
McNamee, Bowen: 82
McWaters, Robert: 146–147
Magruder, John Bankhead: 140, 157, 166, 169
Mallory, Stephen: 134
Manso, Leonardo: 35
manumission laws: 114
Marshall, John: 190
martial law: 138, 149, 215
Martin, Francois Xavier: 107–108
Mathews, Wilkes & Wood: 250
Maximilian (emperor of Mexico): 152, 163
Mayor Aldermen and Inhabitants of Galveston v. Michel B. Menard: 72–77. *See also* Flats Case
Menard, Michel: 72–77; photograph of, 72
Merrill, James: 39–41
Mexican War: W. Ballinger's enlistment in, 26; Battle of Monterrey, 27, 30–31; Battle of Palo Alto, 28; Battle of Resaca de la Palma, 28; Camargo, 29–30
Mexico: 27–31, 152, 163
Military Reconstruction Act of 1867: 196
Miller, Samuel F.: 177–180, 224–229
Mills, Andrew G.: 199
Mills, Ballinger: 200
Mills, John: 93
Mills, Robert: 110, 199
Mirabeau, Doctor: 58
Miss Hull's French School: 198–199
Missouri Pacific Railroad: 239, 248
Mobile *Register and Advertiser*: 81
Moise, T. S.: 137
Monroe Doctrine: 152, 163
Monterrey, Battle of: 27, 30–31
Monthly Catalogue of Reliable and Efficient Practising Lawyers: 81
Morris, William: 71, 93
Mott, Marcus: on W. Ballinger, 5; as partner at Ballinger law firm, 231–232; photograph of, 232; and railroad law, 243, 244; and bureaucracy, 252
Muldoon, Miguel: 68–69

Murrah, Pendleton: as governor of Texas, 155; resistance of, to Confederate induction of state militia, 155–157; and cotton impressment, 157–159; and Texas as French protectorate, 162–164, 170; and R. Lee's surrender, 166; and Civil War, 169; and Texas surrender, 170
Murray, John: 145–148
Murray, Oscar G.: 234
Murrow, J. S.: 112–113
Murrow Case: 112–113

N

Napoleon III (emperor of France): 152
National Union Convention: 193
nativism: 28, 91
negligence: 233–234. *See also* tort law
"negligent misconduct": 236
Neutrality Acts of 1818: 53
New Departure: 202, 204–205
New Orleans *Picayune*: 81
New York *Herald*: 81
New York *Tribune*: 81
Nichols case: 70
Nixon case: 237
Northern Pacific Railroad: 210
Norton, A. Howell: 54
Nott, Josiah: 112
nuclear family: 101

O

"Oaks": 98–101; photograph of, 99
"Obnoxious Acts": 205–206, 214–215
Ochiltree, William: 134
Odin, John Marie: 110
Ohio Volunteers: 30
"On the Greek Revolt Against Turkey" (Ballinger): 151
Oration: 79, 91–92
Orr, James L.: 194
Ottoman Empire: 151

P

Palmer, Edward Albert: 108
Palo Alto, Battle of: 28
Panic of 1873: 209–211, 230
Parrott, Mr.: 68–69
Paschal, George: 186–190, 192, 195
Pease, Elisha M.: 191, 195, 196, 224, 225
Peck, George: 252

Index

Penn, William: 13
Philadelphia: 86
Pierce, Franklin: 54, 55, 56
piracy: 41
Pitt, William: 15
poll tax: 215–217, 220–222
Poole, J. E.: 245
Potter, Henry: 32, 134, 136
Powell, Peter: 35–36
Pullman, George: 2

Q

Quakers: 13–17, 86

R

racism: of W. Ballinger, 29–30, 164–165, 175–176; of Anglo-American Texans, 35; and mob violence, 91; and slavery, 112; and emancipation cases, 115; and interracial marriage, 201
radicals: revenge policy of, 177–178; and national elections of 1866, 194; and Texas elections, 196–197
railroad law: 1–4, 11, 211, 232–245. *See also* law
railroads: railroad law, 1–4, 11, 211, 229, 232–245, 251–253; Galveston, Houston and Henderson Railroad Company, 2–3, 80–81, 232–240; travel by, 136; as Ballinger law firm clients, 184, 211, 229, 232–245, 248–249, 251–253; Northern Pacific Railroad, 210; and Panic of 1873, 210, 230; transcontinental railroads, 210; Galveston, Harrisburg & San Antonio Railroad, 232, 248; and tort law, 233–239; Gulf Colorado and Santa Fe Railroad, 234, 237, 248, 250; Missouri Pacific Railroad, 239, 248; International & Great Northern Railroad Company (I&GN), 240–243; Texas & Pacific Railroad (T&P), 240–245; Houston Tap & Brazoria Railroad (HT&B), 241–244; and bureaucracy, 249–250, 252; and "free use of the wires," 249, 250; Atchison, Topeka & Santa Fe, 250, 251–253
Reagan, John: 212
real estate law: Mexican land grant nullification, 34–36; Grayson Case, 67–71; and railroads, 229, 251–253. *See also* land grants; law
Reconstruction: Northern backlash against Confederates, 169–186; Federal occupation of Texas, 171, 196–197; general amnesty grant for Confederates, 173; pardons for Confederate officials, 176–182; and treasonable offenses, 176–182; S. Miller opinion of, 177–178; and Executive Bureau, 180; and Johnson-Union club, 193; politics of, 193–195; end of, 197, 205; and Texas Constitution of 1876, 219. *See also* Civil War; Confederacy
religious bigotry: 21, 38–39
Republican Party: 129, 133, 223
Republic of the Sierra Madre: 51
Resaca de la Palma, Battle of: 28
Revolutionary War: 14
Reynolds, Joseph J.: 196
Richardson, Willard: 110, 220–221
Roberts, Oran: 4–5, 77, 116–117, 186, 191, 258

S

St. Clair, , Arthur: 14
St. Mary's Catholic College: 9, 19–21, 24, 95
salaries: 106–108, 215
Sands, Benjamin F.: 170–171
San Jacinto, Battle of: 43
S. Cochran & Company: 82
Sealy, George: 250, 252
secessionists: W. Ballinger's opposition to, 7–8, 124–132, 162, 226; and Democratic Party delegation, 122–123; Galveston assemblage of, 127–128; and A. Lincoln election, 128; and "Lone Star" movement, 128; and Federal occupation of Texas, 171; and National Union Convention of 1866, 193. *See also* Civil War
"Secession Speech": 124–125
sectionalism: 120–121, 123, 130
Sellers, William: 194
Sequestration Act: 83, 141–145
Seward, William H.: 108, 178–180
Shearman & Sterling: 1, 241–242, 244, 246–247
Sheridan, Philip H.: 171–172, 196

329

Sherman, W. T.: 160
Slave Codes: 175
slavery: end of, 8; Ballinger family ownership of slaves, 13–14, 82, 111; smuggling of slaves, 39–41; and abolitionism, 82, 85, 93, 165; and W. Ballinger, 82, 85, 93, 111–112, 117–119, 129; in Texas, 111–120; education of slaves, 112; emancipation cases, 112–118; and flogging, 112; forced emigration of emancipated slaves from Texas, 114–115; and manumission laws, 114; "slave catching," 118; treatment of slaves, 118–120; conscription of slaves into Confederate Army, 164–165; and Emancipation Proclamation, 173; Slave Codes, 175. *See also* freedmen
Smith, Ashbel: 170, 171, 194
Smith, Doctor: 255
Sontag, Henriette: 85
Sorley, James: 143
Southern Home School: 199
Spanish civil law: 75
Speed, James: 180
"spoils system": 42
Stancel & Stancel: 116
Stewart, Alexander T.: 82
Stockdale, Fletcher: 202, 204
Story, Joseph: 190
Stuart, Hamilton: 94, 110
suffragettes: 199, 217
Sullivan, George: 247, 258
Sullivan & Cromwell: 247, 258
Supreme Court. *See* Texas Supreme Court; U.S. Supreme Court
Sutcliffe: 239
Sydnor, John: 93, 134

T

T&P. *See* Texas & Pacific Railroad (T&P)
Taylor, Richard: 146
Taylor, Zachary: 26, 32
Terhune: 143
Terry, John Wharton: photograph of, 246
Terry's Texas Rangers: 231
Texas: and secessionism, 7–8, 127–132, 162, 171; economic evolution of, 8–9; land grants in, 33–36, 74–76, 232; nullification of Mexican land grants in, 34–36; and rebellion of J. Carvajal, 50–57; land as economic base of, 67, 142; slavery in, 111–120; forced emigration of emancipated slaves from, 114–115; sectionalism in, 120–121; response to Lincoln's election in, 127–128; "Lone Star" movement, 128; armaments purchases for, 134–138; martial law in, 138, 149; Sequestration Act, 141–145; as cash poor state, 142; conscription laws affecting, 149, 155–157; and industry, 153; frontier defense act, 155; native Confederate troops protected from leaving state, 155–157; cotton impressment by Confederacy, 157–159; as French protectorate, 162–164, 170, 203–204; nativism in, 163–164; peace negotiations after Civil War, 169–173; cotton production in, 171; Federal occupation of, 171, 196–197, 205, 206; "Juneteenth" in, 173; pardons for Confederate officials, 176–182; Constitution of the Republic of Texas, 189; and freedmen's suffrage, 195; and post–Civil War election of Confederates, 195–196; and Thirteenth Amendment, 195–196; and voting, 195, 199, 203–204, 215–217; and New Departure, 202; and "Obnoxious Acts," 205–206; and corrupt elections, 206; Constitution of 1876, 211–220; and education, 215–218; "Black Belt," 221; railroad's impact on, 229–231; and mourning for W. Ballinger, 259–260
Texas & Pacific Railroad (T&P): 240–245
Texas Bar Association: 258
Texas Cavalry Regiment: 231
Texas Confederate Constitution: 189
Texas Constitution of 1845: 189
Texas Constitution of 1866: 189
Texas Constitution of 1876: W. Ballinger's involvement in, 211–220; and election postponement, 212–214; amendments to, 214; and executive authority, 214–215; and governor's salary, 215; and poll tax, 215–217; and free public education, 217–218; and disposal of public lands, 218; and judiciary reform, 218; public

endorsement of, 222
Texas Ordinances of Secession: 189
Texas Supreme Court: W. Ballinger's appointment to, 8, 206–209; T. Ballinger's appearance before, 11, 77–78; and W. Ballinger's appointment as U.S. district attorney for East Texas, 42; and *League v. Nichols*, 70; and *Mayor Alderman and Inhabitants of Galveston v. Michel B. Menard*, 73, 77; Ballinger law library offered to, 186; reform of, 191–192; legislative advisory role of, 192; salaries of, 218; and railroad law, 243
Thirteenth Amendment: 195
Thompson, Edward: 247
Thompson, L. A.: 77
Thompson and Goldthwaite: 73, 231
Throckmorton, James W.: 195, 196
Tipton, Major: 242
Toombs, Robert: 226
tort law: development of, 233; and negligence, 233–234; and livestock, 234–235; and contributory negligence, 235, 236–238; and concomitant assumption of risk, 236; and fellow-servant rule, 236, 238–239. *See also* law
Trans-Mississippi Military Department: 155, 157
treason: and Confederate officials, 169, 173; J. Love pardon for, 176; W. Ballinger pardon for, 176–182; and death penalty, 179
Tredegar Iron Works: 135
Truehart, H. M.: 249
Truehart and Company: 249
Twiggs, David: 30

U

ultra vires: 243
unemployment: 210
Unionists: and sectionalism, 120–121; opposition to sucession by, 123–126; and "Lone Star" movement, 129; loyalty to Confederacy, 129–130, 133; and "home rule," 175

U.S. Constitution: 155, 189
U.S. Supreme Court: and impressment of private property, 157; and W. Ballinger's pardon for treason, 177; W. Ballinger's appointment to, 223–228
university education: 19–20. *See also* education
Uriah Bartley v. The Georgia Railroad and Banking Company: 235

V

Van Dorn, Earl: 134, 135
Vicksburg: 152
voting: and freedmen, 195, 203–204, 206; women's suffrage, 199, 217; terrorism as prevention of, 206; and poll tax, 215–217, 220–222; for aliens, 217

W

Walker, LeRoy Pope: 134
Walker, Robert: 39
War of 1812: 15
Webster, Betsy: 113–118, 145, 148
Webster, Daniel: 51, 52, 53
Webster Case: 113–118, 145, 148
Weiss: 143
Wheeler, Royall T.: 67
Whig Party: 121, 123
Wigfall, Louis T.: 134, 154–155
Wiley, Doctor: 197–198
Williams, Samuel May: W. Ballinger's services for, 32–33; children of, 33, 105; and Flats Case, 72–77; photograph of, 72
Williams, U. S.: 19
Williams, William Henry "Beaver": 33, 105
women's suffrage: 199, 217
Woods, William B.: 227
Woolf & Gillespie: 83
Worth, William J.: 30, 31–32

Y

yellow fever: 161, 224–225, 255
Young Men's Lyceum: 91

Z

Zachary, M.: 68–69

COLOPHON

The typeface used for the text is Janson, designed in 1937 by Stanley Morison, who based his design on a much earlier one by Nicolas Kis. The display face, Trajan, is based on the inscriptions on Trajan's column, and was designed in 1990 by Carol Twombly.

One thousand copies printed at Edwards Bros., Inc., Lillington, North Carolina, on 50 lb. Glatfelter.

www.ingramcontent.com/pod-product-compliance
Lightning Source LLC
Chambersburg PA
CBHW031232290426
44109CB00012B/265